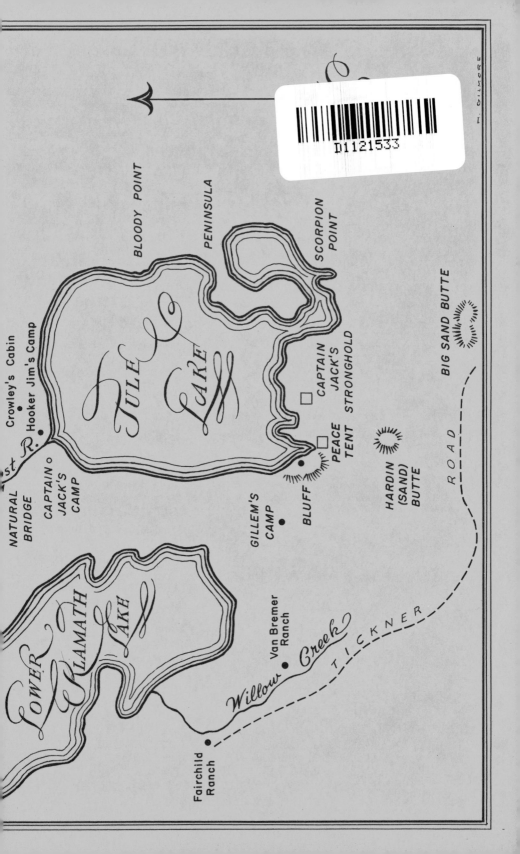

LOWER KLAMATH LAKE

TULE LAKE

NATURAL BRIDGE

CAPTAIN JACK'S CAMP

Crowley's Cabin

Hooker Jim's Camp

St. R.

BLOODY POINT

PENINSULA

SCORPION POINT

CAPTAIN JACK'S STRONGHOLD

PEACE TENT

BLUFF

GILLEM'S CAMP

HARDIN (SAND) BUTTE

BIG SAND BUTTE

ROAD

Van Bremer Ranch

Willow Creek

TICKNER

Fairchild Ranch

I. GILMORE

D1121533

BURNT-OUT FIRES

BURNT-OUT FIRES

Richard Dillon

PRENTICE-HALL, INC.,
Englewood Cliffs, New Jersey

for
Brian Dervin Dillon

Library of Congress Cataloging in Publication Data

Dillon, Richard H
Burnt-out fires.

Bibliography: p.
1. Modoc Indians--Wars, 1873. I. Title.
E83.87.D5   1973 979.4'04   72-5846
ISBN 0-13-090993-9 ©

CONTENTS

INTRODUCTION

Exactly one hundred years ago, California suffered its only major Indian conflict, the Modoc War which broke out in November 1872. The major causes were familiar ones—the basic antagonism of cultures underlying all of our Indian wars and the land-lust of white settlers. The immediate causes were the usual combination of civilian duplicity and pressure on government, a worthless treaty, Indian Bureau bungling (more stupidity than perfidy) and Army folly and overconfidence. Thus, in many ways, the Modoc War is worthy of attention as a key to the story of *all* of our sad and unnecessary Indian wars. Nowhere else has history so consistently repeated itself as in what Teddy Roosevelt, unconscious of the irony of his phrase, called the winning of the West. When someone wins, someone has to lose. It is not necessary to study every frontier war and skirmish; the Modoc War was all the Indian wars of this country, rolled into one. To paraphrase Quintilian, "For exploring human nature, one war is large enough."

On the other hand the Modoc War was special, more dramatic than most, even unique. Gen. John Schofield was correct in describing it as a "conflict more remarkable in some respects than any other before known in American history." It resembled a Tennessee mountain feud crossed with a Greek tragedy almost as much as an Indian campaign. The Army found that its enemy consisted not of war-painted, feather-bonneted nomads but pidgin-English-speaking natives who wore Levis and gingham shirts, who worked as part-time cowboys for California ranchers who were their genuine friends and protectors, and who fought from barricades, rifle pits and trenches like Prussians, not Indians.

The Modocs, dispossessed from their homeland on the California-Oregon border by an unratified treaty of 1864, refused to go into exile on an alien reservation under the guns of Fort Klamath. Their feud was not with all whites but with the local speculators and squatters who coveted their grasslands for grazing purposes. Self-interest was the only principle of many of these frontiersmen. Since 1789 it had been first tradition and then law that the Indians owned their land; it could be taken from them only with their free consent or by right of conquest in a war. Only the Government could extinguish Indian title to public lands. Therefore, an Indian war was in order.

The Modoc War correspondent of the *London Illustrated News* blamed the conflict upon the "scoundrelism" of the border settlers, going back to pre-Civil War days. He oversimplified. While the Modoc War was not a tragedy without villains, neither were all of the settlers ruffians. But all felt a racial superiority over the Indians which they believed gave them carte blanche. So it was that even well-meaning whites brought calamity to the Modocs and Klamaths, just as their cultural arrogance had done to the tribes further east. And all in the name of civilization. A typical attitude was that of one Oregonian who urged citizens to erect a monument to the white "martyrs" of the Modoc War because they had lost their lives in the first effort "to plant a school on the ancient site of the savage wigwam."

As pure story, the Modoc War is remarkable. Irony and tragedy play larger roles than in similar conflicts. Captain Jack, *de facto* chief of the so-called renegades, was a man of peace, not a warrior. Yet he was forced to war and even to murder by his jingoist braves who, when all seemed lost, promptly turned traitors and hired out to the Army to track him down. When the Army virtually drew straws to choose scapegoats for hanging, Captain Jack was elected, of course; the most murderous of his band were granted immunity from punishment because they had helped the Army. As a final indignity, a posthumous humiliation, the American Government exemplified its social Darwinism as much as its scientific zeal by lopping off the heads of Captain Jack and his chief lieutenants for study in the Smithsonian Institution. Less shocking than this brutal confirmation of assumed cultural superiority was the anticlimactic and unworthy termination of the Modoc story. The half-scalped and shot-up survivor of the Modocs' massacre of the United States' Peace Commission led a theatrical lecture tour in which the stars of his troupe were the very Modocs who had tried to murder him, while the chief of the Army's Indian scouts parodied the Modoc War with a Wild West show and, later, prostituted his Modoc War reputation in order to peddle quack medicine. Thus was the sacrifice and suffering on both sides in the Modoc War defiled by the rampant commercialism of American civilization.

The Modoc War took place in as bizarre and difficult a battleground as the Everglades of Florida's Seminole Wars, a *malpais* or badland called the Modoc Lava Beds today but known to the Indians as the Land of Burnt-Out Fires. This jagged jumble of volcanic rocks, hillocks and caves was a worthless wilderness to the whites but a natural Gibraltar to the Modocs, as the Army learned to its sorrow. It was, even more than J. B. Priestly's Arizona desert, geology by day and astronomy by night.

Captain Jack probably never mustered more than fifty-three braves in a battle, yet for six months he stood off an Army that came to number almost a thousand men, including infantry, cavalry, artillery and Indian scouts, with their small-arms supported by mountain howitzers and mortars supplied by pack mules, wagons and whitehall boats on Tule Lake.

At the most, Captain Jack lost only *six* men by direct combat action, while the Regular Army, militia, civilians and Indian scouts paid for the land-grab with 165 dead and wounded. The cost of the Modoc War in money was about half a million dollars more than the usual budget for

Fort Klamath and other garrisons that attempted to keep the peace on the post-Civil War frontier of Oregon and California. In relation to the number of enemy in arms, it was probably the most costly of all our Indian wars.

Captain Jack, who was overromanticized after the war into a fair copy of one of Rousseau's noble redmen, was a skillful civil leader betrayed by his own ego. By the need to save face, he was maneuvered into murdering Gen. E. R. S. Canby, one of the few high-placed friends he and the Modocs had. Canby was the only general killed by Indians in our history. (George A. Custer had the permanent rank of lieutenant colonel at the time of his death at the Little Big Horn.)

Jack's most trusted comrade is little-known today, but as a field commander and tactician he ranks with Osceola, Crazy Horse and Chief Joseph. The only battle which the Modocs lost—the turning-point in the war—was the only one in which Captain Jack displaced Scarfaced Charley as commander. Like Captain Jack, Scarfaced Charley was a man of peace. But, when driven to war, he whipped the Army every time. In the Battle of Hardin Butte, called the Thomas-Wright Massacre by the military, Scarfaced Charley fought what was perhaps the classic, most perfect battle in Indian war history. With twenty-two braves, he ambushed a force of sixty-six regulars supported by fourteen Warm Springs Indian scouts, killing every officer but one, who lost a leg. The soldiers panicked and hid in the rocks or ran pell-mell for Army headquarters, less than four miles away. Scarfaced Charley could have annihilated Thomas's command but he tired of killing and, content with twenty-seven of his enemy dead and seventeen wounded, he called off his men and shouted to the terrified survivors, "All you fellows that ain't dead had better go home. We don't want to kill you all in one day."

The splendid defense by the Modocs of their homeland against such overwhelming odds immediately appealed to the underdog-favoring American public. The people began to question the origins of an apparently needless war, and out of this criticism of the minor Modoc War grew the organized Indian reform movement in this country. It was begun by half-scalped A. B. Meacham and continued by Helen Hunt Jackson, author of *Ramona* and *A Century of Dishonor*. Newspaper editors, even during the war, became as ambivalent as the public itself. At one moment, especially after the dastardly murder of General Canby, they cried for genocide as the only cure for the depredations of a tribe earlier despised as a lot of bandy-legged riffraff in cast-off settlers' clothing. The next moment, the Fourth Estate was busily metamorphosing Captain Jack into a Rob Roy of the Lava Beds.

Poets emoted in sarcastic doggerel:

> "...In truth it was a gallant sight
> To see a thousand men of might
> With guns and cannon, day and night
> Fight fifty dirty Indians

For every foot of Lava Bed
They threw a pound of hissing lead
A ton for every Modoc head
In three day's roaring battery...

We'll bless you when you've killed them all
The men and women, great and small
And not a babe is left to squall
Its hatred of our victory

For this is Freedom's chosen land
The heritage of all that's grand
And the millennium's at hand
So great is our humanity.

Sgt. Michael McCarthy was no poet but he had no illusions about the immediate cause of the Modoc War: "The War Department, in its usual wise way, sent only enough soldiers to pick a quarrel and drive them into a war." Pvt. Maurice FitzGerald was converted, too. He saw that the conflict was not what his faith called "a just war," so he wrote of his opponents, "They were fighting for what they deemed an inalienable right to retain possession of a locality that had belonged to them and their ancestors from time immemorial and from which it was sought to forcibly eject them, for no good reason." Even Oliver Applegate, whose pioneering clan stood to gain much by the removal of the Modocs, admitted that far too many Indian wars had been caused by white man's greed and ruffianism. In this he was only echoing the earlier words of such Indian fighters as Col. William S. Harney and Kit Carson.

As early as the 1850s the Army realized it was being "used" by greedy settlers and Christian crusaders in the Indian Bureau, and it resented the fact. Gen. Ethan Allen Hitchcock at that time damned the whites who invaded Indian lands, provoked violence and then screamed for protection from the Army—which thus countenanced their aggressions. Gen. John Pope during the Civil War added that the Army was held responsible for Indian hostilities by the very people who brought violence about by their treaties. Gen. John Schofield in 1875 was insisting that no one was more desirous of peace in the West than the Army: "There is no glory to be won in savage warfare, and when to this feeling is added the conviction that the Indians have been driven to war by injustice and outrage, the indignation felt by honorable soldiers can easily be imagined."

Perhaps the Modoc War was exceptional too, in the number of men—on both sides—who worked so hard to avoid war. These were the real heroes of the story, as much as Canby, Captain Jack or Scarfaced Charley. Peace Commissioner A. B. Meacham was outstanding, but also notable were rancher John Fairchild, Judge Elijah Steele, squawman-interpreter Frank Riddle and his courageous Modoc wife, Toby. These Oregonians and

Californians really believed what the country's Founding Fathers had said—that the utmost good faith must be observed toward our Indians. Meacham urged a policy of citizenship and justice for the Indians both during and after the Modoc War as the only solution to the nation's Indian problem, warning, "The cost of this war has not yet been footed up... [but] the results stand in ghastly monuments, calling in thunder-tones on a triumphant nation to stop in its mad career and *think*...."

But there was no time to stop and think in a hustling-bustling, confident and go-ahead industrialized nineteenth-century America. And tradition was too strong. The belief of racial superiority, whether blatant, subtle or unconscious, was so deeply ingrained in westering Americans that they scorned Indian customs, refused to recognize Indian property rights and absurdly reckoned the country to be undiscovered, "unknown," simply because no white man had ever squatted there. The Indians must assimilate or perish. Indian Bureau policy has to make them as comfortable as possible on the reservation, as uncomfortable as possible when off. Secretary of the Interior Francis Walker put it bluntly: "Such of them as went right should be protected, and such as went wrong should be harassed and scourged without intermission."

Small wonder that Col. James B. Fry would reply for the Army, "Driven continually behind our rapidly advancing frontier, plundered and abused by the more powerful and agressive race, without one particle of redress for any wrong done him by the white man, and knowing no law but retaliation and vengeance, it is not strange that the barbarian should indulge in bloody deeds."

Even in 1873 it was axiomatic to some—the Fairchilds and Meachams—that wars solved nothing, that nobody won a war—certainly not an Indian war, in which even the nation's self-respect was forfeit. But even had these men of peace been as skillful at their peace making as wet-coopers at their trade, they were doomed to fail. They were men born ahead of their time. Not for another hundred years would it dawn on a majority of the people that it was folly for an Army to fight an unjust war largely to regain face, or honor. Only a tiny minority in 1873, who personified the legendary voices crying in a wilderness, sensed what Lawrence Clark Powell recently put into words: "Win or lose, war and honor are incompatible. To life, and to life only, is honor due."

The Modoc War was a small but grotesque Grand Guignol drama. Of all our Indian wars, it was perhaps the least "necessary" and, theoretically, should have been the easiest to prevent. And yet all the labors of the peace men were in vain and a bloody war came, as if by some inexorable, primordial urging. With the ritualistic inevitability of a Greek tragedy, the unwanted Modoc war unfolded as part of our Manifest Destiny, which was the "civilizing" of the North American continent from sea to sea.

"It has always been observed that Indians settled in the neighborhood of white people do not increase, but diminish continually."

Benjamin Franklin, 1754

"Kill with bullet don't hurt much; starve to death hurt a heap."

Captain Jack, 1873

CHAPTER ONE

CIVIL WAR IN OREGON

The echo of Gen. P. G. Beauregard's cannons firing against the red-brick ramparts of Fort Sumter was slow to reach the Far West. When at last they did resound on the Pacific slope, some three thousand miles from Charleston harbor, it was natural that big and muscular California should take the lead in responding to the Federal Government's call for help in fighting a civil war. After all, the census enumerators of 1860 found only 52,465 souls in Oregon as compared to 379,994 Californians.

The Golden State not only put two units into the field in the war-torn East, the so-called California Regiment (actually the 71st Pennsylvania) and the California Hundred of the 2d Massachusetts Cavalry, but also filled the ranks of a Washington Territory regiment while mustering within California no less than a half-dozen infantry and cavalry outfits. Besides these units, California offered a First Battalion of California Mountaineers and even a squadron of Mexican lancers, Don Andrés Pico's Native California Cavalry.

The California regiments performed well in securing the strategic Pacific littoral for the Union, in keeping open the overland trails and in holding hostile Indians in check during those parlous days when the Regulars had to be diverted to the East. California's volunteer army went on to win considerable fame beyond the state's borders by means of Indian skirmishes from Apache Pass in the Southwest to Idaho Territory's Bear River and, particularly, in the march of Col. James H. Carleton's California Column all the way from the Coast to the Rio Grande, retaking Arizona and New Mexico from the Confederates while en route to Texas.

Where California led in the West, Oregon lagged badly, trailing even its sparsely settled satellite, Washington Territory, in patriotic zeal and military glory. The state considered itself to be far removed from the conflict and of much less strategic

1

and economic importance than California. Moreover, Oregon had far fewer Copperheads, Confederate sympathizers, than California to worry over. Hence, Gov. John Whiteaker did not choose to respond when President Lincoln called to the country for seventy-five thousand volunteers. The appeal reached Oregon by May 11, 1861, but Whiteaker turned a deaf ear to it. His friends said that he believed the state was so remote it was virtually exempted from participating in the fratricidal struggle and could sit out the war. The governor's enemies and critics accused him of being soft on Secession.

Whether Whiteaker was a pacifist, a Copperhead or merely a do-nothing politician, the Union cause in Oregon had rough sledding during the initial months of the Civil War. Col. George A. Wright, the able commander of the District of Oregon, requisitioned the governor in June of 1861 for a cavalry unit, and A. P. Dennison, ex-United States Indian Agent at The Dalles, was chosen as enrolling officer. But so suspect were the loyalties of both Dennison and Whiteaker that Wright thought better of it, jettisoned the plan and disbanded the company before it was fully mustered. The general had to apologize to the loyal majority of Oregonians for the War Department's seeming willingness to abandon the Pacific Northwest at a critical hour, but reminded them that the Government had to give higher priority to the preservation of the Union itself.

When the exasperated Wright was promoted to brigadier general and given the command of the entire Department of the Pacific, he decided not to trust the defenses of Oregon to men loyal to a possibly "Secesh" governor, so he began to garrison the state's few military posts with California and Washington Territorial Volunteers after the regulars were recalled. As Federal troops on station in the Northwest began to dwindle away to nothing, Oregonians of whatever feeling toward Jeff Davis began to be haunted by the spectre of a largely undefended Indian frontier only a few years after the bloody ambushes and skirmishes of the Rogue River and Yakima wars. They pressed the governor to take action, and when he proved himself as dilatory as ever, various localities began to form their own irregular militia companies.

One of these militia units almost certainly prevented a tragedy and probably a massacre in the summer of 1861. Lindsay Applegate led a forty-five man party to Bloody Point on Tule Lake in August after several murders were reported on the California-Oregon border. They were blamed on the Modoc

Indians, although the Pit River and Snake Indians may have been involved. Just in the nick of time, Applegate's force arrived at the promontory jutting into the waters of Tule Lake near the southern fork of the Oregon Trail. There they found an emigrant company surrounded by Modocs led by John Schonchin, Black Jim and Scarfaced Charley. Like a pack of wolves circling a wounded buffalo, the Indians were closing in for the kill. Applegate's opportune arrival not only scattered them and saved the train but kept the border calm during the remainder of the 1861 traveling season.

The Federal Government finally gave up all hope of stirring Governor Whiteaker into action. The War Department appointed Thomas R. Cornelius, a veteran of Pacific Northwest Indian wars, to command the First Oregon Volunteer Cavalry. This regiment was to be composed of ten companies of men signed up for three-year hitches. The minimum strength of each company was set at sixty-four men, the maximum fixed at eighty-two. Enlistments were encouraged by the bait of a one-hundred dollar bounty to be paid at the expiration of the enlistee's term of service, plus a land warrant worth 160 acres.

Although an annoyed Gen. Benjamin Alvord later reminded a new governor, Addison Gibbs, that California had put as many regiments into service as Oregon had fielded companies, the handful of Webfoot Volunteers had no real trouble in curbing rebel sentiment in Oregon. This proved to be the case even though only seven of the ten authorized companies were actually raised between November 21, 1861, and August 10, 1863. The military suppressed those newspapers adjudged to be seditious, like Joaquin Miller's *Democratic Review* in Eugene, and put a stop to surreptitious, nocturnal meetings of such subversive groups as the Knights of the Golden Circle, whose opposition to the Civil War was considered treasonable.

The most important role of the volunteers in its peace-keeping mission was the maintenance of the scatter of existing Army posts in Indian country, and here the force had its work cut out for it. Patrols and reconnaissances had to be continued, for the real threats to Oregon settlements were not Confederate sympathizers but hostile Indians. The latter were always alert to exploit any weaknesses they could detect in the defenses of the state's exposed settlements and ranches. And Oregon's citizens knew that the mere presence of military power, the "showing of the flag" by forts and outposts and patrols, did more to keep the peace on the Indian frontier than all the treaties ever sent to Washington, to lie unsigned in the Senate.

There would be no Gettysburgs or Cold Harbors in the Far West, but the Oregon Volunteers performed well in the few skirmishes that came their way while they were playing a constabulary role akin to that of the Royal Canadian Mounted Police. They protected peaceful whites from hostile Indians and peaceful Indians from hostile whites. In short, they kept the peace.

Oregon's volunteer army carried out deep and skillful exploration of wilderness areas as far as lonesome Steen's Mountain by means of prodigious marches. It safeguarded emigrants by escorting wagon trains, patrolling the main roads and maintaining fast expresses. The enlisted men of the First Oregon Cavalry proved to be a higher class of men than peacetime regulars. (John Smith, Indian agent at the Warm Springs reservation, was once asked if he did not want some regular troops to protect himself from hostiles. "No," he exclaimed, "I prefer the raids of the Snakes to the presence of the soldiers.") Many volunteers, officers and men, signed up for lofty motives of duty and patriotism, hoping to fight in the East although the recruiting posters correctly stated the regiment's duty to be the provision of frontier protection. They were, in fact, the "citizen-rangers" of Thomas Hart Benton's speeches of the 1850s, as opposed to the senator's "schoolhouse officers and pot-house soldiers" of the peacetime Regular Army.

Col. Thomas Cornelius reached Fort Walla Walla in Washington Territory, just across the line from Oregon, in July 1862 with two companies of the 1st Oregon Cavalry. They were shortly joined by three more companies, raising regimental strength to six hundred men. Col. Justus Steinberger replaced Cornelius when the latter resigned and served under Brig. Gen. Benjamin Alvord, commanding the District of Oregon, which included not only the state but all of Washington Territory and that portion of Idaho Territory lying west of the Rockies.

The most dangerous—even explosive—Indian situation existed in southern Oregon, from the base of the Cascade Mountains all the way to Idaho. Congregated there were not only the largest number of Oregon's Indians but the state's most unruly tribes, the Modocs, Snakes and Paiutes. The Oregon Snakes were actually Shoshonean-speaking Northern Paiutes, closer kin to the Nevada bands than the true Snakes or Shoshoni who had greeted Meriwether Lewis in 1805. During the Civil War the Snakes were the hostiles most feared by Army and settlers in

Oregon. General Alvord likened them to the Comanches of Texas.

During the summer of 1862 Alvord sent Lt. Col. Reuben F. Maury and three cavalry companies to escort Oregon-bound travelers. This was a big job for there were some eight thousand wagons and ten thousand persons to guard. Maury was also charged with the impossible task of arresting the Indian murderers of a number of travelers. To better control southern Oregon, the Army planned two new forts. One near old Fort Boise (a trading post), would anchor the eastern end of the dangerous zone of desert and mountains. The other, destined to become Fort Klamath, would protect the last leg of the Applegate Trail or Cut-off, the Southern Road of the Oregon Trail.

The forts were necessary because of the utter failure of the Army's plan of the 1850s for a no-man's-land in southern and eastern Oregon. Gen. John E. Wool had tried to make the area into a vast Indian territory from which whites would be barred. But the fact of a transcontinental trail through its middle, plus the discovery of gold in the Powder River and Salmon River country, doomed Wool's scheme. Mining camps boomed in the forbidden area similar to Dakota's equally off-limits Black Hills. So many disbanded Confederates alone came to eastern Oregon to prospect for gold that wags in Portland called their camps "the left wing of Sterling Price's Missouri Army."

Although Colonel Maury's thousand-mile march to the Owyhee, Malheur and Snake rivers during 1862 was free of untoward incident, the settlers of Auburn, the Powder River mining center near Baker, were not sure that the Indians' awe of the bluejackets would last. Therefore, in August 1863 some fifty Auburners fixed their names or X's to a petition addressed to the Federal Government. The memorialists asked for military protection against the depredations of Snakes and Bannocks who were rustling thousands of head of stock and taking a few lives, too. The Oregon Legislature responded by requesting Congress to remove the Indians to reservations where they could be closely watched and controlled. To put down Indian marauding, they asked for more military posts. This was just what General Alvord was planning, and in November he sent Maury out again, along with Captains George B. Currey and John M. Drake. Fort Boise was established, fittingly, on the Fourth of July 1863, and Fort Klamath a few months later.

In April 1864 the Army finally caught up with the elusive Snakes. But when Lt. James A. Waymire found them, it was in such God-neglected country that he had to leave his horses and close in on them on foot, only to see the enemy slip away into the wilderness it knew so well.

Poor pay rather than a paucity of patriotism was responsible for Oregon's so-so showing in recruitment. It was asking a lot of the Beaver State's young men to trade their comfortable civvies for a uniform available in only three sizes. Base pay for a private was only thirteen dollars a month, the food was bad, the work hard and the hours long. Hardly were recruiting posters tacked in place before they were joined by help-wanted signs offering young men jobs paying forty and fifty dollars a month. But the recruits did not yet know that there was a lot more boredom than excitement and danger to a soldier's life, so a sufficient number of men abandoned the lucrative gold camps, where a miner could earn five dollars a day, and rallied to Army service.

Although the Government provided them with uniforms, Springfield rifles and bayonets, the volunteer cavalrymen had to furnish their own horses and gear, or "horse furniture" as the Army called it. The longer they served, the worse off they were, because Congress in the middle of the Civil War repealed the Act of 1861 that had allowed pony soldiers forty-cents-a-day allowance for forage. Nor were the small luxuries of life provided by a paternalistic government, and the troopers had to pay thirty-three cents at the post sutler's store for a spool of cotton thread, sixty-seven cents for a comb and two dollars for a half-ream of notepaper on which to write home complaints about the God-awful food. Still, the love of adventure was strong in many young men, and the fires of unbanked patriotism were fanned by visions of a hundred dollar bonus.

Most of the soldiers, when they found that there was a lot more wood chopping or road grading than fighting Injuns, made the best of it. (The words of Tombstone's Sid Wilson apply to the history of Oregon as well as to Arizona: "There was a hell of a lot more postholes dug out here than guns shot off.") Most of the Oregonians made a joke of their rugged life, many singing the popular parody of a back-East jingoist tune by Septimus Winner titled "Abraham's Daughter":

> *I'm a raw recruit with a brand new suit*
> *One hundred dollars bounty*
> *And I've just come down to Ashland town*
> *To fight for Jackson County.*

Not all of Oregon's officials were of Whiteaker's stamp. The state's first Adjutant General, Cyrus A. Reed, was something of a Union firebrand. He exhorted his fellow citizens to service: "There is no state in the Union so deficient in arms as Oregon and I may say that none stands so much in need of them. . . . Surrounded as we are by savage tribes of Indians, we should at least be sufficiently organized to defend ourselves. Every able-bodied man should be a soldier, ready to take to the field. . . . Shall we then, here in Oregon, lie supinely upon our backs while the great battle of freedom is being fought?"

Opposed to the enthusiasm-rousing oratory of Reed was Army grub. In Oregon this ran to moldy or wormy flour and salt junk (antique pork) with an occasional lapse to beef which stunk up the plates of the wearies, or enlisted men. Beans and desiccated vegetables did the troopers little good in throwing off either scurvy or low morale. Occasionally meals were, quite literally, the bread and water of penitentiary legend. And often the bread was almost a token offering, a single piece of hardtack, more symbol than substance, like the Host at Communion, albeit very dissimilar in consistency or, better, density. Hardtack, or "flour tiles" as the soldiers called them, water biscuits exactly 3 1/8 inches by 2 7/8 inches in size, were so constructed as to defy teeth and jaws as well as appetite. Although weevils drilled tunnels and adits in them like merry sappers and were not above taking in maggots as house guests in their borings, the stony breads would shatter only if addressed with the butt of a Springfield rifle. Then they could be powdered into crumbs to thicken soup, or thrown into the coffeepot to make a swill uninspiredly called hardtack-and-coffee. This was definitely an acquired taste even on the Oregon frontier, like the Klamath Indians' roasted crickets. If soaked interminably, the biscuits took on the rubbery complexion of gutta-percha. If left strictly alone, they could have been used to load Coehorn mortars against Modocs.

Small wonder that pinch-gutted soldiers appreciated the dubious kindness of a sutler or post trader in letting them go into hock by buying items on tick, and the philanthropy of local settlers in giving away potatoes at a dollar a bushel. The Army wasted no tears on the personal famines of the volunteers; at one Oregon post, not Fort Klamath, the Old Man was accustomed to throw troopers into the guardhouse for the heinous crime of saving some of their rice from the midday dinner in order to eat it with the cruel farce of an Army supper—coffee and bread. Of course, the evil-minded C.O. did not give a damn, really, *when* the men ate their rice, but he suspected his wards of hoarding food not for solitary banquets at eventide or to bolster their thin suppers but, rather, for the purpose of bartering for the favors of the Indian damsels of the area.

On June 10, 1861, twenty-seven citizens of Siskiyou County's Butte Creek, east of Yreka, added California voices to Oregon's clamor for military protection. They asked Brig. Gen. Edwin Vose Sumner, then commanding the Army's Department of the Columbia, for a company of troops until there were miners enough to protect themselves. They reminded Old Martinet, as Sumner was called behind his back, that there was no force available to restrain possible incursions of hostile Modocs and Klamaths since U.S. troops had been moved north from the Klamath Lake area.

The settlers claimed that both Klamaths and Modocs were making inroads into their settlements, plundering their cabins, driving off their livestock and keeping everyone in constant apprehension, even anxiety, over the safety of their very lives. There was no mistaking the need for a show of military force in the vacuum of the border area. Even Judge A. M. Rosborough of Yreka, one of the closest friends the Modoc Indians had, signed the memorial. Next, Maj. Gen. R. M. Martin of the California Militia told Sumner that the Indians had ordered the settlers to leave Butte Creek or they would run off all their stock. Martin urged that a token force, at least, be sent to protect the Siskiyou Mountains and lake country frontier.

Finally, on January 27, 1863, General Wright ordered Maj. C. S. Drew of the 1st Oregon Cavalry at Camp Baker, near Jacksonville, to reconnoiter the Klamath Lake country, to provide him with a word sketch of the country and to advise him as to the necessity for a military post in the area. On February 20, Drew was back at Camp Baker to report that he deemed a post indispensable for the public's safety and that it should be founded as soon as possible, whether or not a projected treaty with the local Indians should be carried through.

Drew's communiqué satisfied Wright. He forwarded it, with his approbation, to Washington. There it won the War Department's stamp of approval and, that summer of 1863, Drew began his search for a site for Fort Klamath. Three times he marched out of Camp Baker with an escort of Oregon Volunteer cavalry before he made his final decision. He examined the south and north shores of Klamath Lake but found no site. According to Dr. Henry McElderry, post surgeon at Fort Klamath in 1874, Drew located the site for the post between July 10 and 20, although the founding was delayed until September 5, 1863.

To the surprise of everyone, even the delighted burghers of Jacksonville, seat of government for Jackson County, Oregon, Drew chose none of the obvious locations near Klamath Lake, Link River, Lost River or the Applegate Trail. He also passed up the old (1860) location of Camp Day on Spencer Creek near the Klamath River, twenty-two miles west of Linkville (Klamath Falls, today). Instead, he opted for a site on little Linn Creek, now Fort Creek, a tributary of Wood River. This stream lay in the lee of the high Cascade Mountains dominated by Mount Scott, some twenty miles to the north, and by Mount Thielsen and Mount McLoughlin, all nine-thousand-foot peaks. The latter, twenty-five miles to the southwest, was still called Mount Pit at the time of Drew's exploration. It had been named for the holes of pitfalls dug as game traps in its sides by the Indians, much like those of California's Pit River. More often than not it was misspelled Pitt.

In 1913, Uncle Jerry Martin recalled the founding of Fort Klamath for the editor of the *Klamath Republican.* He had been with Major Drew when the latter came near building the new post near the springs at Pine Grove, where he was camped. But someone suggested that he was not close enough to the thickest settlement of Indians, so he decided on the ultimate site of Fort Klamath. It was, indeed, fairly close to an Indian area, but the redmen were the tolerably peaceful Klamaths rather than the feared Modocs or Snakes. According to Drew, he chose the particular spot for other reasons. He liked the looks of the lush grass that grew there in well-watered meadows and clearings, offering a sharp contrast to both the densely wooded Cascades to the west and the dry land of pumice and alkali to the south and east, where the lye-burnt soil of the Modoc Plateau merged with the basin and range country of Nevada's true desert. There was enough forage in the loamy meadow north of Upper Klamath Lake to sustain whole legions of dragoons, even if the grass was not of a quality to excite the jealousy of a Nashvillian or a blue-grass Kentuckian. The thick native grasses were low growing, and the yield of hay would prove to be only a ton an acre on the porous, infertile soil. But later, with irrigation, tame grasses such as timothy and alsike clover or legumes improved both forage and soil, and Fort Klamath became a source of large quantities of nutritious hay. The waters of Linn Creek and the other streams impressed Drew, too, with their clarity and sweetness. In 1874, the British traveler J. W. Boddam-Whetham was there. He remarked on the clarity of the brooks and verified the local Indians' name for Fort Klamath's prairie—"The Beautiful Land of Flowing Water."

Drew's chosen prairie was ringed with great stands of ponderosa pine and tamarack or lodgepole pine, ripe for the axe. There was wood enough for centuries of barrack construction or fireplace stoking right within the environs of the fort. The site's southern exposure guaranteed the garrison the last bits of daily and seasonal warmth that the declining sun had to offer an area with cold nights all year and frost a good part of the year. (On August 25, 1873, Lt. Col. Frank Wheaton would note that he had a good fire going.) The southern exposure also offered a magnificent view of the Hudsonian heights of the Cascades on the one hand and the great spread of the Klamath Basin toward far-off Mount Shasta, looming up in snow-clad splendor all year, a hundred miles to the south in California.

Lt. Stephen Jocelyn of the 21st United States Infantry Regiment, who was stationed at Fort Klamath in 1874, exulted over its limpid streams, crowded with five-pound trout, and its beautiful plain: "This is the loveliest spot I have seen in Oregon."

Major Drew was pleased to learn from the local Indians that Upper Klamath Lake seldom froze over for more than a few weeks per year and that the tribal stock managed to winter safely only a few miles from the location of his fort. When an inspector, Capt. James Van Voast, was sent to check on Drew's choice of site between October 10 and 20, 1863, he agreed that the site at 4,200 feet of elevation was an excellent one. He described it as being in the most beautiful and pleasant part of the valley, where there were at least six townships of good land adjacent to the post to induce people to settle in the area. The valley ranged in width from six to sixteen miles and trended southward from Sun Mountain to blend into the expanse of the Klamath Basin. The shore of Upper Klamath Lake was just six miles south of the post-to-be. Wood River Valley was called I-ukah by the Indians, meaning Between the Mountains, because it was sheltered not only by the high sierra of the Cascade range on the west but hemmed in on the east by a range of wooded hills of some four to six hundred feet of elevation called Sullix, meaning Mad, by the Klamaths. The odd name was bestowed on the heights presumably because of the eerie, deep echoes that bounded back from the cliffs.

Major Drew's choice of a location for Fort Klamath was not universally applauded. Although slightly elevated over the surrounding terrain, the site was surrounded by impenetrable marshes in the spring and early summer from the melting snow and the runoff of streams gone over their banks. When the marshes finally dried in late July or early August, the change was signaled by the assaults of millions of mosquitoes and the advent of what Surgeon McElderry called miasmatic diseases caused by the prevailing winds sweeping over marshy areas and bringing germs to Fort Klamath. Luckily, the cold nights at the post seemed to keep disease at a distance; it was not an unhealthy place.

Drew had, unknowingly, placed Fort Klamath at the border of the wet Canadian zone of the Cascades and the arid Transition zone of junipers and sage. Notwithstanding its advantages in terms of water and grass, pines, Douglas fir and western larch, its reasonably healthy climate and beauteous setting, critics charged that Drew had blundered. Fort Klamath, about ten miles south of the then virtually unknown Crater Lake, was simply in the wrong place. It was considerably removed from the Indians it was meant to awe and the settlers it was meant to protect. No matter, went Indian Bureau and Army thinking; the Indians could be brought to a reserve near Fort Klamath. The only settlement in the area was Linkville, now Klamath Falls, thirty-six miles away at the falls of the Klamath River. The Lost River heartland of the dangerous Modocs and such Applegate Trail troublespots as Bloody Point were even farther away. Lindsay Applegate, who had largely secured passage of a resolution in the Oregon Legislature asking for a Fort Klamath in 1862, wanted it much further south, between the Modocs and Yreka, California, in fact. He felt that bad men in that mining town "tampered" with the Modocs. He later told Gen. Benjamin Alvord: "While I was in charge [of the Klamath Indian Agency], I managed to athwart their schemes and to keep the peace, but after my removal they became more embolden." He felt that Drew had defeated the very purpose of Fort Klamath by locating it sixty miles north of the Modocs (who *had* to be watched, of all southern Oregon's Indians) and where there was neither road nor settlement to protect.

On the other hand, the new post was able to provide a

geographical link between the Applegate Trail (and the military road to the desert country and Idaho) and the trans-Cascade settlements of the upper Rogue River Valley, once a good trail could be hacked across the mountain chain. Drew planned to build such a route and also to run roads north from the fort to the John Day Turnpike and south to intercept the Yreka Road to Oregon, which ran over the Siskiyou Mountains. Because the mining boom was beginning to pull prospectors and settlers over into the area of east-central Oregon as well as the state's southeastern area, the more northerly location of the fort seemed proper.

Capt. James Van Voast agreed with Drew and predicted a network of roads overseen by Fort Klamath, routes that would carry triple the amount of traffic then using the Applegate fork of the old emigrant road past Tule Lake: "There can be little reason to doubt that, soon, cavalry stationed at this fort will find roads in all directions by which they can operate and hold in subjection the Indians in all the surrounding country."

It was no secret that the town of Ashland favored the location of Fort Klamath on Lost River near the emigrant road. Jacksonville, sensitive to the advantage such a location would give its rival in furnishing supplies to the military and in outfitting travelers in general, opposed the choice and urged one that would be more convenient to the county seat. Drew chose a location not particularly close to either city limits, but the road he cut over the high Cascades ended at Jacksonville, not Ashland. Hence his choice was everywhere accepted as a victory for the county seat over Ashland, although the Army post lay almost a hundred miles away over some of the roughest terrain in the West.

Accusations of politicking and misconduct by Drew developed out of his choice of location for the outpost. News of the hubbub reached the ears of the Army brass in San Francisco's Presidio and an inspector was sent to make an objective investigation. The Department of the Pacific chose its investigator well. James Van Voast was technically only a captain of the 9th Infantry, but in 1863 he was also provost marshal at San Francisco and charged with the detection of disloyal plots in the West. His orders were to make a critical examination of everything pertaining to the military in and around the new Fort Klamath and particularly to inquire into adverse reports on the conduct of its commanding officer, C. S. Drew, now a lieutenant colonel.

Captain Van Voast found that virtually all of the complaints] had been made by a disgruntled Indian sub-agent, Amos E. Rogers, in communications addressed to J. W. Perit Huntington, the Superintendent of Indian Affairs for Oregon. These all boiled down to two basic accusations. First, that Drew's choice of a site guaranteed that the post would be of little or no use to the Indian Department in controlling its wards and of no use to the military in protecting either settlers or immigrants from such warlike tribes as the Modocs. Rogers' second accusation, in Van Voast's paraphrase, was that "Colonel Drew has openly declared himself inimical to the policy of the Indian Department and has taken every opportunity to insult its dignity, weaken its power, lessen its influence and to destroy its authority." These were strong words but the tune was a familiar one, part of the clamor and clangor of the great undeclared war in the West—between civil and military authorities in general and between Indian agents and Army field commanders in particular. Almost never did they see eye to eye on correctives for what both euphemistically called the Indian problem.

Because it was late in the season, Van Voast could not be as thorough as he would have liked. He did not personally examine the country lying around Fort Klamath, but he did collect verbal as well as written reports by interviewing twenty persons of the Jacksonville and Yreka areas. The results confirmed his first impression that there was no question about the fitness of the place for a fort in terms of health and economy. To Van Voast it appeared to offer advantages of strategic position, too. "Indeed," he summed up, "with the limited means at Colonel Drew's disposal for the construction of a new fort in that location of the country, it is hardly possible that one could have been located which would have afforded greater advantages and have secured like protection to emigrants and to citizens."

When the provost marshal asked Drew about Rogers' second claim, the colonel assured him that it was untrue. He was always willing and ready to cooperate with Rogers—when such cooperation added to the public safety or reflected credit to either department. Van Voast, for his part, could find no one to cite any incident in which Drew had failed to cooperate that could be considered cause for censure. He heard out a few complaints against the colonel in Jacksonville in regard to the manner in which he supplied his troops, but Van Voast left the citizens convinced that the causes for complaints were more apparent than real. He found that strictly proper transactions—Army style—were simply not understood by the citizenry. The chief source of critical comment was Drew's choice of a contractor named Glenn who was suspected and accused (without any proof) of Confederate sympathies. But since Glenn had taken the required oath of allegiance and was in partnership with a strong Unionist, Van Voast was quite willing to let Colonel Drew be the judge of his loyalty. He blamed most of the strong feelings against the colonel on petty jealousies, personal interests and party prejudice.

The Army liked Drew's choice of a site for Fort Klamath, concurring completely with the opinion of its inspector, Van Voast. Gen. Benjamin Wright, commanding the department, informed Washington: "I have little fear of murders on the emigrant road, where they are said usually to have occurred, if Fort Klamath is occupied by cavalry. During the winter the troops at Fort Klamath will hold completely at their mercy all the tribes in the vicinity of the Klamath Lake Valley." After checking with Capt. Robert S. Williamson of the Engineer Corps, who had explored the area in a railroad survey, Wright gave his full approval of Drew's choice of site. He noted that the complaining Indian sub-agent had "subsided" and apparently resigned after Van Voast's visit, and he ended his endorsement by stating flatly, "I believe it is the best position we could occupy in that country."

In the summer of 1863, Capt. William Kelly, a forty-odd-year-old Irishman from Galway, was ordered to accompany Colonel Drew to the Klamath and Modoc country to construct and garrison the new Fort Klamath. From the fragrant, flowery meadow on Wood River he was to build a new road (really a trail) across the Cascades some twenty miles south of the existing Rogue River Trail. Kelly marched his men out of Camp Baker, which he had commanded, probably not knowing that the success of his new post would mean the death of his old command near Jacksonville. Later that year, Captain Van Voast recommended the abandonment of Camp Baker as Fort Klamath proved itself. Kelly headed up seventy-nine men of the rank and file of C Company, 1st Oregon Cavalry. His subordinate officers were First Lt. Frank B. White and Second Lt. D. C. Underwood, the latter officer acting as both his quartermaster and commissary. Kelly left behind him only a skeleton detachment of men to forward supplies to the new outpost and to keep watch on the Indians and any stray Secessionists who might be lurking in the Siskiyous.

Perhaps it was just as well that the men of C Troop found themselves scuffling with boulders and windfalls rather than hostile Modocs or Snakes that season, if they were half as poorly armed as were their comrades stationed at Fort Hoskins in western Oregon. Corp. William Hilleary described the arms issued to the soldiers there as looking like weapons abandoned in the pell-mell retreat from First Manassas. Some were bent, almost all were damaged in some fashion, and a few even had burst breeches or barrels.

However, the condition of the armory proved to be of little import to the Fort Klamath garrison. Since troopers in the mid-nineteenth century provided the cheapest labor supply this side of the Old South and its "peculiar institution," and Army posts were often derided as Government workhouses, it is not surpassing strange that the weapon most often used at Fort Klamath during the Civil War years was neither the carbine nor the Colt revolver but the axe. The men of C Company (the cavalry's designations of troop and company were still interchangeable in 1863) chopped a narrow trace through the pines under the general supervision of Captain Kelly and the direct supervision of Lieutenant White. This track, perhaps by the grace of God as much as good engineering, managed to miss all the major precipices along the route. In fact, though damned as a poor excuse for a road until 1900, at least the shortcut over the Cascades was good enough to handle sawmill machinery on jolting pack mules. Known as Drew's Road or the Mount Pitt Road, and sometimes as the Fish Lake Road, it was best known as the Ranchería Trail because it cut through Ranchería Prairie on Butte Creek north of Mount Pitt (now Mount McLoughlin). Because it was considered to be such a rough road, in 1865 it was replaced, to cries of good riddance, by a new road laid out by another Fort Klamath commander, Capt. Frank B. Sprague. This route arched over the Cascades near Crater Lake via Union and Annie creeks blazing the way for Route 62, the Crater Lake Highway of today. However, the Ranchería Trail fell back into favor and is today part of the popular Winnemucca-to-the-Sea Highway, Route 140.

Drew's soldier-built road past the pyramidal cone of Mount Pitt, said by world-travelers to be a dead ringer for the Bernese Oberland's Niesen Peak, was no Boston Turnpike. But Van Voast praised its uniformed navvies, saying that their road was fully as good as could be expected and that the work expended upon it showed that the men had labored with more than ordinary industry to get it finished in so short a time. From Jacksonville the road ran to Butte Creek, Ranchería Prairie, Four Mile Lake north of today's resort of Lake of the Woods, and thence near Denny Creek, the site of the 1846 ambush of John C. Frémont by Klamaths. From that stream it turned up along the west shore of Upper Klamath Lake to Seven Mile Creek, Wood River, and finally, reached Fort Klamath at Linn Creek, since renamed Fort Creek. (Linn was the civilian contractor who constructed the post.) Once a sawmill was established on the east side of the creek opposite the fort, construction was rapid and most of the buildings at Fort Klamath were of box lumber rather than rude log cabins. The steam-powered circular mill operated at a capacity of about two to three thousand board feet of lumber a day. It was operated under lease or contract until 1870. Located adjacent to a pine forest, Fort Klamath was destined to be a wooden fort although there was superior sandstone for the quarrying in the hills southeast of the Klamath Agency, which was founded next door to the post in 1864.

Fort Klamath itself was officially founded on September 5, 1863, and it shot up as Drew skipped the usual Army practice of advertising for bids by contractors. He did not want to wait for the lowering skies of winter; he wanted his men out of their tent bivouac and into solid shingle-roofed quarters. So he simply hired carpenters and had no difficulty in getting his plans and estimates approved. Using one-inch pine lumber, Drew built a line of quarters for five officers a few rods in front of Linn Creek, and a long (139 feet) duplex-type barracks building running east and west on the southern edge of the parade ground. This structure was composed of two dormitories joined by a double stone fireplace and a flimsy common wall or partition, plus rooms for first sergeants. The quarters were capable of sheltering two hundred men, but normal strength for Fort Klamath was two companies. In late 1873, for example, the barracks held forty-five men of C Company, 1st U.S. Cavalry, and fifty-one men of F Company, 21st U.S. Infantry. Although the twin barracks were raised a foot and a half off the ground for good drainage and had full verandas, front and back, ten-foot ceilings and plenty of windows besides two doors, no sooner were the stables built than some of the men were grousing that their horses had better housing than they possessed. This may have been true; certainly Captain Van Voast found that the horses, all American- or Oregon-bred, were in fine shape when he made his inspection. Possibly the men's opinions were affected by the periodic fires caused by the red-hot stovepipes poked through the shingled roofs with only a light zinc flashing for protection. Time after time, the white-washed structures of Fort Klamath were smoke-blackened, and several burned down over the years thanks to the cast-iron stoves that supplemented the inadequate (and, shortly, ruinous) double fireplace.

Kitchens and mess halls were followed by quarters for the post's four laundresses and the post trader's store, the latter three hundred yards in the rear of the officers' quarters. The sutler or post trader had a billiard room for officers in his building, and later there was even a good restaurant for the post and a room set aside as an officers' mess. Once Drew and Kelly had their horses and men protected from the oncoming winter, they built that essential structure of any Army post—the guardhouse. It was a forty-by-forty-foot building of six-inch sawed and hewn lumber. They also put in a hospital with a twelve-bed ward at the northeast corner of the parade ground, a bakery and quarters for the adjutant and the quartermaster. Drew's double storehouse resembled the enlisted men's bar-racks. Two units were joined by a common wall and made the strongpoint or bastion of the post by the addition of a blockhouse at either end.

Van Voast applauded Drew's economies as much as his diligence. The warehouse's sections were eighteen feet by thirty-eight feet. This was quite modest for a two-company post on a frontier some 300 miles from headquarters and the nearest quartermaster in Portland, and 130 miles distant from the nearest fort, Camp Warner. And the distances were across very rough terrain. Still, Drew managed to cram six months' subsistence into the double warehouse. His economies hurt the post, however, during its moment of crisis in 1873, when it became headquarters for the Modoc War effort. When troops in the field needed canteens and haversacks these were requisi-tioned from Fort Klamath, but none were to be had in the too-small warehouse.

In the center of the parade ground stood a 125-foot flagpole set up as a kind of beacon or guide for travelers as well as a symbol of U.S. authority when Old Glory flew from the top of the staff. It also served as a base point from which surveyors could run their lines of measurement. Just north of the 1,050-acre military reserve lay a lush area of bunch grass, the fort's 3,135-acre hay reserve. At first the troopers had the fatiguing duty of cutting fodder atop their many other "police" duties and drills. But, later, contracts were let to civilians to provide hay at from four to five dollars a ton, and the soldier's life became a happier one. Hay proved to be Fort Klamath's major crop. Overly optimistic was Van Voast when he ventured that the sandy loam of the Klamath Basin and the dry black-sage bench lands to the east of the fort would produce grain and vegetables in profusion. He believed that Fort Klamath, within a year or two, would be sustaining cavalry as cheaply as the Rogue River Valley. But the Army's official *Outline Description of U.S. Military Posts and Stations* put the case more honestly as well as succinctly in 1871 when it reported on Fort Klamath's agricultural potential: "Soil (pumice stone) not arable. . . . No vegetables or corn can be raised at the post."

Of warring at Fort Klamath there was even less than cultivating. Forts Bidwell and Boise and Camps Warner and Harney and others, plus the nameless desert camps ringed with rifle pits, were closer to the bellicose Snakes than Fort Klamath. Fort Klamath was a watchdog over the Klamaths, turned peaceful, and the Modocs who, for some reason, were largely off the warpath during the Civil War. Perhaps it was the very presence of Fort Klamath that kept the Modocs in line. Still, the post was not entirely removed from Indian campaigning. Command of it fell to Lieutenant Underwood when Drew led thirty-nine men of C Company out on his Owyhee Expedition between July 1 and October 18, 1864, and, later, Capt. F. B. Sprague led two subalterns and seventy men of C Company and I Company, 1st Oregon Volunteer Infantry, on a march to Alvord Valley in Oregon's eastern desert.

Part of the success of Fort Klamath's role as watchdog was due to an early boost Captain Kelly gave to peace rather than Indian warfare. When the compassionate and generous Irishman saw that the Klamaths were destitute and on the verge of starvation that first winter of Fort Klamath's existence, he advanced them food on his own initiative and responsibility. Kelly handed out 9,921½ pounds of beef and 11,401 pounds of flour in addition to other articles of subsistence. When he presented Superintendent of Indian Affairs Huntington with a bill for $2,518.40 to forward to his superiors, Huntington urged them to pay it. He heartily approved of Kelly's measures to keep the Indians peaceful and well fed. Huntington wrote: "The course of Captain Kelly, in my judgement, had a most salutary effect in conciliating the Indians and rendering future control of them easy and economical. It is but justice that the Government should sanction the expenditure." Kelly's bill was paid.

CHAPTER TWO

THE KLAMATHS

The last major land cession in Oregon history, some twelve to fourteen million acres or approximately twenty thousand square miles, was made as a result of the founding of Fort Klamath. On October 14 and 15, 1864, J. W. Perit Huntington, Superintendent of Indian Affairs for Oregon, secured the vast area from the Klamaths, Modocs and Yahuskin band of Snakes in exchange for the Klamath Reservation of 768,000 acres to be set up adjacent to Fort Klamath, some annuities and other treaty considerations. Unfortunately, Huntington's otherwise bargain of a treaty also sparked the fuse already laid to the Modoc War, which finally detonated at dawn on November 29, 1872. Where the Klamaths entered willingly upon the treaty negotiations and accepted reservation status, the Modocs participated most reluctantly in the proceedings and with a latent hostility toward both whites and Klamaths. There was good reason for this; the reservation site was plunked down in the midst of the Klamath nation, alien territory to the Modocs and less genial in climate than their own Lost River country to the south. Located first on the lakeshore, the agency was later moved three miles north of Upper Klamath Lake to a point in a pine grove where a creek called Beetle's Rest issued from a spring to form a pond and then a tributary to Crooked River. Here the Klamath sub-agent placed a sawmill and gristmill. The former, particularly, figured in the tragedy of the Modocs and the crisis of Fort Klamath.

Huntington's Treaty of Council Grove near Fort Klamath culminated a trend toward a pacific existence on the part of the Klamath Indians. This was the result of a *volte-face* by the tribe, however, for not long before, the Klamaths had gone into warfare as a kind of business venture after a long tradition of isolationism. The brief adventure into bellicosity had come as a result of the Modocs and others demonstrating its profits—in horses, in captives, in other booty—to the Klamaths. Largely spared the raids of the Nez Perces, Cayuses and Snakes by the inhospitable terrain of the upper Deschutes Valley, the buffered Klamaths led an uneventful life until about 1825. Living was easy in a land where the larder included not only ducks, brant, geese, herons, cranes, swans, coots (mudhens), mallards, loons, pelicans and sage hens, as well as squirrels, blacktail and whitetail and mule deer, antelope, elk, foxes, beavers, otters, mountain sheep, trout and suckers, but also such delicacies as crickets, grasshoppers and moth-chrysalis grubs roasted and eaten like choice Virginia goobers. The Klamaths apparently had everything—snow-clad peaks, crystal streams, azure skies and deep blue lakes with green shores. Densely wooded mountains alternated with wide-open spaces and attractive meadows and marshes. The climate of the Klamath Plateau was dominated by a dry atmosphere, with hot days and cold nights much of the year. Fort Klamath's mean annual temperature proved to be 40.47 degrees Fahrenheit. In winter, although there might be four feet of snow on the ground and thick ice in the lakes, the water almost never entirely froze over.

During the late 1820s, the Klamath country was penetrated by such Hudson's Bay Company *bourgeois* or "booshway" leaders of fur-trapping parties as Peter Skene Ogden, Finan McDonald and John Work. With the barriers broken down, a few Klamaths were taken as slaves by the Nez Perces, enough for the masters to be called Pierced Noses when it was the slaves, mostly, who had their septums perforated and decorated and their heads flattened, as well. In the eyes of the first white visitors, the Klamaths were comfortable if isolated aborigines. They enjoyed a high standard of living compared to the so-called Diggers of California and Nevada, who gleaned a meager existence. The Klamaths ate well of game, salmon and other fish, and bread. Their staff of life was *apaws,* the gray-green, slick pond lily seed that was cured, parched and ground into a flour for cakes and mush by means of stone mortars and pestles. They lived in snug semisubterranean houses or winter lodges. But, curiously, they knew little real wealth when Ogden first visited them, and he reported that the tribe owned only a single horse.

Slowly the Klamaths began to change. They gave up piercing their noses and flattening the foreheads of their infants. The latter practice had led them, and their near kin, the Modocs, to address the despised Yahuskin and Walpapi Snakes as "Conical Heads." They adapted rather easily to the white man's ways, being light-skinned and capable of blushing where the Modocs could not, tall like the whites—even lank and wiry (although their wives were fat like Modoc squaws)—and with small hands and feet. They were dreadfully naive, at first, and when Ewing Young, the fur-trapper-cattleman, passed through their country and left behind some flour and a bag of sugar, they knew nothing better to do with the treasures than to smear on the flour as face powder and to hide the sugar in a safe place—a running stream.

The Klamaths, who originally called themselves and the Modocs Maklaks or Muckalucks, were quite different from the other Indians of Oregon. The two tongues or the two variants of the Klamath-Modoc tongue composed a unique language family not related to such other language groups as the Shoshoni or Sahaptin. The word Maklaks, like Hopi, apparently signified simply The People. But it may also have had a connotation of The Encamped, or The Settlers, to indicate their sedentary life. Later they took the very apropos name of Eukskni—Lake People. Individual names among the Klamaths often were actually nicknames assigned a person for some deviation from a norm of body build, features, gait or so forth; thus, Big Belly, Grizzly Nose and Crooked Neck.

As the Klamaths lost their isolationism, they began to turn up as travelers in the Willamette Valley and on the Columbia. They also began to lust for guns, horses, trade goods, the white man's food and (especially) drink. Large numbers found their way down the Deschutes to the Columbia River at the Dalles, and so many trudged over the Cascades Mountains via Santiam Pass that a relationship, prompted by intermarriage and the exchanging of vocabularies, sprang up between them and the Molallas way down the Willamette near Salem. The wanderers also visited what passed for civilization in Oregon Territory— Oregon City—once it was founded at the falls of the Willamette River.

With more and more contact with the Warm Springs Indians on the Deschutes just north of the Klamath Lake country, the Eukskni decided to become slave traders. They became the brokers or middlemen, in fact, between slave-hunting Modocs and the market—the Warm Springs country. Sometimes the Klamaths accompanied their wilder Modoc kinfolk, but it was mainly the latter who marauded into Shasta and Pit River Indian country. The slaves, particularly women, were bartered for horses and guns. War, or more precisely slave trading, became so profitable that it changed the character and life-style of the Klamaths, as John C. Frémont learned to his sorrow.

The Pathfinder further shattered the isolation of the Klamath nation when he made a traverse of it in 1843, at which time it was peaceful. Then, in 1846, Frémont was back. He crossed Lost River, which he named McCrady River, and made his way up the western shore of Upper Klamath Lake when he left the Modoc country. He was bound for a marsh village he had visited in 1843. While distracted by the arrival of a messenger—U.S. Marine Lt. Archibald Gillespie, with still-secret orders in case of a war between the U.S. and Mexico—Frémont was jumped by Klamaths (presumably) at Denny's Branch, or Denny Creek, on the west shore of Upper Klamath Lake. Two of Frémont's praetorian guard of Delaware Indians, Denny (for whom Frémont named the creek) and Crane, were killed, along with his French-Canadian aide, Basil Lajeunesse, before Frémont, Kit Carson, Alex Godey and the others could rally and drive off their attackers. Carson took a Hudson's Bay Company half-axe from the dead chief of the raiders and smashed in his head. In the chief's quiver they found forty steel-tipped arrows, which did not raise the Honourable Company in the esteem of Carson and Frémont. Carson was familiar with both Plains and Rockies Indians but he gave the palm to the Klamath armorer-artificers who made such beautiful—and deadly—bows and arrows. A missionary of the same period reported that Klamath bowmen could drive a shaft clear through a horse.

Although Oregon pioneer Lindsay Applegate, who was in the area at the time, blamed the Hot Creek band of Modocs for the ambush, Frémont—and most historians—believed it was the work of the Klamaths. The explorer retaliated by striking the Williamson River village of Ya'ak. Even if the tribe were guilty, these particular villagers were innocent of any responsibility for the ambuscade. Like Black Kettle's flag-waving Cheyennes on the Washita, these Klamaths became the hapless victims of an ambitious and egotistical officer. The latter's agent of revenge was Christopher (Kit) Carson.

Frémont's vengeance ended for a time the era of Klamath amity with the whites. The November 26, 1846, *Oregon Spectator,* for example, reported a Klamath raid on a wagon train bound north into Oregon from California. In this strike, two travelers were killed and one wounded. The introduction of the diseases of civilization worsened matters, but the Klamaths were a sagacious people, always testing the wind before making a move, and they did not lose their heads—either actually or figuratively—when the Cayuses murdered the Whitmans at Waiilatpu near Fort Walla Walla in 1847. True, the Klamaths politely heard out the harangues of the Molalla chief, Crooked Finger, and allowed themselves to be recruited for his grand alliance of Umpquas, Rogue Rivers, Pit Rivers, Klamaths and Modocs. This league was supposed to drive the whites from Oregon during the winter of 1847-1848 in a kind of half-baked race war. When Crooked Finger was at last ready to strike, he received the surprise of his life. The settlers were very much on guard, and they turned a victory at Butte Creek into a subsequent slaughter of the Indians at Abiqua Creek, just east of Silverton and Salem. There, Klamath chief Red Blanket was killed with a dozen of his eighty followers. The white settlers showed mercy on the humbled Klamaths by giving them just three days to leave the Willamette by the Klamath Trail over Jefferson Pass. They needed no urging; they pulled out with Red Blanket's mournful widow escorting his corpse back home to the Klamath Basin. This March 1848 debacle proved to the Klamaths that it was not good business to fight with the whites, so they settled back down to their middle-manning of the slave trade. Later, because of this defeat, they were said to hate and despise the serviceberry-eating Molallas, even if the latter did speak a bastardized Klamath tongue.

Chief Chiloquin, who led some of the Klamaths' forays, told whites that his tribe's enemies, and particularly the Snakes, originally provoked the Klamaths into warfare. But he said that it was true that when they found it profitable they extended their attacks from Snakes to Shastas, Rogue Rivers and Pit Rivers, with the help of their blood-allies, the Modocs. Nevertheless, warfare was not in their blood, as it was with the Modocs. Chiloquin explained: "We found we could make money by war, for we sold the provisions and property captured for horses and other things we needed. . . . We made war because we made money by it and we rather got to like it."

When an Oregon newspaperman, Samuel A. Clarke, interviewed Chiloquin circa 1873, he could hardly believe that the little fellow—all of five feet and sixty-five years of age—could have once been the terror of the Pit Rivers. But he then reminded himself of the stature of Napoleon and Grant and concluded, "Generalship, and even statesmanship, are not matters dependent on size." Chiloquin bragged to him: "The Klamaths were a great nation and, though they have never [sic] fought the Bostons and have not resented the evil acts of Boston men against them, they sometimes made war against all the tribes around and never were beaten in any great battle." Chiloquin's boast must be taken with a grain of salt, but it was probably true that his Klamaths thrashed three hundred invading Snakes in the 1820s when the latter got themselves lost in a tule fog, or dense ground fog, and were scattered on the ice and snow of Klamath Marsh where the Klamaths, on snowshoes and familiar with the low fogs, picked them off in small groups, almost at leisure.

Such successful battles led to a shift in power away from civil chiefs and shamans, or Klamath medicine men, to warriors. The latter began to double as chiefs. They included the tongue-twisting trio of Monchnkkasgitk (usually rendered Mogenkaskit by whites), Kokdinks and Gumbotkni (alias Cumtucne, who died about 1866) and the more famous and euphonic Lileks and Chiloquin. Strangely, the warrior who rose to head-chief of the whole Klamath nation, Lileks, started off on the wrong moccasin. As a youth he was a *berdache,* a transvestite homosexual. But he underwent a supernatural experience on Mount Scott during one of the meditative pilgrimages or spirit quests that were common to both Klamaths and Modocs and discovered his manhood and prowess as a warrior. Never again did he affect women's dress or the ways of a squaw. He led his people to war and dominated the Klamath confederacy of tribelets or bands at the time the whites established hegemony over southern Oregon.

As early as 1844, Indian Agent Ephraim White urged the Klamaths to unite under a single head-chief (directly opposed to tribal tradition, as was also the case with the Modocs) and Lileks succeeded in becoming that key man. He was as lucky in love, with seven wives, as he was in war, and he became wealthy to boot. Having lived long enough at the Dalles to acquaint himself with the anything-but-inscrutable Occidentals, he adopted such hallmarks of their civilization as a code of law, centralized authority and punishment by flogging for everything from aggravated quarreling right on up (or down) to murder. He established *skookum* houses or underground prisons, with jailers, based on the guardhouse at Fort Klamath. And by 1866, Lileks accomplished the impossible, changing a basic tenet of his tribe's religion by substituting the white man's burial for the redman's traditional cremation of the dead. He also created titles of rank for his subordinates, again borrowing from Fort Klamath. He sub-chiefs became *sajints* or sergeants.

Unfortunately, like many other "essential" men of history, Lileks did not know when to quit. When he did not step down from his high office as he grew senile, Klamath Indian Agent Lindsay Applegate had to remove him for "imbecility" and loss of influence over his people. It was difficult to replace the old codger, and Applegate's first choice, Charlie Preston, interpreter at Huntington's 1864 treaty powwow, balked because of a lack of ambition. But Allen David, who had attended the Council Grove treaty as Boos-ki-you, agreed to replace Lileks.

Almost as famous as Lileks was Chiloquin, for whom an Oregon town is named. He was almost part of a dynasty. He was the son of a Klamath Marsh chief. His sister was also a chief, and his brother, Beaded Hat, was a sub-chief. As the Klamaths aped the whites more and more, headmen came to bear such prosaic names as Allen David, Dave Hill, Charlie Preston and Henry Blow, although there were still nonconformists like Captain George and Link River Jack. Unfortunately for historians, little Klamath history was preserved from pre-white times because the tribe's religion forbade the mention of a dead person's name, under penalty of death. Naturally, a great oral tradition was impossible under such circumstances.

Hardly had the dust of the Levi Scott-Jesse Applegate exploratory party of 1846 settled before the covered wagons of emigrants were rolling westward over the new South Emigrant Road via Applegate's Pass. They moved right through Modoc country and on the edge of Klamath country. Because of the Molalla War, in part, an armed escort was formed by Oregonians in 1848. Murders on the trail in the late 1840s were probably the work of Modocs, if not Pit River Indians. The Klamaths managed to avoid trouble with the overlanders, although Jesse Applegate cast covetous eyes on the well-watered Klamath basin and introduced a bill in the state legislature to charter a Klamath Company. The colonization bill failed to pass because opposing legislators believed Oregon's territorial government did not have the power to grant such concessions.

When settlement finally came to the Klamath basin and highlands, it was peripheral to the Klamaths' homeland. Much of the latter was off limits to squatters in any case, because of the great expanse of the Klamath Reservation and Fort Klamath military reserve after 1864. And even the few sooners who came in the 1850s tended to settle more on Link River and Lost River country, on the border between Klamath land and the Modocs' territory. Wallace Baldwin was an early arrival who ran fifty horses and some cattle from the Rogue River to the Link River crossing area when he was about nineteen years old. He was so peaceable that he did not even have a gun with him, trusting to his fishing pole and the provisions he had brought. He was welcomed by the Indians, who made him presents of game and *apaws* seeds. When Judge F. Adams came in 1856 to graze two thousand head of beef cattle in the area of later Keno, Oregon, he had no trouble, probably because he first secured permission from the local natives.

One of the first Californians to regularly visit both Klamaths and Modocs was Mart Frain, a trapper and Yreka trader who reached the Link River ford on April 30, 1857, with five pack mules loaded with beads and other trinkets. He found Klamaths, Modocs and even Snakes and Cayuses camped together and trading among themselves by the river. Frain swam his mules across to join in the barter, and a squaw in a tule (reed) *balsa* or canoe conveyed his goods across, using her feet—projecting through a hole in the bottom of the craft like an inverted Eskimo kayak—as paddlewheels. He traded his goods for twelve hundred skins, then watched the Indians gamble away all their precious new beads in the ancient odd-or-even game of chance. Frain came back several times to trade beads, looking glasses, red calico, copper and tobacco for marten, mink, beaver and otter furs and deerskins during the next few years. He always insisted that the Klamaths and Modocs were peaceful folk, at least until whites killed some of their men, from time to time, without provocation.

The pressure of settlement was much more on the Modocs than the Klamaths since the south fork of the Oregon Trail passed directly through their country. The Modocs reacted to white hostility with violence while the Klamaths bent over backwards, like India rubber men, to oblige the pale-faced newcomers. They became neutral in the strife between the whites and the Modocs and, eventually, became allies of the former against their kin. During the so-called First Modoc War of 1852, when Captains Ben Wright, Charles McDermit, Jim Crosby and John Ross were campaigning, Crosby pursued some Modocs all the way to the Silver Lake area, then killed some Klamaths at Klamath Marsh, on the Williamson River, and on both sides of Upper Klamath Lake. With remarkable forbearance, the Klamaths held their tempers in check and refused to let this outrage precipitate a war. Chiloquin, much later, explained his tribe's self-control: "Even if they felt like avenging the deaths of the people, they knew they could not contend against the whites long, for they had learned they were as numerous as the trees on the mountains."

In 1853 and 1854, armed escorts again accompanied the wagon trains rolling through the Modoc country, but early in the latter year four whites were killed in Lower Klamath Lake Valley. Settlers retaliated by falling upon some Indians at Klamath Ferry. The most objective people to be found in a highly biased society, honest civil and military officers, placed the blame on whites for the growing violence. Some even suggested that the settlers were invoking a policy of extermination, although the term genocide was not yet used. Small wonder, then, that some of the settlers transferred a smidgeon of their hatred from the Indians to certain Army officers and Indian agents.

On August 21, 1854, Joel Palmer, Superintendent of Indian Affairs for Oregon, took the first formal steps toward pacification of the western end of Applegate's South Road. Guided by a Warm Springs Indian, he powwowed with the Klamaths and Modocs at Upper Klamath Lake. Before distributing presents, he warned his audience through an interpreter of the swift and sure punishment that would follow any acts of violence or theft against the white man. He wrote in his pocket diary, "The council broke up with an apparent good feeling." The superintendent considered his brief *wa-wa* to have been a bona fide treaty council with the Klamaths, although no written document was forthcoming. In his report, Palmer denigrated the Klamaths as warriors although he was impressed with their elk skin shields, impervious to the sharpest arrow. He said: "They were once numerous but wars with the surrounding tribes and conflicts among themselves have rendered them meek. They now number about four hundred and fifteen souls. . . . They possess a few horses, and among them I saw four guns, but they had no ammunition. The bow and arrow, knife and war club constitute their weapons."

Palmer had a plan that would have demoralized the Klamaths and Modocs even sooner than was the eventual case. Like Applegate, he liked the appearance of the Klamath basin and sought to colonize it, but with trans-Cascades Indians rather than white Americans. Luckily for all concerned, Palmer's idea of exiling all the troublesome West Side tribes to the Klamath country was killed by his own superiors who, for once, respected the unwillingness of Indians to make such an insane move.

The next major visitors to Klamath country were Lieutenants R. S. Williamson and Henry L. Abbott, surveying a route for a possible California-to-Oregon railroad. They largely agreed with Palmer's estimate of the Klamaths, although the few horses of 1854 had grown to "many" the following year and the tribe now boasted at least one Yankee wall tent, properly erected with ropes and tent pegs. The explorers had no trouble with either Klamaths or Modocs even during these nervous—Rogue River War—times in Oregon.

Some straying Klamaths finally did get themselves involved in the Rogue River War, however, but not as combatants. Thirty-five braves were with the friendly Umpquas collected by a special Indian agent to move onto a temporary reserve during the trouble. The Klamaths surrendered their guns and ammunition quite willingly. In April 1856 there were 141 more of them forming part of a camp of 1,440 friendlies being moved to reservations. Chief Lileks hurried to Oregon City and secured their release and return to Klamath country by wagon, with supplies of beef and a military escort.

The Klamaths were accused by some settlers of setting war fires on the Klamath Trail over the Cascades and of having "evil intentions" in general, but most of the warnings of Indian Agent George Ambrose and of the scared citizens of Marion County during the Rogue River War were unfounded. Still, in 1856, shortly after the killing of thirty-nine emigrants and the presumed kidnapping of some women and children, Umpqua squaws showed up in settled country in white women's clothing—which was a good way to get killed, especially if the gingham bore bloodstains. When questioned about their garb, the women alleged they had obtained the garments from Indians at Klamath Lake. The Klamaths, now always ready to placate angry whites, summarily executed three suspects in the murder of five prospectors on the Rogue shortly after this interrogation of the Umpqua women. One wonders if they even bothered to get the right men, so prompt was their punishment.

One reason the Klamaths became involved in the murders way over on the Rogue River was the fact that the miners' corpses were found by Indian Agent G. H. Abbott while on his way to talk to the Klamaths and Modocs. He hoped to follow up Joel Palmer's offhand "treaty" with the genuine article. He thought that there was a chance the Bannocks and Paiutes might sign, too, and he planned to select a site on which he could concentrate all of the different tribesmen. This was the program being put forth by the settlers; group the Indians together, irrespective of tribes and natural geographical distribution, in reserves where the military posts, like Fort Klamath, could keep a sharp watch on them. Then the settlers could get on with their plowing and stump-burning. Then the Applegate Trail would be turned from a gauntlet to be run into a great highway, skirting both the Blue Mountains and most of the Humboldt Desert and pouring population into southern Oregon.

During the 1858 and 1859 territorial sessions, legislators directed their Congressional delegate to press for the establishment of a fort in the country of the Modocs and the Klamaths. But nothing happened. In 1859, Agent G. H. Abbott was in charge of a Klamath Lake Sub-Agency, but it was strictly on paper. There was no office or property, no reservation. Abbott lived in the town of Jacksonville while he was responsible for 472 Klamaths, 310 Modocs and 250 Yahuskin Snakes—a couple days' travel across the Cascades in snowless weather.

The campaign for a Klamath fortress was renewed in 1860 when the legislature memorialized Congress to this effect and also asked that a military road be cut across the Cascade Mountains and all the way to Boise from Eugene City. However, the outbreak of the Civil War drew Congress' attention from Klamath Lake to such nearer bodies of water as the vulnerable Potomac and disaster-haunted Manassas Creek.

About this time both Klamaths and Modocs grew restive, and there were bloody incidents with whites and between the two Indian tribes as well. Chiloquin, the pint-size chieftain of the Klamaths, ran into a Modoc enemy near Bogus Creek one day. The fellow had threatened to drink blood from the chief's heart. Although the most redoubtable warrior of all the Modocs, Scarfaced Charley, was the man's companion, Chiloquin (or so he said) haughtily ordered him out of his way and proceeded to kill his rival in combat. Remembering his victim's boasts and threats, Chiloquin then completed his revenge by cutting the cadaver open and drinking blood from the heart.

In 1861, Indians raided toward Yreka, but an uneasy peace largely prevailed in the land of the Klamaths and Modocs as the Civil War opened. That same year, Lindsay Applegate of Ashland Mills urged that an Indian agency be established in the Klamath country, not only to protect the emigrant road but because he wanted the Indians off the land. He saw it as good stock-raising country with considerable mineral potential. He was right about the first point and wrong about the second. In 1862, even the Klamaths were tempted to exploit the weakened military posture of Oregon, as regular soldiers were drawn off for Civil War duty. With the Modocs, they harassed settlers and travelers and extorted one hundred dollars from Joseph H. Chaffee for a license to operate a Klamath River ferry. But their greed knew no bounds. When he crossed seventeen men and twenty-seven animals, the Indians demanded a toll from the emigrants, too. They then charged the travelers one dollar a night for grazing rights and, after only two weeks, drove the ferryman away. Chaffee reported gloomily on the situation in the Klamath country: "When the party is small and defenceless, they rob them of what they have. The Indians are well armed, having in most instances two revolvers apiece, plenty of rifles and a good supply of ammunition. The Indians engaged in this work are the Klamaths, Paiutes, Snakes and Modocs. They assert that, in case of difficulty, they will be supported by all these different tribes of Indians."

The situation in the Klamath country had grown critical. The Government answer was not long in coming. Maj. C. S. Drew made his surveys and then founded Fort Klamath on September 5, 1863. He also recommended treaties with both Lileks' and Old George's bands of Klamaths and with the Modocs, most of whom acknowledged Old Schonchin as chief. He made his recommendation although he had only minute faith in the Indians as treaty signers, saying: "The Indians of the Klamath Lake region are justly denominated hostile. . . . The Klamath Lake, Modoc and Pah-Ute Indians, so far as relates to their general character, are virtually one tribe and none of them are in the least reliable for any good whatever. On the contrary, it is susceptible of the clearest demonstration that they are a horde of practical thieves, highwaymen and murderers, cowardly sycophants before the white man's face and perfidious assassins behind his back."

Drew's eloquent if intemperate opinions were at wide variance with the conclusions held by Superintendent of Indian Affairs J. W. Perit Huntington. According to him: "The bands near the Klamath Lakes are friendly with the whites and have been for some time. Their desire to treat for the sale of their lands has been known for some time."

Chiloquin agreed with Drew only in that the Klamaths and Modocs (not the Paiutes) were kissing kin, more or less. He knew that his people were not assassins, as did Huntington. He could not speak for the Modocs. In regard to the occasional friction between Modocs and Klamaths, as exemplified by his own killing and modified cannibalizing of the Modoc warrior at Bogus Creek, Chiloquin blithely said: "The Modocs and the Klamaths were, in the beginning, one people, and there never was any open trouble with them until after they first made war on the whites. The different bands sometimes quarreled and fought but that soon passed over, for we were really the same race and had a common interest, and the men of our band frequently married the women of another band." Klamath Chief Henry Blow agreed. "There never was any general war with the Modocs, for the tribes were friendly and had constantly intermarried. They went with us in raids on the Pit River country and some of them joined with us on other war parties."

In truth, some of the Klamaths were almost becoming white themselves. As they grew used to the settlers amongst them, they began to imitate them, as did the Modocs. The Klamaths grew more ambitious and materialistic than before, although they clung to their old tradition of burning the possessions of the dead, even (sometimes) a warrior's Pit River slave. A settler named More learned this, to his disgust. When his Klamath mistress died, her people burned up all the fence rails the couple had so laboriously split. Another religious privilege should have appealed to the mores of southern Oregon. It was, in Stephen Powers' words, "the envy of civilized men." The Klamaths were allowed by their faith to kill their mothers-in-law. Actually, this was no longer a common custom by the time the whites came.

The Klamaths' religion was close to that of the Modocs, but a little less dramatic perhaps. They worshipped a god, The Chief Above, who gave them everything and taught them to make elk skin boots, leggings and hats, and showed their squaws how to weave skullcaps. The Klamaths were careful never to dislodge stones or pebbles if they could help it because The Chief Above liked to walk from stone to stone on earth and was angry when one was misplaced by man. The Klamaths also revered certain animals, as did the Modocs. And with good reason; it was common knowledge among the Klamaths that fire had been lost everywhere in the world until Coyote and Wolf had stolen it from its hiding place and restored it to the people. Coyote carried the secret of fire in his toenails and passed it on to Turtle, who clambered slowly up into the mountains and communicated it to stones and trees so that the Klamaths could summon it by striking stones (flints) and drilling wood.

Both the Klamaths and Modocs were in a stage of demoralization during the 1860s. The conflict of two such opposing cultures—the Indian and the European—was tearing them apart. The case of the Klamaths was dramatized by an event of that period. Although they wore the white man's Levis and cotton or wool shirts, bore his weapons and traps and rode his horses or wagons, picked up American names and a smattering of the English language and even substituted burial for the traditional Indian cremation of the dead, the Indian in them kept breaking through the superficial "civilizing." Thus, when two of Captain George's Klamaths got drunk on white-man's firewater and not only disobeyed his commands but insulted him to his face during their war-whooping binge, the Chief coolly reverted to the old ways. He drew his bow and fitted a reed arrow to it and shot one dead where he stood; notched another shaft and shot the second man to death. Thus, Captain George settled a case of lese majesty, and the dead men's relatives did not dare protest the murders.

CHAPTER THREE

THE MODOCS

One of northeast California's historians, William S. Brown, likened the Modoc country in the 1850s to Daniel Boone's Dark and Bloody Ground of Kentucky of a century earlier. So, too, did Modoc War combatant Col. William Thompson. Certainly the small Modoc tribe earned a reptuation for ferocity during the 1850s that was little less than that of Boone's Shawnees. The prevailing attitude toward the Modocs on the Oregon-California frontier was displayed by Gov. Lafayette F. Grover of Oregon when he explained, or tried to justify, the Modoc War to Gen. John M. Schofield. He described the Modocs as a band of robbers and murderers, the most treacherous and bloodthirsty savages west of the Rockies, who occupied a country peculiarly adapted to protect them from successful pursuit after their forays. Grover claimed that the Modocs tortured, mutilated and murdered travelers indiscriminately, sparing only a few girls for slaves. "Over three hundred emigrants are known to have been slain in this manner by these Indians, ascertained by actual count of bleaching bones upon the soil, before the establishment of the military post at Fort Klamath in 1863. This post was established for the protection of the immigrant trains," concluded the governor, "and to make end to the slaughter and rapine of which the savages were constantly guilty."

The governor exaggerated the number of victims; it may have been half of his three hundred. Nevertheless, his indictment was accepted by Oregonians and some Californians. Col. William Thompson was a newspaperman of the period and he suffered even more from adjectivitis than the governor. He depicted the Modocs as fierce, remorseless, merciless, cruel and relentless savages. He considered the Modoc butcherers-of-emigrants to be as cunning and treacherous as the Apaches. Borrowing Voltaire's words for the French, he described them as being half monkey and half devil.

34

Even the friends of the Modocs were not enthusiastic. Historian Hubert H. Bancroft damned them with faint praise: "Not such a bad specimen as savages go, but filthiness and greed are not enviable qualities and he has a full share of both." Stephen Powers, the pioneer anthropologist who first studied the tribe in anything like a scientific sense, was ambivalent. He had a liking for them but nevertheless found them dull, cloddish and indolent in peace. In war they were tough and brave and notorious, as he said, for keeping Punic faith. Perhaps the Modocs' appearance was against them, in white men's eyes. Their faces were heavy, with low, somewhat flattened foreheads. Their most striking features were their heavy-lidded eyes; they all looked sleepy. Modoc mothers in the infancy of their children not only flattened their heads in the manner of some Washington tribes but also tugged and pulled at their eyelids to give them the dozing look they fancied. Besides this drowsy look, the Modocs had yellowish eyeballs and deep black pupils that made for a mean, surly appearance. Many, too, had inflamed eyes, and blindness was rather common among them because of the near-constant smudge of the fires in their poorly ventilated earthen winter lodges.

The Modocs were darker of skin than were the Klamaths and were more Mongolian-looking, with their high cheekbones, although they were not very prognathous and had strong nasal ridges. The hair of their heads was straight and dark. They removed their sparse body hair with tweezers except for their eyebrows, of which they were quite vain. Not as well proportioned physically as the Klamaths, the Modocs had more rugged physiques than the Shastas and the Sacramento Valley Maidus and other neighbors. Although they were a little slow (or reluctant) to express thought and emotion, they led an active and vigorous life of hunting, fishing and digging and were quick on their feet. Most remarkable of all—particularly with their numerous eye afflictions—was their power of vision. This would be made dramatically clear in the first battle of the Lava Beds, fought in a dense tule fog. Anything but merry, the few dances of the Modocs were confined to celebrations of war, death and the taking of scalps.

A small minority of whites, mostly Californians, got along well with the Modocs and genuinely liked them. A larger group of Californians and Oregonians feared them, and the largest group of all despised and denigrated them. The latter saw them as a half-dangerous nuisance, like coyotes, to be cleared from valuable range land as soon as possible. Given the presence of Fort Klamath, there was not much need to fear a small and debauched gang of bandy-legged, polygamous bucks chiefly adept at cadging whiskey and bumming grub from the tolerant, fun-poking citizens of Yreka when they were not busy pimping for their dusky wives, daughters and sisters. So their chief critics saw the Modocs.

Of course, the truth about the Modocs lay lost somewhere in between the extreme positions. They were neither "noble redmen" of a Delacroix painting nor villainous subhuman pests. As befitted the northernmost, the farthest-flung of all California tribesmen, the Modocs were the most rugged of individuals. They were stubborn go-it-aloners who were suspicious even of their own kissin'-kin, the Rock Indians of only a few miles away, and wanted no truck at all, most of the time, with their nearest other relatives, the Klamaths. The Modocs made up in aggressiveness what they lacked in numbers, and were as stubborn and stolid as oak stumps.

Modoc culture diverged markedly from that of all other California tribes and considerably from that of their neighbors and kinfolk, the Klamaths of Oregon. Their character was dominated by pragmatism. Right and wrong were translated into that which worked and that which did not work in an area where the living was seldom easy. This cultural trait made collision with the whites absolutely inevitable. Since the end *did* justify any means in the Modoc mind, the jumpy settler was right, for once, in seeing his red-skinned neighbor as a creature almost without ethics or morals, ready to stalk him like a wild beast any time that his mood might shift from indolence to violence. Once the Modoc considered himself at war with the settlers, he could strike when and as he pleased since his code of conduct carried no restrictions of fair warning or fair play.

But while the Modocs were a warlike people, more proficient at warfare than the Sacramento Valley folk to the south, they were not constantly on the warpath. Quite the contrary. Less aloof culturally from the whites than many redmen, the Modocs dressed like whites, took their names and nicknames, mixed with them in town and worked for them as ranch hands. They even adopted the whites' canvas tents in place of their own traditional lodges and learned to survive "civilized" diseases, after smallpox killed off 150 of their number in 1847. And when the white men went to war with them in 1872, they found that the Modocs fought like American troopers or

European grenadiers—only better—rather than like the hit-and-run savages of the Great Plains and Southwest. They used trenches, fortifications, strategy; they seldom mutilated or tortured their victims and only scalped an occasional foe in order to have a symbol for the victory dance after a battle. B. F. Dowell and many other men acquainted with them asserted that the Modocs became more loyal and kind as they adopted Yankee ways. Stephen Powers disagreed. He found them "churlishly exclusive," and their new loyalty to the whites to be merely fear. "My observation," he said, "which is not limited, gives painful proof of the fact that the younger and English-speaking generation are less truthful, less honest, and less virtuous than the old simon-pure savages."

Small wonder that politicians, press and public were perplexed by this curious race. The Modoc warrior was a mixture of contradictory and incongruous qualities. He was *sui generis.*

The Modocs' enemies were legion. The tribe maintained a live-and-let-live arrangement with the Klamaths and an uneasy peace with the whites between 1852 and 1872. All other peoples were more or less lumped as enemies, present or potential. Originally, Klamaths and Modocs had been one and the same people, members of the Maklak or Muckaluck tribe. But during the eighteenth century the southern peoples of this tribe or confederacy rebelled over a demand for tribute in the form of fish from Lost River. During the proper season this stream became one of the most remarkable fisheries in all America. The red suckers so crowded the river near its mouth that it was impossible to cross it by the fords. The minority of Maklaks who pulled away, to become as different from the larger group as Yankees from Britons, were dubbed Modocs. The word was said to mean Near Southerners or People to the South, but another tradition has it that they earned the name because they were so unfriendly, the term Moadoc meaning enemy in the Shasta tongue.

Modoc society featured a tripartite separation of powers. Not only were church and state separated, but so too was the military. Thus there was for each band of the tribe a civil chief or *Lá gi,* leader; a shaman or medicine man who combined the curate's calling with that of aboriginal general practitioner and psychiatrist; and a war chief. The *Lá gi,* had strictly a political function. His domain was the domestic scene, and he yielded to the warrior chief in times of strife. Still, he was the most powerful of the three in the view of the whites because he was more permanent and more easily recognized and identified than the shaman with his limited, mystical-medical sphere, or the war chief who was usually selected by a sort of *ad hoc* nominations committee of braves when the tribe decided to go on the warpath. Unlike the Klamaths, only men were chiefs and, apparently, homosexual *berdaches* need not apply either. A man's wealth and the number of persons in his household (thus, a guaranteed following) could help him attain the status of leader, but the prime requisite was oratorical ability. The long-winded were almost certain of success in Modocdom. General Canby, for example, found Captain Jack to be the most tireless haranguer he had ever met. To the Modocs, still water ran shallow. Like the American electorate, the tribe believed that the man who talked well would be an intelligent and successful leader, to boot. Judgment and diplomacy were expected to follow oratory just as surely as tail followed snout. Eventually, the top talker of the bands became the spokesman of the entire tribe and even a true, overall tribal leader like Old Schonchin. Since chieftainship was not hereditary, Schonchin and other chiefs either had to do a lot of fighting or a lot of talking.

When Modoc-American relations finally broke down circa 1872, so too did the old mores, and Captain Jack, really a sub-chief who doubled as a temporary war leader like Hooker Jim or Scarfaced Charley, was forced by circumstances and his own personality to also absorb the role of *Lá gi*. But the true civil chief, Old Schonchin, never gave it up, and even Captain Jack's breakaway band, if pressed, would probably have cited Schonchin as their chief and Jack only as their temporary war leader. It was the old problem of *de facto* versus *de jure* status. Jack never formally deposed Schonchin, and the burden of his double role so vexed Jack that he turned into a truly tragic feature, hag-ridden by indecision, a kind of Hamlet of the Lava Beds. Luckily, he was not saddled with the chores of a witch doctor, too. He had a capable shaman in Curly Headed Doctor, who took charge of all magic and ritual and "gave his people a good heart." And his incantations were highly effective in the Lava Beds battles. Otherwise, Captain Jack, the melancholy Dane of the Lava Beds, might have broken under the strain.

Captain Jack's white opponents saw him as the totalitarian leader of an army. They could hardly have been more wrong. He won his post by the strength of his personality, but he would hold it only as long as success came his way. Captain

Jack was virtually chairman of a committee of the whole, deposable by simple voice vote at any time, rather than a despot or dictator. Only the prestige of success and his powers of persuasion could save him from an ouster if he failed in leadership. And although the Modocs fought much more like a civilized army than other Indians, there was little military discipline as such, only the self-discipline of the guerrilla. The proficient warrior was listened to and followed. That made him an interim chief. If his skills failed, his following abandoned him for a better bet. In a very real sense, a Modoc band such as Captain Jack's was a more perfect—or at least more uninhibited—democracy than a New England town meeting or an inkwell-hurling French Assembly.

The *Lá gi* or chief was arbiter and peacemaker for the tribe or band, but the final authority lay in a lax community assembly, so informal that voting was almost unheard of and the chief had to keep an ear constantly to the ground to sense public opinion. The latter, again democratically, was what shaped and determined Modoc policy. Village gossip rendered decisions that the chief, the shaman and the war chief implemented. Custom and courtesy demanded that every point of view be heard and heard out, no matter how long-winded the citizen. But the mores also insisted that the majority ruled, absolutely, and that the minority must follow.

In a culture conditioned to violence and killing, there were four different kinds of homicide recognized. There was deliberate murder, including that attributable to witchcraft; manslaughter in a brawl; unintentional killing, most often in hunting accidents; and justifiable homicide, committed in anger and usually involving the dehorning of a cuckold. Indemnities and vengeance and feuds were all concomitants of intra-tribal torts, but the survivors of an adulterer were not likely to get a settlement from the wronged party. The code was anything but Draconian for Modocs. On the other hand, warfare was the almost inevitable result of the killing of a Modoc by a foreigner, white or red.

Serious crimes other than homicide included theft and, properly in a society geared to public speaking, slander. Suicide was rare and confined almost entirely to women. According to old Usee George, Captain Jack's first wife hanged herself with a buckskin rope because she was "jealous of a man." Most self-murders were by hanging or by the poison so popular with the more suicidal Paiutes, wild parsnip.

The "nation" the Modocs inhabited straddled the Oregon-

California border right on the Pacific flyway for migratory fowl. Its borders more or less ran from Mount Shasta northward along the Cascade crest to Butte Creek and Butte Lake and thence to the Klamath River to Klamath Falls, then eastward in a line between Lost River and Sprague River, touching Yainax Butte, to the west side of Goose Lake. This body of water the Modocs shared with other tribes. From the south end of the lake the line ran southwestwardly back to Mount Shasta. Violations of these boundaries meant war just as surely as salmon ran in the Klamath. But, with the coming of the whites, borders and boundaries in the tribal sense began to lose their meaning and the Modocs liked to hang about Yreka, once that town was founded in 1851, as much as around Lost River. Still, they only tolerated the Klamaths, and intermarried with them to produce the Gumbatwas or Rock Indians. They did not really like them. They despised, terrified and enslaved the Pit River Indians and looked down upon the Paiutes as well as hating them. Curiously, it is said that they feared the Shastas in addition to hating them, although the concept of a fearful Modoc brave is a little hard to swallow.

Because of the powerful Modoc ego, it was only natural that the tribe's early cosmogonists should place the exact center of the world—which was a flat disk—in the middle of Modoc territory. It lay, in fact, on a hill on the east shore of Tule Lake. The center of the known world of the Modocs was itself divided into three provinces that were strictly geographical, not political or ethnic. In the west was the land of the Gumbatwas, or Rock Indians, called People of the West; in the center were the Paskanwas, the River People; and on upper Lost River, beyond Lost River Gap and modern Olene, Oregon, and especially in Langell Valley were the easterners of the tribe, called People of the Far Out Country, or Kokiwas. The westerners were concentrated on the sunset side of a line drawn along the ridge separating Lower Klamath Lake from the Lost River Valley and then along the west shore of Tule Lake to the Lava Beds and southward to the bulk of Shasta. The main area of concentration was in the region of Willow Creek, a tributary of Lower Klamath Lake, paralleled by two other streams feeding Little (Lower) Klamath Lake, Cottonwood Creek and Hot Creek. This was the Willow Creek of the west, not to be confused with the more easterly stream of that name. The latter, feeding the flooded crater basin called Clear Lake or Wright Lake, dominated the area to which Captain Jack fled in the closing days of the Modoc War. There was even a third Willow Creek involved in the Modoc story: the stream that watered Fort Bidwell in Surprise Valley near Goose Lake. Along its banks marched U.S. Army reinforcements during the Modoc War.

The Modoc heartland, the land of the Paskanwas, lay on the lower stretch of Lost River's valley, or Kóketat, and the northern rim of Tule Lake. Some claim that the name Modoc means neither Southerner nor Enemy but is simply a corruption of the old name for Tule Lake, Moatak. This huge body of water was apparently without an outlet and drained only by evaporation but remained fresh. It was fed by Lost River at its northern end, a deep stream with only two crossings on its lower reaches, Stukel Ford and the Natural Bridge. These were strata of marls heaved up through the volcanic sandstone, pumice and egg-size black scoria to form vaults over and under which the waters of Lost River could pass. The Modocs were riparian folk because theirs was a hot and dry country in summer and all game, from reptiles, amphibians and fish to wildfowl and deer, congregated on the riverbanks and around the ponds, lakes and bubbling springs where there were cottonwoods and willows to provide shade and green grass in oases of a volcanic land verging on desert. Trees were few, otherwise—just yellow pine and a scattering of western cedar on the hills plus the ubiquitous juniper and piñón in the more Nevada-like areas.

Since the fisheries were there, settlement was there and, likewise, much of Modoc history. The lower Lost River was both the site of Captain Jack's birth and of the great tragedy of Modoc history, the Ben Wright massacre of 1852. There, too, was the capital of the Modocs, its Paris and Rome rolled into one. The Modoc metropolis was the west-side winter village of Wa'chamshwash, some fourteen semi-permanent earth-covered slab lodges, as comfortable as those the Mandans offered Lewis and Clark in 1804, plus a tribal crematory and a fine *temescal* or sweathouse. (In summer the Modocs roamed and contented themselves with wickiups of brush and willow boughs.) The Modoc War began when cavalry troopers "jumped" Wa'chamshwash in November 1872 while a ragtag band of irregulars, civilians playing soldiers, hit its suburb across the river, Na'kosh. From the twin villages the Modocs fled to the Lava Beds and the dramatic last stand that fascinated the whole world.

Essentially, the Modocs formed a closely knit tribe of no more than a thousand souls, counting mewling infants and drooling ancients. By the time of the Modoc War, long after the height of their power, they numbered probably only 250 persons. The U.S. Army was *never* able to accept the fact that its hundreds of troopers were fighting just fifty-odd braves led by Captain Jack. The geographical subdivisions of the Modoc nation did not impair the basic unity of the people, nor was there much social stratification, although wealth was recognized as being not only respectable but desirable.

Poetry, songs and myths were strong among the Modocs because of their powerful religion. They resembled the ancient Greeks not only in their cosmography but in their faith. Their pantheon was headed by Kumookumts, sometimes rendered Kumush, who was The Old Man, The Creator, Our Father. This Zeus of the California-Oregon line was a humanoid, and hermaphrodite, cultural hero and the greatest of a Noah's Ark of mythological beings or divinities. He was a trickster and a wanderer who traveled in the guise of an old crone despite a well-developed eroticism. He was revered by all, especially by the shamans who understood him more readily than the Modoc laity. According to the dogma of the priests, he had disappeared from the earth long before, but his footprints remained—like those of the mythical beast, Bigfoot, in the lower Klamath River Valley. Other anthropomorphic superanimal heroes of Modoc mythology included the ubiquitous and cunning Coyote, as well as Weasel, Spider and Eagle. The latter was the greatest of Kumookumts' adjutants, for although his home was on Sprague River, he liked to perch atop mountains and gaze for hundreds of miles, even as far as the *salt chuck* (Pacific Ocean). Eagle was the bringer of good luck, too, and if the all-wise avis flew overhead, it was sure to guarantee success in war and gambling (nothing was said of love) to the Modocs below. Eagle also gave all the other animals their names.

Bears, of course, were powerful beings, believed to have human intelligence, and snakes were immortal because they shed their skins and grew new ones. But more powerful than these fellows was Frog. He was as lucky as he was powerful, and if a Modoc killed a frog he would find that the spring where it lived would go dry, as punishment for the meddling human. The Modocs addressed their prayers not only to Frog and the other animal beings but, like most primitives, prayed also to sun, moon, stars and Mother Earth for good hunting. Nor did they neglect to pray to some of Mother Earth's offspring (in hopes of getting a juicy haunch of venison) such as mountain peaks and lakes. The *temescal* or Modoc sauna was not exactly a church or temple, but the sudatory did serve as an altar in that it was the place where Modocs most commonly offered up their prayers. In conjunction with their prayers, the natives also erected piles of stones along trails. Passersby would add a stone and a prayer in itinerant devotionals. Travelers who halted sometimes made offerings of food, Chinese fashion, to the spirits. The more devout Modocs liked to intone an orison as they arose with the dawn. It was with superstitious awe that N. B. Ball, a militiaman with Capt. Jesse Walker's company, heard the chants of early risers as the troops lay in ambush around a Modoc village in 1854, waiting for the braves to fill the notches of their rifle sights.

Dreams constituted the old and new testaments of the shamans, as well as of the lesser clergy called dream doctors and the ordinary laymen engaging in the soul-searching that ethnographers and others of their ilk term "crisis quests," which resembled a combination of Christian pilgrimage and the religio-philosophical insights of cosmic consciousness.

The Modocs did not believe in an immortal soul but rather in a life force in the heart that escaped through the top of the head. This force mixed with the air like the hydrocarbons of modern America. The dead were cremated, never buried, and were burned only by day, never at night. The Modoc religion was the opposite of Shintoism; the dead were *deliberately* forgotten, and as quickly as possible, and never mentioned. Although the women, particularly, mourned the dead for a long time with cropped hair and faces smeared with pitch and wild plum seed charcoal, all possessions of a dead person were disposed of to reduce or eliminate all visual reminders of the departed. Even dreaming about the dead was held to be a portent of very bad luck for the Modocs.

Omens were seen, heard and sensed everywhere. A barking coyote meant a death in the village, likewise the hoot of an owl or the insane call of a loon in the night. Good luck charms were worn to offset the danger of a full moon setting off old *canis latrans* into a fit of ululation. Eclipses were the fault of gluttonous Bear swallowing either the sun or the moon. Luckily for the Modocs, Frog had only to urinate on *ursus* and he would speedily regurgitate his planetary meal. Since Frog's aim was sure and his bladder always full, the Modocs were never left long without sun or moon. On ecliptic occasions the Modocs shouted like genuine lunatics, rooting for Frog to use Bear as a *pissoir.*

Through dreams and spirit quests, some of which may have taken a few intrepid Modocs even to magical Crater Lake (of which the Klamaths were terrified), shamans—mostly men, but not all—derived real power. The individual's "call" to the vocation of witch-doctoring came usually in a dream, for there was nothing hereditary about shamanism. The medicine man among the Modocs needed very little specialized hardware. He bore no rattles or drums to enhance his bedside manner when curing the sick, nor did he wear distinctive dress except for the small badge of office which was a red buckskin skullcap decorated with clustered and pendant woodpecker feathers. And, figuratively speaking, his black valise was nigh empty. It would contain probably a pipe and a buckskin band to which feathers were attached, and perhaps a necklace of bear claws. If he were a quack not really able to withdraw foreign bodies from a patient by mumbo jumbo and sucking, his pack might hold a few pebbles, feathers and thorns which he could palm during his treatment as proof of his efficacy.

The shaman was feared and given a wide berth by run-of-the-riverbank Modocs. He could depose a chief. Most Modocs believed that the killer of a medicine man would die within a year of the deed, from supernatural causes. On the other hand, it was commonly believed that the profession was as dangerous as it was powerful, for few shamans died peacefully in bed. The medicine men possessed spirits or familiars—Frog, Rattlesnake, Fish Hawk—who provided diagnoses and cures for man's ills, both natural and spiritual. When they failed him and he lost a patient, he sometimes paid with his life. Captain Jack's eradication of a shaman for malpractice was one of the many causes of the Modoc War.

Most of the Modocs, however, were more concerned with life on their flat little earth than they were with death and dreams and spirit quests. In the eyes of white travelers, Kumookumts' realm looked only marginal. It was far better than Nevada's Black Rock Desert, which lay not very far away, but was no Willamette or Sacramento Valley by a long shot. Still it was paradise enough for the hard-working, hard-hunting Modocs, who were said (by an apocryphal story) to call their land ''The Smiles of God.'' At least, before the digging of drainage ditches and the building of dikes, it was a land blessed with many lakes and streams, if arid between the watercourses.

When March's sun melted away the snow, the Modocs dismantled their winter lodges to let the foundations dry out for the next season and moved to their regular fishing sites in time for the spring run of red suckers. This fish, despite its unfortunate name, was good eating, tasty and not bony. When they spawned they ran up from Clear Lake in great numbers, where they could be easily shoveled ashore with baskets by the laziest lout of all the Paskanwas. The women dried the fish and then gathered turnip-like desert parsley roots in April and May before moving to the higher, moist meadows elevated four to seven thousand feet where the best digging grounds for *apaws*—so-called wild potatoes—were to be found in May. This crop, dug with fire-hardened sticks of mountain mahogany and carried by the squaws in woven baskets on their backs, was the soft and milky root, under a thin brown rind, which was the staple of the Modoc diet, their daily bread. It could be roasted, boiled or dried. John C. Frémont described it as the most agreeably flavored of all the root crops of the Far West. Raw, the *apaws* tasted half-way between a potato and a carrot, with a dash of celery to intrigue the palate. Some whites even thought that the Modocs got its name from wandering, forgotten Spaniards who called it *apio,* or celery. Cooked, the roots tasted like roasted chestnuts, the *marrons* of Paris.

The Modocs also fished for trout—black, speckled and silver-sided—which appeared each year in Tule Lake and the Bonanza River. Some of these fish weighed fifteen pounds each, and a few record catches ran up to twenty-five pounds. The fishermen stretched seines across the bows of their canoes and simply paddled them about until the nets were filled. (Salmon did not venture up to Modoc country because the gravel beds necessary for their spawning all lay below the first rapids of the Klamath River.) Next, the Modocs moved back to the high meadows, this time to dig a kind of bittersweet *camas,* as pungent as ginseng, in June or July to dry and store as winter rations. They then shifted to the poisonous white *camas,* or death *camas,* having learned to render them edible by leaching, much as the California Indians made their acorn flour palatable by rinsing out all of the puckery tannic acid.

Summer was the hunting season for pronghorn antelope on the plains and mountain sheep in the Lava Beds. While the men were hunting, the women were gathering *wocus*, the farinaceous seeds cupped in the poppy-like pods of an aquatic plant similar to the water lily. This seed, the mainstay of the Klamath diet as the *apaws* or western false caraway was to the Modocs, was made into a bread or *panada.* Even American settlers, picky about Indian food, learned to like *wocus*. They would gather and parch the seeds for eating in a bowl of milk as a breakfast cereal. The Modocs also ate *icknish* or Indian celery, wild plums, and even tules, bullrushes, for food.

A second run of suckers drew the Modocs back to the river banks in late August and September while the women hunted and dried serviceberries, chokecherries and such other fruits as the wild plum. Now the men hunted wapiti or elk, using a brush and rope enclosure (the so-called chute and pound of the anthropologists) combined with a drive of the animals. They also hunted the herds of mule deer that were the equivalent of buffalo to the Modocs. By October they were back in winter quarters on Lost River near Tule Lake, building new homes or repairing their old lodges. The skilled fishermen amongst them, employing hooks, traps and spears to take chub, suckers, buffalo fish or mullet, minnows and freshwater shellfish, also enjoyed a last run of steelhead in December and then reinforced their winter larder by ice fishing. When winter tightened its icy grip on the countryside, the Modocs opened their hoards of iron rations—dried *camas,* piñón nuts (the so-called pine nuts of the market), dried fish and the seeds of buckwheat, dock, tarweed, lamb's-quarters and other plants and grasses. Although their caches were secret, pilfering was common because of the might-makes-right moral code of the tribe. Still, the more provident Modocs were usually spared the annual "starving time" which each winter brought to the Pit Rivers.

The Modocs not only survived in their austere land but actually thrived because of splendid adaptation to their environment. Atop the gleaning, fishing and hunting base of their economy they grafted warfare and slaving to enhance their standard of living. War parties in ancient times numbered a dozen men. Against the Pit River Indians or the Shastas or Paiutes, the aggressor Modocs of the 1840s would mount a war party of up to a hundred men, counting Klamath auxiliaries. They marauded for two or three days on rations of roots and dried meat so that they would not be encumbered by women, to whom all cooking was delegated. The Modocs became natural tacticians because of these raids, keen at picking advantageous ground for their fights—as the U.S. Army would learn. They sometimes wore armor of wooden rods or, better, a cuirass of elk rawhide sewed with sinew. In cold weather they wore robes of skins and furs, sometimes decorated for gala occasions with the splendid colors of duck scalps. But since the warriors preferred to fight in summer, they usually wore only a breechclout and moccasins, for ease of movement.

There was complete freedom to join or to resign from a war party. This proved to be the fatal weakness in Captain Jack's fight with the Army. A sense of loyalty and military discipline was almost entirely lacking. In such a tightly knit people there was no intratribal warfare. The nearest thing to it in Modoc history was Captain Jack's separatism, when his insurgents split away from the main body of the tribe under Schonchin. Even under the great stress of the Modoc War there was no civil war as such, although some of Jack's lieutenants sold out to the Army and turned against him, again because of a moral code that seemed inside-out to white observers. Seldom did the Modocs raid in winter or during bad weather, and seldom did they have much to fear, themselves, in these times. This explains the complete lack of preparedness for the raid by Fort Klamath cavalry on Captain Jack's village on a cold November dawn of 1872. Finally, the Modocs differed from most other tribes in that they were not particularly interested in collecting scalps as trophies of coups. A scalp or two as a token of victory would do quite as well as a dozen in the ceremonial scalp dance of victory. Being materialistic by nature and tradition, the Modocs preferred live slaves to dead scalps as souvenirs of their triumphs over enemies. They were a much better investment, and a victory without the booty of slaves was an empty one.

The Modocs were only mediocre craftsmen. Naturally, living in a land of pumice, scoria and *aa* or *pahoehoe* lava, they made little pottery for the lack of suitable clay. Their baskets were excellent, if not as notable as those of the Pomo and Washo. Their best work was in the making of handsome willow baby baskets. They had little art other than rock paintings. The Modoc canoes were few and were either crude dugouts or tule *balsas*. Simple rafts outnumbered canoes, although they knew how to use adzes and horn wedges and how to control burning by the use of pitch. Canoes were both paddled and poled, but the Modocs did not excel as watermen. Their half-subterranean homes were comfortable and well made, but in summer they abandoned them for mat-covered huts of willow poles or rude sagebrush windbreaks. The sweathouse was their community center.

In aboriginal times, Modoc clothing varied from a loincloth of tule, swamp grass or sagebrush bark to the rabbit skin cloaks of winter decorated with brilliant mallard feathers. The pelts of coyotes and groundhogs were used, too, as cloaks. Later, the influence of the Plains Indians reached the Modocs either via the Klamaths or the Paiutes and they changed to buckskins. With the coming of the whites, they changed costume for a third time, adopting with alacrity the Levis and flannel shirts of the settlers. The squaws imitated their lighter-skinned sisters by changing to calico dresses. Moccasins were of skin in summer and of woven fibers in winter. Leggings were worn by both men and women and in summer and winter alike. Women wore the tribe's fine basketry hats more than did the men. Often the latter preferred a cylindrical hat of cottonwood bark or the inner bark of the pine. In winter they would doff this headgear and don a fur hat.

There was little face painting among the Modocs, compared with the High Plains tribes, but during the Ghost Dance craze, face painting of magical designs became common. They did little tattooing, but nose ornaments were sometimes worn in the pierced septum and the women pierced their lobes for earrings. Beads and shells, particularly the rare tubular seashell called the dentalium, were the principal articles of jewelry and, together with clamshell disks, doubled as money.

Because the Modocs looked and acted so differently from surrounding tribes and because they were so adept at mimicking white customs, it was natural that a legend should grow that they were either the decayed remnants of the Aztecs or part white, the result of an admixture, long ago, of Caucasian blood. Supposedly, this infusion came from an unrecorded visit of Spanish explorers. Much more likely, it came from the quite recorded visits of Hudson's Bay Company trappers and early Yankee squawmen. Where Indian Agent A. B. Meacham and pioneer Oliver C. Applegate attributed the Modoc uniqueness to Aztec origins, many other whites thought they found a Christian God and Hell and a Savior and a Heaven in Modoc mythology. There were even said to be tales in the Modoc oral tradition that could only be of the forbidden fruit of the Bible. And if Lot's wife was not turned into a pillar of salt by Kumookumts, he did turn a woman into stone.

The Modocs really came to the attention of California and Oregon settlers in 1846, quite aside from their supposed involvement in the ambush of John C. Frémont near Upper Klamath Lake that year. That same season, pioneers Levi Scott and Lindsay Applegate, who had come to Oregon with Dr. Marcus Whitman in 1843, set out from the Dalles to blaze a new

Oregon Trail, a southerly route to the Willamette Valley from the Hudson's Bay Company trading outpost of Fort Hall, Idaho. Leaving on June 20, 1846, the Scott-Applegate party camped near the Frémont ambuscade site on the twenty-ninth before crossing Lost River on the incredible underwater arch of the Natural Bridge. This bizarre ford was typical of a crazy river that played hide and seek with the explorers. Between its head in Clear Lake and its mouth in Tule Lake, the confounded river not only coursed in almost a full circle but, several times, vanished from sight to flow underground before popping up again to surprise the explorers.

Among the followers of Applegate and Scott were Moses (Black) Harris, one of the most famous of Rocky Mountain men, and David Goff. The latter introduced the Oregonians to the Modocs. Starting off after a band of mountain sheep which he spotted in the rugged and unexplored Lava Beds lying on the south shore of Tule Lake, Goff became separated from his comrades and then lost. Before long, the hackles of his neck began to warn him that he was being stalked. In the very nick of time the main party found Goff, and the Modocs who had been trailing him pulled back and took to Tule Lake in their canoes when they saw how well armed was the force of palefaces.

Otherwise, the Modocs gave the expedition no trouble, and it laid out a new trail from Tule Lake across the plateau now called the Devil's Garden, thence to the south shore of Goose Lake and over the Warner Range via Fandango Pass and Surprise Valley to Massacre Lake, which the Applegate-Scott party gave the unflattering but less alarming name of Mud Lake. From there they ran the trail across the bleak Black Rock Desert of Nevada to Soldier Meadows and Rabbit Hole Springs until they reached the safety of the well-watered Humboldt River portion of the Oregon-California Trail, which they followed up to Fort Hall. The Oregonians were back home by October 3, 1846, having proved the feasibility of an alternate route to the Blue Mountains-Columbia River road. They may have left an unwelcome guest behind them because, according to Modoc tradition, smallpox swept the tribe shortly after their entrance into the Tule Lake country.

Lindsay Applegate and his friends did not make their reconnaissance in order to plan a toll road that would fatten their purses. Rather, they had in mind a free route that would bypass the Hudson's Bay Company-controlled northern approach to Oregon. They were, in fact, playing a hand in the game of Manifest Destiny which, shortly, would find Uncle Sam winning the pot (the Oregon Territory) from John Bull. The Applegate Trail, or South Road, provided a low and rather snow-free passage into both California and Nevada to emigrants all too conscious of the dangers of the High Sierra after the Donner Party disaster of the winter of 1846.

The one major drawback of the South Road was not demonstrated fully until late September 1850. A badly wounded man staggered into Jacksonville to report himself to be the only survivor of a party of eighty persons that had been attacked by Modocs just as the teamsters were bringing the wagons into the circle which was the customary corral and defensive position of all emigrant trains when they camped. Surprise was complete. From the rimrock facing Tule Lake's eastern shore, the war-whooping Modocs fell upon the caravan and massacred every person except the exhausted courier who had fallen, wounded and unconscious but unnoticed, into a screen of tules on the lakeshore.

An armed party led by Col. John Ross rushed to the lakeshore promontory now called Bloody Point and found it a ghastly site. Stripped and mutilated bodies of men, women and children lay amidst the charred ruins of prairie schooners. According to the reports of the would-be rescuers, babies and small children had been swung by their heels to dash out their brains against wagon wheels. From the grouping of some bodies it appeared that husbands and fathers had been forced to witness the slaughter of their loved ones before being put to death themselves. The men of that rescue party never forgot the shocking sight that met their eyes at Bloody Point, and never forgave the Modocs. One of them was sixteen-year-old Ivan D. Applegate. While he did not bear a burning brand of hatred for the Modocs all of his life as did some of his comrades, he did not forget the fate of the unfortunate emigrants and he could never trust the Modocs. Not once did he pass the site in his long life in Oregon without pausing to remove his hat in memory of the murdered travelers of the fall of 1850.

Sparsely settled southern Oregon and northern California were in no position to retaliate. But the settlers were not about to write off such an atrocity to experience. A year after the massacre, Capt. John F. Miller and a company of Jacksonville volunteers performed escort duty on the Applegate Trail. They arrived at Bloody Point just in time to prevent a repetition of the tragedy of 1850. Miller rescued a party that had been harassed for several days by Modocs, then patrolled the trail but did not attempt to attack the redmen. Once, however, when his men spied smoke rising from the reeds of a dried-up bay of Tule Lake, he captured several Modoc squaws. Some of the volunteers, remembering the dismembered carcasses of Bloody Point, wanted to kill the Indian women out of hand because some of them still wore ragged and blood-smeared garments obviously stripped from the corpses of white women. It was with great difficulty that Miller restrained his men from vicious reprisals.

The next atrocity attributed to the Modocs occurred either on Willow Creek or on Crooked Creek in California's Siskiyou County south of Lower Klamath Lake. An emigrant party estimated to number one hundred persons wandered off the Applegate Trail. According to Siskiyou tradition, every soul was systematically killed and thrown into a stream where the bleached bones and half-burnt wagons could still be seen in 1873. Only two sisters, about fourteen and sixteen years of age and sometimes identified as the Reed girls, were spared. The younger girl died first and, eventually, two Modoc warriors quarreled over her sister, and one of the rivals ended the argument by grabbing her by her hair, throwing back her head and cutting her throat. He then threw her body over the rimrock near Hot Creek. A witness to the throat-slitting was Scarfaced Charley, then only about sixteen years old, himself. When he worked on John A. Fairchild's ranch, he told his employer about the incident. Fairchild, in turn, told two members of the Oregon Volunteers during the Modoc War, and these two men, C. B. Bellinger and William Thompson, secured leaves of absence and made a search for the girl's remains. Near a burnt wagon on February 18, 1873, they found a skull, a rib and an arm bone. They were just about where Scarfaced Charley had described the murder, a ledge on the right side of the road leading from Nat Van Bremer's ranch to Pressley Dorris's place, and not far from the latter. Bellinger and Thompson tried to learn something of the ambushed party but were unsuccessful. They took the bones to Jacksonville, packed them in a box and expressed them to David Rafferty of East Portland for his specimen cabinet.

Full reprisal for the Applegate Trail murders waited until 1852 and the organization of several para-military companies of Yrekans by Captains Charles McDermit, Jim Crosby and Ben Wright. All three were given the title of captain, but Wright proved to be a born leader as well as a ruthless man. Although born and raised a Quaker, the charismatic Wright already enjoyed a growing reputation as an Indian fighter when he became a squawman in northern California. He lost caste, to be sure, in polite society because of his marital arrangements but not one whit of his reputation as a frontiersman, which counted for more in Victorian California. He soon won a strong mixture of approbation and detestation as he sought an eye for an eye, in the most unmistakable terms. An apocryphas story had him inviting Modocs to a feast of beef he had spiced with strychnine, to celebrate the murder of eighteen travelers that season. The story is probably not factual—not that the ruthless Wright would have blanched at such a strategem. In fact, it is almost sure that he did buy poison to "exterminate the red rats," as Elijah Steele quoted him. But either Wright's Indian interpreter tipped the Modocs off, as Steele believed, or the Yreka druggist, Dr. Ferber, so adulterated the poison to increase his profits that it was not toxic enough. Or perhaps the Modocs, familiar with toxins, were just too wary for Ben. In any case, Steele claimed only one Modoc died of poisoning, and Wright certainly fell back on tried-and-true methods of exterminating Indians.

Shortly after he rescued a peaceful overland party on September 3, 1852, from a Modoc attack where Bloody Point pinched the trail against the ten-foot-high beds of tules of the lakeshore, an ambush occurred in which four men were killed and mutilated and another man wounded through the back and lung by an arrow. Captain Wright took two Modocs prisoner. He sent one as a messenger to the band and held the other as a hostage. When a Modoc messenger appeared, he brought a proposal for a peace treaty which included the surrender of the two captive girls of whom Wright had heard rumors. Wright led his forty-three-man force, which included at least five Indians— Bob, Bill, Joe, Penache and Sail—and had his three lieutenants and a sergeant place them in strategic positions around the Modoc camp near Natural Bridge. But there was no fight and the Siskiyou County Rangers spent three days in peaceful if inconclusive powwowing. No white captives appeared, but the Indian population began to swell at the same time that some of Wright's men drifted away. On the fourth day he is said to have had only eighteen men to back him up. By now he was sure that the Modocs meant to do to him what he had planned for them. Tired of their buying time with tall stories and false promises, he decided to anticipate their treachery with a taste of their own medicine. He positioned his men so that they could cover the entire village of some forty-five warriors with their rifles, then stalked boldly into the middle of the village. He was wearing his *serape* or blanket poncho to keep off the morning cold—and to hide the loaded pistol he held in each clenched fist. Wright walked up to the chief and demanded that he make good on his promise to release the kidnapped girls. Again according to the story, which has not been accepted as gospel even in pro-Wright Yreka, the Modoc chief insolently told him that he had no captive women and had never meant to keep his promise anyway. He said to Wright, "You hold our men as hostages and we outnumber you so much we shall have to hold you as such," or something to that effect. It was enough for Ben. Hardly had the chief finished his words before Wright lifted his revolvers clear of his *serape* and shot him dead in his tracks. He then broke into a zigzag run for cover on the perimeter of the camp as his men poured a volley into the lodges to cover his retreat. Once he was safe back in his lines, Wright turned and led his men in a charge on the village. The Modocs broke and fled, puzzled and surprised by the deadliness of the fire of these whites who fought like demons—or Shastas—instead of cowering and begging for mercy like the peaceable farmers trapped at Bloody Point. Some of the Indians jumped into Lost River to escape and were there shot like ducks. Others hid in the sagebrush from which they were routed by the Siskiyou Rangers' methodical search. They were shot down like jackrabbits as they were flushed from their hiding places. Those hiding underwater, in the river, betrayed by bubbles, were jabbed with long poles and shot. At the cost of only a few men wounded, Ben Wright left the Modoc capital a shambles, with many women and children slain along with their menfolk. One estimate placed the Indian dead at forty-six; another—Elijah Steele's—had forty of forty-seven killed and one poisoned by strychnine. Among those killed, of course, was the chief. (Supposedly he was the father of Kientpoos or Captain Jack, but a contrary tale had Jack's father being killed in a battle with Warm Springs and Tenino Indians near the headquarters of the Deschutes when Jack was only a child.) It would take twenty years, but eventually the Modocs had their revenge during the Modoc War.

The Ben Wright massacre effectively ended the Modoc threat to travelers on the South Road for most of the following two decades, although, in the words of Col. James B. Fry, "The

heathen treasured up the example these Christians set him."
Wright's men paraded the streets of Yreka as heroes though
they were as penniless, ragged and as brutalized by their
campaign as their recent foes. Some of the men waved trophies
in the form of Modoc scalps at the cheering crowds. Ben Wright
himself was feted like a sagebrush Caesar with public demonstrations, bonfires, banquets and—sublime irony—appointment
as an Indian agent. Although one of the company. E. P. Jenner,
in later years insisted that each one of Wright's rangers had
risked his life with no expectation of remuneration, the fact is
that claims were promptly filed with the state and promptly
paid. The legislature in 1853 appropriated $23,000 in payment
for services rendered by the Siskiyou County Rangers. By New
Year's Day 1855, warrants had been issued by the Board of
Examiners to the sum of $14,987. Privates were paid $4 a day,
and Wright received a total of $744 for his service from August
24 until November 24, 1852. He did not have long to enjoy his
cash or notoriety. The day after Washington's Birthday of 1856,
Frémont's old guide, Enos, trusted by Wright, led a massacre of
twenty-five whites at Gold Beach. Enos personally killed Wright
with an axe, mutilated his corpse, cut out his heart and cooked
and served it to his fellow rebels.

This kind of atrocity bred not only retaliation but an
unreasoning hatred of all Indians, without distinction, among
the white settlers. Stephen Powers was shocked at the murderous disregard held by the Oregonians for the Modocs. He
wrote, "I have more than once, when sitting at the fireside in
winter evenings, listened to old Oregonians telling with laughter
how, when out hunting deer, they shot down a 'buck' or a
squaw at sight, and merely for amusement, although the tribe to
which they belonged were profoundly at peace with the
Americans."

The Ben Wright Massacre on Lost River, which many
knowledgeable frontiersmen felt was completely justified, put a
stop to large-scale trouble with the Modocs. Little was heard of
them, although in 1854 some of them bragged to Superintendent of Indian Affairs Joel Palmer that the tribe had killed
thirty-six whites in the preceding four years. That same year,
Chief Schonchin is said to have made an informal treaty of
peace with Capt. James Walker. Attacks on travelers shifted to
the east and west, involving the Paiutes on the one hand and the
Rogue River Indians in the Siskiyous. The latter interdicted
travel on the California and Oregon Road or Siskiyou Trail and

brought on the bloody Rogue River War. Neither the Klamaths nor the Modocs took any real part in this struggle, although a Captain Judy claimed to have had a battle in 1854 on the Klamath River north of Yreka with a force (strange allies, if true) of Modocs and Shastas. More likely true are the tales of Modocs joining Klamaths to fight Shastas and some Trinity River Indians in 1855 over an obsidian quarry north of Shasta Butte. But in 1859 there were reports of Modoc raids, and a five-man party of whites was murdered by an Indian war party that included two of Chief Lileks' Klamaths. He had the three perpetrators of the raid seized immediately and executed. Lt. Lorenzo Lorain and Lt. Alexander Piper then led sixty-eight soldiers from Fort Umpqua across the Siskiyou Mountains to pacify the Modocs in 1860. The soldiers established short-lived Camp Day, but the Modocs needed no chastising. They were not, at the moment, interested in bothering civilians or soldiers. The outbreak of the Civil War emboldened them, however, and some Modocs were believed involved in the attack by Paiutes and Pit Rivers on a cattle drive in Hot Spring Valley near modern Canby, California. Three men driving the stock to feed Virginia City's hungry Comstock miners were killed, a fourth cowboy was wounded, and 910 head of cattle were rustled. But the mere presence of Lieutenant Piper and sixty-two men of the 3d Artillery in the Klamath-Modoc country brought tranquility and peace to the land again.

Chief Schonchin of the Modocs virtually sued for peace, telling the whites that it was their stupidity that caused warfare between them and his people. He said that they could not distinguish between Modocs and horse-thieving Snakes, or Pit Rivers. But, he sadly concluded: "I think if we kill all white men, no more come. We kill and kill but, all time, more come and more come like grass in spring. I throw down my gun. I say 'I will fight no more.' My heart is sick. I am old man."

For the moment, Old Schonchin's people followed his example, and in 1862 Oregon Superintendent of Indian Affairs, William H. Rector evaluated the Modocs as more of a nuisance than a real problem. On September 2 of that year, in fact, he suggested that they be subjugated and governed like a colony, with their chiefs and sub-chiefs acting as policemen.

CHAPTER FOUR

COUNCIL GROVE

Most Americans in the nineteenth century made no serious attempt to accept the Indian on his own terms. They either saw the Indians as candidates for civilized society or romanticized them as noble redmen—or, at the other extreme, as sneaking human wolves. But the Modocs and Klamaths had a few genuine friends among the white settlers of the border, men who accepted them pretty much on their own terms. Most prominent were Judge Elijah Steele and A. M. Rosborough of Yreka, two of the wicked Californians who incited the Modocs to violence—in the eyes of many Oregonians. The Modocs not only liked the two, they respected them and dubbed the former "Joe Lane's Brother," likening him to the old Indian-fighting governor of Oregon Territory. Both served their state as Indian agents, and it was Steele, in 1864, who tried to ward off impending disaster for the Modocs by means of a Valentine's Day treaty. In the summer of 1863, Steele was appointed Indian agent for Northern California, and in this official capacity he interceded to end a guerilla war between the Klamaths and Modocs on the one hand and the Shastas on the other. The treaty was a result of this action.

Apparently in fear of being punished by the soldiery at newly established Fort Klamath, a band of Modocs and Klamaths came to visit their friend at his Yreka home. Steele was absent, but when he returned he found that his wife had been lecturing them on how to live in peace. Well she might. Not only were the Modocs again warring with the Shastas and Pit Rivers, but they were blaming white settlers for aiding the Shastas against them and, in revenge, were beginning to steal cattle and rob travelers. Even the now-docile Klamaths were aroused to violence, and Colonel Drew had to arrest and execute Old George, or Captain George, while another hostile chief, Skookum John, was killed by Drew's troopers in November 1863 while resisting arrest. George had known enough English to understand the gravity of the Civil War and to dream of uniting the Indians in a racist war against all whites while they were distracted by their own rebellion.

Steele powwowed with Lileks of the Klamaths, Schonchin or Sconges of the Modocs, Josh and Jack of the Shastas, John of the Scott Valley tribe and Jim of the Hamburg Indians. Present was a prominent Modoc sub-chief Kientpoos (Kintpuash), whose name was understood by Lt. George W. Kingsbury as Fornicate-Too-Much. Apparently the lieutenant was being fooled by the Modocs or else he misunderstood sign language. Kientpoos really meant Having-the-Waterbrash (pyrosis), that is, Man-with-Heartburn. For an Indian, he was a nervous, sensitive fellow with the acid stomach that accompanies the more Western temperament. Presumably Steele did not like the name (small wonder!), so he dubbed him Captain Jack either because he resembled a Yreka miner of that name or, less likely, because he was fond of hand-me-down uniforms and buttons from Fort Klamath. Steele was deservedly proud when he got the disparate group of aborigines to agree to abandon the warpath. The cost of his treaty was some grub and forage for his Indian friends plus the gift of exactly two blankets. He reported to his superiors, "I have faith to believe that this conference has saved the country a bloody war with the numerous bands of Indians inhabiting the western slope of the Nevada mountains to northern California and southern Oregon."

The Indians agreed to live in peace and friendship with each other and in amity with the whites, Negroes and Chinese of the frontier. Any individual violating the agreement was to be surrendered to the soldiers at Fort Klamath for punishment. Free passage through the Indian country was guaranteed to all travelers, without toll. The only such charges allowed were for ferriage of rivers or guidance across unknown country. The Indians agreed not to get drunk or to steal when in the white man's towns or camps, were never to carry bows and arrows in settled areas unless they were hunting, and under no circumstances were to enter towns armed with rifles or pistols unless for the sole purpose of having them repaired. They were to stop selling Indian children and squaws as slaves, although Steele had no objection to a woman being traded off if the buyer agreed to marry her before a judge. The Indians further agreed to stop raiding the Pit River tribal settlements and to submit to the regulations of Fort Klamath officers. The Modocs and Klamaths were granted permission to visit all settlements and to submit to the regulations of Fort Klamath officers. The Modocs and Klamaths were granted permission to visit all settlements and guaranteed protection while there, as long as they provided themselves with passes issued by Fort Klamath's officers.

Unfortunately, while Judge Steele knew Indians he did not savvy Washington bureaucracy. His highly successful treaty was unauthorized in Indian Bureau eyes and therefore null and void. Historian H. H. Bancroft accused him of going ahead with it even though he knew that he had no authority to transact such a treaty, and certainly not when it pertained to Indians in Oregon as well as his own California. Even in California he was apparently not empowered to enter into treaties on his own initiative. But Steele acted because he saw a power vacuum. He sought to fill it before warfare should occupy it. Even Bancroft admitted that he did what seemed best in the circumstances. When Steele reported on his action to the Commissioner of Indian Affairs, William P. Dole, he mentioned the strained relations between the Superintendent of Indian Affairs for Oregon and the military at Fort Klamath: "Because of the fact that an unhappy difference existed between the Agency at Jacksonville and the military department, and in view of the impending danger, I deemed it my duty to call the council."

Congress, like the bureaucracy of the Indian Bureau, chose to ignore Steele's treaty completely. Had Washington slashed red tape, for once, and approved the Yreka agreement of February 14, 1864, the tragic Modoc War might have been averted for all time. Steele understood and liked the Modocs and enjoyed their respect and trust. *They came to him.* Needless to say, most treaties were foisted upon the Indians by whites. The treaty was a fair one and its stipulations were clear. The Modocs left Yreka peaceful and content. Like the other Indians who were party to the council, they assumed that they now had a binding agreement with the Great Father.

That summer, Colonel Drew wrote his San Francisco head-quarters from a camp in the field to reassure the Presidio brass that slackening discipline at Fort Klamath had been fully restored and that he expected that the acting commander, Lieutenant Underwood, would have no trouble with either Klamaths or Modocs. He was right, of course. The Modocs and Klamaths, believing that Steele's treaty was in force, were very models of virtue. When some Indians jumped a pack train led by a man named Richardson near Goose Lake on June 12, a Modoc warrior actually brought to Colonel Drew three of the mules run off by the raiders. This was an astonishing testimonial to the respect they held for Steele's treaty.

Unfortunately, rumors reached the Modocs that the Great Father considered their friend's treaty to be just a scrap of paper. They did not, of course, understand the professional obduracy and stupidity of governmental minions and believed themselves betrayed by Washington.

Luckily, the idea of a treaty with the Modocs and Klamaths was not dead in the capital. It was just that Steele's treaty was not "proper." Four months after the Yreka parley, the Acting Commissioner of Indian Affairs requisitioned ten thousand dollars for Superintendent J. W. Perit Huntington to effect a treaty with the two tribes and the Snakes as well. He was to extinguish their title to the land except for a reservation. The acting commissioner believed the job could be done for less, so he advanced only half of the amount appropriated by Congress. But Huntington needed the full sum to deal with three different tribes.

Senator John Conness of California disliked Steele, and although President Lincoln balked at first, eventually Conness legislated him out of his post. He was replaced by Austin Wiley, who was immediately named a treaty commissioner with Huntington. On June 22, orders were issued to initiate talks and to negotiate a proper treaty. Huntington went to Fort Klamath for a preliminary conference with the Indians who would be signatory to the document. He found some 1,200 to 1,500 Klamaths, all friendly and willing to move onto a reservation.

Huntington arranged for a grand formal council to open on October 8 which would culminate in the signing of a treaty of peace and friendship. Huntington wrote Washington that he anticipated little trouble in making a favorable treaty with the Klamaths and Modocs, and he reiterated his strong belief that it was cheaper to feed Indians than to fight them. In fact, he estimated that even placing the Snakes and Bannocks on a reservation, far more difficult than settling the Modocs and Klamaths, would cost but one tenth of asserting military control over them.

About August 20, 1864, Chief Lileks of the Klamaths called at Fort Klamath to see his friend, Capt. William Kelly. Lileks and his delegation urged just such a treaty as Huntington envisaged. On October 9 the superintendent returned to Fort Klamath with one of his Warm Springs Indian agents, William Logan, in lieu of the absent California commissioner, Wiley.

Twenty chiefs and lesser headmen, led by Lileks and Chiloquin, represented the 710 Klamaths present. Four chiefs, headed by Schonchin, represented the 339 Modocs. Kiletoak and another chief spoke for the twenty-one members of the Yahuskin band of Snakes present. These Shoshones ranged the Summer Lake and Silver Lake country to the northeast of Fort Klamath. Wily Paulina of the more bellicose Walpapi Snakes, born raiders, was expected to come in but did not attend the council.

Huntington, who had taken office on April Fool's Day, was a dedicated if not terribly enlightened Indian official. He was something of a mild reformer for his day in that he saw Indians not as worthless oafs but as childlike wards of the Government who would profit from the manual-training program he hoped to establish on the reservations. He wanted them to make careers for themselves, just as did whites. Huntington also preferred to issue them practical trade goods rather than the cheap trinkets and gewgaws of tradition. Acting Commissioner Dix left the details of the treaty to him, only reminding him that it was not Government policy to admit title (to recognize property rights) in the case of "wandering tribes." He urged him to work out a treaty of genuine peace and friendship that would be guaranteed by the Indians agreeing to inhabit a proper reservation, one with natural resources and adapted to both grazing and agriculture. This, in Dix's words, was so that "in the course of time they shall be reclaimed from their present wild and barbarous mode of life and induced to turn their attention to more civilized pursuits." Then, added Dix, "There will be no necessity for a new treaty and then removal to a new country."

Chief Mogenkaskit recalled how the important and impressive treaty conference of Council Grove, six miles from Fort Klamath and about a mile north of the site chosen for the Klamath agency, appeared to the Klamaths. He went there with seven Warm Springs Indians and met Lileks and Chiloquin of his tribe, Schonchin, Chief George and Kientpoos (Captain Jack) of the Modocs, and Huntington and his "secretary." The Indians gathered for about a week, of which October 14 was largely devoted to the treaty making per se. The first campfire was built under a great pine tree and Huntington made a speech of welcome. He showed fishhooks, blankets, buttons and red paint to the gathering, then said, "I have come from Washington, from the Great Father, to see about buying your land, and I have brought with me the things to pay for it. Tell me how much land you want to save for yourselves."

The chiefs walked back to their respective camps and pondered and powwowed amongst themselves. They returned to ask for the land that lay between the Three Sisters mountains in the Cascades, 100 miles north of Fort Klamath, and Steens Mountain, about 180 miles to the east of the Army post, then south along the range just east of Goose Lake to the California boundary and along that invisible but important line (big medicine to the whites) but including all of the Modocs' Tule Lake-Lost River area to the Cascade Range and thence back up to the starting point.

Huntington shook his head with great emphasis and objected. "That is too much land for you to take care of and hold, and I want you to go back to your camp and think it over and then point out to me land near your home which you can hold and take care of." After many hours the chiefs agreed to a much smaller area proposed by Lileks. Huntington accepted the compromise, saying, "That is all right. The matter is now finished. You will now be closed up like in a high fence so that no one can get over to you, or their cattle get over, nor can you get out to them without permission. So, tomorrow, I will issue you all the things I have and tonight we will have a big dance."

The final terms of the twelve-article treaty reached the Interior Department on February 24, 1865, too late for Senate action during the winter session. The treaty, along with verbal amendments of July 2, 1866—supposedly agreed to by the Indians over Captain Jack's objections—was not ratified until December 1869. Not until February 17, 1870, was the treaty formally proclaimed by Washington. And, incredibly, not until March 14, 1871—more than four and a half years after the Council Grove powwow—did President U. S. Grant, by Executive Order, reserve the 768,000-acre tract for the treaty Indians. This governmental procrastination, whether s.o.p. or not, was absolutely disastrous to Modoc-American relations, following as it did the unilateral abrogation of Elijah Steele's Yreka treaty. Again the Indians believed they had been tricked. None of them was more alienated than Captain Jack, who argued against acceptance of the belated treaty and repudiated his "signature" on the original document. Gen. E. R. S. Canby commented, "This long delay made the Indians who were parties to the treaty very suspicious. . . . When the treaty, as amended by the Senate, was interpreted and explained to them, Captain Jack, the present leader of the troublesome Modocs, protested that it did not represent what they had agreed to. He was, however, convinced by the testimony of the other chiefs and finally assented to it." Canby misread Jack's grudging "assent"; he was not convinced, only overruled.

The Klamaths signed the treaty willingly; the Yahuskin Snakes much less so; the Modocs reluctantly—and Captain Jack and a following disavowed the whole thing. The Modocs were now uprooted from their own land and made to go and live on the land of the Klamaths. This was a lot for the proud Modocs to swallow. By the treaty of Council Grove they relinquished all title to all lands except a portion of the tract reserved for the three participant tribes. There they must remain, forever, unless the Indian agent should grant them temporary leaves. On the other hand, no white men except for reservation officials and Army men from Fort Klamath were to be allowed to remain on the agency. However, the Government reserved the right to build roads or railroads across the reservation and, shortly, it granted a twelve-mile-wide swath across the best portion of the Klamath Reservation, including the Sprague River Valley, for the speculative development of the Oregon Central Military Wagon Road Company. It was never finished, but the damage was done to Indian relations. Not until 1889 was the Government able to retrieve the lands granted to developers alongside the unconstructed portions of the road.

Other than in the area of roadways, the Indians had exclusive rights to develop their land's resources, including its roots, berries, fish and timber. In exchange for their cession of their tribal lands, the three nations were to receive eight thousand dollars a year for five years, then five thousand dollars a year for the next half-decade, and a final three thousand dollars per year for a last period of five years. The Indian agent was to apply these funds to the promotion of the well-being of the Indians, to advance them in civilization and especially in agriculture, and to secure their moral improvement and education. The annuities could not be used as payment of debts contracted by individual Indians. An extra payment of thirty-five thousand dollars was authorized beyond the gift articles distributed at the time of signing. This sum would subsist the Indians for the first year on the reservation by allowing them to purchase teams, tools, farm implements, seeds, clothing and provisions. Also, the money could be used to hire white men to teach the Indians agricultural and technical skills.

The Government promised to provide for a fifteen-year period a superintendent of farming operations and a farmer, a blacksmith, a carpenter, a sawyer and a wagon maker who would double as a plow maker. For twenty years, a doctor, a miller and two schoolteachers would be provided, and the Government would erect, maintain and supply for a twenty-four-year period a sawmill, flour mill, smithy, carpenter shop and wagon wright's shop, plus a manual-labor school and a hospital.

Alcoholic drink was completely forbidden on the Klamath Reservation, and any Indian who drank liquor or even brought a bottle of spirits on the reservation might have his part of the tribal benefits withheld for as long a time as the President of the United States might direct.

The Government reserved the right to allot in severalty the reservation lands. That is, it had the only right and discretion to grant lands on the reservation to Indians as individuals, as landholders. These lands had to be held free from levy, sale or forfeiture. The individual tracts were to be inalienable, were to be held in perpetuity and were not to exceed 40 acres in size for a single man and 120 acres for the head of a family. The exact size of a married man's allotment was to depend on the number of his dependents. The Government planned to establish rules to secure survivors' title to the allotments used and improved by a family head.

The Council Grove treaty demanded the acknowledgment by the tribes of their dependence upon the United States Government and their subjection to such laws and regulations as the Government might enact. The tribes further promised to live in peace and amity with U.S. citizens, to refrain from committing depredations on their persons and property and to cease waging war on other tribes. They were even to abstain from any communication with hostile tribes. The U.S. Government claimed the right to add other tribes to the Klamath Reservation at its discretion, but it would prevent their encroaching upon the rights and privileges guaranteed to the signatory tribes.

The assembled Indians concurred in a desire to see Lindsay Applegate as their resident Indian agent. He, along with Dr. W. C. McKay of Warm Springs, was serving as Huntington's counsellor and interpreter during the powwow.

If legend is correct, when Chief Schonchin signed the Council Grove treaty he swore that "that mountain shall fall before Schonchin makes war against his white brother." He was willing to make the best of a bad treaty, a bad treaty from the viewpoint of the Modocs, now dispossessed from their traditional homeland. Legend again cites Schonchin Butte in the Modoc Lava Beds as the target of the chief's outstretched arm and finger, but since the low Butte is some fifty-odd miles from the powwow site, the landmark which never fell—because Schonchin *did* keep his promise—was more likely a height much closer to Fort Klamath. Making a grudging "X" alongside Schonchin's mark were his unwilling subchiefs, Kientpoos or Captain Jack and the Chief's younger brother, John Schonchin. Old Schonchin had the last word. Reviewing recent Modoc history, he orated, "Once my people were like the sand along the shore. Now I call to them and only the wind answers. Four hundred strong young men went to war with the whites; only eighty are left. We will be good if the white man will let us, and be friends forever."

The Indians and the Government, even with the best of intentions, could never agree on the exact metes and bounds of the Klamath Reservation. The redmen wanted the boundary lines to follow the lay of the land, as on a California rancho *diseño*, between the landmarks noted and established as corners of the reservation. They did not understand or accept the straight air-lines of the surveyors who finally ran the boundaries in 1871. The Indians could reckon direction and distance only by pointing and by citing the number of days or fractions of a day's travel necessary to traverse a given area. So, even when one disregards the errors of the original surveys, the transit lines cut out huge areas of land the Klamaths and Modocs honestly believed to have been guaranteed them by Huntington, speaking in behalf of the Great Father in Washington. Not until December 18, 1896, did the members of a Klamath Boundary Commission file their final report, fixing the exact, correct borders of the Klamath Indian Reservation. The commission found that the inept initial survey had "shorted" the treaty Indians by some 617,490 acres worth $533,270.

A more disastrous result of the Council Grove treaty than its topographical confusion and the puzzling of the Indians with talk of rods and chains and compass points was the compressing of Snakes and, particularly, Modocs into a *Klamath* reservation on land that was and had always been Klamath country. The Government could be counted on never to learn anything by experience in Indian affairs. Such "convenient" doubling up of suspicious and even hostile tribes was always explosive. It had not worked, long before, with Seminoles and Creeks, it was not working with Navajos and Mescalero Apaches in New Mexico's

Bosque Redondo concentration camp, and it would never work with Modocs and Klamaths on the new Oregon reservation. Still, the Government proceeded to force the Modocs to join the Klamaths on "their " reservation, as the latter saw it. About half of the Modocs went along with Chief Schonchin, but many of the disgruntled younger men split off to follow the leadership of a faction led by Captain Jack and John Schonchin. They refused to move onto the reservation.

Colonel Drew arrived at the Council Grove conference on the last day of it. He was glad that he had not been required to help draft the treaty. It was not that he thought that Huntington's treaty was dishonest or a particularly bad instrument, as treaties went. But he was sure the Government would fail to honor its provisions. He was both right and wrong. For once, the Indian Bureau seemed willing to honor the letter of the treaty (slowly and belatedly, to be sure), if not always ready to honor its spirit. But Drew, like Canby and other military men, was wise enough to see how deep was the division among the Modocs over their forced move to Klamath land, and he feared that the resentment would smoulder and eventually flame into warfare.

The Secretary of the Interior, for his part, was pleased as punch with Huntington's treaty. He was, of course, in nigh complete ignorance of the climate of opinion among the Modocs, and he exuded confidence in his annual report of 1864: "We may then hope to see the end of the long course of expensive hostilities with the Indians of southern Oregon and to find the great highways of travel safe for those who frequent them; while the Indians themselves may be expected, under their new relations to the Government, to participate in the great benefits to be derived from their being reclaimed from a wandering life and settled upon reservations, which have resulted so happily in the case of their brethren in the northern and western portions of the state."

But the Council Grove treaty was not enough. The Secretary wanted Congress to pass a law that would effectively bottle up the Indians on their reservations, where they could not interfere in the exploitation of valuable land by diligent farm folk. Punishment for straying without permission was to include the withholding of annuities. As justification for his request, the Secretary of the Interior posited a possibly hypothetical situation that was almost a prognostication of subsequent events in Modocland as well as a jaundiced review of the current situation on the Oregon-California border:

"A large part of the labors of the Agents and their incidental expenses in this Superintendency are caused by the constant efforts of a part of the Indians to leave their reservations and live about the white settlements. If this is permitted, the Indians become an intolerable nuisance to the whites and the effect upon themselves is most pernicious. They are always drunken and debauched, their women become prostitutes, and all soon are infected with loathsome diseases. There are found in every community a few white persons who are vile enough to associate with them and desire their presence. These persons naturally acquire the good will of the Indians and have much influence over them. By enticing them to leave the reservation, notifying them of the approach of the Agent, and assisting them to conceal themselves from him, they often defeat the object of the Government in keeping the white and red races apart." Having neatly disposed of Yreka squawmen and lusty Fort Klamath troopers in one half-paragraph, the secretary next took care of such solid Siskiyou citizens as Steele and Rosborough: "Another class of citizens, who are respectable and do not furnish them whiskey or debauch their women, thoughtlessly encourage their presence to secure their services upon their farms or at other labor. But once away from the reservations and beyond the control of the Agent, they unavoidably come in contact with immoral influences and the effect is the same as if the motive was bad."

In his next annual report, the Secretary of the Interior referred to Huntington's economy in receiving twelve million acres of Indian land for just ten thousand dollars, a moderate-size reservation, and some annuities and services for a twenty-four-year period. He pointed out, too, that the treaty provisions were very favorable to the United States (which would hardly be classed as news, treaty-wise) but that Huntington had been fair to the 1,200 to 1,500 Indians of Council Grove, the largest number ever included in an Oregon treaty. "The reservation is not likely to be traversed by any important line of travel and but a small portion of it will be coveted by whites for settlement. I consider it, in every respect," reported Huntington, "well adapted for the purpose for which it was designed."

A good part of the future Klamath Reservation was desert but it also included some fine grazing pastures and seed-gathering and root-digging country around Klamath Marsh. There was excellent fishing in Upper Klamath Lake and in the Williamson and Klamath rivers, and enough arable land near the mouth of the Williamson alone to support all the Indians who would ever be placed in the reserve. The superintendent was apparently sincere in his attempts to be on the square with the Klamaths and Modocs. In determining the bounds of the reservation, he told the Secretary of the Interior he had in mind the advantages for supporting a colony of Indians engaged in industrial pursuits. Scarcely less important to Huntington was his desire to locate the tribes so that their separation from whites would be as complete as possible.

Besides distributing presents at the close of the treaty making, Huntington left nearly sixteen thousand pounds of flour with Captain Kelly at Fort Klamath, to be issued to those Indians who chose to remain encamped adjacent to the post even before the Klamath Agency could be established under Sub-Agent Lindsay Applegate. He was sure that this largesse would quiet them and also convince them of the White Chief's good faith. As early as May he had been optimistic over the future of the Klamath Reservation, although he had little hope of getting money to bring in the Walpapi Snakes of Paulina. (In fact, he feared that the taming of them would mean their extermination.) But should they come in, he would have a good place for them: "I do not know of a location more adapted to their wants or less objectionable when the interests of the whites are considered than the tract reserved for those purposes in the Klamath Lake country. The post, Fort Klamath, is near the northwest of the tract. . . . I hope that the operations of the military department will meet with such success that it will be practicable to include the roving bands of Snakes as well as the Klamaths and Modocs."

Huntington, already sanguine of success, must have convinced himself that he had a lucky star immediately after he left Fort Klamath upon the conclusion of the Council Grove treaty. Certainly it made easy the task of treating with the Snakes of Oregon's desert country. While riding with Agent Logan in advance of his party on the road from Fort Klamath to Warm Springs, he came upon two Indians who fled into the brush but who were flushed and apprehended by his military escort. They proved to be Walpapi Snakes of bloody Paulina's band. Huntington had his party encamp at once, and Lt. James Halloran of the Washington Territorial Infantry, commanding his escort, sent out scouts. Late in the day they found a camp of the Snakes on Mill-ke-ke Creek about fifteen miles from its junction with the Deschutes River. The soldiers captured five men, three women and two children and brought them into camp. There, Huntington's luck almost changed. As he recalled, "I was congratulating myself that I had, at last, the long-desired opportunity of communicating with the hostile Snakes when the five men suddenly made an attempt to seize our guns, which were standing around some trees in camp. We were compelled to commence firing upon them at once and three of them were killed, the other two escaping, badly wounded." Later, Superintendent Huntington learned that one escapee died during the night and only one brave reached Chief Paulina's camp. But to his great delight, after this setback Huntington learned that one of the squaws in custody was Paulina's wife. He took her and the other captives to Fort Vancouver for safekeeping.

On November 8, 1864, Paulina came into Fort Klamath in response to Huntington's invitation and guarantee that he would be allowed to depart unharmed. He told Captain Kelly that he was tired of war and desired to make peace if he would be protected by Huntington from his enemies. The superintendent assured him of this, of course, and laid plans for a treaty in the chief's country as soon as the melting of the snows would permit him to travel through the mountains. General Alvord was delighted by the news although he was not counting on Paulina to hold to any agreements. But he ordered the Warm Springs Indians to cease all attacks on the Walpapi Snakes and he told Lt. Col. R. C. Drum at Fort Vancouver, "It will remain for us to test the sincerity of this submission, but if it shall turn out to be sincere, it is a very auspicious event for the peace of the Indian frontier."

Alvord promised Paulina that he would send his wife and the children to Fort Klamath where the chief could visit them, once winter was over. The General then asked Huntington to bring onto the Klamath Reservation all of the warriors under his control. This was in November 1864, but the severity of the winter was such that Huntington could not even visit Fort Klamath, so he wrote to Captain Kelly on December 12 to ask him to tell Paulina that his messages had been received and given attention. Huntington promised him, as had Alvord, that the Warm Springs Indians would no longer make war on the Snakes and that the soldiers of Fort Dalles were also being called off. He told Paulina that he was prepared to provision him and his people on the Klamath Reservation if he would commit no more depredations and would stay away from Warm Springs. Huntington promised to come to Fort Klamath to see him as soon as spring should clear the roads. He then advised Kelly: "I am glad to know that he desires to submit to the Government and cease war, but he cannot expect that the Indians and whites whom he has been robbing and trying to kill for many years will refrain from shooting him if he goes where they are. If he makes a treaty and observes it he will then have a claim to the protection of the Government."

In February 1865, General Alvord asked that Fort Klamath be shifted to his District of Oregon from its incongruous place in the California district of operations, especially since Paulina was coming in. Gen. Irwin McDowell then requested Governor Gibbs of Oregon to reinforce Fort Klamath with the newly mustered I Company of the 1st Oregon Infantry. On May 10, orders were issued at Fort Vancouver for Captain Kelly to hold ready C Company, 1st Oregon Cavalry and an officer and twenty-five men of I company to take the field on or about June 1. However, it was not to be an escort for a treaty-making Huntington but an expedition to protect travel on the road to Canyon City, Boise and the Owyhee mines. Lieutenant Underwood was authorized to hire the necessary transportation, and Captain Kelly was ordered to chastise any Indians he might find. Col. Reuben F. Maury's orders left tactics to Kelly but suggested that the Irishman set up a depot, garrisoned by his twenty-five infantrymen, near Silver Lake on the Yreka-Canyon City Road, and then scour the countryside during the summer and fall with his cavalrymen. On May 11, Maury warned Kelly that earlier operations in the field both to the north and east were likely to drive hostiles into his section of the country.

Kelly's beat was a huge slice of Oregon, from Harney Lake to Diamond Peak in the Cascades and from the headwaters of the Deschutes northward to the eastern branches of that river. He was to leave enough cavalrymen at Silver Lake to act as escorts for travelers for as long as thirty to forty days at a time. And, should he fall in with Byron J. Pengrá, surveying the Oregon Central Military Road from Eugene to Boise, he was to extend him all necessary protection. Maury cautioned Kelly to be careful and not to stray too far or be too long absent from the traveled roads. "The experience with these Indians is that in such cases small parties will get to the rear of the command and seek opportunities of committing depredations upon unsuspecting parties."

In June 1865, Colonel Maury received orders to suspend all operations. He considered the Fort Klamath escort operation so important, however, that he requested special permission to send it out. But Departmental Headquarters adamantly reiterated that *all* operations were suspended. The reasons were probably a combination—the end of the Civil War; Paulina's apparent willingness to come in; and, just possibly, the unsettled conditions at Fort Klamath. Controversy had hovered over it from its founding because of its location, Kelly's unauthorized feeding of Indians, and a general lack of discipline. When Maury informed Governor Gibbs of the suspension of military operations in southern Oregon, he remarked cryptically, "I fear the troubles which appear to hang around Fort Klamath are the cause of this suspension, which I hope is only temporary. Yet it stops the preparations and must cause delay." As he wrote, a Regular Army officer, Capt. Joseph Stewart of the 3d Artillery, was conducting an investigation of the condition and management of Fort Klamath but whatever the trouble there, it was hush-hushed and is unknown to this day. It may have been nothing more serious than the excessive fraternization of soldiers—and officers—with local squaws, which shocked a number of Indian Bureau officials.

Despite the halting of all military maneuvers, Huntington started out to deal with Paulina that June of 1865. He took the Paiute or Snake squaws and children with him but had to leave one woman and child at Warm Springs when he found them too sick to continue traveling. He pressed on with the others and some "partially friendly" Klamaths to Fort Klamath, where Captain Kelly got in touch with Paulina. Kelly also managed to provide him with an escort from Fort Klamath, the one exception to Colonel Maury's no-escort orders.

One of Kelly's troopers was Pvt. O. A. Stearns of I Company, 1st Oregon Infantry, who later became a pioneer settler of Klamath Falls and testified in the 1896 rectification of the reservation's boundaries. He recalled that after several days of difficult haggling with Paulina at Council Butte on Sprague River, some forty miles east of Fort Klamath, Huntington overcame the chief's fear of retribution for his long war on whites and Indians alike. There the superintendent secured another of his bargain-basement treaties on August 12, 1865. He forwarded it to the Interior Department on September 1 as a sort of addendum or codicil to the Council Grove treaty with the Modocs, Klamaths and Yahuskins. In it, Paulina's Walpapi Snakes or Paiutes agreed to go onto the Klamath Reservation. Huntington could not help crowing a little over his ability as a treaty negotiator: "The two treaties, taken together, will be found to include a greater number of Indians, cede a larger extent of territory, and anticipate smaller expenditures than any other treaties ever negotiated in this region." Because of the beastly terrain of southeastern Oregon and the fierce character of the Walpapis, he estimated that "ten good soldiers are required to wage successful war against one Indian. Every Indian killed or captured by the military has cost the Government fifty thousand dollars at least. Economy, then, indicates that it is much cheaper to feed them than to fight them."

With Huntington at Sprague River that August was Lt. John McCall. He was destined to become Fort Klamath's Acting Assistant Quartermaster and Acting Commissary of Subsistence. Still later, McCall became the husband of Lindsay Applegate's daughter, Theresa. McCall wrote: "Pelina [sic] and a portion of his band came in today. . . . They are a miserable looking lot of rascals apparently capable of committing almost any fiendish act. Their wardrobe is in a seedy condition, giving evident token that they have either been very unsuccessful in their recent plundering excursions or else they have a cache in the mountains somewhere. They bring news of the willingness of other hostiles to make terms of peace."

Superintendent Huntington, so often right, was unfortunately wrong when he reported that the Walpapi move to the Klamath Reservation meant the bringing in of all other hostiles and the end of Indian warfare in Oregon. Instead, Paulina led his men off the reservation in the spring of 1866 and back on the warpath; Captain Jack ultimately followed suit. Gen. George Crook had to carry out a very difficult campaign, which included the battle at Infernal Caverns in California, far to the south of Fort Klamath.

But, for the moment, all looked well in Oregon and northernmost California at the Civil War's end. The Klamaths, Modocs and Yahuskins had given up all claims on some twelve to fourteen million acres of land, the Walpapis were coming in, and Lindsay Applegate was beginning improvements of the Klamath Reservation even before there was any money appropriated. He placed some Indian farms on Klamath Lake and soon had two thousand Indians in his charge. He considered them to be good raw material for citizenship, except for those who were becoming debauched and diseased from living too close to the Emigrant Trail or South Road, Fort Klamath, or California mining towns.

Progress at the Klamath Agency was slow. Lindsay Applegate first erected buildings on the northwest point of Upper Klamath Lake at Kohasta, but in 1866 he asked permission to move the reservation's headquarters to a little creek at Beetle's Rest so that he could set up a water-powered sawmill and gristmill at the edge of the pines. In 1868, his request was granted and the Klamath Agency moved. In 1867, he had no hay tonnage to report to his superiors, unlike the Umatilla or Grande Ronde reservations, nor did he have any hogs. But at least he did have 632 horses grazing on the reserve, worth $12,640. Schonchin's Modocs were joining the Klamaths in building cabins and fences and splitting fence rails for sale to whites. When the Government sawmill began to operate, dressed lumber was sold by the Indians to settlers. All was quiet along the Wood River.

CHAPTER FIVE

GARRISON LIFE

Because the enthusiasm of many militiamen began to wane concurrent with their enlistments in the fall of 1864, Governor Gibbs encouraged men to join a brand-new outfit to be led by Indian chaser Col. George Currey. The recruiting drives of the 1st Volunteer Oregon Infantry featured pretty young things singing patriotic ditties like "Stand Up for Uncle Sam, My Boy." Either their sex appeal or Oregon patriotism paid off; the regiment was duly mustered and I Company reached Fort Klamath as a reinforcement in 1865. The Jackson County volunteers had gathered at moldering Camp Baker for speeches and presentation of a flag before marching over the Cascades. During their arduous trek they bolstered their government-issue rations with elk steak and fresh trout. The footsloggers were met at Williamson River by a cavalry detachment from Fort Klamath, which escorted them to Wood River and a welcome by Captain Kelly. Capt. Franklin B. Sprague brought two subalterns and seventy-eight enlisted men with him. It looked like an army to the cavalrymen of C Company, now down to a strength (on paper) of only forty-five men.

Not that Fort Klamath needed reinforcing, for the post's slumber in the dewy meadow was hardly disturbed either by the Civil War or Indian wars. Typical of "action" around Fort Klamath was Captain Currey's earlier request to Captain Kelly to keep an eye on local Indian renegades (that is, would-be hostiles). The latter could only find a few braves among the Klamaths who had been at Yamhill after the Rogue River War, but Currey immediately pegged these men as either renegade Klamaths who had fought the whites in that war or else Rogue Rivers masquerading as Klamaths under the very guns of Fort Klamath. He told Kelly that they should be held to the fate that their complicity in the Rogue River War merited. But if Currey expected a new Rogue River War to erupt around Fort

Klamath, he was doomed to disappointment. Neither the renegades nor anyone else threatened the fortress.

The volunteers damned the dulling isolation of Fort Klamath as fervently as would their successors, the regulars, after the Civil War. The post lay four hundred miles from its supply base at Portland and, with freighting rates at $5.25 a pound, all fuel, hay—600,000 pounds a year—and straw had to be procured locally by the local labor force, the garrison. Grain, flour and smoked meats could be had in Jacksonville, but salt meat had to come all the way from Portland. Isolation was, of course, most annoying between December and July when snow in the mountains closed all the roads to the west and blocked direct contact with Ashland Mills and Jacksonville, more than a hundred miles to the west, where daily coaches of the California and Oregon stage line running between Redding and Roseburg connected the ends of the stalled railroad, which would not meet to bind the two states together with steel until 1887.

Of course there was always the blessed U.S. Mail. Every Wednesday, military mail reached Fort Klamath from Henley or, later, Yreka. A horse trail to the latter, 120 miles from the fort, was kept open year-round, so important was mail to operations—and morale—at the fort. The quartermaster's courier left Yreka early Monday morning, rode to Ward's Ferry on the Klamath, Brown's Place and Linkville before reaching Fort Klamath on Wednesday afternoon. He began his round trip on Thursday.

As the Civil War waned, the guerrilla warfare of the Indians increased but—unfortunately, as the garrison saw it—most of the action took place far from Fort Klamath. Thirty-nine men of C Company, 1st Oregon Cavalry, marched with Colonel Drew (July 1 to October 18, 1864) on his Owyhee Expedition, but the remainder were cooped up in Fort Klamath because Drew feared that Snake Chief Ou-a-lucks would persuade the Klamaths, Modocs and Goose Lakes to join him in a great anti-Yankee alliance and crusade to spread warfare from Canyon City to the lakes country. Drew explained to San Francisco headquarters, "With the aid of the other Indians named, he would doubtless extend his operations toward this post and elsewhere." To see that this did not happen, Drew left Lt. D. C. Underwood in command of Fort Klamath, describing him as zealous, faithful and "entirely conversant with the Indian character, and with his knowledge in this respect and the completion of the defenses I have ordered [two blockhouses], I do not fear the result should the Indians conclude to make an attack upon him."

Drew was not afraid of bogeymen; while there was no assault on Fort Klamath by the Indians, they did begin to raid closer to its pickets. On June 24, 1864, for example, John Richardson's seven-wagon train was attacked not far from the fort and three of his fifteen men were wounded, six oxen stolen and three thousand pounds of flour destroyed. Troops on scout rescued the travelers without the need of Fort Klamath's assistance, but Underwood did send an ambulance to bring the wounded to his hospital. Colonel Drew blamed the raid on Modocs and Klamaths in league with Ou-a-lucks and advised the San Francisco Presidio: "I shall march slowly toward the Goose Lake country so that I may be within express distance of Fort Klamath should more troops be required there or in the vicinity. I have directed the issue of rifles and ammunition to the workmen at the Fort, if necessary." But Fort Klamath's soldiers and workmen waited in vain for an Indian attack. It never came.

There were a number of scraps with the Snakes in the 1860s but most involved men from Fort Dalles or other posts, not Fort Klamath. This was the case in the draw or defeat of Lt. James A. Waymire and Joaquin Miller's civilians by the Indians in April 1864 near John Day River, and the May 18 defeat of Capt. John M. Drake's force by Paulina near Crooked River, in which Lt. Stephen Watson was killed along with two enlisted men and seven were wounded. Fort Klamath was largely an observer of the great reconnaissance of Colonel Drew and Captain Currey during the summer of 1864. It bogged down, anyway, at Camp Alvord in the desert, though not because of Indian resistance but from an epidemic of the "bloody flux" or dysentery. Paulina had laid an ambush for Drew on the south side of Warner Mountain but had gotten cold feet when he saw the colonel's "fire-belching wagon," his howitzer. But Paulina let nature take its course, and soon Drew had 106 of his 134 men on sick call. Both his surgeon and Currey's hospital steward were out of medicines and using an Indian remedy suggested to them by Currey, wild geranium root tea.

While Drew's once-formidable force was lying ill at Camp Alvord, the Indians again struck close to Fort Klamath. They wounded a guard, Henry Wilkinson, with an arrow through the arm, as T. L. Davidson's wagon train wended its way westward in September. A few days later in a gorge, a shower of arrows greeted the travelers. Davidson sicked two savage dogs on the attackers but only one of the animals returned, and with an arrow driven into its chest.

Fort Klamath was playing a role in this drama although it was not a fighting one. The fort and Captain Kelly were "under fire," but not from the Indians. Kelly was not only feeding Indians in distress from Fort Klamath stores, he was selling provisions to hungry emigrants and giving away food to those who were destitute. A busybody commissary of subsistence in San Francisco challenged Kelly's accounts: "There is no authority in the subsistence regulations for giving or selling subsistence stores to citizens not employed by the Government. This is the second time that Captain Kelly has come to the relief of indigence at the expense of the Government, without authority. I would recommend that the issue be disapproved." The compassionate Kelly reminded his superiors that there was no other source of foodstuffs but Fort Klamath until the emigrants were safely in the Rogue River Valley. General Wright finally endorsed Kelly's actions but drew the line for him: "I recommend that the issue be approved. I shall direct Captain Kelly not to sell or give provisions to emigrants except in extreme cases. Emigrants must not expect the Government to supply them unless some great calamity has befallen them."

Captain Jack and the Modocs gave Fort Klamath no nightmares in 1864. Far from it. He was hanging around Yreka with his men and on October 14 actually made the paper. When a Shasta squaw killed another belle in a jealous rage over a white lover, the Shastas buried the dead woman in a coffin, Yankee-style, in a gulch near the sawmill at Forest House, not far from Yreka. There was the usual singing and dancing and presentation of beads (fifty dollars' worth) to the corpse, but the newspaper most remarked the presence of an unlikely mourner at a Shasta burial—Captain Jack. The Modoc sub-chief was there, armed with a bow and arrow and a rifle with a white rag tied around its muzzle. With a small fire burning before him, he delivered a eulogy or speech of some kind about the departed.

In September 1865 the men of Fort Klamath had another of their rare opportunities to see action when Captain Sprague reconnoitered Drew's new military road all the way from Fort Klamath to Camp Alvord. He took two subalterns and seventy men of C and I companies. It was a march virtually without incident, but hardly was he back in the compound before word reached Fort Klamath that the Indians had cut the road. On October 17 he left the fort again, with eleven men. He saw no Indians but picked up some sign and pursued two unseen mounted redmen who gave him the slip. Barely was he back at the post when Major Rinehart, on October 23, sent him out once again. This time Sprague was to join a force at Camp Bidwell for a joint move against the Snakes around Alvord. He left with ten men and reached Surprise Valley on the twenty-eighth, finding Capt. Augustus W. Starr of the 2d California Volunteer Cavalry in command. Since he was already under orders to move to Camp Crook, and the snows of winter were threatening, Starr could not join in Sprague's projected sweep, but he did lend him a lieutenant and ten men with which to double his force for a reconnoitering mission. It was well that he did, for Sprague finally found his Indians. Or, rather, they found him.

The Californians and Oregonians moved northeastward from Camp Bidwell to Warner Creek or Joanna Creek, south of the Warner Lakes, and then proceeded along the lakeshore trail where it pinched against the water. In these narrow confines Sprague's detachment was ambushed, front and rear, by Snakes in trenches. There was no escaping a fight; the lake was on one side, bluffs on the other. Somehow Captain Sprague managed to turn his force around and dash for Camp Bidwell. Although the Snakes in front of him were armed with rifles and the ambushers of his rear guard with bows and arrows, he made his escape without a man or horse being hit by enemy fire. Three days later the Snakes improved upon their military tactics. They struck Camp Alvord, killed a guard and ran off sixteen head of cavalry horses.

Sprague had to admit that the closing of Drew's Road between Fort Klamath and Camp Alvord was now no longer a rumor but a proven fact. "In my opinion," he reported on November 11, 1865, "direct communication by express with Fort Klamath, until the Indians are driven from the route, is impracticable. And, in any event, is so in the winter, on account of the snow in the Steens' and Sierra Nevada Mountains." Sprague's lack of success substantiated the observation of Oregon's ex-Senator and ex-Superintendant of Indian Affairs, Joel Palmer, on Indian fighting on the California-Oregon border: "By dividing into small and prowling bands they are enabled to pounce at any moment upon remote settlements, isolated mining camps or passing pack trains. Their stealthy presence is never indicated except by a consummated murder or robbery, while their parties are so small and perfectly on the alert that pursuit is useless."

Fort Klamath's strength remained low during the Civil War and in the post-war years. For example, on paper it numbered only forty-four men in November 1865—including but one officer, the post commander. Actually, only twenty-one men were fit for duty. Three others were under arrest, one more was sick and the remainder were off chasing Indians. And some of the men carried on Fort Klamath rosters were "ghosts." In March 1866, for instance, Capt. John B. McCall asked permission to drop Pvt. Lorenzo B. Harris from the roll of A Company since he had never seen him and could not discover his whereabouts or even find a description of him although he was supposed to have transferred to Fort Klamath from the 2d California Volunteer Infantry in September 1864.

How hollow must have sounded Cyrus Reed's ungrammatical bombast at war's end to the men of Fort Klamath. The Oregon Adjutant General orated: "When the story of those times shall be impartially written, every soldier, whether he done service in the Army of the Potomac, in the Valley of the Mississippi, or hunted the savage on the desert plains of Oregon, will share equally his country's blessing. . . . I can say without fear of contradiction that for long and tedious marches, excessive privations and hardships, that our own troops can produce as fair a record as any."

Captain McCall's B Troop, 1st Oregon Cavalry, was stationed at Fort Klamath in the fall of 1865, but the process of '61 was soon reversed and regulars were ordered to replace volunteers in frontier garrisons. Both of the cavalry troops, A and C, were marched to Fort Vancouver between June 1 and 10, 1866, to be mustered out, leaving the infantrymen of Company I to hold the fort. With the nation at peace, officers and men alike found it harder than ever to endure the monotony of Fort Klamath, a life Army wife Martha Summerhayes of Arizona summed up in a synonym for garrison duty on the frontier—"glittering misery." On July 12, 1866, Major Rinehart wrote Captain McCall, then at Fort Vancouver, to tell him of the mad pace of life at Fort Klamath: "We are just where you left us—our suspense has not abated a particle. What the deuce is to become of us is still the daily topic. I think when the odd fractions of companies can all be found there will be a grand muster-out. The Vol's are already whittled down to an allspice and 'our souls go marching on.' I have been expecting lightning to strike in these parts so long, in the shape of orders, that I would not be surprised at anything." At least Rinehart could report some news. The new road was within a few days of being ready for travel (Sprague's Road, replacing the Ranchería Trail), and he had captured seven Snakes, some of "Huntington's treaty of amity boys."

Snakes or no Snakes, Indian fighting remained in short supply around Fort Klamath. Only Lt. H. B. Oatman managed to find any. He took ten men of I Company on October 5, 1866, and pursued Chief Paulina's Walpapi runaways from the Klamath Reservation because they had stolen Modoc and Klamath horses in their departure. His men killed four of the renegades near Sprague River. Oatman left Fort Klamath again on a similar mission on the 15th, bound for the Chena-kau Valley with twenty-two men of I Company. With the help of troops from Fort Bidwell, he hit the Snakes again near Lake Abert, killing fourteen and wounding (he guessed) about twenty or thirty more. Oatman lost one enlisted man and had one Indian scout wounded. Although the Snakes were severely chastised by Oatman, they refused to go back on the Klamath Reservation.

Not until July 8, 1867, were the last Oregon volunteers relieved at Fort Klamath and marched to Jacksonville to be converted back into civilians. They were replaced by the fifty-four men of A Company, 1st U.S. Cavalry, from Fort Bidwell, the first regulars to enjoy the all but unbroken peace and quiet of Fort Klamath. First Lt. John F. Small replaced Captain Sprague in command of the fort but was later succeeded by Capt. Thomas McGregor of A Troop. The Federals began an immediate renovation of the somewhat rundown post, and new buildings started in 1867 were finished the next year. Troop A was destined to remain in garrison at Fort Klamath until 1870 when it was relieved by Capt. James Jackson's B Troop, in time for the Modoc War.

There was a little action around—or out of —Fort Klamath in the years following Appomattox. Capt. William Kelly brought C Company of the 8th U.S. Cavalry into Fort Klamath that July of 1867 but marched them right out again, bound for Camp Warner and an engagement in April of the following year on the Malheur River, which earned Kelly a major's brevet for gallantry. Lieutenant Small had a crack at combat duty in the fall of 1867. He took fifty-one men of A Company and ten Klamath scouts including Dave Hill for a twenty-day reconnoiter of the Silver Lake country to the northeast of the fort. Small killed twenty-four hostiles, captured nineteen women and children and destroyed two camps before returning to Fort Klamath on the twenty-second of September. For his Silver Lake fight on the eighth of the month he was given a captain's brevet for gallantry in an action in which, according to Army records, he killed or captured more of the enemy than he had men with him. His only casualties were two enlisted men and one Klamath scout wounded.

That was about the sum of Indian fighting in which Fort Klamath was even remotely involved. Mostly, its men kept an eye on the Klamath Reservation where discontent was growing out of food shortages and the fact that the Klamaths were lording it over the Modocs and Yahuskins, whom they treated as intruders on their domain. The Klamaths were even refusing them permission to hunt or fish on "their" land. The annual report of the Secretary of War for 1870 carried a warning about this wrangling at the agency: "Should these difficulties become aggravated or assume the complexion of hostility to the whites, it may be necessary to strengthen the garrison." But things never got that bad and, in the opinion of the nonstrengthened garrison, apparently never would.

Tired of worrying about the potential danger from Klamaths or Modocs, the soldiers and officers trapped in the abrasive boredom of the post might find the most exciting bit of news of a season (except for a once-only, abortive revolt over bread) to be a company council of administration auditing the accounts, or a board of survey like the one that found boxes of bacon and sacks of rice short of weight. In the latter case, Acting Commissary of Subsistence John McCall was found innocent of malfeasance; the vanishing stores were blamed on leaking, shrinking and evaporation. "News" in Fort Klamath's compound might involve nothing more extraordinary than the decease of an Army mule. One of Sgt. Rudolph Giesy's beasts died of cold and cramps on an expedition to Jacksonville in December 1865. Since McCall was responsible for all Fort Klamath property, he had the noncom sign an affidavit in regard to the critter's passing: "I furthermore swear that the death of the above mule was without any fault or negligence on the part of the aforesaid Captain J. McCall."

Fort Klamath was such a peaceful and healthy post that it was spared the shock of the deaths and illnesses that made news in most frontier garrisons. The death of nineteen-year-old hospital patient Pvt. Greenberry Tedrow, of enteritis on

November 30, 1865, was almost unique. It was, of course, a great blow to his buddies. But it paled as a tragedy when compared to the death of Pvt. Stephen T. Hallock in the spring of 1866. Hallock was reported absent without official leave after a half-dozen soldiers of I Company were given a furlough to the Rogue River settlements. Only five of the six returned over the mountains to Fort Klamath on the crusted snow of the Ranchería Trail by the deadline, March 1. In the opinion of his bunkies, Hallock was the last person on the post who would have gone AWOL, the very last to be a candidate for "Company Q," as prisoners of Fort Klamath's "Hotel de Crossbar" (the guardhouse) were derisively called by the men.

Hallock had not showed up at the agreed-upon time and place for the hike back to Fort Klamath, so his five friends had set off without him, urged on by threatening skies. Assuming that he would overtake them on the trail, they started off at a normal pace and covered the hundred-mile journey without any real trouble, although the snow became rotten underfoot during the middle of the day and they had to travel early and late when it was frozen hard enough for good footing. When Hallock failed to arrive, the Fort Klamath morning report had to carry his name as a deserter and he was dropped from the roster, but his comrades-in-arms were reluctant to believe him guilty of desertion.

It was on April Fool's Day 1866 that Fate played its cruel trick on Hallock's Fort Klamath comrades. One of the soldiers wandered over to Wood River after lunch on April 1 for a bit of fishing. He followed the road to the old pole bridge across the stream. Suddenly, he stopped and stared. The body of a man lay half on a stringer of the bridge and half in the icy water of the stream. The soldier hurried forward and found that the man was the missing Hallock, his muddy clothes frozen to his body, his face blue and swollen. But he was alive, barely. The angler shouted for help and with some of his buddies carried their unconscious friend to the hospital. Every known cure for frostbite was tried. He was rubbed with snow, dosed with brandy, wrapped in warm blankets. But all these efforts proved futile, and Hallock died before Reveille on April 2. His friends now did what they cursed themselves for not having done earlier; they backtracked him. From the evidence on the trail they were easily able to put together the sad story of Stephen Hallock's last days.

Delayed by business in the settlements, Hallock had not been able to reach the rendezvous at the departure time he and his pals had set. He started back over the Ranchería Trail just one day behind them. He was almost halfway to Fort Klamath before the going became difficult as he reached the snow level on Ranchería Prairie. Unluckily for Hallock, a rainstorm blew up and drenched him, his clothing and his blankets. It also made his progress agonizingly slow through a now soft and slushy snow. He was a short fellow and it took him several days to plow and clamber his way through an area easily covered in a day's march by his comrades ahead of him. Unable to start a fire, he was forced to spend the nights shivering in the cold, getting little rest for the next day's march in the dubious shelter of overhanging tree boughs. Because he knew that his leave was expiring and that he would get in trouble, he tried to hurry at the very time he should have been hoarding his strength. He began to travel both night and day. On the evening of March 31 he reached Seven Mile Creek and, while trying to cross it on the log bridge, slipped and fell into the ice-cold stream. He abandoned his blankets and empty knapsack where he crawled out of the water, and the backtrackers found them on the log where he left them. He now lost his way and wandered along the valley, but stumbled again on the road from Crater Lake and Annie Creek and was able to follow the parallel black tracks of wagonwheel ruts down which the melting snow water ran. The trailers could see where he had staggered and fallen, time after time. They even found black powder scattered on the snow like pepper where he had tried to reload his Colt revolver to fire signal shots to summon help. They then found his Colt revolver with all the percussion caps on the nipples snapped but with only one chamber discharged. The powder in the other chambers of the cylinder was too soaked to explode. When no help came after his single shot, Hallock began to crawl the last mile and a half to the Wood River bridge.

As they stood there in the snow examining their friend's misfired pistol, the full horror of the incident dawned upon the men. Hallock had been within sight and sound of Fort Klamath, dying slowly. Almost certainly he had heard Reveille on April 1 before he lapsed into unconsciousness from fatigue, starvation and exposure. Worse, his single signal shot *had* been heard by one of the sentries on duty in the morning. The guard, remembering that it was April Fool's Day, dismissed the gunshot as someone trying to play a joke on him. He did not report it to the sergeant of the guard. And so Stephen T.

Hallock died on Fort Klamath's doorstep.

To add to their scanty supply of reading matter imported from the settlements, the soldiers of Fort Klamath started a weekly paper of their own, *The Growler*, edited by Orson A. Stearns. It was written in longhand on foolscap since there was neither press nor type at the post. On a good day it would run twelve or more pages. The men contributed poetry and prose essays as well as news, although the editor invited the latter particularly. When there simply was no news at Fort Klamath, a common occurrence, the editor and his contributors invented it. The "Correspondence" box was often full of imaginary happenings, and these humbugs were read not only by the entire garrison but by the little guard unit stationed at the Klamath Agency and even in Jacksonville, where the soldiers traded copies of their latest issue for copies of the Oregon *Sentinel.*

It was probably this swapping of the homemade Fort Klamath paper that brought its greatest scoop to the attention of the outside world. Pvt. Thomas S. Warren, who had been reading (perhaps too much) in Bulwer-Lytton's *Last Days of Pompeii*, captioned a story "Tremendous Earthquake at Fort Klamath" and signed it, with deliberate illegibility, "By Order of Comstock." Naturally, the *Sentinel* thought that the account was ok'd by the brass and signed "By Order of Commander," and it reprinted the story. It was a modest sensation. American papers picked it up and it was cabled to Europe for the Continental press.

The yarn was a good one. Earthquakes, after all, had been felt by Oregon military posts, so it was believed: "This morning at daylight we were startled from sleep by the precipitate shock of an earthquake immediately followed by the noise of distant thunder . . . the whole heavens were full of a very black cloud of smoke; the air had a very sulphurous smell and ashes of a brownish color fell fast as ever I saw it snow. We had to use candles in the mess room. Most of us went to breakfast but had only got fairly into our seats when, horror upon horror! The earth seemed rolling like waves of the ocean. Everyone was thrown to the floor and regained his feet only to be placed in the same position again. With the rattling of dishes, crashing of window glass, crackling of timbers of the buildings and the screams of frightened boys, you could not imagine a more perfect chaos. Some of us gained the door and such a sight as met our eyes!

"The tall pines around the fort seemed to be lashing

themselves into fury. The wagons in front of the stable were engaged in pitched battle; horses and cattle lying crouched upon the ground, uttering the most pitiful moans; dogs howling and the unearthly yells of the Klamath Indians encamped near the fort completed the scene. We imagined we were amid the wreck of matter and the crush of worlds. The sutler's store was thrown about twenty feet from its former position. There were no lives lost and no serious accidents to anyone, but there were quite a number of bruised shins and skinned noses. No serious damage to any of the buildings, all log or frame houses; but I do not think there is a whole pane of glass left at the post.

"There are many speculations as to the cause of this most singular freak of nature but most of us are of the opinion that a volcano has broken loose near the Klamath Marsh, as a continuous volume of smoke is seen ascending in that direction. Some of the soldiers have volunteered to go up and find out if we have a monster vomiting fire near us or not. There was about a half-hour between the first and second shocks; the first was only perceptible; the second lasted, as near as can be judged from various opinions, from two to three minutes."

The War Department became interested in seismic Fort Klamath but soon smelled a hoax and ordered that the writer of the humbug be sent to Vancouver Barracks in irons. Private Warren is said to have begged editor Stearns not to tell on him and the latter kept his mouth shut about his sources. Not until after the volunteers were mustered out was the correspondent's name revealed and, according to Oregon historian Buena Cobb Stone, Orson A. Stearns was still getting letters from scientists in 1914 querying him on details of the great Fort Klamath earthquake.

Although Fort Klamath was a healthy post, with only one death from disease in its first nine years of existence—and that, according to Post Surgeon Henry L. McElderry, a case of enteritis contracted before the man took station at Fort Klamath—life there was dull, damned dull. There was certainly no news value in the diet. It was the same Civil War issue of fresh pork and fresh beef with beans, bread, hard biscuit, rice, dessicated potatoes, hominy, tea and Costa Rican or Rio de Janeiro coffee, brown and white sugar, salt, syrup, vinegar and, thank heaven, both "common whiskey" and "superior whiskey," the latter for the officers and gentlemen of the post.

Still, Fort Klamath's muster ate better than the fellows out chasing the Indians. Perhaps their lots balanced out. When Lt.

John Bowen wrote to McCall from the field at the end of March 1866 he had had no meat for ten days and the detachment was due to run out of flour in just ten days more. The expedition was hardly a smashing success, either, and not worth such privations. Although but one man had been lost, shot to death with arrows near Harney Lake, Bowen felt that the campaign was already played out. "We have done considerable scouting during the winter but have accomplished nothing. The country is now so flooded that it is impossible to get about to any purpose." Yet virtually every man in Fort Klamath's dull barracks would have exchanged places with Bowen for a crack at hostile Indians. This was so even though they realized that Lieutenant Small was right in describing the pacification expeditions as "one of the most dangerous and inglorious modes of warfare—hunting Indians on the mountains and deserts of Oregon."

For the trooper stranded within the confines of Fort Klamath and not unlucky enough to be detailed to the strenuous and detested road-building duty, one day was like every other one. Reveille at 5:30 A.M. was followed by breakfast and then Stable Call at 6:00. At 7:30 both Fatigue Call and Sick Call were sounded and, a half-hour later, "Boots and Saddles" for mounted drill. Guard mount and dismounted drill would follow at 10:30, and at 11:45 the men heard the welcome notes of Recall, followed by dinner at noon. Miscellaneous drills occupied the afternoon from 1:15 until 3:30, then "stables" at 4:00, retreat at 5:15 and supper at 5:30. The day—and virtually every day—was closed with tattoo at 9:00 and taps at 10:00.

The officers were not kept busy enough even with the endless rounds of paper work—morning reports, weekly reports of forage, returns of provisions, ad infinitum—and all of them engaged in extracurricular activity. Some were accused of dalliance with the local squaws. McCall, on the other hand, helped plan a Southern Oregon Military Road Company as a result of his experience with Pengrá's escort and the subsequent time on his hands in Fort Klamath. The company was actually founded in 1868 with a capitalization of twenty-five thousand dollars to be realized by the sale of stock to subscribers at one hundred dollars a share. But the road, as such, was not built.

Capt. Frank B. Sprague, for whom Oregon's Sprague River was named, succeeded Maj. William V. Rinehart in command of

Fort Klamath on August 21, 1866, Rinehart having replaced the post's co-founder, Kelly. Sprague was apparently well liked. When he visited lonely Camp Lyon in Jordan Valley, Corp. William M. Hilleary contrasted him with his own detested commander, "His Excellency" Lt. James A. Balch: "Being a plain man, he prefers to stop with the soldiers instead of the high falutin' Regulars." Sprague tried to make Fort Klamath more endurable for the men by relaxing the bread rule, which the men resented, and by using post funds to add vegetables and fruit to vary the garrison diet. But he also believed strongly in keeping his boys busy, and thus out of mischief. Perhaps taking his cue from Oliver Applegate who, with two Indians, opened a new road from the Dalles to Fort Klamath, Sprague scouted a new route over the Cascades with the mulatto hunter and frontiersman, John Matthews, and then set twenty men of I Company to build a road that would better the Ranchería Trail. Nor was road building confined to the Cascades. When the expedition was sent to establish Camp Alvord in September 1865 as a winter headquarters for moves against the Snakes of the Steens' Mountain area, the soldiers had to build not only a road but a poor excuse for a corduroy road across the mirey and treeless area of the Warner Lakes by cutting tules, or marsh reeds, and laying them out as a roadbed. Much of the time it more resembled an artificial or floating pontoon bridge than a road. The men then had to haul wagons out of the morass by hand when even the fort's tough mules bogged down. This bit of road building led directly to Fort Klamath's only mutiny, the so-called Bread Riot of 1865. The sixty-odd soldiers, pinch-gutted from slim rations and the hard labor of a road gang, and building Camp Alvord with logs that had to be hauled a mile or two from the hills, marched home to Fort Klamath through snow, mud and rain. At Sprague River Narrows their scanty supplies were further reduced by the raids of half-wild Indian dogs, and when they arrived at the fort they were not too distantly removed from starvation. So ravenous were the young men that they ignored orders and instead of delivering up their just-distributed flour ration to the post baker to be made into bread (the baker returning fourteen ounces of bread for every eighteen ounces of flour given him, to make the labor worth his while), they prepared to enjoy a great pancake feast in their mess using *all* of the flour issued them. Ordered to turn in their flour to the baker as was customary, they refused and were arrested for mutiny. They finally complied with orders, but not before Major Rinehart had made an example of sixteen-year-old Pvt. James Corwin Fullerton, the first soldier to refuse to obey orders. Rinehart had him strung up by the thumbs with his toes just brushing the ground. As night fell and a snowstorm howled about the bastions, the rebellious troops heard the ominous rattling of rifles by the guards in company headquarters. They feared the worst. But before the would-be mutineers could plan a genuine revolt or a surrender, Fullerton was returned to the guardhouse, where it was a case of standing room only, as almost the whole garrison was under arrest. The major then joined them and read the prisoners the Articles of War, advising them that the crime they had committed was punishable by death, but since the Civil War was over he was not even going to court-martial them. He released them with a warning, and so the Bread Riot ended on a peaceful note.

Young Fullerton went on to become a lawyer, judge of the Circuit Court and Oregon state senator. The punishment of the teenaged soldier was cruel but not unusual for the times. A drunken baker at Fort Hoskins, for example, was given a taste of "bucking," his wrists tied together and his arms drawn down over his knees and a musket passed over his arms at the crook of the elbows and under his knees, rendering him as cramped and helpless as a trussed pig. He was released shortly, but not all soldiers were so lucky. Punishment of peaceful local Indians was more severe. Those "guilty" of drunkenness were given twenty lashes, then packed with thirty pounds of sand and made to march in circles. Tipsy squaws got off easily; they were merely disgraced by having their heads shaved by the Army. When Captain Sprague took command from Rinehart, he abolished the bread/flour quota system and imitated Fort Walla Walla, where a hundred percent bread return on issued flour was the policy.

During the opening of Sprague's Road to Union Creek and the Rogue River via Annie Creek Canyon, along the line of today's Highway 62, the troopers of I company rediscovered Crater Lake. The great caldera or volcanic cauldron in ancient Mount Mazama, from which, eons before, twelve cubic miles of Oregon had been blasted by the pent-up forces within the earth, was twenty-five miles in circumference with waters two thousand feet deep. It was—and is—rightly considered one of the wonders of the world. The spectacular lake had first been found by miner John Wesley Hillman on June 12, 1853, while he was searching with a group of prospectors for the legendary

Lost Cabin Mine. The Oregon argonauts named it, descriptively, Deep Blue Lake, and more poetically, Mysterious Lake. It was again visited on October 21, 1862, by six miners led by Chauncey Nye, who, unimaginatively, named it Blue Lake. It was more or less forgotten until two of Fort Klamath's roadbuilders, John M. Corbell and F. M. Smith, found it and clambered down its steep thousand-foot bluffs to the water's edge to gaze in awe at Wizard Island and Llao Rock. The entranced troopers named it Lake Majesty. Captain Sprague wrote a description of Lake Majesty for the newspapers, but the name did not take. It became known as Crater Lake after it was explored by five people in a knockdown wooden rowboat in 1869, though the name Mystic Lake clung to it for a time, also.

Although Crater Lake lay only twenty-two miles northwest of Fort Klamath and but three miles off Sprague's military road, its existence was almost unknown and was, in fact, hidden from the men and officers of the post by the Klamaths. Chief Allen David finally explained that it was forbidden to the Indians as the home of the Great Spirit and of monsterlike men called llaos. When, long before, a Klamath had dared to look upon its waters, he became stronger than other warriors but made the mistake of killing one of the fish-men, and hordes of llaos then set upon him, carried him to the top of a cliff, cut his throat with a stone knife, chopped his body into pieces and threw them into the lake to feed the other llaos. Said Allen Davis, "Such shall be the fate of every Klamath brave who, from that day to this, dares to look upon the lake." Even as late as 1890 the superstition surrounding Crater Lake was so strong that the Indians feared to visit it. W. G. Steele, the pioneer Oregon outdoorsman, wrote, "There is probably no point in America that so completely overcomes the ordinary Indian with fear as Crater Lake. From time immemorial no power has been strong enough to induce him to approach within sight of it."

Curiously, it was the thumb-stringing Major Rinehart rather than the kindlier Captain Sprague who put an end to the misuse of Fort Klamath soldiers as common road laborers. He did not like to see A Company hacking down trees or leveling roadbeds while the boys of other companies chased Indians. He complained loudly and all the way to the Adjutant General of Oregon, Cyrus A. Reed. The latter was convinced and took up Rinehart's cause as his own. He roundly denounced the practice in his annual report for 1865-1866. Reed found such manual labor to be highly detrimental to the service. It was wrong to recruit men to fight for their country for sixteen dollars a month under the iron rule of the military service and then to force them to take up axes and scythes to cut timber or hay or build roads. "Being poorly fed and still more poorly paid," said the adjutant general, "there is no wonder that the soldier would soon learn to curse the service that treats him so, as well as the officers immediately in command of him."

Reed became interested in the plight of the Fort Klamath slaveys largely as the result of a letter Rinehart sent him in 1865, which read: "The troops at this post have been working instead of campaigning. They have made a good wagon road over the Cascades to Rogue River Valley, which has reduced freight one cent per pound. This saves the Government at least three thousand dollars per annum. The soldiers cut and put up two hundred tons of hay last season and cut their own wood. This year, they have the same work to do. I wish you would make a point in your report against employing troops at hay making, etc. It has this effect—drills, parades and all *military* duties are suspended during such fatigue duty (fatigue duty does not actually express it, it is actual labor), the men become careless and neglect their personal appearance, lose all pride, which is indispensable to the true soldier, their efficiency in drill and the duties of a soldier are destroyed or, at best, impaired, discipline cannot be kept up, insubordination creeps in and makes them more like a set of railroad hands than soldiers. The ration that a man drills and stands guard on becomes too little when he chops cordwood or rakes hay. A man is excusable for growling when he is hungry.

"On a campaign, I would not [have it] but that soldiers should cut roads, build bridges, etc., to add to their comfort, efficiency, etc.; but in garrison we should not require such work from soldiers. Yet the practice is kept up and sustained on the plea of *economy*. It may be economy. It would be economy if I should hire and bind you to sort lace and then force you to dig potatoes, instead. A great Government like ours should not practice such economy. Other nations turn out model soldiers and so can we, but not of those from the hay field." Rinehart wanted his men to be of the sort praised by Gen. Charles P. Stone, who said, "For the work I have seen a squadron of United States cavalry perform on the plains, Germany would send two regiments and deem it hard service."

Garrison duty on the frontier, especially in winter, was hard enough without the sentencing of "volunteers" to hard labor.

As Captain Currey saw it, it was "the dullest of all monotonous times. . . . I do not think a better system could possibly be devised than the present garrison duty system to alienate men from their officers and render the officers unsympathetic with their men, chill the enthusiasm of troops and sap the foundation of patriotism." Withal, Fort Klamath was a happy post, and not one of the verminous sod or adobe forts which General Sherman urged should be exhibited in Boston by a new breed of abolitionists as examples of cruelty and inhumanity to slaves in blue uniforms. Nevertheless, desertions began to increase at Fort Klamath in the late 1860s and early 1870s.

Rinehart's complaints had their effect and Fort Klamath ceased to be a workhouse. When the next major east-west artery was needed, to tie together the settlements of northernmost California, it was not built by privates from Fort Klamath but by a civilian, H. C. Tickner. He finished the Tickner Road in December 1871, except for a few necessary wells along its route, which he completed the following year. It ran from the Ball Mountain Road at Bull Meadows, entered Butte Valley at the Ball ranch and ran eastward to the Boyes ranch and Red Rock Valley to pass south of Van Bremer Mountain, now Mount Dome, and skirt a little-explored and much-ignored volcanic badland that would soon become known all over the world as the Modoc Lava Beds. From there it struck the Pit River Road in Hot Springs Valley at the Boiling Spring a few miles east of modern Canby. In the spring of 1875, Tickner also finished the first wagon road up the Klamath River, via Shovel Creek and the Topsy Grade to Linkville.

The increased roads of the Klamath country were both symptoms and causes of the growing civilization—or, at least, settlement—of the region. By 1866, there was a pony express from Fort Klamath to Henley twice a week, and canoes were ferrying travelers across the Williamson River as well as the little Link River. This last was perhaps the shortest river in the world, only eight thousand feet long, connecting Upper Klamath Lake and tiny Lake Ewauna, which, in turn, fed the mighty Klamath River rushing to the Pacific Ocean. Link River was also one of the most curious streams in creation. At times it was almost solid with frogs; at other seasons it was a mass of writhing water snakes and blue racers. When the south winds blasted it properly, they hustled its waters back into Upper Klamath Lake and literally blew the river dry except for a trickle in the bed.

With thousands of steelhead and mullet lying on the newly exposed banks, even the laziest Indian could pick his fill.

During the early years of Fort Klamath's existence there was no town on Link River. Linkville waited for George Nurse, a New Yorker of Scots descent, who had come to Fort Klamath in 1863 at the age of forty-three to cut hay in the meadowland. He was later employed to clear windfalls and other obstructions on the Ranchería Trail until Sprague's new road could be finished. The Ranchería Trail, however, was not abandoned. Many travelers and troopers continued to use it, and it was kept open after Sprague's Road was in business. Nurse got eight dollars a day for this road maintenance, and he earned every penny of it. He moved on to become sutler, or post trader, at Fort Klamath with a silent partner, Alexander Miller, who put up all the money and let the rugged and ambitious Nurse do all the work.

But on March 12, 1867, as Captain Sprague and three men were saddling up to hunt some Indians who had stolen horses from the post's herd, they saw Nurse leaving Fort Klamath with a wagonload of supplies. Sprague later recalled: "I asked him what he was planning to do and he said he looked for the fort to peter out soon and felt he could make himself some money by trading with the Indians for furs. . . . Nurse said he had everything he owned loaded in that rig." Sprague pushed on south and cut the Indians' trail. Shortly, he jumped the four rustlers and recovered four of the Army mounts, but the thieves got away. He remembered, "We were somewhere deep in the lava break country about 100 to 130 miles south of the fort and felt we had already gone too far with only the four of us, so we turned back." A few days later, en route to Fort Klamath, the quartet of riders saw a smudge of smoke on the horizon and turned west toward it. Sprague found Nurse camped between Upper and Lower Klamath Lakes. He had already set up shop in the form of a rude shelter and was trading with Indians from the supplies unloaded from his wagon.

Captain Sprague and his men camped with Nurse that night, shared their rations with him and yarned with him around a campfire. Next day, Nurse gave Sprague a note for the sawmill at Fort Klamath which listed the lumber he needed for a trading post or store. He also gave him a letter to the sawyer and one to Alex Miller, asking that the sawed lumber be rafted down to him at Link River. On May 1, he sought permission from

Jackson County to establish a ferry on Link River just about where it opened out into Lake Ewauna. Earlier, Indian Joe had been paid fifteen dollars a month from Fort Klamath funds to keep a ferry across Link River.

Nurse had a boatwright provide him with a ferryboat and he got the lumber rafted down safely and built a cabin on a rocky point of the river bank. George Nurse just squatted, like everybody else, probably encouraged by the news of Congress' July 1866 announcement of a list of public lands for sale and the granting of preemption rights. He did not have a deed until the United States transferred the land to the state of Oregon in July 1872. Until then, squatter's rights sufficed. In 1872, T. H. McCann, in whose name the first Linkville deeds were registered, gave Nurse a warrantee deed for a dollar.

The site Nurse chose for his settlement was where the road (really a trail, then) from Fort Klamath crossed Link River on its way to Henley and Yreka, California, and to the military posts of eastern Oregon. First called simply Link Ferry, Nurse's Ferry and Klamath River, the name settled down as Linkville until modern times, when the town was renamed Klamath Falls. All business was first transacted in "Uncle George's" name, but Alex Miller was still his silent partner and exchequer. Nurse platted the townsite and offered lots for sale, but there were no takers. Everyone just squatted where he pleased, as Nurse had done. Three miles to the south, for example, his near-namesake, William or Wendolin Nus (a German, not a Scot) built a cabin on the east bank of the Klamath River and set up a rival ferry. Nus, the first permanent settler of the Klamath basin, had ranged cattle in the upper Klamath River Valley since 1858. After a stay in the John Day mines, he squatted three miles west of Link River crossing in 1866 and began to supply beef to Fort Klamath, then imitated Uncle George Nurse.

Even as remote an area as the Klamath basin received a psychological lift from the thudding sledges of the gandy dancers driving rails toward Promontory. Although no railroad came to Linkville for many years, the web of dirt roads brought farmers and cattle ranchers and sheepmen. Above all, they attracted prospectors in those early years, men ready to freeze in icy streams to the east or keel over from sunstroke in their coyote holes for a chance at getting rich quick. By 1868, Nurse was so busy freighting supplies into Linkville by pack train from Yreka that he had to hire a gardener to take care of the vegetables, the orchard and the berry patch he had set out. Fort

Klamath and the scattering of sodbusters and ranchmen provided a market that was not satisfied by the soldier-green-grocers who had established a truck garden at Burnett's Point on Upper Klamath Lake. From the latter, whitehall boats were soon hauling produce to the Klamath Agency landing. As early as May 1865, Bob Whittle had proved that freighting by water was practical when he moved 1,300 pounds of freight across Upper Klamath Lake. A flatboat of fifteen to twenty tons capacity was built by a Rogue River man to handle the soldiers' harvests, and the crew worked it across the lake and up the Williamson River through floating logs to a rendezvous with the waiting wagons from Fort Klamath.

Yreka liked the idea of waterborne freight since it hoped to supplant Jacksonville as the supplier of Fort Klamath. Thus the Yreka *Journal* on June 30, 1865, rather prematurely pointed out the advantages of lake travel and reminded its readers that the land route around the lake was almost free of snow even in winter while Captain Kelly, in June, was still trying to open the Ranchería Trail, clogged with drifts of snow up to twelve feet deep. But the paper was honest enough to realize that the shallow lake (forty miles long, from five to twenty-five miles wide, but only some eight to ten feet deep!) could be choppy and treacherous in a blow. To prove it, the paper on May 26, 1865, ran an account of one of the earliest Klamath cruises.

Captain Kelly took some soldiers on a sail that turned out to be mostly a row from Williamson River to Link River, forty miles away by water. Returning, he had a fair wind, but it freshened as he neared his home port. An anonymous crewman told of the denouement of the watery expedition: "Captain Kelly can handle a company of soldiers but is not familiar with a whitehall sailboat. Missing the channel of the river in coming in and bringing her to, we turned turtle and spilled the Captain and four of us into the lake. He will not go out without old sailors again. It was a rough lake but he took it in good part and the boys had a good laugh on shore."

When Ivan Applegate got married, he took his bride and some guests on a cruise in a boat that was sometimes powered by a two-horse treadmill but which, this trip, used only sails and oars. A squall hit and the party was almost swamped and shipwrecked, having to camp on a small island until the storm blew over. In 1871, Samuel Grubb, a Klamath Agency employee, built a flat-bottomed scow in which he hauled freight between Pelican Bay and Kowasta. The following year, a sailboat with a genuine keel was placed on the lake by an old salt named Moody. It connected Klamath Lake with Link River and Agency Lake and Williamson River. The vessel was named either the *Mary Moody* or the *Maggie Moody* (Klamath memories fail this test) for either the sailor's squaw or his daughter. Most of the freight she carried was lumber from Klamath Agency and goods bound for the reservation or Fort Klamath's sutler's store. About the time of the Modoc War, square-rigged barges, real windjammers, made their appearance to run freight from Rocky Point to Agency Landing, being poled up creeks when necessary. But boats on Klamath Lake did not provide the answer to the transportation problems of the border country. More and better roads, and wagon trains in place of pack trains, were the answers.

The wagon road to the Central Pacific Railroad at Reno Station in 1869, via Fort Bidwell, was 450 miles long and open only from May to December. An alternate route was the all-year wagon road from the railroad terminus at Red Bluff (later, at Redding), California, to Ager, Linkville and the fort, 340 miles long and "all-year" in name only. During the three heaviest months of winter it was usually closed. There was also a road from Portland to the Dalles and thence to Fort Klamath by the Deschutes River, and the long and difficult but effective pack train trail from the port of Crescent City, California, to Jacksonville and the Sprague Road over the Cascades to Fort Klamath. But pack mules could only carry two hundred pounds each, and a round trip on this twisting trail took from two to three weeks. Freight costs were six cents a pound on the ship from San Francisco to Crescent City and five cents a pound for the muleback portion of the journey. This route, too, was really open only from July to November.

Still, with no road being anywhere near perfect, trade in the Klamath, basin was increasing, and in 1871, Lt. Greenleaf A. Goodale, C. O. of Fort Klamath, recommended the establishment of a post office at Linkville. That was the year Nurse decided to put up a fine hotel there. The following year Linkville got its post office, with George Nurse its postmaster at a salary of twelve dollars a year. A new Fort Klamath Commanding Officer, Maj. G. G. Huntt, described the route from Yreka to the fort via Ward's Ferry and Linkville as a real road (in part), open at all seasons for pack animals if not yet for wagons. A round trip could now be made over this line of communication in only four days. A contract was let to a Mr.

Kilgore of Ashland to carry mail from that town to Lake City, California, via Linkville. The mail contract paid about four to five thousand dollars a year for the weekly trips of Kilgore and his sons on horseback, in a light wagon, and sometimes on foot. In 1872, a U. S. Land Office was placed in Linkville and jack-of-all-trades Nurse was appointed receiver. But he did not qualify and was shortly replaced. On the eve of the Modoc War, in 1872, George Nurse's little empire was a small boomtown for land-hungry Americans. It had forty permanent residents and many more seasonal drifters, a store, post office, hotel, blacksmith shop and feed stable. There was a saloon, of course, a carpenter shop and even a suburb—two homes were built across the river. His sturdy wooden bridge with a corduroy approach now replaced his ferry. The structure was said to have cost him between twelve and fifteen hundred dollars, but Nurse could afford it. He had prospered by ferrying wagons at two dollars a crossing, horsemen at fifty cents and animals from two-bits for a horse or a mule to a nickel apiece for sheep and hogs. Good times had come to the Klamath basin. As early as 1868 the Yreka paper was crowing, "There is no snow between here and the Fort. The grass in Klamath basin is splendid and the country is full of people traveling toward Goose Lake and Pit River. The Indians are busy gathering the winter supply of *camas* and the valleys are dotted with their tents."

From their front-row seats the cavalrymen of Fort Klamath could watch all this activity and see the squatters moving onto low-grade land, now that most of the good range was gone. These "swamp grabbers" were hooted, at first, for taking over worthless marshes which overflowed in winter. But they were wise enough to secure large holdings and to ditch them for drainage. Before long the "swamp grabbers" were sitting pretty—and high and dry—in the Klamath basin.

Substantial cattle spreads began to spring up all over the country vacated by the Modocs and Klamaths. George S. Miller settled in Langell Valley and replaced that area's antelope, sage hens and prairie chickens with herds of cattle. He prospered. Just before the Modoc War, when Indians stampeded one of his herds near Alturas, they ran off between three and four hundred steers he was driving to Arizona. N. B. Ball was a Kentuckian who pioneered Butte Valley and soon had five hundred head of cattle on his three-thousand-acre ranch on Butte Creek. Even more prominent was John A. Fairchild, a Southerner who came to California on the Gila Trail in 1849.

The Mississippian gave up mining to become a rancher on some 2,700 acres on Butte and Cottonwood Creeks near Meiss Lake. Before long he was running three thousand head of stock. He was elected to the State Assembly to represent Siskiyou County, and he became perhaps as good a friend of the Modocs as Squire Steele in Yreka.

More and more ranches appeared, including the Van Bremer place on Willow Creek, Charles Boyes' spread on Butte Creek, the Hole-in-the-Ground Ranch near modern Dorris and, on Lost River itself, a string of farms and ranches of which probably Dennis Crawley's place was best-known.

In September 1869, forty-five privates of K Company, 23d U. S. Infantry, came to Fort Klamath as reinforcements from Crescent City. Once on the post they helped the cavalrymen build target ranges on which they could practice in accordance with Blunt's *Small Arms Regulations*—as if there was any need for sharpshooters at quiet old Fort Klamath! At least it meant a change, and the troopers placed target ranges, a hundred by a thousand yards in size, at the southeastern edge of the post where the ridges would backstop them. Short-range targets revolved on vertical axes. The troopers made fun of the new broad-bladed spade bayonets of the foot soldiers, a combination weapon and entrenching tool, until challenged to a sham battle. At the sound of a starter's gun the cavalrymen were to charge from the south end of the military reservation toward the north edge, where the infantrymen were to dig in at the same signal. To the amazement of the horse soldiers, by the time their galloping mounts carried them to the infantry positions they found the footsloggers dug in and waiting for them with rifles at the ready. The yellowlegs took it well. What the hell, it was all just a game, anyway.

The whole fort now seemed an anachronism as the Klamath basin began to settle up. It was no longer a frontier, what with mining, ranching, farming and freighting booming all around. The post was a throwback to a time when the Indians were a real threat. Now, with the industrial revolutionary nineteenth century transforming the Oregon and California border, the redskins were all tucked away on their reservation except for the miserable handful of Modocs bumming about with Captain Jack. They had been the source of several letters of complaint to the Fort Klamath commander in 1869, from Butte Valley and Lost River settlers, but it would not be any trouble to round them up and boot them onto the Klamath Reservation.

CHAPTER SIX

RENEGADES

Jesse Applegate hoped that the advent of the 1870s would bring good fortune for the Modocs and Klamaths. The Oregon pioneer respected Lt. Greenleaf Goodale, who became commanding officer of Fort Klamath in 1869. He sharply contrasted the latter's Christian character with that of some of his predecessors, whom Applegate chose not to name: "Previous to 1869, Fort Klamath had been under the command of Army officers who were indifferent to the Agent's protestations against interference with his people. Already there were evidences of shameful civilizing, through soldiers' agency, among the Klamath children, some of the mothers with unblushing pride claiming that their half-breeds were entitled to fatherly protection by the officers of the Fort. The United States Army is sometimes disgraced by bad men in high office. These cases are exceptions and Fort Klamath was unfortunate in being sometimes under the command of officers who dishonored the uniform they wore by associating with Indian women of ill fame."

Lindsay Applegate, Jesse's brother, was a sound choice as Indian sub-agent for the Klamath Reservation. While not as close a friend of the Modocs as John Fairchild, Elijah Steele or A. M. Rosborough, he was respected by the Indians and acceptable to them as their shepherd. He had almost thirty years experience on the frontier and, in the words of Indian Superintendent A. B. Meacham, he "thoroughly understood Indian character, habits, customs and peculiarities. He was in every way qualified for the position." Lindsay's brother, Jesse, was naturally biased, but was truthful when he echoed Meacham's sentiments and added, "Lindsay liked the Indians under his care and during his agency, they made rapid advances." Indeed, from his May 1866 arrival with an ox-drawn wagonload of supplies—including seeds, a breaking plow, axes, wedges and other tools—Lindsay Applegate worked hard to

97

make the Klamath Agency a success. But the promised manual training school did not materialize, and although he had as many as four thousand Indians on his hands by 1870, the Klamath Reservation was not even formally established until March 14, 1871. Until his thousand dollar per annum salary began, Applegate worked diligently on faith and his good credit.

Congressional purse-pinching—Maj. William V. Rinehart called it "niggardly parsimony"—caused not only a teetering economic situation but also a bad political climate on Oregon's Indian frontier. With the scant weapons for peace at his disposal, Applegate was unable to arrest the deterioration in intertribal relations. Paulina had hardly brought his Walpapi Snakes on the reservation, after suing for peace in late 1864, before he bolted again. This time he left for good. Next, the usually tractable Klamaths—certainly so when compared to Modocs or Walpapis—became altogether too "civilized" for Applegate. As they grew more ambitious and materialistic, they began to confiscate Modoc lumber in their quest for property and wealth. Soon they were annoying Modoc squaws and interfering with Modoc fishermen. Chief Schonchin, who had brought most of the Modocs onto the reservation in the fall of 1867, was as peaceful and patient as a Moravian and willing to turn the other cheek. But the younger men, led by Sub-Chief Captain Jack, refused to tolerate this bullying and exaction of tribute. Small-scale bickering between Klamaths and Modocs began to grow into a vendetta.

Agent Applegate got precious little help from Fort Klamath in enforcing law and order at Klamath Agency. Impatient with its laissez-faire attitude, he formed a force of Indian police at the reservation to arrest any of his wards supplying the hostile Snakes of Paulina. But all of his gendarmes were Klamaths, a fact that further alienated the Modocs. And when he turned some prisoners over to Fort Klamath, the culprits were not tried for their crimes by the Army officers. Applegate blamed the citizens of Yreka for the refusal of Kientpoos to return to the reservation. He accused attorney Elijah Steele and other "bad white men" of tampering with the off-reservation Modocs. As early as 1863, he had tried to get the Army to locate Fort Klamath not on Wood River but between Yreka and Lost River as a buffer between Steele and the Indians. Although the sub-agent and the Fort Klamath military seldom saw eye to eye, in this matter Applegate was in complete agreement with Major Rinehart, who later said: "The advice of Squire Steele to the

Modocs on several occasions while I was at Fort Klamath seemed to me to be leading them into a course of defiance and insolence towards the U.S. authorities. I regarded Steele as a very bad advisor, and so informed the Modocs."

Nor did Rinehart have a high opinion of those who consorted with the local Indian girls. Most of his fire was directed at civilians, of course, rather than at the soldiers and his brother-officers who had been blasted by Lindsay Applegate for their sexual impropriety. "Those who understand the circumstances may find some grains of allowance for our early pioneers who took squaws to wife, such as Col. Craig and Dr. Newell, but there can be no charity for our modern squawmen. They are usually outlaws, fleeing from the justice of the law to begin with, and besides exercising a baneful influence in their lives and conduct, their civilization at best is of a very low order."

Unfortunately for the Modocs, the crisis in their relations with the Klamaths and whites came at the time of an abrupt, albeit brief, about-face in American Indian affairs which muddied further the already turgid waters of Indian diplomacy. Vacillating President U. S. Grant, succumbing to War Department pressure, took control of a number of Indian agencies away from religious-oriented civilians and placed them in the hands of Army officers again. Grant had been badgered by get-tough civilians and by officers right on up to Maj. Gen. Henry W. Halleck. In the 1866-1867 annual report of the Secretary of War, Halleck expostulated: "Whatever may have been, or may now be, the effect of our Indian system east of the Rocky Mountains, where the Indians are organized into large tribes and governed by powerful chiefs, it has proved worse than useless on this coast, where they live in small bands with no well recognized and responsible head. The farce of Indian treaties should be entirely abandoned and these savages be taught that they are not independent nations but the *subjects* of our Government, and that while they are amenable to our laws they are entitled to receive our protection. It is useless to expect the whites and Indians to live together in peace. In revenge for savage barbarities, the frontier settlers kill the Indians without regard to their individual innocence or guilt. The military are powerless to prevent this and the civil courts will not punish a white man for killing an Indian. Consequently, the Indians retaliate by murdering innocent whites without regard to sex or age. The only way in which this murderous frontier can be terminated within a limited period is to remove the Indians to some large and well-defined reservations placed entirely under military authority."

Over the protests of the Indians and Lindsay Applegate, the Government replaced the latter with Capt. Oliver C. Knapp in October 1869. Knapp secured his discharge from the Army but was still a soldier in his thinking, if a civilian in fact. Immediately the situation worsened on and around the Klamath Reservation. The ex-soldier *tyee* had no idea how to handle the troublemakers. Lindsay Applegate, four years later, recalled with good memory but bad orthography, "While I was in charge I managed a thwart their schemes and keep the peace but after my removal they became more embolden."

Indian Superintendent Meacham was hardly surprised by Knapp's inability to keep the peace among four different Indian nationalities, however small, crammed onto a single reservation in a "consolidation" so much sought by Washington. He knew that Knapp really had no heart for the job and largely went through the motions of administering the agency. "Why should he do more?" asked Meacham rhetorically, "the position came to him unsought. He knew nothing of Indian character; he did not care to know. That he performed his duty honestly in the financial management of the Agency has not been questioned. That he felt the contempt for the Indian so nearly universal among officers of the Army is certainly true."

Meacham was no more disturbed at the switch of the Indian agencies from Interior Department administration to Army control than was the Commissioner of Indian Affairs in Washington. In his annual report of 1868-1869 he warned that "Our true policy towards the Indian tribes is peace and the proposed transfer is tantamount, in my judgement, to perpetual war." Claiming that past experience had shown military management of Indian affairs to be a failure, the commissioner ended his plea in despair: "It is inhuman and unchristian, in my opinion, leaving the question of economy out of view, to destroy a whole race by such demoralization and disease as military government is sure to entail upon the tribes."

The experiment did not last long. Government policy soon reversed itself. In 1870, Congress passed a law prohibiting Army officers from holding such civilian positions as Indian agents. The military men were withdrawn and replaced by church-sponsored civilians in a pendulum-swing back to the opposite extreme of "Quakerism" from the hard-nosed attitude of the

Army. A. B. Meacham applauded what he saw as the Government's return to sanity and predicted that there would be no more bullying sentinels and blasphemous teamsters to tutor the Klamaths and Modocs in their civilized vices, no more Indian mistresses in the sub-agent's quarters and no more bacchanals of firewater.

But the change was too little and much too late for the Modocs. A. B. Meacham, who probably knew the Indian situation on the California-Oregon border better than any other single individual, described Lindsay Applegate's ouster as a critical turning point toward Indian resistance to authority, followed by violence and open warfare. He remarked, "The sad sequel to the removal of a peace man to make a place for an Army officer marks one of the darkest pages of our history as a nation."

Meacham attempted to save the situation by a daring move in the last days of 1869. He would talk Captain Jack and his renegades back onto the reservation. After speaking to Knapp, Meacham sent a messenger, Modoc Sally, to tell Jack to come and talk with him. Captain Jack responded that Meacham would have to come to him. And he added, pointedly, that he had no desire to see him. Meacham went ahead with his plans nonetheless, asking Fort Klamath for an escort. In keeping with the Army's unwritten law of no cooperation with Indian Affairs officers, Captain Goodale demurred. He did so even though an ex-brother officer, Knapp, was now Klamath sub-agent. Later, perhaps because of second thoughts on the subject of officerly camaraderie, Goodale reconsidered and grudgingly extended to Meacham and Knapp a non-com and a squad of men from Fort Klamath.

The superintendent added Ivan Applegate and some Warm Springs and Klamath Indians to his party and set out with the soldiers following him. He left his escort and his wagons at Link River on December 22, 1869, telling the noncommissioned officer to wait there for orders from him. Then he cut cross-country to the west bank of Lost River and Jack's village of a dozen huts. The lodges stood about a mile downstream from the Natural Bridge.

When Meacham was within a few miles of the Modoc village, four Indians cantered up on ponies. Each warrior was armed with a rifle and a pistol. They ordered the party to halt, then demanded to know the nature of Meacham's business. Although he explained it, the mounted sentinels said that their people did not want to see anyone. They told Meacham to turn back. Instead, he assumed a bold front and swung around the horsemen, giving them a good look at the Colt Navy revolvers and sixteen-shot Henry repeating rifles with which he had armed his party. He approached the village at a brisk pace. Although it appeared deserted, he noticed that the four guards hurried ahead of him and, dismounting, ran to the crude steps of the largest lodge and entered.

Superintendent Meacham dismounted at the village and prepared to lead his men into the lodge when a Modoc lookout halted him, shouting, "One man come! No more!" Meacham entered to find a sullen Captain Jack staring at him, unwilling to shake hands, smoke or even speak. The superintendent coolly lit his pipe while the perennial peacemaker of the tribe, Scarfaced Charley, tried to soothe Captain Jack's ruffled temper. Speaking for the adamantly mute chief, he asked Meacham what he wanted. Charley heard the superintendent out, then explained carefully that Jack would come to Meacham's house *if* he wanted to see him. But he did not want to see him now. Therefore, Meacham and his party should go away. But at this point Jack could contain himself no longer; he broke in to accuse all whites of being liars and cheats. He said that he could not believe half of what he heard from them. Still, he would listen to Meacham.

First, the superintendent asked him for permission to let the rest of his party into the lodge. This was granted. In fact, Jack abandoned his bad manners and ordered a camp prepared for his visitors. A rude shelter was thrown up, sagebrush was collected for a campfire and some of his followers caught fish and roasted them for their callers. Meacham's powwow was put off until the next day. That morning, his wagons came up and Meacham invited the Modocs to a feast. Not forgetting Ben Wright and his poisonous marinades seventeen years earlier, the Modocs would not eat a thing until the whites and Klamaths had first dug into the food. Then they put away beef, bacon, hard bread and coffee with sugar in proper fashion, with gusto. With a full stomach, Jack was ready to parley but Meacham held up progress until he could get squawman Frank Riddle and his Modoc wife, Toby, to translate for him, although he already had Ivan Applegate, a pretty fair country translator.

Finally, Meacham made a big speech during which he exhibited a copy of Huntington's treaty of Council Grove. Captain Jack insisted that he had never signed the 1864 paper.

Technically, this was true. But Meacham, who had the word of Chief Schonchin of the Modocs and Chief Henry Blow of the Klamaths, reminded Jack that he had *accepted* its terms. He therefore demanded that Captain Jack observe its requirements. Neither Jack nor any of the other Indian "signers" apparently could write, and they were not asked to make X's alongside their names, neatly lettered by Huntington's scribe. Since the treaty was not approved in December 1869—and Jack knew this from his friends Steele and Rosborough—it was not binding on him even had he signed it. To him, his comings and goings were none of the business of Meacham or Knapp. Jeff Riddle recalled what Jack said. "I did not sell my country. I have said to the Americans that if they wished to emigrate here, they could live here. But I did not sell this country. He, Schonchin, sold it."

Captain Jack began to weaken before Meacham's arguments, asking what portion of the Klamath Reservation was set aside for his occupancy. Jack's soothsayer and conjurer, Curly Headed Doctor, now butted in. The shaman got to his feet and said loudly in Modoc, "We will not go there." With these words, the atmosphere in the lodge chilled. The Modocs now said that they were done talking. Meacham, fearing a treacherous attack, quietly told his men to leave. At this, the Modocs sprang to their feet and seized their weapons. The visitors did likewise. Toby now rose to argue with her people and to urge acceptance of the treaty's demands that they go on the reservation. According to her husband, Jeff Riddle, she shouted to her kin, "You be quiet! Listen ye to my speech. You do not understand well this thing and on both sides. Meacham is your friend. He spoke to your benefit for the purpose of you to live comfortably. Quietly here, sitting down, listen to him, not being wrathful. Then the Americans will make it straight. All of ye sitting down, lay down your guns! Now, with ye whites the Indians again desire to debate."

Jack ignored the eloquence of the squaw and prepared to leave his lodge. Meacham detained him and said, "Don't leave me now. I am your friend but I am not afraid of you. Be careful what you do. We mean peace but we are ready for war. We will not begin it, but if you do, it shall be the end of your people. We came for you and are not going back without you. You must go." Asked by Captain Jack what would happen to him if he refused, Meacham went out on a long limb and answered, "We will whip you until you are willing." Jack replied that he would be ashamed to fight so few whites with so many warriors. But he agreed to give Meacham an answer in the morning.

After Captain Jack withdrew for a conference with his headmen, the whites and their Indian friends spent a cold, sleepless and nervous night around the campfire in front of their flimsy wickiup. During the night Meacham managed to send a secret courier to the corporal's guard he had left at Link River, twenty-five miles away. He ordered them to move up near the Modoc camp but to move in on it *only* if they should hear gunfire. Of course, the troops, fortified with Dutch courage by some Linkville grogshop, rode noisily into camp as if they were the Light Brigade. Captain Jack and John Schonchin, armed with rifles, faded into the brush but did not shoot. While they appraised the situation, Meacham seized opportunity by the horns and sent the squad clattering in a circle to cover the indecisive Modocs, perhaps two hundred in all, counting women and children. He assured them that they were in no danger and gingerly disarmed the braves. Now he breathed easier, and he quickly issued rations to the Modocs, rounded up their ponies and prepared to move out.

Mary, or "Queen Mary of the Modocs" to sarcastic whites who observed her liaisons with five or six different whites in succession (she stayed only long enough to clean a man of his money, they said), came to Meacham to plead for her brother, Captain Jack. The superintendent got her to go to the Lava Beds hideout of her brother, and she agreed to take Meacham's scout, Gus Horn, with her. She was to assure Jack that nobody had been harmed, that no one would be harmed, and that he should come in.

Next day, Meacham started with his entourage for the Klamath Reservation, camping at Link River that night. On the following day, Captain Jack and a few followers overtook him. According to Samuel A. Clarke, Captain Jack was an artful hypocrite who now played the role of penitent and vowed to remain on the reservation at the same time that he told Indian confidants that he did not intend to stay there long. Whether Jack was dissimulating or not, he agreed to go on the reservation—on one condition. Ever fearful of losing face with his people, over whom he held such tenuous sway, he begged Meacham to prevent the Klamaths making fun of him as a coward who had run away from a tiny force. Meacham did more than that. He sent the Fort Klamath troopers ahead, to avoid embarrassing the sub-chief by having him enter the reservation under a small military guard. A grateful Jack made excuses, saying that the soldiers frightened his women and children.

Meacham's next crisis came when he reached Modoc Point on the reservation. Some of the agency's Indian idlers met the newcomers and invited them to participate in friendly games of chance. The superintendent had to issue a temporary order restraining them. His antigambling ordinance was most unpopular, but he feared that gaming losses might create ill will between Klamaths and Modocs before he had the latter securely in their new home. That might ruin his peacemaking coup.

At the agency, Meacham called an impressive council, larded with ceremony, to recement cordial relations between Modocs and Klamaths. Boundaries were drawn to separate them on the reservation. When the Klamaths had gathered beneath a huge pine to meet the Modocs, Captain Jack took a position near their chief, Allen David, as Meacham orated: "You meet in peace today to bury all the bad past, to make friends. You are of the same blood, of the same heart. You are to live as neighbors. This country belongs to you, all alike. Your interests are one. You can shake hands and be friends." He then laid a hatchet on the ground between the two chiefs and gave each one a pine branch. The two stepped forward and covered up the symbol of war with the boughs of pine needles. By twos, the prominent headmen of each tribe met to pledge friendship. Chief Allen David then made a speech exhorting all to live in eternal friendship. Captain Jack responded in the same vein. In the quaint language of interpreter Jeff Riddle, the Indians promised "at no time to get incensed. In a common home they would live and to the Americans they would keep friendship."

Meacham then wound up the festivities by issuing to the Modocs their treaty goods (clothing), which they had earlier forfeited by refusing to come to the reservation. The Modocs moved off to their camp on Modoc Point and began to prepare a grand feast with the flour and beef Meacham gave them, while the superintendent's teamsters built a huge bonfire to celebrate the reunion of, and realliance of, the two tribes. The fire also was an attempt, a vain one, to ward off the cold of a winter's night, for it was New Year's Eve. A frosty wind appeared to be trying to sweep in the new year of 1870 from across Klamath Lake, where ice creaked and groaned a mournful accompaniment to the fire-lit celebration.

The Klamath sub-chief, Henry Blow, promised to become a

Christian. Old Link River Jack asked Meacham to reexplain the Christian faith to him, then changed the subject and asked how whites could predict eclipses. He finally examined Meacham's watch and got the superintendent to demonstrate his big medicine by signaling the appearance of the New Year by firing off his pistol. Meacham did so just as the hands of the dial came together at midnight. The superintendent's superbly conducted (one might almost say "staged") *wa-wa* ended on a suitably religious or mystical note and the explosion of good gunpowder.

The era of good feeling that began before the first dawn of 1870 lasted only a few weeks. Allen David and Henry Blow could not control their young bucks. The latter began to harass and bully the Modocs again, especially Jack's newcomers. They seized logs the Modocs had cut and they took the eight thousand rails they had split to fence their allotted land. Timber was the one great resource of the Klamath Reservation—sugar pine, tamarack or lodge pole pine, and the fine-grained, lightweight ponderosa pine. The latter (also called bull pine, Western yellow pine or Oregon white pine) was especially valuable for boxes, sashes, doors and general lumber—the Modocs' only "money crop." Should the Klamaths be allowed to seize their lumber with impunity, the smaller tribe would be reduced to poverty, dependent entirely on the annuity handouts of the sub-agent.

The Klamaths were told to share and share alike with the Modocs and the handful of Snakes, but they could not forget that these people were interlopers on Klamath land. Thus they said, "The timber is ours. You may use some of it but it is ours. From our land the rails you have cut. The land belongs to us. The Modocs are bondsmen."

Captain Jack immediately protested to Captain Knapp, who promised to make things right. But he could do nothing with the young Klamaths. He did not return the stolen rails nor secure payment for them, as Captain Jack asked. The Klamaths became even more offensive and, this time, took all the newly cut rails left to the Modocs, some five thousand of them, according to Riddle. Jack appealed to Knapp again, complaining bitterly that he did not come to the reservation to work for the Klamaths for nothing. He insisted upon being paid for the fence rails. Knapp could only advise him to move his Modocs from Modoc Point to a distant area on the Williamson River. Jack accepted his proffer but, of course, the Klamath tormentors followed him there and continued their bullying and thieving. Even when Knapp tried to help, he bungled. He alienated John Schonchin by moving him to Williamson River after promising him an allotment next to his friend, Link River Jack.

When an exasperated Captain Jack came to him a third time for help, Knapp did one of two things. According to his defenders, he told Jack to pick his own site on the reservation, any place he liked. If Knapp's detractors are correct, he roughly told the sub-chief that if he came and bothered him again he would put him where he would not cause the Government any more trouble. The latter seems more likely, and Jeff Riddle, as honest as anyone concerned, quoted (or paraphrased) Knapp thus: "If you come here again, then I will lock you up where the Klamaths will not bother you any longer."

If Jack swallowed his pride at this rude rebuff, he soon disgorged it. He called a secret council of the Modocs while Chief Schonchin was away fishing on the Williamson River, and they voted by a large majority to abandon the reservation they had grown to hate. They would return to the heart of the Modoc country, Lost River, some seventy miles to the south. On April 26, 1870, the day Knapp stopped issuing rations to the Modocs, Captain Jack led his followers off the reservation. In the words of ethnologist Stephen Powers, he was "emboldened by the imbecility which reigned on the reserve." About 150 Modocs followed him. There were some sixty warriors, including some, such as Sub-Chiefs Charley Riddle and George, who later claimed they went involuntarily, too fearful to oppose the popular tide of opinion.

Jack, again eager to save face, claimed he had been starved out and that the promised double blankets had been cut until each Modoc was issued only half of a single blanket. This was probably nonsense. Meacham had given him a supply of blankets and other woolens. There were fish in Klamath Lake; Knapp had issued ample provisions of flour and beef. In the face of these facts, Jack still asserted solemnly that he had been given nothing to eat but some sour barley. He claimed he had had to kill seventeen of his horses to feed his squaws but, nevertheless, some of them who had weighed 200 pounds were now down to 140 pounds. Jack used a gun, but he was stretching a long bow now. Even if he and his people were not as well provided for as Sub-Agent Leroy S. Dyar insisted, his hungry cohort could not have eaten up seventeen horses in just two months even if his dieting squaws had managed to drop as much fat as he claimed. When not even Jack's white friends in Yreka would swallow these whoppers, he switched his tune and accused Knapp of trying to "trap" him and his people at Yainax Station, some thirty miles from the Klamath Agency headquarters. This did not hold, either, because Knapp was obviously trying to separate the Klamaths and Modocs and had put Commissary Ivan Applegate in charge of Yainax to protect them. But wherever Jack went on the reservation the Klamaths dogged him, and Knapp's failure to stop this harassment was critical. It was also, in Stephen Powers' words, "fatuousness worthy of the Indian Bureau."

Old Chief Schonchin settled down peacefully at Yainax in the Sprague River Valley with most of the remainder of the tribe after Captain Jack left with his partisans. But not all Modocs were in these two major groups. There was a band at Hot Creek and Willow Creek, friends of Californian John A. Fairchild and his neighbor-ranchers, and another group, the Big Springs band, on the site of modern Bonanza, Oregon, on the upper Lost River east of Linkville. But they made no trouble for anyone, and it was Jack's band of dissidents that aroused the ire of white Oregonians because they settled right back in the grazing range of the Lost River Valley and Tule Lake, which the Applegates had touted to would-be settlers.

An attempt to move the wild Snakes of the Camp Harney area to the Klamath Reservation failed, but they remained quiet, although they refused to budge. The public's attention was drawn to Captain Jack's so-called renegades when Jesse Applegate reported Modoc "depredations," with no real evidence. He was more correct when he later recalled that tribal morale and discipline were breaking down, adding, "Schonchin being the legitimate chief of the Modocs, Captain Jack lost control over them. They would not obey him. He admits, himself, that they would not." This was true, or at least half-true. Jack's Modocs wandered about between Linkville and Yreka, pretty much as free agents. They were working here and bumming there, certainly not raiding settlers. By and large they were tolerated or even liked by the Californians and ignored by Oregonians outside of their tribal lands, now being settled by farmers and ranchers. Stephen Powers could accuse them at this period of nothing more grievous than *annoying* the settlers and creating "intolerable pother." The commonest accusations thrown at them were claims of trespass and petty thievery. Their most cardinal sin seemed to be the killing and butchering of a few strayed beeves. There was no talk of Captain Jack going on the warpath. In the opinion of the townspeople of Linkville and Yreka, and the soldiers of Fort Klamath, he just was not up to it. He and his tattered dissidents in cast-off Levis and workshirts simply could not be taken very seriously. They peddled their women and cadged drinks on the seamier side of such settlements as Yreka. The pioneer Oregon newspaperman Samuel A. Clarke claimed that Jack's main source of income was a tax he levied on prostitution. But the journalist also admitted that it had long been just good Modoc manners to lend squaws or trade their favors for ponies or blankets.

The Applegates and their neighbors were of mixed emotions in regard to the Modocs. Sympathy and hostility each had its season but, generally, the Modocs found the Oregonians more antipathetic than the Californians with whom they came into contact. Stephen Powers was more or less a Californian and he had no use for Captain Jack, calling him a cowardly braggart and bully who had cheated Captain George of the Klamaths out of twenty ponies in a gambling game by threatening him with a force of his followers. Powers insisted that the insurgent was not only a bad loser but "a man of mean quality, a coward, and a thorough-paced scoundrel." He compared him unfavorably to honest and upright Chief Schonchin, who would ride forty miles to renew his leave of absence or hunting and fishing season furlough, although such permission was only a techni-cality, a farce, since there was not a bayonet on the reservation and Fort Klamath could not be bothered with such reservation nonsense.

Many Californians sympathized with the plight of the Modocs, and a few became their close friends. Stockmen John A. Fairchild, Pressley Dorris and others were joined by Yreka townsfolk Dr. T. T. Cabaniss and attorneys Elijah Steele and A. M. Rosborough. They liked Captain Jack's right-hand man (and half-brother), Scarfaced Charley, even more than the sub-chief. His face was hideously scarred, twisted into a sardonic, mocking and cruel grimace by a long cicatrice on his cheek. It was a most unfortunate mask, for it belied Charley's real nature. Although he was one of the best warriors of the tribe, he was a peacemaker who was respected as a man of honor by most of the whites who knew him.

So rich is Siskiyou County's volcanic ashen soil—for the growth of legend, at least—that three stories, or more, explain Charley's deforming scar. The most accepted account is that he hitched a ride on the rear of the stage between Hawkinsville and Yreka when he was a child and that he fell and suffered the deep, disfiguring gash on his face when he either hit a sharp rock or was struck by the rim of the turning wheel. Another tale had him falling from a wagon while drunk (not, presumably, when a mere lad). The third reported him jumping from a moving wagon while a prisoner of war being transported to the stockade or guardhouse at Fort Jones, west of Yreka. In his tumble, he is said to have fallen against a rock that was still being pointed out in recent years by Siskiyou old-timers. After his escape he is supposed to have hidden out in a gully near Gazelle, which still bears the name Scar Face Gulch. This tale is likely folklore, not fact, since Fort Jones ceased operations in 1858 when the Modocs were quiet, although there is a tale that the post was reopened during the Modoc War. But the scar on Charley's cheek was anything but fresh at the time of the Modoc War, and Scar Face Gulch almost certainly was named not for the Modoc brave but for a Shasta with the same name who was lynched near Gazelle during the time of the Rogue River Wars.

Captain Jack's good-looking sister, Mary or Queen Mary, was held in something more than mere affection by the lustier men of Yreka. The squawmen lived with her, *seriatum,* and it is said that there were clandestine goings-on in the more respectable part of town that involved Mary. Jack himself was a drifter during this period but not considered by whites to be their enemy. One of the Applegates tried to again persuade him to go on the reservation and Jack half-agreed. He told him, "If the American Agent will protect me, I will go to the Agency. Also, if Frank Riddle would become Agent." But negotiations failed.

Still, Jack and his followers were not pariahs until June of 1871 when the *de facto,* if not *de jure,* Modoc sub-chief suddenly became *persona non grata* in Oregon and parts of California. Henceforth he had to give Fort Klamath a wide berth. That summer he called in a medicine man to treat a Modoc child suffering from a malignant disease. The shaman may have been a reservation Modoc of Schonchin's band or a Klamath; the record is not clear on the point. Nor is it known why Curly Headed Doctor was not at the bedside, as Jack's resident physician. But when the incantations of the visiting practitioner failed to cure the illness and the child died, Jack revoked the medicine man's license with a vengeance. The punishment for such malpractice was death, and Jack personally shot the man dead. To Captain Jack it was perfectly justifiable homicide. (Chief Seattle had done the same thing in Washington Territory, using a trade musket from Fort Nisqually, and Captain George once had to rid himself of some bothersome Klamath drunks by shooting them to death.) Almost certainly the white population of the border heard a garbled version of the affair, like the one that reached Oliver Applegate's ears: "Captain Jack, having a spite against a Yainax Modoc, perhaps fearing him on account of his being a doctor or magician, watched his opportunity and when the doctor was off near Clear Lake on pass [i.e., from Fort Klamath's officers], Jack, accompanied by four of his leading men, crawled into his tent at night and shot him through the head."

The border settlers were made nervous by the shooting, and Lindsay Applegate reported that the Modocs were conducting themselves more insolently after it occurred and was not punished. Since the victim was "only" an Indian in a period of a blatantly racist double standard of justice, Fort Klamath did not break its neck trying to bring the well-known murderer to the bar of justice, even though it was an open-and-shut case of murder in the eyes of the law. But after Lindsay Applegate's son, Ivan, commissary at Yainax, protested that the murderer must be punished for killing one of his peaceful wards, Captain Jack was indicted by Oregon authorities for homicide. Indian Sub-Agent John Meacham, A. B.'s brother, now in charge of Klamath Reservation, requested Capt. James Jackson, commanding Fort Klamath, to arrest the Modoc sub-chief.

Jackson was willing, but in order not to needlessly jeopardize the lives of nearby settlers by provoking the Modocs to violence, he decided to haul Jack in quietly. The captain knew that the renegade liked to frequent Yreka, especially around the Fourth of July when the holiday spirit made begging particularly rewarding, when whiskey flowed like spring water and gunpowder fireworks provided colorful entertainment. Fearing that Captain Jack would resist arrest, Jackson decided to pick him up in the alien surroundings of Yreka. He thought he would be less likely to fight there where the troopers would be backed by a large population of citizens who believed in civil law. Jackson sent Lt. Henry Moss and ten troopers on a quiet march to Yreka to apprehend Jack. But when Moss slipped into town he found the bird flown. Either the sagebrush telegraph or Captain Jack's white friends had tipped him off. Fort Klamath's C.O. blamed "the squawmen who infested that section of the country." But one wonders if the yellowlegs were as diligent in their search for Jack as they were for ardent spirits in a town celebrating the birth of the Republic. Jack should not have been hard to find. He and his men were lauded in the press for pitching in to help with the fire brigade's engines when a disastrous fire swept the town on the Fourth.

Before his elimination of the witch doctor, Captain Jack had yielded to the urgings of the Indian Bureau and had visited the Yainax location of Old Schonchin's reasonably contented followers, numbering about a hundred people. But with a warrant out for him, Jack could no longer even toy with the idea of going back on the reservation. Meacham did what he could to try to preserve the precarious peace, replacing Knapp with a man he could trust—his own brother, John Meacham. He urged Fort Klamath to stay all military action toward arresting Captain Jack, and he joined Jesse Applegate's surprising support of Elijah Steele's plan for a special, small Modoc reservation on Lost River. Meacham forwarded to Gen. E. R. S. Canby in Portland a map of the proposed area that ex-surveyor Applegate made for him. The result was still another ally for Steele's plan to avert a war. General Canby himself now became a supporter of the Lost River Modoc reservation scheme of Jack's friend and protector, Steele. Canby now revoked the order calling for Captain Jack's arrest, and Fort Klamath relaxed again.

Meacham never knew when to quit. He sent his brother, John, and Ivan Applegate to dicker with Jack. It turned out to be a dangerous gamble; John Schonchin, Hooker Jim and Curly Headed Doctor urged killing the commissioners. Captain Jack, backed by his "prime minister," Scarfaced Charley, managed to shut them up. Jack met the whites in good faith and recited his people's grievances, especially the failure of the Government to protect his people from the Klamaths as had been promised. He told the two whites that he could not be held responsible for the death of the blundering shaman because of their laws. He reminded them that twice he had tried to live side by side with the Klamaths. But he would never do so again, said Jack, and he declined their offer of any site he chose on the reservation. He had had enough of broken governmental promises. When Meacham and Applegate then offered to recommend to higher authority Steele's idea of a Lost River reserve for the Modocs—if he would not trouble the whites while the Indian Bureau made its decision—Captain Jack agreed readily. According to Meacham, he even said that he would bring his men to

Yainax if the decision in Washington should be against the Lost River reservation. If Jack actually said this, he speedily regretted it and recanted, or did not mean it in the first place. But he had no objection to whites settling fairly close to his village, and he promised to keep his braves from molesting them. When his couriers reported to him, A. B. Meacham immediately pressed Washington for the Lost River reservation, a genuine solution to the Modoc problem. As he must have feared, the Commissioner of Indian Affairs did nothing but temporize.

There was little or no trouble that fall and winter of 1871, but the calm was broken on the second day of the new year. J. M. True of Lost River brought a message to Capt. James Jackson, asking him to remove Captain Jack's "threatening marauders" from the area. Next day, True called on Jackson's superior and the new commander at Fort Klamath, Maj. George G. Huntt, and deposed, in behalf of his neighbors and himself, that Jack's men had knocked down fences and turned their ponies in to graze on his haycocks. For several evenings they had not only taken fodder from his haystacks but had had the gall to order him not to remove any of the hay. They had added to their insolence by demanding money from him, had stolen utensils and a halter from two neighbors, and threatened the lives of two other settlers. True was convinced that the Modocs were not bluffing; they meant to carry out their bloody threats.

If the complaint carried by True was not enough to sway Huntt and Indian Superintendent A. B. Meacham to action, the next document filed in *l'affaire Modoc* did the trick. Meacham received a petition from forty-four citizens of Jackson County, Oregon, demanding the removal of the Lost River Modocs. Not one of the petitioners was involved in True's earlier protest. The forty-four said they were backed by the most influential settler in southern Oregon, Jesse Applegate, "a stock raiser equally interested with us in their removal." They described Jack's Modocs as a fractious band of Indians refusing to honor their treaty commitments and partly blamed this upon the evil influence of citizens of "an adjoining state" who were busily engaged in an illicit trade with the Modocs.

Meacham now abandoned all hope of Judge Steele's plan for a small, separate Modoc reservation on Lost River. He forwarded the memorial to Gen. E. R. S. Canby, commanding the Army's District of the Columbia, and accompanied it with a request that a force of soldiers from Fort Klamath be sent to move the Modocs to Yainax on the Klamath Reservation. He thought that fifty troopers would be sufficient for the task. Meacham was so confident that Canby would go along with him that he made arrangements with Ivan Applegate to subsist the runaways at Yainax after apologetically explaining his request to Canby: "I regret very much the necessity of this action but the peace and welfare of white settlers and Indians demand that it be done promptly."

Since there was now no conflict between Indian and military departments of the Government, such as that which had prevented Lindsay Applegate from bringing Jack on the reservation, the petitioners asked for the prompt removal of the bothersome band, reminding Canby that the cavalry force that they had asked for two years earlier was ready and waiting at Fort Klamath. According to the signers, the Modocs were now so emboldened by their successful defiance of white authority that ranchers were hustling their families across the Cascades to safety in the face of Modoc threats of arson and murder. "We have been repeatedly on the verge of a desolating Indian war with this band of outlaws who, by your delay to enforce the treaty, have been led to despise rather than respect the authority of the Government." After thus overstating the gravity of the situation, the petitioners asked rhetorically, "Shall a petty Indian chief with twenty desperadoes and a squalid band of three hundred miserable savages any longer set at defiance the strong arm of the Government, driving our citizens from our homes, threatening their lives and destroying their property?"

Canby was impressed by the memorial, but he surprised both Meacham and the petitioners by replying that he still felt it unwise to send a force to bring in Jack. He thought the Modocs should be allowed to stay put, for the time being. The general had not yet given up his forlorn hope that Squire Steele's Modoc reservation plan would carry the day in Washington. He stated: "I do not think that the immediate application of force, as asked for, would be either expedient or just. They should at least be notified that a new location has been selected for them and provision made for their wants. . . . I am not surprised at the unwillingness of the Modocs to return to any point on the reservation where they would be exposed to the hostilities and annoyances they have heretofore experienced (and without adequate protection) from the Klamaths." Canby also thought that the natural resources of the Klamath Reservation were insufficient for the number of Indians being concentrated there, and added, "With their imperfect reasoning powers, and natural suspicions, they have concluded that they were intentionally deceived and now distrust the agents of the Indian Department."

General Canby was pleased when Maj. Gen. J. M. Schofield, commanding the entire Military Division of the Pacific, backed him up. But although Jack's Modocs were left alone, Canby did notify the commanding officer of Fort Klamath to take adequate measures to protect the settlers from hostilities, if necessary, and to be ready to remove Jack's band should forcible measures become obligatory. He also asked Fort Klamath's C.O. to notify him immediately of any reports of Modoc depredations. Realizing that there were provocateurs in both camps—"evil-disposed persons," in his terms—Canby now tried to prevent a clash by interposing a force of cavalry between the whites and Indians. Both to keep the white agents of discord in line and to awe the Indians and reassure the frightened settlers, he ordered fifty to sixty troopers from Fort Klamath and Camp Warner. Canby suggested Camp Yainax as a likely site for their bivouac. But he was still optimistic about peace: "As I am fully satisfied that the Modocs will gladly settle at any point where they can be protected from the hostilities of the Klamaths, I consider it very important that all proper means to prevent a collision should be adopted."

The general spelled out his intentions carefully. The cavalry force was to avert war with the Modocs, not to make war on them. It was to keep the peace. Canby specifically warned his subordinate officers that the depredations of individual Indians must not be taken as proof of the guilt of an entire band or tribe. Subscribing to Teddy Roosevelt's later philosophy of walking carefully but carrying a big stick, Canby added a codicil to his orders, however: "If hostilities should actually be commenced or be inevitable, the most prompt and energetic measures must be adopted to suppress and punish them."

When Indian Superintendent Meacham responded to Canby's program, he advised the general that he had had no action from Washington on his suggestion that Steele's plan for a Modoc reservation should be followed. Worse, he reported both Applegate at Yainax and J. N. High, sub-agent at the Klamath Agency, as describing Modoc hostilities as imminent. Meacham was as ambivalent now toward the so-called renegades as Canby. He still believed as he had in 1871: "Actual experience demonstrates the impracticability of consolidating tribes of Indians together although, in theory, it looks well." He predicted resistance and feared war; but the settlers were entitled to protection. Of the Modocs, he said, "Had they behaved honestly and on their part maintained peaceable relations with the white settlers, they might have remained at Modoc Lake [i.e., Tule Lake] undisturbed. Such has not been the case and, much as I regret the necessity for forcible arrest and return to the reservation, I can see no other way to secure peace and mete out justice. I would respectfully recommend that the commander of Fort Klamath be instructed to arrest the chief and five or six of his headmen and hold them in confinement until some further orders shall have been received from the Department at Washington City."

Meacham alerted Washington of his actions, asking the commissioner to countermand them by telegram, if need be. Otherwise the arrest would be made and war might result. Possibly all this was a bluff to smoke a decision out of the Indian Bureau by this heavily veiled threat. Certainly he made a last try at securing Squire Steele's six-mile-square Lost River reservation for Jack on the Oregon-California border, writing Washington: "I have suggested in my annual report (1871) an alternative but it has not received any attention known to this office. I should regret bloodshed but I am powerless to prevent it without I am authorized to locate these people on a new home." If it was, indeed, a final gamble by Meacham, who was about to be replaced as Superintendent of Indian Affairs for Oregon by a hard-nosed "realist," T. B. Odeneal, it was a dangerous hand he was playing, with both white and Indian lives at stake. Unfortunately, the idea of a Lost River reservation was already a lost cause. Much later in the year, Ivan Applegate explained to Odeneal why this was so. The better lands along Lost River and Tule Lake were already preempted by whites, since the Modocs had extinguished their title to them by "signing" the Council Grove Treaty in 1864. Wrote Applegate: "Nearly every foot of it fit for cultivation has been taken up by settlers whose thousands of cattle, horses and sheep are ranging over it. The country where those Modocs are is a pastoral region, not an agricultural country, and to undertake to maintain them on a small reservation would probably cost more than to provide for them and the Klamaths on this reserva- tion. . . ." Finally, Applegate got down to cases. "The white settlers are very opposed to establishing a new reservation for this band of desperadoes, and their determined opposition would keep up a continual conflict. . . ." A week later (October 16, 1872) he reiterated this point to Odeneal in a letter. "One very bad feature in the matter is the fact that there is a very bitter feeling among the settlers against the Modocs. The delay in removing them has made some of the settlers almost desperate and it is hard to reason with such people and keep them from doing some act that might bring on a general massacre."

Earlier in the year, Jesse Applegate threw his weight behind the petitioners. He reminded Meacham that Jack's men were not the usual quiet and orderly Indians of the rest of Oregon but outlaws or renegades who held the settlers of Lost River at their mercy. Very critical of Washington's policy of moral suasion, promulgated by the humanitarians of the Indian Bureau, he believed physical punishment was what the Modocs understood best. Jesse Applegate was not completely self-deluding when he described himself as a friend of the Modocs, and he took the pains to explain his change of position to Meacham. "I am, as you know, much in favor of treating Indians with forbearance and humanity and, as there were some just grounds for the discontent of this band of Modocs, I fully approved of your purpose last summer to place these Indians on a reservation to themselves." But now, he argued, breaking up Jack's city of refuge near Tule Lake would be for his own good. If the band were not rounded up, war was sure to come with the settlers. The latter, he said sarcastically, were not likely to appreciate the "right" of the redmen to rob them; they would violently resist Modoc "tax collectors" bent on driving off their horses or butchering their cattle.

Applegate warned Meacham that action would have to be taken during the winter of 1872-1873. "If this is not done before spring opens it cannot be done this year. As well expect to collect the coyotes out of that region of rocks, mountain and morass as the Indians in the summer season." Applegate then proved himself to be a good prognosticator in the light of the later Lava Beds campaign. He observed of the Modocs, a squalid band of desperadoes in the eyes of his friends, that "no kind of force can pursue as fast as they can retreat and the military force on the Pacific is insufficient to hunt them out and rout them from their fastnesses."

Canby apparently discounted Applegate's dire warnings, if Meacham did not. Probably this was because Major Huntt reported on February 18, 1872, that the Modocs were not giving anyone any trouble, although just two days later Gov. Lafayette F. Grover got Meacham to renew his plea for the arrest of Captain Jack by informing the Indian superintendent that the settlers were actively preparing for war—or, as the governor put it, for "defense."

Although Ivan Applegate wrote Capt. John McCall at Fort Klamath in March to cross his fingers, saying "Meacham seems to hold on pretty well and may be retained," the superintendent was not continued in his $2,500-a-year post. He was replaced by "no-nonsense" T. B. Odeneal. Curiously, the latter had served his apprenticeship with a Quaker agent among the Osages and always professed to be very sympathetic toward the redmen. He preferred to rule Indians by peaceful means, even though he felt that Indians considered whites to be their natural enemies and that some frontiersmen responded by urging a policy of virtual extermination of the native Americans. Odeneal made his statement: "Believing as I ever have that many acts of injustice have in the past been committed against them by representatives of the Government, as well as by individual white men, all my sympathies are enlisted in their favor when I see any attempt to trample upon or disregard their rights." In reality, for all his fine talk, Odeneal displayed little knowledge of the Indians, especially the Modocs, and even less sympathy for them.

The rub, anyway, was that Odeneal considered the Modocs to be an exceptional case. Jack's band was a small group of roaming outlaws who had cut themselves off from the tribe and who (he said) bragged of their murders of both Indians and whites. He was also quite convinced that they were egged on in their depredations by Yrekans who made money by running guns to them. Hence his hard position: "I believe that to subdue them now is not only the most merciful and christianlike [way] but the only safe way to deal with them."

In compliance with General Canby's request to give a show of force his personal attention, Maj. Elmer Otis led a detachment of forty-odd men from Camp Warner. By the time his twenty-seven pack mules had negotiated the miles of standing water, mud and thin crusted snow that passed for the military road to Fort Klamath, his animals were so worn and jaded that he had to remain at the post for a full week to allow them to recuperate. While he added a Fort Klamath unit to his command, consisting of twenty-three enlisted men and ten pack mules under Lt. Henry N. Moss, aided by Acting Asst. Surg.

C. W. Knight, Sub-Agent J. N. High and Ivan Applegate, he sent his half-breed scout, Donald McKay, and four Indians to arrange a conference with the Modocs at Lost River Gap, ten miles east of Link River.

Otis made camp at Juniper Springs and at noon on April 3, 1872, began his powwow with Captain Jack and thirty-nine warriors. He noticed immediately that the braves who crowded into the rude, half-floored Galbraith log cabin were armed to the teeth with carelessly concealed weapons. Some settlers joined the council as Jack denied all allegations that he had scared white womenfolk and children or had stolen cattle, broken fences and trampled fields. He blamed these depredations on the Klamaths—if, he added, they had indeed been committed at all. But when Otis warned him that he must restrain his men and punish them for misdeeds or the Army would do it for him, Jack promised good behavior and convinced the major that he would mind. Otis reported the prospects for peace to be good when he advised Canby. "This certainly will be assured as long as the troops are in their vicinity and probably his conduct will be much improved by the visit of the troops, as he was much frightened when he heard that the troops were coming."

After ordering Captain Jack to keep his men away from the settlers and telling him to go to Camp Warner if he needed supplies, Otis took testimony against the Modocs from twelve settlers, including Jesse Applegate. They told of thefts and demands for compensation for lands occupied by their ranches. Perhaps the interview of George Nurse by Klamath Sub-Agent J. N. High was typical: "From your knowledge of Captain Jack's band of Modocs, do you apprehend any danger to the lives or property of settlers from them?" Nurse replied, "I do, to both, from the fact that they have come to my place and fired into my barn, knowing there was men in it at the time. They have torn down my fences and turned their stock into my fields. Armed parties have come here and made hostile demonstrations, causing fear in the minds of myself and the people here. They have stated to me that they claim the Lost River country and if the white man wants the water and grass they will have to pay for it."

To the surprise of Major Otis, two white settlers opposed to the majority accompanied Captain Jack to the *wa-wa* and spoke in his behalf. They were Henry Miller and N. B. Ball, who lived closest to Jack's semipermanent village, about ten and six miles distant respectively. They testified to Jack's peacefulness, and bachelor Miller told Otis that he hired Indians as cowboys, or herders, and that he had never had to pay the Modocs a nickel for the land he held. Moreover, he did not believe they extorted payment from the other settlers. He thought that Jack wanted only a thousand-acre Modoc reservation on Lost River. As for the reputed hostility of the Modocs, Miller snorted and said, "The Indians are not more insolent to whites than whites are to whites." He reminded the officer that he had raised stock for two years without trouble from the Modocs. He had been forced to leave his ranch only once, from July 1870 till February 1871, and then only because rumors of Indians killing cattle had brought in troopers who chased the Modocs away, leaving him no cowboys. He also reinforced Jack's guess that (from the pony trails he had seen) the Klamaths, not the Modocs, were guilty of cattle raiding.

Ball told Otis that he had lived for ten years near the Modocs and since October 1871 within a half-dozen miles of them. He apprehended no danger to the settlers although, yes, he had heard of trouble over hay at Charles Monroe's ranch, only six miles from his own spread. But he believed that Monroe had reneged on a promise to pay for his land, in hay, and that Jack's men were merely collecting on a bad debt when they hit his haycocks.

The Lost River Gap talks of Major Otis were a failure in that Captain Jack still refused to go back on the Klamath Reservation. But they were a success in that they bought a little time for all concerned; there was no war that summer. Originally, Otis had given the Modocs a clean bill of health, writing Canby, "I do not anticipate any serious trouble." Now, however, after mulling over the results of his powwow, he did a complete *volte-face* and ended up by warning the general, "I am f opinion that if left where they now are, it will probably lead to a serious outbreak, in time." He advised the withdrawal of Meacham's permission (of August 1871) for the Modocs to remain on Lost River until a decision to move or not to move could be made by Washington. In any case, he wanted Jack moved sometime after September when the winter season would favor his well-equipped Fort Klamath troops over the Indians, should they resist. Major Otis even went so far as to recommend banishment for Captain Jack and Black Jim, suggesting they be exiled to the Siletz Reservation, far from Modoc country.

About the same time that Otis changed his tune, Canby caved in to settler pressure and wrote (April 17) his superiors that the opposition of local whites now made a Modoc reservation inadvisable. He suggested an alternative (which he must have known the Modocs would spurn), to give the Sprague River Paiutes a new reservation in their old country and to turn their vacated area over to Jack's Modocs. But Sprague River as well as Yainax was exposed to Klamath intimidation, and it was the Klamaths, not the handful of Snakes or Paiutes, who had made reservation life a hell for Captain Jack.

Indian Superintendent Odeneal made one last gesture for peace. On March 14, 1872, he sent Ivan Applegate and the new sub-agent on the Klamath Reservation, L. S. Dyar, to dicker with Jack at the abandoned Army campsite of Juniper Springs. (Jack still refused to come to Linkville for talks.) Although the peacemakers brought Chief Schonchin and other reservation Modocs along to try to persuade Jack to join them, he would not leave Lost River. Odeneal had granted his agents permission to discuss other areas of relocation if Jack turned thumbs down on Yainax, but they reported there were no suitable alternatives; all of the good land had been declared state grazing lands or taken up by squatters except for the lower Lost River, where Jack was located, and the nearby settlers were determined and insistent that no aboriginal island should be left in a settled pastoral area.

During the Otis powwow Captain Jack had not been as forceful in his refusal to move as he had been earlier. Ivan Applegate now learned why. It was not that his obduracy was any less, but he was trying to avoid war and still retain his leadership. When Applegate asked him if he would not come in, Jack would not answer the question directly. As he hesitated, Black Jim and others warned him in the Modoc tongue that it might be dangerous. Forgetting that Applegate understood his lingo, Jack blurted in Modoc that it was best not to answer the question at all, in order to avoid a dispute with the whites. Wisely, Applegate appreciated Jack's delicate position as a moderate leading more than a few war hawks and did not press the question. Instead, he heard out Jack's speech:

"We are good people and will not kill or frighten anybody. We want peace and friendship. I am well known and understood by the people of Yreka, California, and am governed by their advice. I do not want to live upon the reservation, for the Indians there are poorly clothed, suffer from hunger, and even have to leave the reservation sometimes to make a living. We are willing to have whites live in our country but we do not want them to locate on the west side and near the mouth of Lost River, where we have our winter camps. The settlers are continually lying about my people and trying to make trouble. . . . Say to the superintendent that we do not want to see him or talk with him. We do not want any white men to tell us what to do. Our friends and counsellors are men in Yreka, California. They tell us to stay where we are and we intend to do it and will not go upon the reservation. I am tired of being talked to and am done with talking."

The whites, for their part, were just about done with talking, too. General Canby again transferred Fort Klamath to Oregon's District of the Lakes from its incongruous position in the Army's California Department. That same month, September 1872, he ordered Fort Klamath's new commander, Maj. John Green, to make one last attempt to talk sense into Captain Jack. Green was quite a good choice for the job. He was an experienced and courageous career officer who had replaced Maj. George G. Huntt at Fort Klamath on July 17. On September 9, Green left on his mission, taking Captain Jackson's B Troop, 1st Cavalry, and sending a messenger ahead of his patrol to inform Jack that he came in peace, not in war; that he came to talk, not to arrest him. When he reached the vicinity of the Lost River lodges, Green dramatized the peacefulness of his mission by turning his cavalry horses out to graze along the river. Still Jack refused to come out of his lodge. He remained there, sulking; he would not talk with Green or even greet him. The limping excuse of the Indian for his gross manners was that his mother was ill. (But he also groused via an intermediary that the whites talked altogether too much, which was certainly true.)

Wisely, Major Green took no umbrage from Jack's bad manners and inhospitality but simply continued his unhurried reconnaissance. He swung eastward along the South Emigrant Road and visited California's Camp Bidwell. This was a lonely outpost the Army had plunked down in the glacial graben of Surprise Valley, dessicated except for three large alkali lakes, eastward across the Warner Mountains from Goose Lake. It flanked the Modoc country on the southeast as Fort Klamath did on the northwest. Green then reconnoitred his way to Camp Warner on the west side of Warner Lake, back in Oregon again. These posts held the nearest reinforcements for Fort Klamath, should they become needed. They were each more than a hundred miles distant as the crow flies and many more miles than that when travel was translated from distance into time, measured by the ruggedness of the military road across the badlands of Oregon.

Major Green ended his scout and found a message at Fort Klamath from General Canby urging him to confer with the District of the Lakes commander, Lt. Col. Frank Wheaton, if his patrol turned up signs of resistance. At the same time Canby informed Wheaton at Camp Warner that he did not consider it likely the Modocs would resist removal or, if they should, that Fort Klamath could not handle the matter. But he wanted military force used to help the Indian Bureau only after all peaceful means had been exhausted. Knowing that Captain Jack might resist and prove to be a handful for Fort Klamath, Canby ordered Wheaton to be prepared for hostilities and to act promptly with all his force to protect the frontier.

But Wheaton was not worried in the least by a scruffy band of Modoc vagabonds. He returned to his headquarters from an October 5 visit to Fort Klamath, and when he wrote Canby it was more concerning road repairs than Modoc dangers. He dismissed the idea of Modoc trouble by citing the opinions of Major Green and Klamath Sub-Agent L. S. Dyar that there would be little difficulty in removing Captain Jack's band in December. Only a fortnight later, Canby advised him that Superintendent Odeneal planned to round them up in mid-November, still anticipating no resistance. Should Jack resist, Odeneal promised to communicate with Colonel Wheaton.

Canby now gave Colonel Wheaton what amounted to a carte blanche. He wrote, "In giving such aid as may be necessary, you will be governed by your own discretion, the commanding officer suggesting only that if the intervention of the troops becomes necessary, the force employed should be so large as to secure the result at once beyond peradventure."

Wheaton advised Major Green at Fort Klamath to keep him fully and promptly advised of Modoc developments by courier. The colonel was ready to move every available man out of Camps Harney, Bidwell and Warner to bolster the Fort Klamath force. But he complained that heavy snows were already a problem and he hoped, aloud, that he would not have to move any troops against the Modocs during the inclement season except from the most strategically located of the Army posts, Fort Klamath. Odeneal may have had some second thoughts about this time. While still professing that he could round up the renegades without help, he decided that a show of force might smooth the operation. For this reason, Colonel Wheaton asked Green to report at once if he needed a larger force than was presently stationed at Fort Klamath. Green hedged. Eleven days later, he replied that a patrol sent to scout the Modoc country had reported it as quiet as when he had made his own tour. Therefore, he did not need his garrison strengthened. But he thought it a good idea to keep Capt. David Perry's troop of cavalry at Camp Warner, in readiness for a quick march to Fort Klamath should it prove necessary. There was no arguing Green's reasoning, "If they [the Modocs] refuse to go, the larger the force that can be brought against them the quicker the matter will end."

The Indian Bureau was as nervous about the Modocs in 1872 as was the Army. Rumors had Jack's band foraging—raiding—as far away from Lost River as Surprise Valley. These tales led the settlers to reiterate their fears of trouble. Their earlier appeals had already started into motion the cumbersome bureaucratic wheels of Washington. Grinding out letters, memoranda and telegrams, the Indian Bureau in April instructed Odeneal to move Jack's Modocs to either the Klamath Reservation or to a Lost River reserve, if they still refused to budge. This victory for Meacham and Steele was quickly snatched away, however, by a countermanding telegram on July 6, 1872, that dealt the deathblow to hopes of peace. Commissioner of Indian Affairs F. A. Walker advised Odeneal that he *must* remove Jack to his "proper place" on the Klamath Reservation, where his renegades would once again be under the guns of Fort Klamath.

This was fine with Odeneal. He considered Jack's rumored marauding to have invalidated Meacham's 1871 guarantee that the dissidents could stay where they were until a *final* decision should be made in Washington. He thought that they held sway over the peaceful Modocs because their insubordination went unpunished, and he believed that they imagined themselves too powerful to be controlled by the Government. Finally, the moralizing side of Odeneal's character held advancement in civilization impossible for the Modocs under such leadership as that of Captain Jack. He told Washington that one might as well expect youths to practice Christian virtues after growing up under Montana road agents or Mexican guerrillas. He concluded: "They must in some way be convinced of their error in this respect, by such firm, decided action as will leave no doubt in their minds in regard to the fact that we intend that they shall be obedient to law and faithful to their treaty obligations. This need not—and with proper management will not—require the use of force. When they all have thus been convinced, we can with reasonable hope of success, commence the work of civilizing and christianizing them, and transforming them into peaceable, self-controlling and self-sustaining men and women."

In a sense, Odeneal overruled his principal Indian advisor, Ivan Applegate, who considered Meacham's guarantee of no-molestation to be still in force. (So, in fact, did General Canby.) He bluntly told Odeneal that a move against Jack would be considered treachery by the Indians and that the Army would be averse to taking an action in obvious violation of the 1871 *status quo* agreement. Odeneal ignored Applegate's warning and, now very sure of himself, explained the situation in oversimplistic terms to the Commissioner of Indian Affairs in Washington. He blamed Jack's defiance on "evil-disposed" Californians who were out for gain. "It is my experience that nine tenths of the trouble with the Indians in this Superinten-dency is brought about by meddlesome white men giving them improper advice and dealing illegally with them." He promised to put a stop to the machinations which he had dreamed up, although he must have known he would have his work cut out for him in putting a stop to attorney A. M. Rosborough, Judge Elijah Steele, rancher John Fairchild and all the others who sympathized with the beleaguered Modocs.

Steele and his friends were still trying to salvage peace on the California-Oregon border. When Jack conferred with him, Squire Steele cautioned him not to resist any force from Fort Klamath. Steele and his friends promised to act as the Modocs' attorneys; they surveyed a proposed Lost River Modoc reserva-tion and in a last, hopeless maneuver urged Jack to dissolve his tribal band on the chance that he and his men could settle on their own tribal land in severalty, as homesteaders. The Senate, as usual, spurned this theory that native Americans could legally hold land as individuals.

Steele's defeat mattered little at this point, in any case. Superintendent Odeneal left Salem and reached the Klamath Agency on November 25, 1872. Too proud or too timid to go to Captain Jack himself, he sent Ivan Applegate and O. A. (One Armed) Brown to formally announce the Government's final decision. Jack and his men were to be moved to the Klamath Reservation. He also had his representatives spell out his promises to advance the Modocs' welfare and interests and to invite Jack to come to Linkville for a further discussion on the 27. Jack's patience was worn threadbare by garrulous couriers. He treated the emissaries with insolence, vowing with more vehemence than ever that he would never go back. This could not have surprised them. A man less familiar with the situation, Stephen Powers, asked rhetorically in 1873, "Who blames Captain Jack for not wanting to go back to it, if he could help himself—back to that accursed pest house?"

But One-Armed Brown and Applegate were startled, and frightened, to hear some of Jack's hotheads urge the killing of the two messengers in order to get a war started. Jack vetoed the idea, possibly, as L. S. Dyar suspected, in order to try to catch bigger fish—like Odeneal. On the other hand, Jack's white friends were sure that he wanted to avert war.

When Applegate and Brown returned safely to Linkville they advised Odeneal to arrest only Captain Jack and his praetorian guard—Black Jim, Scarfaced Charley, Boston Charley and Curly Headed Doctor. Once these henchmen were safely locked up in Fort Klamath's sturdy guardhouse, Applegate was sure that the other Modocs would come in quietly. "I feel confident," wrote Ivan Applegate, "that in winter they could be removed quite easily by the troops stationed at Fort Klamath." Still, a spine of doubt pricked his assuredness, and he warned Odeneal that fifty or sixty troopers would be necessary and, to avoid real trouble, they would have to act with "*great caution*"—and he emphasized the words.

On November 25, Odeneal importunately advised Colonel Wheaton that he wanted as large a force as could be spared so that he could awe Jack's force, which might total eighty men. He would tolerate no more delays. He was ready to implement the final, peremptory order that he had just received from Commissioner of Indian Affairs F. A. Walker: "You are directed to remove the Modoc Indians to Camp Yainax on Klamath Reservation, peaceably if you possibly can but forcibly if you must." To get things rolling, Odeneal dispatched Applegate and Brown to Fort Klamath for a force of yellowlegs. Squawman-Kentuckian Jeff Riddle, married to the Modoc girl, Toby, explained in pidgin Modoc-English to his red friends what Odeneal's orders were: "Remove the Indians to the agency, not boisterously. They not going, drive them there."

CHAPTER SEVEN

LOST RIVER RAID

The nightmare of the Modoc War began just after dawn on November 29, 1872, as Scarfaced Charley and Second Lt. Frazier A. Boutelle exchanged gunshots on the west bank of Lost River. The immediate chain of events leading to the fight began quietly enough at 5 A.M. Thursday, November 28, as a rider reined to a halt at Fort Klamath. He was Ivan Applegate, Indian sub-agent and commissary at Yainax Station on the Klamath Reservation, the outpost set up to receive the Modocs and Snakes after it became obvious they would never get along with the Klamaths.

Once his horse was taken care of, Applegate let the sergeant of the guard escort him to the quarters of Lieutenant Boutelle, who was officer of the day. Applegate bore an important message to the post commander, Maj. John Green, from the new Superintendent of Indian Affairs in Salem, Thomas B. Odeneal. In his communication, Odeneal reported that Captain Jack and his splinter group of Modocs had defiantly declined his invitation to a Linkville powwow on the twenty-seventh and, in fact, had reiterated their flat refusal to leave Lost River and return to the Klamath Reservation even in the face of the Indian commissioner's final order to do just that. The crux of the letter, therefore, was Odeneal's request for a force of soldiers from Fort Klamath to compel the Indians to go back on the reservation at once. "I transfer the whole matter to your department," Odeneal wrote Major Green, "without assuming to dictate the course you will pursue in executing the order aforesaid, trusting, however, that you may accomplish the object desired without the shedding of blood, if possible to avoid it."

When Applegate asked Boutelle if he thought that his superior would send troops, the lieutenant replied in the negative. He was sure Major Green would not send troops since Fort Klamath was understrength and Canby had ordered no

127

military moves until the Army was sufficiently strong to place the result of such actions "beyond peradventure." On paper, there were fifty-three cavalrymen of B Troop at Fort Klamath and fifty men of F Company, 21st Infantry. But in Canby's official report for October, there were only four officers and ninety-nine men on duty at Fort Klamath, if no one was on sick leave at the moment.

Odeneal still felt, or hoped, that there would be no fight. Applegate had advised him that Jack had only about half of his band with him. The number of warriors was estimated from a low of forty men to a much too high guess of eighty. Should the Modocs resist his order to move peacefully to the Klamath Reservation, he wanted the ringleaders, Captain Jack, Scarfaced Charley and Black Jim, arrested. The tone of his letter was calm, for he believed that a show of force from Fort Klamath was all that the situation required. He closed, "I think they might be induced to surrender and come upon the reservation without further trouble."

Oliver C. Applegate, at Yainax, was not so sure. On November 28, he ordered three sixteen-shot Henry carbines and six hundred rounds of ammunition from a San Francisco dealer via a Jacksonville store. The Modocs were uneasy, too. George Marsten Miller, though only a boy of eleven years at that time, remembered in later years that Scarfaced Charley came to the ranch of his father, George Miller, at Langell Valley to ask for caps and powder, saying "I go kill deer." The elder Miller, thinking that an Indian war was as sure as shooting, not only said no but lost his temper and shouted at Charley, "Get the hell out of here!" Charley went—off to war.

Odeneal later made excuses to his Washington superiors. He pleaded that the impression among Fort Klamath's officers was that, because of the winter weather and other conditions averse to the Modocs, they would not resist but would surrender and go in without a fight. He told Indian Commissioner Francis A. Walker that he considered the force at Fort Klamath to be too small, however, and reminded him that he had sent messengers One-Armed Brown and Dennis Crawley to warn settlers of the danger of an Indian war.

Three hours after Boutelle told Applegate that there was not a chance of Fort Klamath sending a force to round up Captain Jack, the lieutenant was astonished to hear Capt. James Jackson, his company commander, ordering him to get B Troop ready for a quick march to the twin Modoc villages on Lost

River, fifty-six miles to the southeast of Fort Klamath. Boutelle was so amazed at the unexpected order that he screwed up his courage (for a shavetail did not usually question a major's tactics) and reminded Green of General Canby's order to Colonel Wheaton not to go off half-cocked, which Wheaton had passed on to Fort Klamath. Boutelle told Green he was convinced that Jack's Modocs would fight and that Jackson's force was not strong enough to bring the renegades in—but was adequate enough to provoke a fight. Green answered in curious fashion. He said nothing of tactics, merely referring to the continuing criticism of Fort Klamath by settlers for its do-nothing strategy toward the Modocs, and saying, "If I don't send the troops, they will think we are afraid." Green might have added that he had few options and could always fall back on Canby's earlier orders, in any case: "You must be prepared to act vigorously if the necessity comes upon us." Jesse Applegate, Ivan's uncle, believed Green knew what he was doing; that he sent a small force deliberately so as not to alarm Jack. If he had taken the time necessary to mount a genuine offensive by collecting together a large number of soldiers, he would only have allowed Jack's band to melt away in the Lava Beds.

Uncle Johnny, as the troopers called the German-born Major Green, had few, if any, doubts about the ability of his men to corral Captain Jack. Since Odeneal gave him carte blanche, he gave marching orders to Captain Jackson without waiting to consult General Canby or even his immediate superior, Colonel Wheaton at Camp Warner. Not until December 3, 1872, did Green report to Canby on Jackson's move. He explained lamely at that time, "It was believed that the Modocs would submit to go on a reservation if surprised by the troops; if not, the leaders were to be arrested, if possible, in the hope that the balance would surrender." Of course, he did inform Wheaton on the 28th that he had dispatched Captain Jackson on his mission, stating, "How the matter will end is yet to be seen." He was cautious enough, however, to ask the colonel for the troop of cavalry at Camp Warner which he had reserved as an emergency reinforcement for Fort Klamath. In the copy of Green's rash Order No. 93 to Jackson which he forwarded to Wheaton, the key points were: "He will arrest, if possible, Captain Jack, Black Jim and Scarfaced Charley. He will endeavor to accomplish all this without bloodshed, if possible, but if the Indians persist in refusing to obey the orders of the Government, he will use such force as may be necessary to compel them to do so and the responsibility must rest on the Indians who defy the authority of the Government."

Major Green was not operating in ignorance of the Modoc situation. He was party to all sorts of precautionary plans and provisos made in anticipation of the time when Odeneal would finally call for the arrest of Captain Jack. He had personally assessed the situation in a September 1872 reconnaissance. He was also an experienced and courageous officer, first commissioned in the 2d Dragoons in 1855, who had won brevets twice during the Civil War. He would receive the Congressional Medal of Honor for bravery during the Modoc War. His regiment, the 1st Cavalry, was the proudest in the Army. Authorized by Act of Congress of March 2, 1833, as the 1st Dragoons, it was the oldest U.S. cavalry outfit. The First had seen action in the Seminole War in Florida, the Mexican War and the Civil War before serving against the Apaches of Arizona just prior to its transfer to Oregon in 1872.

Thirty-five enlisted men rode out of Fort Klamath, plus four men bringing up the rear with a pack train. Jackson and Boutelle led the way, accompanied by Second Lt. and Asst. Surg. Henry McElderry. The yellowlegs were not afraid of the ragged Modocs; they were, in fact, itching for a fight to break the monotony, and hoped that the patrol would be long enough. After all, Green had only ordered three days' rations issued to them. No trooper thought of the Modocs in the terms of the romanticizing pioneer ethnologist, Stephen Powers, who called them chained tigers and warriors with "that supreme audacity which armors its breast only with a little red paint against a sixteen shooter." The Indian superintendent had muttered something about a dozen or fifteen soldiers being able to handle it. For nine years Fort Klamath had been about as exciting as a tomb, a headquarters for crushing boredom. Perhaps Jack and his bowlegged braves would liven things up a little for the boys.

Some of the troopers' early enthusiasm was leached away by a penetrating rain sluicing down from the sky into their faces, especially when it turned into a numbing sleetstorm before they reached Linkville, twenty-three miles short of their destination. There they rested, took supper and fed their horses while Jackson talked to Odeneal. Since the captain was required by Canby to implement the superintendent's plans, the latter's advice amounted to an order: "When you arrive at the camp of the Modocs, request an interview with the headmen and say to them that you did not come to fight or harm them but to have them go peaceably to Camp Yainax on Klamath Reservation where ample provision has been made for their comfort and subsistence and where, by treaty, they agreed to live. Talk kindly but firmly to them and, whatever else you may do, I desire to urge that if there is any fighting, let the Indians be the aggressors. Fire no gun except in self-defense after they have first fired upon you." Odeneal assigned Ivan Applegate to Jackson's force as its guide and interpreter and as his personal representative.

Perhaps some of the soldiers, jawing with each other as they tried to dry out their soaked clothing, remarked on how carefully Odeneal looked after his skin. When setting up a tentative Linkville powwow, he had sent Applegate and One-Armed Brown to meet Jack. Now, instead of accompanying Jackson, he was sending Applegate as his proxy.

At Linkville, Ivan ran into his brother, Oliver C. Applegate, Odeneal's choice to take care of Jack's band once it should come in at Yainax. He had just arrived from the reservation. When he learned of Jackson's planned surprise call on Captain Jack, he hurried toward Lost River with a settler, Charlie Monroe, and the Klamath scout Dave Hill. They hoped to come upon two Modocs reported spying on the advance of Jackson's force. However, when the captain reached Lost River before dawn he found Oliver and his two companions, armed with two revolvers and a Henry rifle, standing guard over their route of advance. They had seen no spies. But Oliver told his brother that he and his friends were going to cross the river near the Lone Pine to Dennis Crawley's cabin on the east side of Lost River near the "stone bridge" or natural ford. Presumably, he meant to back up Jackson from across the stream. Eight or more settlers hurried to join Oliver's makeshift force. Twenty years after the event, Jackson claimed that his civilian auxiliaries were detached by him to take post at Crawley's to protect the family there and to prevent any attack on the rear of B Troop.

If the makeshift militiamen had any campaign strategy it was minimal. They first hid in a gully four hundred yards from Hooker Jim's village on the left bank of Lost River, not knowing exactly what to do and perhaps waiting for Jackson to give them a cue. Apparently they meant to deny the Indians the use of their canoes to go across the river to oppose Jackson. When a shot was heard from the river, they saw the village before them begin to stir. One of Applegate's men rode half a mile upstream to a point opposite Jack's village, then hurried back with word that the Modocs were surrendering. Emboldened by this highly premature and, in fact, erroneous news, the settlers-turned-soldiers decided to imitate the captain and to capture themselves a village. They first met Miller's Charley and persuaded him to surrender his gun. Then they rode into the Modoc camp and shook hands with a dumfounded Curly Headed Doctor and others. Hooker Jim sensed something was amiss. He made for the river, but Brown halted him and forced him to give up his gun. Miller's Charley then snatched up the weapon but had to surrender it to the Klamath, Dave Hill. As a military action, it looked like a comical charade, but the harebrained Cincinnati began to realize that they were in a tight spot. They had a tiger by the tail.

Trying to bluff the Modocs, the settlers began to back off. Soon they heard lively firing from the other side of the river, sure proof that Captain Jack had not capitulated. The sound was the signal for a blaze of rifle fire into their own faces. They retreated to Crawley's cabin as fast as their legs could carry them and forted up there. During the retreat, Jud Small's colt went loco from the gunshots, bucking around the village with Jud clinging to the saddle for dear life. Both mount and rider seemed to bear charmed lives, for Small managed to regain control over the animal without either of them suffering a scratch.

Three other civilians, not in on the fight (or not *yet* in on the fight from the Modocs' point of view) were not so lucky. John (Jack of Clubs) Thurber and William or Wendolin Nus, the pioneer, were shot dead. Joe Penning was wounded and maimed for life. He made his escape on his fast horse and was found by the volunteers after he fell from the saddle in a safe area. According to Applegate's pards, the threesome were greeted by the Indians in a friendly manner, then treacherously murdered. They claimed that Thurber died in the act of shaking hands with his murderers. His death was particularly pathetic because he was stone deaf and could not even have heard the firing.

Doubtless the Modocs felt that their murder of Thurber was only justifiable retribution for the squaw and infant hit by a wild blast from George Fiock's double-barreled shotgun as she tried to mount a horse, crying, "No shoot! Me squaw, me squaw!" In the exchange of fire, Miller's Charley, Black Jim and

Duffy were wounded, as were some of the Modoc women, either deliberately or accidentally. The civilians were good enough shots to persuade the Modocs that it would be unhealthy to try to rush Crawley's cabin. Instead, they withdrew eastward.

Lieutenant Boutelle was highly critical of the laymen-soldier's bungled attack. He said they had no more right to attack the village than if it had been located on Broadway. It was difficult to tell just whose side Boutelle was on since he later contrasted the abortive but sneaky attack of the civilians with the "brutal" behavior of the Modocs in sending away two cowboys who strayed into the field of fire, warning them that they were at war with the soldiers but did not want to hurt the cowmen. Boutelle regretted Hooker Jim's later murders but claimed that the Oregon court which indicted him threw in Scarfaced Charley, too, and he was not even with him. A. B. Meacham believed that the civilians started fighting on the left bank only after Jackson was being whipped and Hooker Jim sought to reinforce his fellow warriors. "Had the settlers been content to let the Indians and soldiers fight uninterrupted," said Meacham, "no settler would have been harmed." He reported that Scarfaced Charley, Hooker Jim and Miller's Charley had anticipated Jackson's march and, shortly before the fateful day, had warned local settlers, "You stay at home. You no get hurt. We can whip the sojers." Said Meacham, "If this friendly warning had been accredited and respected and no settler had been present or, being present, had observed neutrality, not one settler would have been injured, no butchery would have followed, no indictments would have found against the Modocs, thereby making peace impossible."

Meanwhile, Captain Jackson's command had followed along the foot of the ridge of hills paralleling the lower Lost River on the south until the troops were within a mile of Captain Jack's camp at daybreak, November 29, 1872. Jackson gave his men, whom he described as a very tired lot of soldiers, the welcome order to halt, dismount and rest. He then studied the winter village and the lay of the land about it near Lost River's mouth on Tule Lake. In order to keep his advance undetected, Jackson had ordered his men off the road as they neared the Indian camp, and the heavy sagebrush had not only impeded and slowed the column's progress in the dark but had also increased the fatigue of the saddle-weary, wet and chilled men of Fort Klamath.

It would have taken a great deal to convince Jackson he did not approach a village of 120 warriors that day, rather than half that many people in all, including women, children and old gaffers. Probably Jack had about fifteen warriors with him, and an equal number were on the other side of the sluggish but deep and unfordable stream. Hooker Jim's cross-river camp was also about a half-mile downstream from Jack's village and near the cabin of Dennis Crawley. Among the warriors with Hooker Jim were Boston Charley, the shaman Curly Headed Doctor, and Slolux. Jack had Scarfaced Charley and John Schonchin with him, also Black Jim, One-Eyed Mose, Watchman, Humpy Joe, Big Ike, Old Tails, Old Tails' Boy, Old Longface and the untidy Shacknasty Jim.

During their rest Captain Jackson had his men tighten the girths of their McClellan saddles. He then split his command into two platoons, placing Boutelle in charge of one while he took the other. Although the temperature was low and his wet overcoat partly frozen, Boutelle at this point took off his coat and said to Jackson, "If I am going into a fight, I want my deck cleared for action." Most of the troops followed suit, despite the frigid temperature, and strapped their coats to the cantles of their saddles. The remounted line of cavalry closed in on the sleeping village at a trot, then halted again at the edge of the group of lodges. It was about 7 A.M. when seventeen troopers dismounted and formed a skirmish line. They stood at order-arms in front of the lodges, awaiting Jackson's command, as their comrades took care of their horses.

Never, since the Ben Wright massacre, had the Modocs been taken so unawares, so completely by surprise. Jackson, with little ultimately to brag about in the affair, boasted in his report, "I have the honor to report that I jumped the camp of Captain Jack's Modoc Indians yesterday morning soon after daylight, completely surprising them." Twenty years later he was still savoring that surprise and blaming Odeneal's hamstringing instructions for the debacle that followed. With the Modocs completely at his mercy he had been forced to *wa-wa* with them because of Odeneal's "peaceably if you can" order. Bitterly, he recalled in later years, "Had they been undoubtedly hostile, there would have been no Modoc War."

Apparently only one Indian was up, perhaps fishing. It was Bogus Charley. He ran up the river bank shouting, "Sojers! Sojers!" Jackson stopped him and demanded, "Where is Captain Jack?" "In his tent," was the answer. "I want to see him," said

Jackson. "What for?" asked the startled Bogus. "I have an order for his arrest." Bogus persisted, "What do you want him for?" Jackson answered rudely, "That makes no difference. Show me his tent."

But another Indian was up and about, unseen by Jackson. Scarfaced Charley was such an early riser that he was across-river, visiting Hooker Jim's camp as the soldiers encircled Captain Jack's camp. At their approach, he fired his rifle—accidentally, he claimed (and Boutelle believed him!), then paddled a canoe back to the main village. As he came up the bank, Captain Jackson drew his revolver and ordered him to halt. Scarfaced Charley had plenty of sand; he ignored Jackson and the pistol and continued on, haranguing his comrades to fight to the death, if necessary. Jackson, hampered by Odeneal's orders, hesitated—too long. Ivan Applegate heard Scarfaced Charley tell the braves that, if they were quick about it, they could kill every soldier without losing a man. Applegate hurriedly translated Jackson's summons to a mysteriously absent Captain Jack, addressing himself to Scarfaced Charley particularly since he was known to be Captain Jack's lieutenant, or right-hand man. He spoke of peace, protection and ample provisions at Yainax. But the scarred warrior was not listening. He pushed past the whites and disappeared into Bogus Charley's tent. According to Jeff Riddle, Jackson now sang out, "You, chief, come here!" But only Scarfaced Charley appeared, to shout, "Jack has not got up yet!" Much later, Captain Jack told newspaperman Samuel A. Clarke that his son (?) had been gambling all night—if Clarke understood him. (Jack had no son.) But perhaps Captain Jack had been up gambling most of the night and was "sleeping in."

In any case, Jack was asleep in bed, naked as a jaybird, when Jackson called to him. The chief yelled to the officer not to shoot, then sent Bogus Charley out to repeat the plea while he pulled on a shirt. But instead of meeting Jackson, he slipped into another lodge. He may or may not have returned to his own lodge to meet with Jackson, but in any case there was to be no Big Talk, and Jack soon made himself scarce, since he was not the fighting man that Scarfaced Charley was. No one among the troops saw hide nor hair of Jack during the raid. Ivan Applegate looked for him but could not spy him. Boutelle later wrote that Jackson could not catch a sight of him, and Jackson himself wrote that Captain Jack took no part in the fight and, in fact, never did put in an appearance. According to Siskiyou

County historian Harry L. Wells, Jack was coming from his lodge, unarmed, with a blanket over his shoulder when shooting broke out. He then drew the blanket over his head and squatted on the ground, where he was taken for a squaw and ignored.

Wherever Jack was and whatever he was up to, Scarfaced Charley assumed the mantle of authority. Jack's more-or-less mace bearer suddenly reappeared by popping his war-painted face up through the smoke hole of Bogus Charley's circular lodge. He then emerged, trailed by Bogus. Both were stripped for battle and bearing guns in their hands. Scarfaced Charley, wearing a sash about his waist, appeared to be nearly six feet tall, a giant for a Modoc. Jesse Applegate called him "a finely developed warrior." He talked excitedly with the other braves, waving his rifle in one hand and not straying far from three or four other pieces lying on the ground, fully loaded.

Although the element of surprise was fraying dangerously thin, Capt. James Jackson's gamble appeared to be winning the day. Ivan Applegate was so sure of it that he walked down to the river to holler across to One-Armed Brown. He told him to tell Oliver that everything was settled. Brown actually started for Linkville, and Odeneal, with the good news of Jack's surrender. At that moment, all hell broke loose on Lost River.

In the confusion of battle, several versions of the spark that ignited it were born. According to young H. C. Rambeau, the Modocs were on the point of giving up their arms when the obstinate Scarfaced Charley raised his gun and said, "I am going to kill an officer." But, whatever the case, when Jackson now demanded that they surrender their weapons, the Modocs refused. The captain then asked his subordinate, "Mr. Boutelle, what do you think of the situation?" Boutelle answered, "There is going to be a fight and the sooner you open it the better, before there are any more complete preparations." Boutelle was probably right; there was no turning back now for Jackson.

The company commander ordered Boutelle to take four men from the left wing of the line of troops and to arrest the Modoc leaders, the men he called the Modocs' "boldest spirits." The latter stood in a line about thirty yards in front of the dismounted cavalrymen who were deployed as skirmishers. According to the lieutenant, he said not a word to Charley. Both A. B. Meacham and Jeff Riddle agreed that, as Boutelle advanced, Charley dropped his rifle onto the pile of arms on the ground. But, according to Riddle, not before Jackson roared to Boutelle, "Take the gun away from him!" and the lieutenant snapped, "You black son of a bitch! Lay down your rifle!" When Captain Jackson ordered him to drop the pistol in his belt, Scarfaced Charley refused and retorted, "You got my gun. The pistol all right. Me no shoot you." Jackson made no response but ordered Boutelle to disarm the Indian. The lieutenant stepped forward and said, "Here, Injun. Give that pistol here, damn you, quick!"

Scarfaced Charley laughed, but there was no laughter in his dark eyes. "Me no dog. Me man. Talk to me like man. Me no 'fraid you. You talk to me just like dog. Me no dog." He then held out the equivalent of an olive branch to the hot-tempered officer. "Talk me good. I listen you." But Boutelle was enraged. He drew his revolver and cocked it. "You son of a bitch! I'll show you not to talk back to me!" Scarfaced Charley did not flinch, but repeated, "Me no dog. You no shoot me. Me keep pistol. You no get him, my pistol." Boutelle leveled his weapon at Charley's chest and squeezed the trigger.

At this moment, Ivan Applegate ran up and added to the mounting confusion by pointing to the warriors and crying out to Captain (and Brevet Major) Jackson, "Major! They are going to fire!" Boutelle called to his own men, "Shoot over those Indians!" He then fired either the first or the second shot of the Modoc War—as Charley saw Boutelle's finger tightening on the trigger, he drew his own pistol and snapped a quick shot at the lieutenant. The two men fired virtually at the same time; the two reports blended as one.

Years later, Boutelle could joke, "Great minds appear to have thought alike," as he remembered the exchange of shots. But it was no joking matter. The slug from Charley's gun tore through Boutelle's upper left sleeve as the left-hander crooked his arm to aim and fire, then cut two holes through his uniform blouse and a slit in his cardigan jacket, but missed both his shirt and undershirt sleeves. It did not even bruise the skin. Ivan Applegate, a witness, reported that the pistol ball smashed Boutelle's gun first and then glanced through his sleeve, but the lieutenant, in describing the fight himself, made no mention of this. He continued to use his service revolver during the ensuing battle, too, so presumably Applegate was imagining things in a tense moment. Boutelle's pistol ball tore the red bandanna Scarfaced Charley wore around his head, but did not draw blood. The Indian dropped to the ground and rolled over and over, downhill toward the river.

The hurried, missed shots of the two antagonists were the

signal for general firing to break out. Bogus Charley led off even before Jackson shouted his command—"Fire!" The troopers poured fire into the Indians, who began to scatter, and put a volley into the lodges. The Modocs were firing from every angle, from every bit of cover they could find. Shots came from the doors of lodges, from the sagebrush to the left of the cavalry's skirmish line, from the river bank. It came especially from Scarfaced Charley's group of braves. The Modoc fire, largely from concealment, grew too hot, and Boutelle's exposed line of riflemen began to fall back. Because the packers had not yet come up and men were needed to hold his platoon's horses, Boutelle had only twenty-three men on the line. (Jackson recalled even fewer on the firing line, giving the figure as seventeen.) First a private was shot to death, then a corporal was severely wounded, followed by two privates. Then two privates and another corporal were less seriously wounded. Boutelle snapped another shot at Scarfaced Charley and thought that he had hit him, for the Indian dropped to the ground and crawled off into the sage. He was either wounded or playing possum, and certainly did not disappear among the lodges as Jesse Applegate reported, "in a comical manner, with all the airs of a conqueror." But Applegate was right when he wrote, "The troops were certain that Charley had been killed, and one man was willing to take an oath that he was dead." The scarred warrior had not received a scratch; his tumble to the ground was but a momentary ruse that the press later embroidered upon: "He counterfeited so naturally that not a suspicion of life was suggested to anyone present."

Lieutenant Boutelle's attention was wrenched away from Scarfaced Charley when he saw a warrior kneel in the opening of a lodge to let fly an arrow at him. Boutelle recalled, "This I dodged, and the subsequent proceedings interested him no more."

Jackson and Boutelle encouraged their men to hold the line, and although eight of their effectives were knocked out of the fight, the lieutenant managed to lead a little charge that drove Scarfaced Charley and his followers from their positions. They fell back slowly, firing as they went. It was hardly a retreat; more of a deliberate tactic to draw the troopers into the open. But after his men had swept through the village, Boutelle halted them in a picket line to defend the captured settlement. Ivan Applegate opined, "Boutelle's calmness saved us." In truth, Jackson's weakened force was overextending itself even in trying to hold the Modoc camp. Apparently the Army concurred with Applegate for, belatedly in 1890, Boutelle was awarded the brevet of first lieutenant for his gallantry in action at Lost River.

For about half an hour shots were exchanged in the din and commotion of battle, clouded with the smoke of exploded black powder cartridges and confused by the mad galloping and kicking of frightened, riderless horses. The Modoc braves kept up their demonlike yells after they faded into the brush without pursuit from the tired and badly battered men of B Troop. The Modoc womenfolk remained in the village, bemoaning their wounded and (presumed) dead menfolk. By and large, the soldiers did not bother them. Boutelle claimed to have "driven" the Modocs away. Actually, they withdrew almost leisurely, and soon the sky to the east reddened with a second sunrise as they burned cabins and haystacks on Lost River homesteads.

Jackson, supposedly the victor at Lost River, was given a brevet in 1890, too, for gallantry on November 29, 1872. But now he fell back, convincing himself (probably from the perjured testimony of the squaws) that he had struck a crushing blow at the Modocs and had killed Captain Jack, Scarfaced Charley, Black Jim and Curly Headed Doctor. Whatever the cause, his report on the battle was wildly unreliable and quite in the fine old "body count" tradition of the Army. A story in the San Francisco *Call* for December 2, doubtless based in part on Jackson's account, reported eighteen Modocs killed along with some men, women and children captured. Lt. Stephen Jocelyn and his brother officers at Camp Warner accepted a figure of sixteen Modocs killed and seven wounded. It was a good story. But it was only a story. The Modocs had about a half-dozen men wounded and only one brave killed, Watchman, whom Col. William Thompson identified (probably incorrectly) as a renegade Columbia River Indian, not a true Modoc. Major Green reported his gratification that no Indian women were killed and only one child shot, accidentally. But other accounts had three children killed by rifle fire besides the squaw shot by Fiock across-river, and a sick squaw burned to death when Jackson fired the village. Some said it was an accident; she was overlooked. Others called it deliberate murder. Jeff Riddle, half-Modoc, told Albert Gatschet that eleven women and children were either killed or wounded, but his figures were never reliable. He figured seven soldiers were killed and seven wounded, for example. Probably more accurate was historian

Harry L. Wells, who estimated that a squaw and a nine-year-old half-breed girl were killed along with two braves. (The Modocs themselves reduced this to one brave dead.)

Boutelle, like his superior, thought that B Troop had killed enough Modocs to prevent further resistance. Therefore he had no objection when Jackson not only let the squaws and children go but also released Captain Jack's horse herd, which a Klamath, Dave Hill, had rounded up after swimming across Lost River. The officers ignored the protests of Hill and Ivan Applegate, who termed Jackson's action "a mad, idiotic piece of folly." Jackson was pleased with three captured rifles and three saddles, which he convinced himself were the personal property of Captain Jack.

Initially, Oregonians greeted Jackson's fight as a victory. B. F. Dowell praised it as a prompt and effective march and attack—in short, a signal success. But even Jackson's whitewashed account admitted that there was no pursuit of the Modocs when they "fled." Jackson's excuse was that his force was too weak to follow them because he had to care for the wounded and protect the citizens at Crawley's ranch. He added, most incorrectly, "The Indians were all around us."

Although Gen. Jefferson C. Davis later described Capt. James Jackson as "a cool and discreet officer," he was obviously a very rattled—if not frightened—commander on the last day of November 1872. He was probably not the coward pictured by Col. William Thompson in his memoir, a man completely indifferent to the fate of settlers exposed to vengeful Modoc wrath because of his indecisive military action. But he lost little time in putting Lost River between him and his "worsted" enemy.

Boutelle guarded the smoldering ruins of the village as Klamath scout Dave Hill, along with Dr. McElderry and a small guard, ferried the wounded across the river in canoes. From the far bank they moved off toward Crawley's ranch a half-mile beyond. Because of high water Jackson could not use the ford at Natural Bridge, so he marched his men the seven miles upstream to Stukel Ford to cross, when a courier brought word of the fight at Crawley's. His rescue proved unnecessary, of course, but he posted the doughty Boutelle in command of his rear guard in case the Modocs should counterattack. Jackson took no action when a few Modoc stragglers burned another house and haystack across the river, but Boutelle repulsed a half-hearted attack on his detachment by a small party of braves. He remarked later, "They had had enough and did not want any more." He followed Jackson to Crawley's, bringing in the dead private, strapped to a horse.

The second act of the Modoc tragedy had already begun, unknown to Jackson and Boutelle. The men of Captain Jack's camp and the women and children of both villages crossed Tule Lake by boat from the mouth of Lost River to the south shore. There the waves driven by the stiff and cold north winds of the plateau lapped at the edge of the Lava Beds, a land of burnt-out fires to the Modocs and a volcanic *malpaís* or badland to the whites. The passage of the thirteen miles of water took the Indians most of the freezing and stormy night. According to the voluminous tradition of the Modoc War, one of the major figures lagged behind. Scarfaced Charley stayed back to warn his white friends of the outbreak of the war. Twice, it is said, he actually took hold of horse's halters and turned the animals around to point out a safe course to travelers.

This was consistent with Scarfaced Charley's character. Despite the fact that Fate had him open the Modoc War with an exchange of shots with Boutelle, he was the least jingoist of Captain Jack's band. In the words of A. B. Meacham, who knew him personally, "Scar Face, as he is generally called, advised the Modocs against resistance and positively refused to participate in any illegitimate warfare, always counseling for peace. At every meeting among his people he voted against shedding blood."

But Hooker Jim, seconded by Captain Jack's demonic medicine man, Curly Headed Doctor, was Scarfaced Charley's opposite. Always the least amenable to authority, he now left a trail of blood and terror behind him as he moved away from Lost River on the north and east shore of Tule Lake to safety in the volcanic jumble of the Lava Beds. With Boston Charley, One-Eyed Mose, Long Jim, Rock Dave, Humpy, Hungry Jerry and perhaps others, Hooker Jim hit every ranch in his path. Only three and a half miles from Crawley's cabin, where Jackson was going on the defensive, he killed the unsuspecting William Boddy at his home and shot his son-in-law, Nicholas Schira, in the head, knocking him off the seat of the wagon he had just loaded with firewood. Hooker and his followers then killed Boddy's young stepsons, Richard and William Crangan, known locally as Richard and William Boddy, while they were at their farm work. The Modocs stripped and perhaps mutilated the bodies. Mrs. Boddy told Colonel Thompson that the Indians not only shot her youngest (thirteen years old) son but cut his throat, too.

The first inkling of Hooker Jim's savage revenge for the surprise attack by the civilians on his Lost River camp near Crawley's came when Mrs. Boddy and young Mrs. Schira saw the team come running into the ranch yard, driverless. When Mrs. Schira took up the reins, she found them slippery with blood. Afraid that her husband had had a terrible accident of some kind, she hurriedly shut up the horses and set off down the road on foot, followed by her mother, who delayed to get bandages and water at the house. The seven or eight Modocs rode out of the brush and rudely stopped Mrs. Boddy, demanding to know if any men were in the ranch house. Still unaware of the violence, she replied that she did not know. She told the Indians, most of whom she knew, that she was hurrying to her son-in-law who had apparently had an accident, perhaps in a runaway. One of the Modocs then held up a bloodstained hand and announced, "This Boddy blood." But he then added, "We Modocs, no make war on women."

Mrs. Schira ran in search of the men of the ranch and was passed by the Modocs, who did not bother her in the least. Returning to her mother, she found the body of the older boy, only fifteen. According to local tradition, he had been shot through the head, disemboweled and his heart cut out. The now-terrified women fled the scene, heading over the wooded ridge toward Crawley's. But when in sight of the cabin they saw it ringed with figures and, fearful that they were Indians, turned away and climbed the snow-covered hills between themselves and Linkville. They spent the cold night huddled together under a juniper and were found in the middle of the second day of their wandering and taken to Linkville. On December 2, Mrs. Schira bravely took a wagon out to collect the dead, but she turned back when she learned that the omnipresent Lieutenant Boutelle was already out on the same mission.

Next day, the Modocs reached the homestead of William, Rufus and W. K. Brotherton, a father and his two sons (eleven and twenty-two years old), about eight miles from Boddy's. They killed and presumably mutilated all three. There they also murdered—"under conditions of peculiar atrocity," according to Col. William Thompson—their own friend, Henry Miller, the man who paid them for the use of their land, who defended them in testimony to the Army, who supplied the Modocs with food. All kinds of stories attempted to explain his murder and possible torture or mutilation. The *Call* in San Francisco reported that the Indians had always been bitter toward him—which was poppycock. But the paper also said he had gone to John A. Fairchild and repudiated his pro-Modoc position, claiming that his life had depended on his giving such answers to the questions of Major Otis. According to this yarn, he had told Fairchild that his answers had been false, and he complained bitterly of the impossible situation in which Otis had placed him.

However, the image of an equivocating, two-faced Miller does not ring true. When Judge Elijah Steele tried to get land for the Modocs on Lost River by having them preempt it like whites and pay taxes on it, he went to Miller for help in describing the area in terms of range, section and quarter-section when the Siskiyou County surveyor refused to help him. And when the Land Office turned down Steele's suggestion that each Modoc be given a quarter-section of land as red-skinned homesteaders, it was to Miller that Steele forwarded the letter, asking him to break the bad news to Captain Jack. Most likely, the Modocs killed Henry Miller for a simple reason: He had failed to warn them of the coming of Captain Jackson and the posse of armed civilians. Not realizing that he had not been privy to information on the raid, they believed their white friend had turned traitor on them. So they killed him.

Mrs. Brotherton would not have trusted Hooker Jim's vow of chivalric treatment of women even had she been aware of it. When she saw her neighbor, John Schroeder, shot off his horse by the Modocs, she prepared for a desperate resistance. Her fifteen-year-old son, Joseph, was with Schroeder but managed to escape the Indians by running for the house at full speed. Mrs. Brotherton hurried out to meet him, revolver in hand, while her younger son, twelve-year-old Charlie, tried to call her back to the cabin, fearful for her safety. When she continued striding toward her other son, who was being closely pursued by the Modocs, young Charlie took out after her. She ordered him to go back to the cabin and get his father's Henry rifle, to elevate the sights to eight hundred yards and to start firing at the Indians. The youngster obeyed and commenced firing. His still younger sister pitched in to help by handing him the .44 cartridges, which she carefully wiped clean of grease and dirt with amazing presence of mind for a child, so that there would be no jamming of the quick-firing ancestor of the Winchester, which, alas, had a reputation for temperament. Charlie kept the lever-action rifle firing until all were safely in the cabin. Mrs. Brotherton barricaded the cabin door with the sacks of flour the menfolk had just hauled from Linkville as the family's winter supply. She and her boys then cut loopholes in the walls of the cabin and fired at the Indians, several of whom were now riding horses from Boddy's ranch. Mrs. Brotherton thought that her fire killed or wounded one or two of the Indians and several of the horses, but this was just wishful thinking in a tight spot. However, the Modocs had no desire to get too close to that Henry, so they moved on. After two nights of fearful waiting in the bullet-pocked two-story box of a house, the family was rescued by Ivan Applegate and some settlers and Klamaths who had gone from Crawley's cabin to Langell Valley and Clear Lake, At Jesse Applegate's place near Clear Lake they had picked up some horses and then had swung by the Brotherton spread.

At least six more helpless men were murdered by Hooker Jim's band, and apparently only one of them, Adam Shilling-law—a cowboy on Louis Land's ranch—was not mutilated. He was also the only man in the entire Modoc War to be killed with an arrow instead of a bullet. Shot through the chest, the tough cattleman managed to ride three miles before falling from his horse. The Modocs spared all women but no men, unless A. B. Meacham was right in that they had the opportunity of butchering the old Quaker sheepman, Tripp, but let him go because he had never once broken faith with them.

Hooker Jim's leniency toward white women befuddled the editor of the Yreka *Journal,* and on December 4, 1872, he guessed that those killed had been the most vociferous in urging the removal of the Modocs from the Lost River-Tule Lake area to the Klamath Reservation. The truth was to the contrary; not a single one of the victims (whose numbers varied in accounts from fourteen to eighteen) was among the forty signers of the petition to have Captain Jack's band moved back under the guns of Fort Klamath. And, of course, Miller was supposed to be a genuine friend of the Modocs, like Fairchild, Dorris, Steele and Rosborough, if the tale of his recanting was false, as seems the case.

Two more men were reported dead, but they turned up safe after separating from Ivan Applegate's party to search for Miller's body. One of them, George Fiock, gave out a bizarre tale of having been cut off at Schroeder's cabin by Scarfaced Charley (who was not with Hooker Jim at all) and a party of

Modocs who fired at him and set his cabin afire. If Fiock's incredible story were to be believed, and it should not be, he got Ivan Applegate to send a friendly Modoc, Schonches (presumably Chief Schonchin), to persuade Scarface Charley not to fight the whites. But the maneuver failed and Applegate had Schonchin fire Schroeder's haystack and barn because the Modocs were taking cover behind them. To top off this absurd story, Fiock recalled that when he got to Linkville he found himself given up for dead and two empty coffins lying in a wagon bed—one of them his.

Obviously, from Fiock's story, hysteria was not limited to women on the frontier. The Yreka *Journal* contributed the next wild tale, one which suggest that ghoulish whites were looting the abandoned ranches. It noted that at Miller's only money was taken, while warm bedding and even a gold watch (easily identifiable and hard to pawn) were left behind by the raiders. (In time, however, the Modocs would admit to robbing the homesteads.)

There was panic in Langell Valley, fed by yarns such as Fiock's. George Miller's house there was converted into a fort, with cellars dug and covered with logs and dirt to make protected trenches extending beyond the house and reached by a hole in the floor. But as tension mounted, the seven families huddled there abandoned their log fortress and started a pell-mell retreat for Linkville. Miller's son, George Marsten Miller, was only eleven at the time but he never forgot the fears of that day. The party was fired on near today's Bonanza, but because of a heavy rainstorm the attackers could not see where their bullets were hitting, so continued to overshoot the party. A man named Fairchild (*not* John A. Fairchild) became so frightened he "froze" on the brake of his wagon and other men had to use force on him to get his vehicle moving again.

The Langell Valley settlers imagined that the Modocs would trap them by an ambush at Lost River Gap so they went the long way, via Poe Valley, to reach the Lost River Ford, near today's Merrill, Oregon, and thence to Linkville and safety. The widowed Mrs. Schira stayed with the Millers in Linkville. According to some stories, Miller never went back to his log fort but settled down in Linkville as a butcher. On the other hand, Corp. Herman Werner talked to a George Miller on a Lost River Valley sheep ranch in 1881. Miller told the noncom that he was afraid of being run off his land by big and bullying cattle ranchers—which throws some light on the causes of the Modoc

War. Unfortunately, he also filled Werner's head with wild tales about Hooker Jim's foray. He said Hooker had been angered by a Lost River settler stealing his daughter and had said to A. B. Meacham, "Have you brought back my beautiful daughter? If not, then blood for blood, and more war!" Werner made no mention of the Boddy and Brotherton raids but passed on stories, doubtless from this Miller, of the killing and mutilating of homesteaders called Maier, Hollinger and John Corvan, with Maier being hung on a rail fence and women and children murdered, too—which simply did not happen.

Where Major Green bungled in sending too few men to round up Captain Jack, now Jackson blundered in spades, to compound the Army's initial error. He did nothing to protect any settlers other than those at Crawley's cabin, not even sending messengers to warn their neighbors. Although his intelligence was fairly good and he wrote on November 30 that the Indians had retired to caves in the Lava Beds south of Tule Lake, he made no move but to send men to the river ford to protect his supply train. Of course, he was nervous, and he reported, "I imagine they will soon be out in war parties." He was not aware of Hooker Jim's bloody trail for two days and did not even realize that no one had spread the alarm to settlers until the day after his fight. And then he merely sent a patrol to alert the Boddy family, some three and a half miles from his headquarters. When the troopers returned to report the cabin standing, he assumed that Boddy and the other settlers had been warned by Superintendent Odeneal's messenger, One-Armed Brown, and had gone to Linkville.

Not till the evening of December 1, 1872, did Captain Jackson finally realize the horrible price of his dilatoriness. Two travelers arrived at Crawley's to report the hideous butchery at Boddy's place which, somehow, the patrol had missed. It was too late for Jackson to retrieve his matter-of-fact report to Major Green, with its all-is-well tone: "The troop behaved gallantly and deserves every praise. The fight was at close quarters and very severe for thirty minutes. The citizens engaged did good service, I learn, and deserve much credit; but for them we would have had a fire in the rear that would have been very destructive."

Odeneal made hurried excuses. He made it known that he had sent his messenger, Brown, to warn all the farmers and stockmen of Lost River and Tule Lake. But he said that Brown claimed not to have known of any people below Crawley's and, since the six men with him had not said a word about them, he had gone no further than Bybee's place. Odeneal refused to blame Brown, or anyone, but stoutly insisted, "I did everything in my power to avert all danger." Col. William Thompson was not afraid to blame the guilty because Mrs. Schira told him that the Modocs had warned the Lost River settlers, time and time again, that they would kill every one of them if the soldiers came for them. Of course, the settlers had demanded of Army and Indian Bureau that they be alerted of any warring moves in the vicinity of their holdings. She wrote Thompson, "If these settlers had been warned in time, not one white person would have been killed, as we all had arms and ammunition sufficient to defend ourselves successfully." But when Mrs. Schira reproached One-Armed Brown for not warning the homesteaders, he only growled that he was not paid to run after settlers.

The nearest thing to a Paul Revere of the Modoc War was not the bungler, Brown, but George Conn of the Land Office at Linkville. He saddled up and rode out at 5 P.M. November 30. He rode all night and spread the word of Indian trouble—but in the safe precincts of Ashland, not in the ranches exposed to danger. Nor was he aware of the magnitude of the massacres; he reported only three men dead, rather than the fourteen to eighteen of later estimates.

Prominent residents of the Lakes country, such as Jesse Applegate, sent messages to the governor of Oregon, via Conn, asking for help. Applegate dramatically informed His Excellency that he was starting to the relief of Clear Lake settlers with a small party of civilians but that he was short of both arms and ammunition and could not hold out long should he have a real fight with the Modocs. Ashland responded to Conn's alert by sending fourteen men with Henry repeaters to the Klamath area, followed next day (December 3) by another party of eight armed men. By the time these volunteers reached Linkville and Applegate made it to Langell Valley, all was quiet and no Modocs were to be seen. They were holed up in the impenetrable Lava Beds.

Californians were warned of the Modoc War by rancher John A. Fairchild, a friend of the Modocs. He also broke the news to the peaceful Hot Creek band of Modocs encamped near his place. Fairchild, like so many, overestimated the number of Modoc warriors as eighty and reminded Yreka that there were only about thirty-five troopers left at Fort Klamath. A dozen men left Yreka that day and were followed by a second relief party next day. Word of the war was telegraphed to San Francisco from Yreka, and it immediately seized the public's attention.

Fairchild hurried to Jack's village in hopes of being a peacemaker, but he found it abandoned and half-burned and all boats destroyed, so he returned to his ranch. En route he heard brisk firing which he could not explain. On December 4, with four rancher friends, he gathered up the Hot Creek band of forty-five, including Bogus Charley, Shacknasty Jim, Steamboat Frank and Ellen's Man George, for their own protection. These Indians, who had no connection with the hostile actions of either Hooker Jim's band or Captain Jack's, were camped near Fairchild's ranch. They were peaceable and anxious to avoid trouble. Fairchild felt that a paternalistic protection of their interests was his proper role. They were quite willing to go on the Klamath Reservation now, and Fairchild and his friends began to escort them to safety there. But at Bob Whittle's place on Link River he was accosted and halted by a small crowd of eight or ten excited whites who were bent on killing the Modocs in his custody. Fairchild told the cowardly group that they would have to kill him first. The stalemate was broken by the arrival of Indian Agent Dyar from Klamath Reservation. He told Fairchild that there was a mob forming to attack him if he tried to cross the river with the Indians. Dyar continued that it was useless to proceed and said he would not allow the Modocs to pass through enraged Linkville until he could get soldiers from Fort Klamath to guarantee their safety and protect them every inch of the way.

John Fairchild was not sure what to do but he was not yet ready to give up. He decided to try to get his charges to the reservation by a roundabout route, bypassing Linkville. However, the Hot Creeks knew enough English to understand the gist of the angry and excited talk of the whites, and the warriors suddenly "spooked." Despite the pleading of Fairchild, the frightened Indians broke and ran for the cover of rocks and bushes, and disappeared from view. They were soon scattered all over creation and only a handful rejoined the squaws and children as Fairchild sadly led them back to the presumed safety of his ranch.

Fairchild learned from Dyar that the Modoc losses claimed by the Army had been scaled down to only nine or ten killed and about the same number wounded. And the word was that

Scarfaced Charley was not dead, after all, although fifty rounds had been fired at him. Through some avenue of communication, the holed-up Modocs were also insisting that the troops had fired first in the battle. Fairchild also learned that Chief Donald McKay of the Warm Springs Indians, already used to scouting for the Army, planned to return to the lakes area with all of his men to protect both white settlers and peaceful Indians. McKay was as worried about the innocent Hot Creek band as Fairchild, pointing out: "The danger now to be apprehended is from a mob who are at war with all who advocate a policy of peace. They ask protection of any white man who may meet them on the way." General Canby immediately issued orders that all peace-loving Modocs be protected and conducted to the security of the Klamath Reservation. He guaranteed payment by the Government of any expenses incurred by a group of Yrekans who hoped to move them, under protective guard, to the reservation by a roundabout route via Rogue River Valley.

But the Hot Creeks did not show up at Fairchild's or at Yreka. Small wonder. Whole towns in Oregon and California were reacting in a mixture of panic and patriotism as Captain Jackson sat at Soldier's Camp, at Crawley's Ranch, presumably pondering the situation and licking his wounds. According to Major Green, one of the panicky souls was Superintendent Odeneal, who fled from Linkville to Jacksonville when he heard of Captain Jackson's scuffle and its bloody aftermath. The Oregon *Bulletin* interviewed on December 3 the most knowledgeable man at hand in Jacksonville, B. F. Dowell. He estimated the chances of the Modoc country settlers thus: "Unless ample protection is timely afforded them, massacre and torture and despoilment may be their fate at the hands of the savages." The San Francisco *Call,* busily gleaning any scraps of information it could find on the Modocs, picked up the story. Dowell, if not misquoted, was bad enough; he confused Captain Jack and Scarfaced Charley, and a composite emerged in his yarn—Scarfaced Jack! The *Call,* however, mangled the facts even more, and after blaming Steele and the other Yrekans for inciting the Modocs to their desperate stand, editorialized: "Had Captain Applegate hanged Scarfaced Jack about a year ago for the murder of another Indian, as he intended to and as Jack deserved to be, perhaps this outbreak would not have occurred."

In one respect, Dowell was right as rain, however. He predicted the Army's difficulties with the Modocs in the Lava

Beds when most civilians and soldiers thought the troopers would give them a whipping in jig time. He stated: "The Modocs in arms number less than seventy warriors but, then, they fight with great advantage over the troops sent against them.... If Jack is living and unharmed, he will be likely to occasion a good deal of trouble if not the loss of lives and the destruction of property before his tribe will be whipped into peace. He is a smart, cunning, active, bad Indian and, while too cowardly to come to the front and risk his own life in a fight, he has the faculty of pushing forward his braves to the utmost. And he is more to be dreaded on account of the influence which some evil-disposed white men hold over him and whose interests will be benefited by the resistance of the Modocs to the authorities and their continuance in the region they claim as their own."

Not until the morning of December 2, almost four days after his fight, did Jackson finally send out a patrol on the Modocs' trail. He had planned to sit tight at Crawley's until enough supplies could be collected, but when men brought him word of the murders of the settlers, he sent out the tireless Boutelle. The latter brought back news of the horrible price paid for Jackson's Lost River "victory." Boutelle found the corpses at Boddy's and met Ivan Applegate's party, which reported the Brothertons and others killed.

Jackson was not only tired but rattled, and he was slow to take action even when the grief-stricken but brave Mrs. Brotherton arrived at his camp with her children. Finally he sent a detachment to Clear Lake to guard Jesse Applegate's family. Ivan Applegate was in Linkville and wrote a hasty note to Capt. John McCall: "Modoc War hot, bloody and savage. I came up last night. Three dead men to bury today and five badly wounded.... People from Clear Lake not heard from. I go there with a small party tonight. George Conn goes to Ashland to get help. Turn out and help him.... We are too few to hold out long. Oliver has gone to Yainax. I will try to keep him out of any more fights and will go where bullets sing as few times as I can. I don't like such work. Am astonished that I am alive today. I could see Oliver fighting on the opposite side of the river but couldn't get to him. His men say he laughed all the time while fighting." Soberly, Applegate ended his note by asking McCall to take care of things for him if it should turn out that he would be "left in the sagebrush."

Major Green, at Fort Klamath, did not suffer the paralysis of decision which afflicted Jackson. The moment he heard of Troop B's debacle, he issued twenty muskets, ten carbines and ammunition to citizens of Linkville, ten muskets to Yainax and ten more to Klamath Agency for self-defense. He then sent Company F of the 21st Infantry, with twenty days' rations, to reinforce Jackson. Since Fort Klamath was only a two-company post and understrength, as always, Major Green stripped its garrison down to a corporal's guard. He did not even have an officer to command the infantrymen he sent, and they marched under the command of First Sgt. John McNamara. The Irishman's orders were to try to link up with Captain Jackson, whose exact whereabouts were still unknown to Fort Klamath, and to take up positions which Indian Agent Dyar should designate, to defend the people against Modoc attacks. Otherwise, the top sergeant was to use his own judgment in selecting his campsites or positions of defense. Green also dispatched a corporal with a wagonload of supplies for Jackson. Green's orders went out on the last day of November, the very day that Jackson reported on his battle and advised Fort Klamath that he would not be returning but would have to stay in the field with his force. He asked Green for the reinforcements that were already en route and for orders as to his future course of action.

On December 3, Green reported to General Canby, explaining Captain Jackson's fiasco by complaining, "The troop made its march as expected and completely surprised the Indians and could have destroyed them had it not been fair to give them a chance to submit without using force."

Slowly, Jackson began to reassert control over the area, with the Modocs flown to the Lava Beds. The squad that he sent to Jesse Applegate's ranch at Clear Lake took up post there. He promised to send Sergeant McNamara's relief column to that area, too, and to protect Langell Valley, which was thought to be particularly exposed to attack. Jackson's forces were bolstered at this point from a completely unexpected quarter. Capt. D. J. Ferree, a Linkville rancher who was A. B. Meacham's brother-in-law, turned up with a company of thirty-six Klamath scouts authorized by General Canby and organized on the Klamath Reservation by Agent Dyar. Jackson immediately sent them out to trail the Modocs to their hiding place and to keep them bottled up so that they could not roam and raid ranchers and travelers until the troops could be moved in to roust them from their lava hideout.

Calmer now, Jackson sent another account of his battle to

Fort Klamath, reiterating to Major Green that the men of his troop, even the raw recruits, had behaved splendidly under fire. He particularly commended Dr. McElderry and Lieutenant Boutelle for their coolness and their gallant and efficient service.

But for days after the blood of slain farmers stained the stubble of Lost River's winter pastures, the commander of the Army's District of the Lakes was unaware of the fighting. There was no telegraph between Fort Klamath and his headquarters at Camp Warner, or anywhere else in the Modoc area. In fact, two days *after* Jackson's bloody rebuff, Colonel Wheaton was ordering Major Green to take a force of 150 cavalry (not the thirty-six to whom Green had given the task) to arrest Captain Jack. And, ironically, he still took the Modocs lightly, believing that a mere show of force would suffice to awe sixty armed warriors into submission. "Only as a dire necessity, and as a last resort, will you permit troops to engage and kill any Modocs."

Once he learned of the true situaton, Wheaton—to his credit—acted with promptness. He felt compelled to do a bit of face-saving, of course, after the bad timing of his optimistic dispatches, so he wrote General Canby that the best-informed officials at Fort Klamath and Yainax and the Klamath Agency had assured him Captain Jack would not resist. Thus, Jack's defiant attitude and killing of soldiers and civilians was not only deplorable but unexpected. But Wheaton did not stop with limping excuses. He promised troops from both Camp Warner and Camp Bidwell by the night of December 5 to reinforce Green's Fort Klamath company. He ordered the Indian-fighting veteran, Capt. Reuben F. Bernard, to reduce his command at Bidwell by every available man, leaving only a small guard at the post. Bernard needed no urging. He marched his men the ninety-six miles from Goose Lake to Crawley's ranch in fast time. But he had only a tiny force, two dozen men, with which to even attempt to carry out Colonel Wheaton's orders, which instructed him to, first, clear and protect the Lake City to Linkville Road, prevent further Modoc depredations on the east side of Tule Lake, and join Green's troops in protecting the threatened ranches and Linkville itself. However, the other men ordered by Wheaton to reinforce Jackson were also on the way. Capt. David Perry and Lt. J. G. Kyle were making a forced march from Riggs' Ranch at the north end of Goose Lake to Crawley's via Yainax. Perry's wagons were sent directly to Fort Klamath to pick up more supplies for the troops in the field.

Wheaton had reacted pretty well, as had Green, to the threat. But still the Army could not take Captain Jack's band very seriously. Captain Bernard's troopers were issued only eight days' rations since the colonel did not intend to detain them long in Modoc country. Wheaton thought that the two companies of cavalry under Jackson and Perry, supported by Kyle's detachment, were more than enough to handle the Modoc rascals. Bernard's real mission, he indicated, was to protect the road and reassure travelers and settlers along it. Incredibly, when he ordered thirty-four cavalrymen and an officer from Camp Harney, he *specified* that no extra ammunition be carried by the men, only that in the individual troopers' cartridge boxes. Acting more like a quartermaster than a field commander, Wheaton explained, "A further supply, if required, can be furnished from the ordnance storehouse at this headquarters."

Capt. Reuben F. Bernard now chimed in, to add his contribution to the Army's chorus of excuses for what went wrong on Lost River: "A dreadful mistake had been made, yes; more than one. . . . The greater sin lies at the door of Mr. Odeneal, who would not trust his precious skin to the council on Lost River but preferred treacherously to send troops with guns in place of an agent of the Indian Department with an olive branch. He was sadly mistaken in believing that the Indians would not fight. He was dealing with desperate men. . . . If he failed to send any word to the settlers on the north side of Tule Lake that troops were coming, he has more to think of than I should care to have."

Late in the evening of December 1, the governor of Oregon learned of the Lost River battle and massacres. He reported the fight to General Canby, blamed the fiasco on Captain Jackson's inadequate force, and informed the general that he was authorizing Ashland to raise a company of volunteers since the Army had insufficient troops to protect the people. He asked his ranking militia officers to be prepared for war, too. Canby calmed the excited governor by telling him that Colonel Wheaton's four cavalry companies and three infantry companies composed a force quite adequate to deal with Captain Jack. In fact, Canby still discounted the reports of disaster at Lost River since Wheaton had assured him of the Army's preparedness and he had not received detailed reports, as yet, on the actions there. Presumably trying to soothe the governor, he hoped aloud that the difficulties on Lost River were not as serious as first reported, and he even hoped that there had not really been any loss of life among civilians!

Fairchild and his friend, Pres Dorris, continued their efforts to substitute peace for war. By December 7, they had much of the Hot Creek band rounded up again, and Dorris wrote a Yreka friend, "All is quiet at present. We don't want any persons to come to our help until we call for them, as we are scarce of blankets. We have made arrangements with the authorities to come and get the Indians, or meet us on the road to the Reservation." On Sunday, December 8, Fairchild and three other ranchers went out to convince Scarfaced Charley and Captain Jack to come in, since they were not blamed for the actions of Hooker Jim, who had been identified by Mrs. Boddy. About twenty-five whites and a few Modoc friendlies waited anxiously for the men's return, some of them feeling that Fairchild was placing too much trust in the friendship of Indian desperadoes. The townspeople of Yreka were even more apprehensive for the safety of Fairchild and his friends. They waited with great impatience for news of the situation from a Fort Klamath courier, the half-breed chief of the Warm Springs Indians, Donald McKay. He was late, having had to make a long detour around a band of unknown Indians near Wheaton's new headquarters at Fort Klamath. McKay brought no news of Fairchild but reported that not only had Wheaton shifted his headquarters from Camp Warner to Fort Klamath but that Major Green had taken personal command of the troops in the field. He would offer Captain Jack terms of unconditional surrender, nothing more. According to the 'breed, "The major says all he wants is plenty of provisions and a snowstorm so he can get Captain Jack. He fought Apaches for five years and has the reputation of being a good Indian fighter."

Lindsay Applegate was considerably less confident of the Army than Major Green. He wrote John McCall, bitterly, "According to the account, seventeen people have already been killed—my neighbors—fruits of the criminal carelessness of the higher authorities of the Military at the Fort."

Major Green was not as yet sure of the exact whereabouts of the Modocs although he knew they were hiding in the Lava Beds on the south shore of Tule Lake. He should have chatted with H. C. Rambeau, who guessed correctly that they would be on watch on the height (later called Gillem's Bluff) at the southwest corner of Tule Lake and in the volcanic "trenches" below it, about six miles from Natural Bridge and twenty from

Linkville. He even pinpointed the hiding place of the squaws and children—it would be in Ben Wright's Cave (soon to be renamed Captain Jack's Stronghold) because it was hard to find and easy to defend. No white, to his knowledge, had visited it since 1866, when his father and Frank Picard had explored it. Rambeau guessed, again correctly, that the Modocs, if pressed on the bluff, would fall back to the natural fortifications in and around Ben Wright's Cave. He was wrong in only one respect; he underestimated the number of effectives at Captain Jack's command because he trusted the Army's claim of Indian casualties at Lost River as fifteen dead.

Among the rumors that now began to fly was one that the Modocs had long been preparing for war and had laid in a year's supply of food and ammunition in the Lava Beds and were actively recruiting the Pit Rivers (their enemies) and Clear Lake Paiutes as allies. Rambeau thought Jack had about forty or fifty braves to face some four hundred soldiers and volunteers in December 1872, but Gov. Newton Booth of California still felt it necessary to send fifty rifles and a supply of ammunition to distribute to Siskiyou County folk as protection against expected Modoc marauding. Bungling in the Modoc War had only begun with Green and Jackson; when the guns arrived in Yreka on the night stagecoach, the ammunition was found to be about three calibers too large for the rifles.

About the time that copy was being set in the San Francisco *Call* to the effect that delightful weather in the Modoc country made everything favorable for a movement of troops against the Modocs, Fairchild and his friend, Pres Dorris, reached Captain Jack. They found him lurking in his stronghold, Ben Wright's Cave in the Lava Beds. Jack was friendly and even loaned Fairchild a pony when the rancher's mount wandered off. The sub-chief (who was turning into a real chief) was bewildered by the unexpected attack on his sleeping village and had had no part in Hooker Jim's massacres. But he was determined to resist being moved to the Klamath Reservation. He told his old friend that he did not want to harm any "Boston" settlers, nor had he ever harmed any of them. That was all Hooker Jim's work. But he would fight soldiers, and to the bitter end, rather than go back to the reservation. He told Fairchild and Dorris to warn the soldiers against coming after him, for he would fight them.

The press tried to report the progress of the Modoc War and managed, this time, to confuse Captain Jack not with Scarfaced Charley but Bogus Charley. The papers reported "Bogus Jack" as justifying his rebellion by claiming bad treatment from Indian agents, especially Lindsay Applegate. The story was that he had moved them from a land of fish and game to a frosty, snowy area so he would have more mouths to feed and, thus, would increase the size of his Government contract. Already the San Francisco *Call* seemed to be more on the Modocs' side in the war than the Army's or the Indian Bureau's. "Here we have a reason for the Modoc War. Whether it be sufficient to palliate the uprising of the Indians or not, it is at least sufficiently explicit to show that they have been most shamefully dealt with."

Applegate replied to the charges but, curiously, by a letter to the San Diego *Union* rather than the *Call* itself. He kept his temper and simply reminded the public of the 1864 treaty signed by the Modocs, in which they had ceded their land and had gone on the Klamath Reservation. He then raised the Oregon-versus-California rivalry factor, stating that Captain Jack's real chiefs were not the Oregon Indian agents but Yreka citizens. Applegate also repudiated the claim that Jack was starved out, stating that the Indians were all treated alike in the distribution of goods and supplies and that the latter were all of the best quality.

However, a counterclaim to Applegate's appeared almost immediately when a Californian named Elijah Heard claimed to have run into Scarfaced Charley near Clear Lake and managed to interview him. If his story was not just a pack of lies to gain publicity, Scarfaced Charley had accused the Government of defrauding the Modocs by issuing them common Army blankets, cut in half, instead of the high-quality double blankets promised them at the Council Grove powwow. He claimed they were also shorted on other articles and had to subsist during their one winter on the reservation, 1869-1870, on barley and bad beef. Charley told Heard that Jack had only about eighty warriors (he was exaggerating) but that they were well supplied and armed and both brave and desperate. The Yreka pioneer believed this, adding that the Modocs—unlike most other western Indians—were dead shots. He predicted that the combination of Modoc resolution and Lava Beds defenses meant that "forty lives will pay for every Indian killed or taken."

Perhaps Scarfaced Charley's rather high estimate of effectives in the Modoc "army" was more prognostication than brag; the Hot Creek friendlies, gathered at Fairchild's, had a change of heart and decided to join Jack in the Lava Beds rather than take their chances in going to the Klamath Reservation. A San Francisco newspaper correspondent actually wired his editor that the squaws and braves alike were making arrows and had poured so much hot lead into bullet molds that they had hatfuls of rifle balls.

The Army was now itching for a fight. It was embarrassed by Jackson's showing at Lost River and meant to counteract it with a splendid victory in the Lava Beds. Although Major Green predicted a long campaign, his superior, Colonel Wheaton, still swallowing Jackson's inflated and absurd claims of Modoc casualties inflicted on November 29, told General Canby's Portland headquarters, "I do not believe we need anticipate a continued resistance from this little band of Modocs." The Army was right in discounting the wild fears of travelers who avoided the Tickner Road and dropped all the way down to Fort Crook because they were sure the Pit Rivers were going to join Captain Jack's Modocs in a grand alliance. But they extended their scorn to the warnings of men such as Heard and Rambeau, too. Capt. David Perry sent out a scouting party from his post at Van Bremer's ranch and reported the Modoc retreat was not as difficult of access as supposed. Col. John E. Ross sent out a party of his Oregon volunteers from Small's ranch, and one of his Klamath scouts came within a mile of Captain Jack's headquarters without any resistance or difficulty. The Klamath even shouted in contempt, "Come out! Come out!" in the Modoc tongue, but to no avail.

The soldiers were impatient to chase the Modocs out of their *malpaís* and awaited with annoyance the arrival of reinforcements and two howitzers and three hundred rounds of ammunition from Vancouver Barracks. The press was enthusiastic about this mountain artillery and its so-called bomb-shells, which could be dropped into Captain Jack's cave from a mile and a half away, to blow him to kingdom come. Some newsmen wondered if the artillerymen could get close enough, however, for such accurate fire on lava tubes, caves and trenches with the newfangled "unwelcome visitors," the explosive shells. The *Call,* for one, thought that riflemen, not howitzers, would still have to clear the Modocs out of their narrow, rocky passages. "Good sharpshooters, well acquainted with the ambush style of fighting, are the kind best adapted to wipe out the Modocs," averred the bellicose editor.

In San Francisco, General Schofield wired Washington

confidently, "General Canby does not apprehend serious trouble, he having provided sufficient force to compel obedience to the orders of the Department." Thus, Gen. William Tecumseh Sherman, in the Capital, was not worried by the Modocs. He advised the Secretary of War, "At this distance it is impossible to judge of the steps necessary to maintain the peace of the frontier, but General E. R. S. Canby is in actual command of all the troops and resources of the country and will doubtless bring this matter to a satisfactory end."

As the Army waited for the right moment to move in and drag the Modocs out of the Lava Beds, there was more explanation of Jackson's debacle and more prophecy of speedy conclusion of the trouble. General Canby conjectured that the unfortunate affair at Lost River was the result of unforeseen and unpreventable contingencies, since he had ordered that all precautions be taken in the Modoc removal. He felt that Jackson had executed his orders properly, and he commended the troops for satisfactory behavior. But he admitted that Fort Klamath had not taken precautions for the possibility of failure of the mission. Schofield, with new information on Lost River at hand just before he sailed for Hawaii, leaving Canby in command of the whole Pacific Coast, was more critical: "A serious mistake was committed in sending a small force to do what, from the defiant attitude of the Indians, would manifestly require a much larger force." But Canby was confident of success. He reminded his superiors that he had an adequate force, now, and that the season was in the Army's favor. The snow would drive the Modocs from the mountains and make them easy to trail. Of course, he admitted, "It will involve some hardship upon our troops, but they are better provided and can endure it better than the Indians."

The old Indian hand, A. B. Meacham, did not share Canby's confidence and put the blame for the Modoc tragedy squarely on the epauletted shoulders of the Army. "The military at Fort Klamath, who had been waiting for eight years at an enormous expense for 'something to do,' were called out and the result was the battle of Lost River. . . . Had no soldiers been employed to forcibly return him [Captain Jack] in 1872, no war would have ensued."

But Stephen Powers had the last word in the widely read *Overland Magazine*. He blamed the Indian Ring and its wishy-washy minions more than the Army, although he wished that General Crook were back in the West instead of Canby.

"Ah, for one day, for one hour, of George Crook!" he wrote. And, with disdain, he added: "The pity of it is—the grievous pity—that it was the settlers who were bitten and not the reservation people. . . . The blood of those poor murdered women and children lies not more upon the bloody-minded Modocs than it does upon the wretched, slabbering, paltering policy which let them loose. What the Modocs need more than anything else is that tremendous thrashing which one brave man gives another and which they can understand; after that, impartial justice—no swindling, no foolery, no generosity."

CHAPTER EIGHT

LAND OF BURNT-OUT FIRES

One of Lt. William H. Boyle's brother-officers of the 21st Infantry at Vancouver Barracks, eager for action, enthused early in December 1872, "I will not have to take that trip to Jacksonville and back, through the mud, without accomplishing anything. . . . You know that as soon as Colonel John Green goes after those Indians, he will clean them out, sooner than a man can say 'Jack Robinson'. . . . Didn't he, whenever he went after the Apaches? He will soon clean out the Modocs, I can tell you that!"

But Lt. Col. Frank Wheaton, commanding the District of the Lakes, was not about to trust the chastisement of the Modocs to Green alone after his—or, rather, his subordinate's—bungling raid on Lost River. While B Troop's battered yellowlegs rested up and their wounded comrades mended, Wheaton got up from a sickbed and on December 21 established his headquarters at Dennis Crawley's miserable shanty on Lost River. There, beset with icy winds, snow and sleeting rain, he awaited reinforcements and howitzers with which he would blast the Modocs from their lava nooks and crannies. He kept himself busy planning the all-out attack of his Modoc Expedition and keeping his enemy under surveillance and bottled up in their Stronghold, as the heart of their Lava Beds defense was coming to be called. He wanted no more hit-and-run raids such as the one that had killed up to sixteen settlers already.

Colonel Wheaton pooh-poohed as arrant nonsense the frightening description of the Stronghold which Jesse Applegate offered. The latter saw the area of the Lava Beds, sometimes called "Hell with the fires gone out," as a once-solid sheet of rock, ten miles square and five hundred feet thick, exploded by Vulcan's mines into a mass of lava rocks ranging in size from that of a matchbox to a church. The underground explosions had heaped the masses of rock high in some places but had left deep chasms in others. Then Nature had placed the area in one

160

of Vulcan's crucibles and heated it up to where the rocks began to fuse and run together, before being allowed to cool. Applegate described the rough surface, honeycombed with cracks and crevices, as ideal for defense. "An Indian can, from the top of one of these stone pyramids, shoot a man without exposing even so much as an inch of himself. He can, without undue haste, load and shoot a common muzzle-loading rifle ten times before a man can scramble over the rocks and chasms between the slain and the slayer. If at this terrible expense of life, a force dislodges him from his cover, he has only to drop into and follow some subterraneous passage with which he is familiar to gain another ambush, from which it will cost ten more lives to dislodge him."

Applegate was a first-rate prognosticator, as it turned out, but the veteran commander simply could not accept the idea of the Stronghold being impregnable. Wheaton wrote Canby, "We will be prepared to make short work of this impudent and enterprising savage. I feel confident that the guns will astonish and terrify them and perhaps save much close skirmishing and loss of life. Unless the Modocs crawl off south through the Lava Beds on our approach, we hope to make short work of them." Only in May, after the Modocs abandoned their bastion, did the Army learn how accurate had been Applegate's warnings. Capt. G. J. Leydecker at that time examined and mapped the rugged lava plateau. Leydecker found that the much-feared Captain Jack's cave was merely an unimpressive kettle or vertical pit (what the geologists called a schollendom) about twelve or fifteen feet in diameter at the surface but swelling toward the bottom. He reported it to be useless as a defensive position, although it offered security from distant fire, as from the howitzers of the Army. But he put his finger on the cause of the Army's monumental overconfidence. His first impression, too, from a distance, was that the Lava Beds formed an immense but level sagebrush plain, with no major obstructions to easy movement of troops in any direction. A closer look disclosed groups of low, rocky ridges which not only broke up the plain and inhibited movement but were admirably designed by nature as defensive battlements and redoubts, even to transversal crevices that furnished excellent lines of communication for the defenders to pass, unseen by attackers, from one lava breastwork to another. And Leydecker found that Captain Jack and Scarfaced Charley were no slouches at defensive warfare; they kept open only the few passages that sixty-odd warriors could safely control, blockading the others with piled-up boulders to prevent soldiers using them to infiltrate the Modoc lines. In fact, the Lava Beds campaign resembled more the trench warfare of World War I (in miniature, to be sure) than the usual Indian wars of the plains and Rockies. The engineer also noted that even the open plateau was hard to cross on foot, and impossible to traverse on horseback. It was littered with rocks and cut by deep ravines which, screened by sage and boulders, were man-traps. As troops gingerly picked their way across the tumbled terrain, they made slow and easy targets for a perfectly concealed enemy in natural trenches and rifle pits strengthened by the Modocs with stone walls four or five feet high. And if skirmishers took refuge in one of the ravines, they were likely (in Leydecker's words) to find it "a slaughter pen for those in it." Not until 1933 and the Civilian Conservation Corps was a reasonably accurate tectonic inventory taken. The C.C.C. boys totted up 224 caves, 16 craters and 75 fumaroles or mud craters.

While Wheaton plotted his attack on a fortress he did not really take very seriously, reinforcements were gathering to bolster the strength of his Modoc Expedition. Maj. Edwin Mason, looking romantically warlike in a fur cap and astride a white "war steed," led a battalion of the 21st Infantry (B and C companies) out of Vancouver Barracks and across the Columbia River to Portland, Oregon, by river steamer, thence by train to end-of-track at Roseburg. From there it was shank's mare over the mountains to Fort Klamath and the combat zone. The two companies, described by a correspondent as "joyous" with anticipation of a scrap, hurried as best they could through rain, mud and snow, fearful that the war might end before they got to Fort Klamath. There were times when Quartermaster Boyle, slimy to the waist with viscous mud, could only coax two miles a day out of his double-teamed wagons, though he started them on the road early in the morning and did not let up on them till nightfall. Even when he ordered soldiers to throw their backs into the job, the mired wagons and fatigued men made agonizingly slow progress over the Cascade Mountains. Sodden and footsore in Green Camp near Crater Lake on December 13, they were cheered (despite a foot of snowfall) when a courier brought word from Wheaton that he would wait for Mason before making his attack. Next day, the foot soldiers slogged on through the driving snow as if in route step rather than in the middle of an impossible forced march. Boyle recalled the change in morale and commented, "There *was* some chance of a fight with the Indians and the trip would not be a fruitless one. . . ." The remainder of the impatient journey was uneventful, as Boyle remembered: "In ten days of hard marches, anxious to get to the Modoc country and close out the war, we arrived at Linkville." After resting for two days, the infantrymen bivouacked at Crawley's ranch next to Colonel Green's cavalrymen.

Wheaton hoped to make his attack on December 27, but neither the pair of twelve-pounder bronze mountain howitzers nor the small arms ammunition he needed had arrived as 1872 faded into history. The Oregon volunteers were growing restive. They had signed up for only three months or the duration of the Modoc War, and only the promise of the cannon kept them from leaving at the earliest moment. Brig. Gen. John E. Ross of the Oregon Militia had given the Modocs just one month of freedom after they had stung Captain Jackson near Natural Bridge. The month was up, and what had been done about them? Exactly nothing. He knew that the Modocs would interpret Army delays as cowardice. But, at last, Lt. William H. Miller brought the howitzers into camp and, within only thirty-six hours, Wheaton had transformed a handful of horse soldiers into two efficient gun crews to operate the cannon.

Apache-campaign veterans among Colonel Green's yellowlegs were appalled at Wheaton's apparent timidity. They shook their heads in disbelief as he waited for howitzers to roust fifty or sixty beggarly, root-digging, red-skinned versions of Sir John Falstaff's scarecrows from a badland offering them neither food nor water nor graze for their horses. Perhaps they were joined in these sentiments by some of the restless Oregon militiamen who remembered the advice Lt. John W. Hopkins of the 1st Oregon Cavalry had written to Captain Currey in 1864: "If the Indians are found occupying such strongholds, they can easily be dislodged by a charge on foot, a few men being detailed to hold the horses. They will choose points not accessible on horseback. It will be found of little account to fire at them while they lie concealed. A charge should be made with loaded rifles. The Indians will be sure to run and can be shot down as they run. They were never known to stand a close charge upon their hiding places."

Captain Jack's Modocs grew as tired of Wheaton's waiting game as did the troopers. So they took the war to the Army, venturing as far from their Stronghold as Captain Jackson's old

Lost River battlefield. There they shouted taunts and dares at the soldiers encamped across the river. When the latter still would not fight, with all this insulting and obscene provocation, they loosed a few rounds at them (which did no damage) and left in disgust. The Modocs were next reported at Van Bremer's Mountain or Mount Dome, keeping an eye on Van Bremer's ranch, occupied on December 12 and fortified, like Crawley's and Fairchild's places, by the Oregon volunteers as an Army outpost. Perhaps they guessed that Wheaton planned to move his headquarters there, to be closer to the Lava Beds.

But when the Modocs struck, it was at none of these Army outposts. On Saturday, December 21, a wagon from Camp Bidwell, laden with firewood, commissary stores and much-needed small arms ammunition, approached the camp of Capt. Reuben F. Bernard's G Troop, 1st Cavalry, at Louis Land's ranch on the bay forming the southeast corner of Tule Lake. The tough veteran of the Civil War and Indian wars had sent for supplies after deciding that the Modocs might keep him in the field more than a few days, after all. Just two miles from Bernard's headquarters, as its escort of six cavalrymen began to relax with their destination in sight, the Modocs struck. A shot from the fifteen-foot bank above the road missed the driver but struck the offside wheel mule, wounding the animal fatally, as it proved. Still the teamster whipped the animals into a mad run for safety. Pvt. Sydney Smith of the escort never knew what hit him; he was shot in the head, abdomen and left leg. He was left behind by his panicky comrades, and the corpse was stripped, mutilated (both ears were cut off) and scalped. (This was said to be the only time in the war that the Modocs scalped a victim.) Another of the squad, Pvt. William G. Donahue, was so badly wounded in the spine that he died on the day following the ambuscade.

As soon as he heard the gunfire, Bernard ordered Lt. John G. Kyle to lead a rescue party. Kyle saved the wagon and supplies and drove back the attackers, whom he estimated to number fifty-six men. If so, Captain Jack had brought virtually his entire army out of his rock fortress. When Bernard's frantic courier reached Wheaton, the colonel sent Captain Jackson and B Troop to back up Bernard. They were too late to gain revenge for their Lost River licking, but Wheaton attached them to Bernard's command. He had great confidence in the ability of the tough Tennesseean. Bernard had come up the hard way, working his way from private and farrier or blacksmith to a captaincy. He had been brevetted twice for gallantry during the Civil War and once more in 1869 while engaging Chiricahua Apaches. Bernard was a fighting fool, a genuine soldier of fortune in Army blue who had 103 battles and skirmishes on his record before he retired as a brevet brigadier general in 1896. But in the little scrape near Land's Ranch, Bernard won few laurels. True, his quick reaction had saved a wagonload of supplies. But in exchange for one dead Modoc, Steve, Bernard paid out two dead troopers and four men wounded, and he lost a mule and four cavalry horses. Small wonder if he cursed the Modoc victory fire in the Lava Beds that night, so plainly visible from his tent.

A foolish but lucky traveler from Big Valley, who did not take the Modoc "trouble" seriously, passed safely through the Lava Beds on the Tickner Road, which the Modocs had cut long before. He reported seeing the Indians driving about a hundred head of captured cattle from the bunchgrass pockets of the Lava Beds to Tule Lake in order to water their walking commissary for the upcoming siege. Shortly, the Ball brothers blamed the disappearance of an entire horse herd on the Modocs, and settlers joined the Army rankers in deploring Wheaton's delaying tactics. There was a growing fear that the Pit River Indians would join Captain Jack, with the result that Jack's force would outnumber the Army once the discontented Oregonians should pull out. The day after Christmas, Oliver Applegate wrote John McCall that he was sending an Indian to the Pit Rivers to persuade them not to ally themselves with Jack's renegades. A greater worry was the watchful body of Indians on the Klamath Reservation, fifteen hundred of them guarded by a Fort Klamath garrison of exactly fourteen soldiers. Oliver Applegate could not pry a regular loose from Wheaton to guard Yainax, but he formed up a small force of volunteers and twenty reliable Indian scouts as militiamen on the day after Christmas and reported to his friend, McCall, "With this force and great vigilance I think we will be able to defend Yainax and keep the Indians there all right. . . . Captain Jack's people here said to the Klamath scouts that they are laying plans to *get* two men (civilians), and that they would have their scalps in a week. That was about ten days ago and Ivan and I are all right yet." When it became clear to Oliver that Captain Jack's threats against the Klamath Reservation were empty ones, he let Wheaton have his militiamen for the attack on the Lava Beds.

But exaggerated fears still gnawed at the confidence of soldiers and irregulars as a settler's rumor made the rounds in Yreka, puffing Jack's strength to one hundred warriors (supposedly verified by officers with field glasses) while Wheaton's three-hundred-odd soldiers were being frittered away in guard posts and escort duty until he was said (erroneously) to have only seventy-five effectives to commit to battle.

Wheaton put up with the rumors and, to make sure that he did not lose his grumbling Oregonian auxiliaries, sent them with Capt. David Perry's troop of 1st Cavalry to Van Bremer's ranch, to keep them occupied. He issued them plentiful rations and forage to improve their morale. Shortly, he sent Mason and Green there, ordered Boyle to follow with his quartermaster's depot and, on New Year's Day 1873, shifted his headquarters to Van Bremer's ranch.

On the night of December 27, Yreka citizens met to form a unit of informal California militia similar to Ross's Oregonians. Pressley Dorris, deputized to confer with Gov. Newton Booth, was surprised to find him inclined toward the thinking of Fairchild, Steele and other would-be peacemakers. Booth actually suggested to California's Senator Cornelius Cole that the Modocs be given a 3,100-acre reservation in their own country, rather than driving them back under the guns of Fort Klamath. But Cole replied in the negative. The die had been cast with the order to Fort Klamath to remove the Modocs. A revocation of the order would be considered a victory by the Modocs, explained the senator. And Washington would not hear of such a thing. Cole, the Indian Commissioner and the Senate were as concerned with losing face as had been Major Green when he sent too few men from Fort Klamath against Captain Jack.

A company of California volunteer riflemen was formed at Wheaton's request. In one of those ironies so frequent in the sad story of the Modoc War, Captain Jack's good friend, John A. Fairchild, was elected its captain and commander, with George Roberts his lieutenant. Fairchild must have been ambivalent about his post; he had a duty to protect the lives of his fellow settlers, but he was very much a peace advocate and friend of the Modocs. But the settlers wanted him as their commander so he accepted. Col. William Thompson but echoed the general sentiment of the area when he described Fairchild as being "as brave a man as ever trod in shoe leather." According to Governor Grover of Oregon, twenty-eight men were mustered (other accounts say from twenty-four to twenty-six) and the unit was called, rather grandly, The Independent Company of California Volunteers. The enlisted men were settlers, *vaqueros* or cowboys, and miners from Yreka. The governor of California sent fifty rifles (or old muskets, as critics of Booth claimed) to Yreka, then enraged the patriots by billing them for the freight charges. Twenty-three of the weapons were forwarded to Fairchild's company and the other pieces were kept in the Siskiyou County seat, now jumpy with worry that Captain Jack would sack and burn fair Yreka. The editor of the *History of Siskiyou County* (1881) noted, "The advent of Lee's army in Washington was no more feared and expected than was the appearance of Captain Jack's spartan band in the streets of Yreka."

In justice to Wheaton, he was not really ready to attack. Major Green had issued thirty Fort Klamath Spencer carbines and almost all the spare ammunition to frightened civilians near the fort after Jackson's November fiasco. Major Mason estimated that his infantrymen had only sixty rounds per man and the cavalry less, perhaps forty rounds each. Wheaton himself guessed that some of his makeshift army, outfitted with Sharps rifles as well as .50-calibre Springfields and Spencers, had only five or ten rounds apiece. (The 45/70 breechloading, single-shot Springfield was not adopted as the standard military arm by Gen. Alfred H. Terry's testing committee until the summer of 1873, after ninety-nine different weapons were examined.)

Since the Regular Army was so dilatory, General Ross sent Capt. Harrison Kelly and ten men of his A Company, Oregon Volunteers, with five Indian scouts for the first close-up look at Captain Jack's defenses. The little command saw twenty Modocs leaving the Lava Beds and hurried forward to cut them off. They failed, pulling back in the face of Modoc rifle fire but without suffering any casualties. Incredibly, in an already incredible war, the interpreter for a second scouting party encountered a squaw wandering about alone. She was none other than Captain Jack's sister, Queen Mary, whom Colonel Thompson, curiously, considered the brains of Jack's band. Instead of fleeing the patrol, she approached and asked if they had any guns with them! As the perplexed scouts left her, they were fired on by a single Indian on a nearby hill, suggesting that Mary was a decoy. The return fire of the men caused the sniper to tumble to the ground, but when they reached the rise the only trace of the ambusher was his bloodied gun. Not to be outdone by farmer-soldiers, the regulars sent out a patrol under Major Green. He reconnoitered the flat-topped butte (soon to be named Gillem's Bluff) that dominated both the Lava Beds and the south shore of Tule Lake. The reconnaissance ended, in Green's words, with "a lively brush with the enemy."

Colonel Wheaton's plans, sketched out in his battle order of Jaunary 12, were simple and seemingly effective. He would move first from Van Bremer's to a point on Gillem's Bluff about three miles from Captain Jack's Stronghold. Next day, he would begin the assault at first light from the base of the butte. He would catch Jack like a fish in a net or, better, like an almond in a nutcracker: While he moved his main force from the west, and the lake cut off retreat to the north, Bernard's force would advance like a pincers from the east and prohibit any retreat in that direction. The key to the assault was the linking up of Green's right wing with Bernard's left flank to prevent the Modocs slipping south, deeper into the heart of the Lava Beds.

By January 15, 1873, the two coveted howitzers were ready for action and all postponements of the attack were ended. Wheaton made one last attempt to persuade Jack to lead his men in peacefully, sending a Klamath messenger to his lava castle. But the sixteen Modocs indicted by an Oregon grand jury for murder, for their massacre of an equal number of settlers on Lost River and Tule Lake, overruled such moderates as Captain Jack and Scarfaced Charley. So an exultant—even cocky— Wheaton prepared to round up the guerrillas in the next day or so and to give them the one thing in the world they needed, the "tremendous thrashing" prescribed by Stephen Powers in the pages of the *Overland Monthly*. According to Governor Grover of Oregon, he had 310 regulars, 25 Californians, and A and B Companies of Oregon Militia under Captains Harrison Kelly and Oliver C. Applegate. Applegate, called *Blywas* or Eagle by the Indians, had twenty Klamath scouts as part of his company.

Wheaton advised his superiors that his army was in better condition than any Indian-fighting troops he had ever seen: "We leave for Captain Jack's 'Gibraltar' tomorrow morning and a more enthusiastic and jolly set of Regulars and Volunteers I never had the pleasure to command. If the Modocs will only try to make good their boast to whip a thousand soldiers, all will be satisfied. Our scouts and friendly Indians insist that the Modocs will fight us desperately but I don't understand how they can think of attempting any serious resistance though, of course, we are prepared for their flight or fight."

On January 16, 1873, Captain Bernard quietly stole up to the pedregal with his one hundred troops from Land's Ranch and began the penetration of the Lava Beds. His men wound their way on foot along a rocky trail from which all landmarks were banished by darkness and a heavy tule fog, or ground fog. Bernard led his men too fast and too far in the gloom. According to Lt. W. H. Boyle, this was because he trusted his own judgment over the advice of his scout, a Yahuskin Snake or a Klamath recruited at Yainax and outfitted at Fort Klamath. The dismounted troopers of B and G Companies stumbled upon the enemy just about the time the barking of Indian mongrels warned each party of the other's nearness. The Modocs were briefly in sight but soon recoiled and concealed themselves in the rocky fastness of their Stronghold, their fire halting the soldiers' advance. Bernard ordered his men to retreat as skirmishers. First, B Troop fell back fifty yards under the covering fire of G Troop; then they reversed their roles, and so forth. When the Modocs began to fire on his pack train in the rear, Bernard ordered a short charge, which cost him three wounded but drove the Modocs back and apparently wounded one of their men, Shacknasty Jim. The subsequent pause in the Modoc fire enabled Bernard to withdraw his force to a hillock on the lakeshore, topped with volcanic boulders that gave him good cover. In this ledge position—called Hospital Rock because the wounded, now numbering four, were cared for there—he forted up to await the grand attack at dawn of the seventeenth.

While Bernard's men huddled in the sage of Hospital Rock, many of them not only exhausted and sleepless but uneasy and discouraged, Green's men across the Lava Beds on Gillem's Bluff were yarning nervously over campfires or boasting of having Modoc steak for breakfast. Others drank "lightning bug" (tanglefoot) if they needed courage of the Dutch variety. According to half-Modoc Jeff Riddle, one Oregon volunteer braggart asked a friend, "How are you going to eat your Modoc sirloin for dinner tomorrow, raw or cooked? I am going to eat mine raw. I don't want to take the time to cook it. I want to clean 'em all up before I stop, the red devils."

The little army in the Modoc camp was neither bragging nor worrying but praying, dancing and singing to ensure the power of their shaman's medicine. Curly Headed Doctor had not only planted eight consecrated stakes in a circle around the Strong-hold, he had reinforced that protective device with a long, red-painted cord of much medicine stretched around a portion of the defense. It was guaranteed to be deadly to whites, he assured his coreligionists, as he puffed on his pipe and called on the spirits and his familiars for help. Lastly, he had called down from the heavens a tule fog, or thick, low-lying condensation fog, to conceal the Modocs and blind their enemies.

At 3 A.M., January 17, 1873, a sentry awakened Colonel Wheaton, and soon a rocket whooshed up into the blackness to warn Bernard to begin to move up. The long roll sounded and the men of the various commands fell into ranks, then moved forward at a steady pace toward the rising sun—which they would not see that day. Wheaton's "first light" remained only a figure of speech. In the dense fog of a supposed dawn, they could not see objects only ten paces away. The next soldier in the line appeared indistinct, ghostlike. Some officers hailed the tule fog as a godsend. They saw it as a screen for their advancing skirmishers. But fog or not, whatever element of surprise Wheaton had counted on was dissipated by Bernard's blunder of the night before and by Perry's noisy sweep of Gillem's Bluff. He had chased off a few Modoc pickets and captured nine freshly-butchered beeves in a companion move to Bernard's, but the potshots of the fleeing Modoc sentries alerted their kin in the Stronghold to an impending attack from the west as well as from the east. During Perry's maneuver a big basso voice was heard giving commands in Modoc. It was believed to belong to the ubiquitous Scarfaced Charley, Captain Jack's field com-mander. Field Marshal Charley was hollering, "There are but a few of them and they are on foot! Get your horses! Get your horses!" But Bernard's *faux pas* was more serious. "A sad blunder," commented Boyle, "for had the troops taken their position at night without the knowledge of the Indians, how different might have been the result of the next day's fight."

From Gillem's Bluff it was as impossible to tell where Tule Lake ended and the Lava Beds began as it was to distinguish night from day in the gloomy fog. The whole Modoc plateau lay swathed in cotton wool. Completely masked from the Army were the obstacles Applegate and Fairchild had warned the officers about, although Mason knew that that plateau's surface was "broken like the waves of an ocean." The lunar landscape of scoria and jumbled, jagged volcanic boulders which the troopers were to storm was leveled and smoothed by the strata of fog lying atop it. The soldiers had no idea how the *malpaís,* called "The Land of Burnt-out Fires" by the Modocs, was pocked with volcanic chimneys, tubes, craters and fumaroles as they advanced gingerly into the fog. Little did they know that cinder cones, crevices and more freshly erupted black lava flows of impassable boulders lay atop the pumice, ash rock and gravel-like rapilli of the desolate, scorched and blackened badlands. They were assaulting a fortress that would have impressed Vauban himself, only they did not yet know it.

Cap. Joel G. Trimble could find only one battleground in all American history to compare in difficulty with California's Lava Beds—the sawgrass jungle of the Florida Everglades during the Seminole Wars. With excellent hindsight, Wheaton finally came to appreciate both his foe and the terrain he chose. He called the Lava Beds a second Gibraltar, and no longer meant it facetiously. He wrote Gen. E. R. S. Canby after the battle, "I have been twenty-three years in the service of the Government and have been employed the greater portion of the time in remote frontiers and generally engaged in operating against hostile Indians. In this service I have never before encountered an enemy, civilized or savage, occupying a position of such great natural strength as the Modoc stronghold, nor have I ever seen troops engage a better-armed or a more skillful foe." Col. William Thompson wasted no words in describing the situation of the Modocs in the Lava Beds and the difficulty of getting them out; they were like "ants in a sponge."

Wheaton had his field commander, Maj. John Green, move into the attack with Major Mason anchoring the north end of the line of troops on the lakeshore. The latter's 21st Infantrymen were supported by Fairchild's Californians on what turned out to be an exposed left flank. Captain Perry's H Troop of the 1st Cavalry held the critical center while the Oregon militia marched on the right flank. Brigadier General Ross was outranked by Maj. Gen. John F. Miller, who had been ordered to the front by the governor of Oregon. Miller showed up but did not choose to assume command and took no part in the fight. Although Colonel Thompson and others guessed that Wheaton had 225 Oregonians alone, the colonel really had only 150 cavalrymen and 64 infantrymen in both pincers of his attack, about 60 poorly equipped Oregonians (with little warm clothing or bedding for a winter campaign), 26 Californians and a company of about 30 Klamaths, plus a few Yahuskin Snake scouts. Thus, Wheaton had a force of about 350 men to throw against the 50 to 60 Modoc warriors. For comparison, Lieutenant Colonel Custer's annihilated command at the Little Big Horn, a little over three years later, totaled 264 men.

No trooper saw an Indian as the bugler ordered the advance with a call that was reiterated by the subalterns' and noncoms' shouted commands, "Forward on the line!" So thick was the condensation fog that Miller's howitzers were able to throw only three rounds into the Stronghold from the three hundred rounds of shell, case shot and canister shot at his disposal. The cease-fire order was quickly given, for fear the artillery, firing blindly, would kill more soldiers than Modocs. Boyle observed, "It was a very unfortunate circumstance for the howitzers that we had waited so long for, as the troops had to depend on their rifles." The cavalry, of course, fought dismounted, as horses were even more useless than the fog-blinded gunners. The first shot boomed in the mist at about 7 A.M. as Nate Beswick of Fairchild's California Sharpshooters heard some Oregonians boasting, "I knew them black devils would run when they learned that we volunteers would get after them. We want Injuns. Show us your Injuns and we will show you some dead ones." They had hardly gone fifty yards when the first shot brought them all to a halt—all except Beswick, who fell, writhing on the broken ground and swearing at his Californians, "Damn your souls! Get me out of here! Can't you see I am shot? My thigh is broke." Two of his comrades jumped to help him and, themselves, drew fire. Volunteers and soldiers alike milled in confusion, for still they could see no enemy. All they could fire at was the occasional flash of a Modoc rifle or, more frequently, aim at the direction the sound of fire seemed to be coming from. The soldiers were now about a mile and a half from the base of Gillem's Bluff as they tried to rally, but Pvt. J. N. Terwilliger saw two of his fellow F Troopers fall nearby. He recalled, "We took Hollis under cover, took off his belts, gave him a drink of water and, as he was badly wounded, we signaled the hospital corps, and two men were shot in attempting to reach him."

Earlier, Fairchild had observed that the men could hardly be kept in line in their eager advance to Gillem's Bluff. He had commented, at the time, to one officer, "Don't fret, they won't be hard to keep back when the Modocs open fire." How right he was. The advance began to bog down in the fog as bravado evaporated under the heavy Modoc fire. Private Terwilliger remembered "the fog being so thick we could almost cut it with a knife." The skirmishers advanced from boulder to boulder, sagebrush to sagebrush—and never saw an enemy. Only the wink of a muzzle blast and a puff of white smoke briefly betrayed the hidden Modocs, as a trooper would stagger and drop. Somehow, Modoc eyes were able to pierce the opaque fog. When they retreated, it was only to a better position to pick off the attackers. Green's advance became a creep, then came to a halt.

Sadly, the men most sympathetic to the Modoc cause suffered the most in the early stages of the First Battle of the Lava Beds. Fairchild's Californians bore the brunt of the first volleys, until Perry ordered them back and placed his regulars ahead of them. Perry's men were eager for a fight, afraid that Bernard's "Apache boys," so-called for their Arizona campaigning, might get all the glory. Fairchild saw Nate Beswick get wounded, then Jerry Crooks and Judson Small. His second in command, George Roberts, was then hit. He was mortally wounded but did not know it. Roberts was still walking around next day with his skull smashed in by a Modoc rifle slug, his brains protruding. He shortly expired. The Oregonians did not have it any easier; two men were shot dead. Then it was the turn of the regulars as Captain Perry was seriously wounded in arm and hip and Lieutenant Kyle also shot, besides a number of enlisted men.

Briefly, some of Green's regulars linked up with Bernard's men at the south end of the two converging lines, but the connection was immediately broken by the Modocs at a deep chasm the soldiers reached at two in the afternoon. It effectively separated Wheaton's two units. Bernard was pinned down after falling back from the critical gorge some three hundred yards to a position of more cover. His trap refusing to spring, Colonel Wheaton now decided to reverse his plan, upon a suggestion from Green. Since a charge across the crevasse would involve a great sacrifice of men, they decided to abandon encirclement on the south for a linkage of the two corps on the north at the lakeshore. Bernard's men were not of much help in this maneuver, being not only in defensive positions but in very much of a defensive psychology by now. They were lying behind hastily thrown up, but effective, little rock forts that they copied from the Modocs. Although Wheaton's new orders were successfully shouted across to them, they were loath to leave the shelter of their rifle pits.

Although the fog was beginning to lift and disperse by 2 P.M., the new encircling movement did not proceed well. It all but petered out as the Oregonians balked at participating in it, claiming that another gash in the lava prevented a junction on the north as well as the south. Colonel Thompson, the Oregonians' later propagandist, reported that they captured "the juniper fort," apparently a rock outpost, and prevented annihilation of Fairchild's, Mason's and Perry's forces. This is hard to swallow since Thompson also had Donald McKay in the thick of the fray, and he was not there at all. Still, Thompson's general "feel" for the battle was accurate; the offensive had bogged down. He heard the zing of Modoc rifle balls around his ears from sharpshooters so well camouflaged with sagebrush that they were unseen when close up. Patrick Maher, he reported, was shot—*somehow*—in the stomach while crawling forward on his belly, and Oregonian Jud Small was shot in the arm by a Modoc he could not see, though the man was only twenty feet from him. The Modocs were as invisible as chameleons. According to Thompson, some frightened soldiers just hid in the waters of Tule Lake, only their heads visible, waiting—and praying—for darkness to come so they could make their escape from the deadly Modoc fire.

With both the California and Oregon volunteers worsted by the Modocs, the regulars now found themselves pinned down singly or in scattered little groups. The skirmish line had vanished. Perry reported, "It was at this point our greatest number of casualties occurred. I was wounded about 4 P.M., having raised myself upon my left elbow to look at a man who had just been killed" The ball hit him in the arm and passed around his hip. He rolled downhill, out of the fight. The *Call* gave Perry's wounding as the turning point of the battle. It disheartened the soldiers just as they were looking to him to rally them in a charge. Whatever starch was left in the soldiers' spines was knocked loose when Kyle was hit, as he assumed command of the charge from Perry. Bernard replaced Kyle with Boutelle. Poor Kyle! The jolly West Pointer from Ohio, whose classmates at the Military Academy wrote of him, "Those who knew the hearty, generous disposition of Kyle, with his ingenuous humor, will long remember his good fellowship," was born under an unlucky star. As his 1870 classmates reported at their 1877 reunion, "He received a severe wound in the shoulder, from the effects of which he never entirely recovered." Hospitalized at Fort Klamath, he returned to duty but in October 1874 accidentally was shot at Camp Bidwell. He spent the next year at Fort Klamath, but from January to November 1876 he was confined to a Government insane asylum in

Washington, where he died on March 30, 1877, at the age of only twenty-eight. Ironically, he was promoted to first lieutenant while insane.

A desperate Green now stood up in plain view and cussed his men to try to move them forward. He ignored the hot enemy fire, and the brave gesture won him a Congressional Medal of Honor, but did not save the disintegrating advance. The often inaccurate Colonel Thompson reported that Wheaton joined Green, waving a sword "taken from a bugler," and that the Oregonians wished to charge the Stronghold but Wheaton would not give his consent. But the chances are excellent that no one wanted to move forward an inch. Green saw his line go to pieces before his very eyes. The only men who made their way over to Bernard's zone were those trapped in no-man's-land and desperately fearful of being taken prisoner by the Modocs as they saw their assault collapsing around them.

By five o'clock the fog had cleared off the entire Lava Beds battlefield and, in Jeff Riddle's words, "Just before sunset, the bank of fog worked its way north like some live monster and settled over the north part of Tule Lake." A beaten Wheaton, in his almost abandoned headquarters, ordered his signal officer, John Quincy Adams, to signal both Bernard and Green to break off all action. The first battle of the Lava Beds was over.

Or so thought Wheaton. But the Modocs were not yet ready to call it quits. They sallied forth from their Stronghold and easily pierced the broken line of troops to get to their rear. The soldiers, their uniforms, shoes and skin torn by the rough lava over which they had been literally crawling for hours, now hid wherever they could until darkness would allow them to retreat, pell-mell, to Gillem's Bluff. The withdrawal resembled a minuscule version of the famous "runaway scrape" of Texas Republic history.

John Fairchild, certainly no coward, was trapped in no-man's-land with Capt. George H. Burton and some of the latter's C Company as the line of skirmishers disintegrated and the offensive passed to the Modocs, who now infiltrated the Army's lines. There was not a ghost of a chance of rescuing the dying, or the dead for burial. The bodies were left lying where they were. At least one soldier was captured alive and taken to the Stronghold to be killed by a squaw in revenge for the death of her man at Lost River. The retreat almost became a complete rout as the frightened and isolated troopers saw Indian signal fires winking in their rear, apparently cutting off their retreat to headquarters. But most of them made it in the darkness.

Fairchild, hugging the ground, ended his military career that day. He had had a bellyful of fighting his one-time friends. On the 24th he wrote a Yreka acquaintance, "I have conversed with several officers, old Indian fighters, who say they never saw Indians fight as the Modoc devils fought the other day. . . . The day was very unfavorable. The fog was so dense we could not see fifty yards. As we charged the Indians they could hear the commands of our officers and always tell where we were and we could not see them. The first we would know we would receive a deadly volley. I have been in a good many close places but that beat anything I ever saw. Our boys were in the hottest of the fight. I am in hopes Governor Booth will change his mind and let us raise some troops. I think the officers believe Dorris and myself told them the facts about the Indians and their location. The Regulars fought well and charged stronghold after stronghold. The Indians would fire and fall back. Colonel Green took more chances than any man I ever saw. He walked the lines and gave his orders during the hottest of the fight and never took shelter or dodged. It looked like a miracle he escaped."

All sorts of excuses were later made for Wheaton's debacle—fbe fog, particularly, but also the unexpected ruggedness of the field. The damned chasm that prevented a linkup of the two corps was an especial target, but so too was the pusillanimity of the Klamaths, the timorousness of some of the Oregonians and the lack of rations or other provisions, which make it impossible to hold even the Army's best positions within the Lava Beds. Boyle was again highly critical of Bernard, who, he said, "did not obey the orders of Colonel Green when ordered to advance his left so as to draw the fire of the Indians."

As the battle dwindled to its end, the Modocs were cutting through the line where Fairchild's riflemen joined Perry's yellowlegs. They then turned the corner as neatly as if Scarfaced Charley had studied Clausewitz in his *wickiup*. They headed north for Tule Lake to outflank and surround the Californians. They were thwarted in this maneuver because Fairchild's men fought stubbornly for their survival and Burton's infantrymen came to their aid. So the Modocs pivoted and headed for Gillem's Bluff, Wheaton's lightly protected headquarters—and possibly Yreka, Portland and San Francisco!

Already the Oregonians had fallen back to the bluff for a

consultation with Wheaton. This led to the colonel signaling Green and Bernard to withdraw. It was an order they would have loved to comply with, but the Modocs would not let them disengage. Official reports later described the Army withdrawal as a rapid but orderly climb to the top of the bluff where Wheaton decided to make a stand. But participants termed the retreat "a wild free-for-all." Even the boastful Colonel Thompson had to admit that he found himself protecting litter bearers and wounded in the rear as the soldiers rushed to Gillem's Bluff, then huddled at its base, afraid to climb to the top as the rumor spread that Jack had seized it. Thompson claimed he personally clambered up and verified the fact that the Army's guards were still there. That night, Lieutenant Boyle asked General Ross what commands he had given in the battle. He answered that his only order, all day, had been "Get up the bluff!" And he stated that he had followed his own command by grabbing hold of the tail of a mule, taking a double-hitch around his arm, and letting the beast tow him up the slope as if "Old Harry" was after him. Colonel Thompson, who liked his nickname of "Governor Grover's Mad-Cap Colonel," euphemized the movement of Green as a "relief column." Actually, the German found his retreat to Gillem's Bluff cut off by infiltrating Modocs and retreated eastward to join Bernard. The Army was saved only by the short military "attention span" of Scarfaced Charley and his men. They had done enough for one day; they let the panicked men climb the bluff.

The soldiers already atop Gillem's Bluff suffered almost as much as the stragglers who made their way up in terror during the night. They did not know they were safe there; the weather was cold; and most of them had thrown away their rations, if not their weapons. Even Wheaton had only coffee and a couple of crackers for his supper. Many of the men were almost barefoot, for the sharp lava had cut their shoes to ribbons.

Colonel Wheaton's grand attack was a grandiose failure, a bloody fiasco saved from complete disaster, perhaps, by the presence of Kelly's Oregon volunteers, who accidentally formed a screen around the colonel's headquarters—with its supplies, ammunition and artillery all packed on mules ready for the order to advance which never came. Since Wheaton had only a guard of ten men, the skulking Modocs might have nabbed the commander himself were it not for the presence of the Oregonians.

Nor had Green's wrong-way retreat been a picnic stroll. He

withdrew all the way to Land's Ranch to get clear of the Modocs, after a breather at Hospital Rock on the Lava Beds shore of Tule Lake. Resuming his retreat at ten-thirty at night, his men marched an average of only a mile an hour on bruised and cut feet. When they finally reached Louis Land's place, practically the whole command fell into a stupor of exhausted sleep. With no litters, the wounded had to be carried out of the lava in blankets held by their comrades or on the backs of a few Indian ponies captured during the battle. Private Terwilliger remembered how a Troop G cook spooked the whole nervous outfit at the Hospital Rock rest when he broke open a cracker box with an axe. "It sounded just like a shot, and every trooper was out of his tent with his carbine."

Boyle reported his horror at hearing the groans of the wounded as they were jostled against sharp lava rocks. He and Lt. William H. Miller both singled out Jerry Crooks of Fairchild's California Company as the bravest of the wounded. He had taken a rifle ball in one leg, which broke the bone so badly he could not be carried in a blanket. So he rode a pony with his leg dangling loosely. When it struck boulders or even stubborn sagebrush, the pain was terrible. Finally, his comrades tied a rope around the leg so that it could be lifted when his mount came to an obstacle. Still, Boyle wrote, "It was sickening to see the expression on his face, and the pain he must have endured was excruciating."

Miller saw another man who was shot through the left arm, the ball severing the artery. He lay in a pool of blood in the red-stained lava, too weak from loss of blood to even move. Barely alive, he was carried all the way to the top of Gillem's Bluff by four comrades who each threw a corner of a blanket over one shoulder to make a stretcher for him. The man, livid as a ghost from shock and blood loss, almost fainted every time his tired buddies lowered him to the ground to change positions as impromptu litter bearers.

Wheaton marched his troops off at dawn to reach Van Bremer's Ranch at two in the afternoon, foot weary and demoralized. There were wagons for the wounded but no food except beef, since the supplies had not come up, and the profiteering Van Bremers charged fifty cents an egg and accepted only cash. Green had to make a long roundabout march from Land's Ranch to Lost River to Van Bremer's to rejoin his superior. Bernard was left to hold Land's Ranch. General Ross moved his dispirited volunteers all the way back to Jacksonville and Fairchild's company began to fall apart, although Ross praised the Californians highly, saying, "They bore themselves nobly, displaying a dauntless courage and bravery." A gloomy Fairchild dashed off a note to R. O. DeWitt on January 22: "There is no telling what the Indians will not do if something is not done for us, and that very soon. You need not be surprised to hear of some terrible murders, as you can readily see we are in a bad fix."

According to Wheaton, he had forty killed and wounded, but this figure later shrunk. Perhaps Governor Grover's figures are as good as any; he reported thirty-seven men killed or wounded among the regulars; two Oregonians killed and five wounded; and one California officer killed and four men badly wounded, two of whom died.

Meanwhile, the Modocs were scouting the battlefield, looting the corpses the Army had had to abandon and taking prisoner two Klamaths, Night Traveler and another unnamed scout, whom they found hiding in a cave. They amused themselves by making their prisoners perform mock war dances and other "monkeyshines," to use Jeff Riddle's term. The Modocs picked up nine Army carbines and six belts of ammunition as well as the arms left by the volunteers in their flight—Spencer sporting rifles, Henry rifles, Remingtons and Ballards. They found loose ammunition scattered all over the ground.

A bewildered and chagrined Wheaton on January 21 decided to fall back to Lost River to establish his headquarters at Lone Pine Ford, later called Stukel Ford, above Crawley's cabin and well upstream from the Natural Bridge. Wheaton had commanded nineteen thousand men at the Battle of the Wilderness in the Civil War. He now found himself whipped by some sixty Modocs. One man, Oregon reporter S. A. Clarke, was not surprised by the outcome of the Battle of the Lava Beds. He wrote: "Your hunter is the raw material out of which your warrior is made. . . . Trained to track his game and bring it down on the run, he feels infinitely superior to the mere parade soldier, who knows the manual of arms and has occasional target practice but is in no practical sense a marksman."

Wheaton planned to remain at Lost River until his battered men were reinforced properly. He hoped to have a boatwright build two flatboats to use as floating mortar batteries for bombarding the Stronghold. He asked permission to secure four whitehall rowboats from Jacksonville to transport supplies across Tule Lake to Mason's base, but later changed his request and asked for two more flatboats, to handle his howitzers. He vowed to surround the Modocs and batter down the lava reefs of the Modoc Stronghold, next time, with mortar and howitzer fire. He was quoted in the Yreka *Union* as saying that one hundred thousand men in one hundred thousand years could not build as strong a fortification as the Stronghold; still, he was sure he could invest it with just one thousand men and some mortars. Wheaton could not know that the Modocs were already losing their fear of artillery—the "guns that go off twice"—and their explosive shells, which the Modocs called "firing cans of powder." As for the soldiers in an open fight, the Modocs had never had any real fear of them to lose.

Wheaton told Canby that he had learned a lot from the battle and, next time, he would whip the Modocs for sure. Governor Grover echoed this line of thought, reporting to Gen. John Schofield on the Lava Beds battle that although the attack by Wheaton had not been successful, it had exposed the difficulties of the battlefield and the character of the enemy. Many must have observed that it had been a very expensive course of study for Wheaton.

The colonel knew he could not carry the Stronghold by a frontal attack without more artillery. But with boats, mortars and howitzers, he was sure he could do the job. Bernard was not so sanguine. He wrote a friend, "Many of the troops would rather serve ten (10) years in Alcatraz for desertion than attack the enemy again in the lava beds." But he liked the idea of boats and howitzers, if effectively used. Still, he told Wheaton it would take a force of seven hundred men to storm the Stronghold—and with the loss of half the force in killed and wounded. Mason approved of the idea of the boats for transporting men without the fatigue of long marches and for moving wounded men without the painful jostling of stretchers and ambulances. And, finally, the gunboats could cut the Modocs off from their water supply.

Lt. Stephen Jocelyn typified the many men who severely criticized Wheaton as an officer who had commanded a division of the 6th Corps in the Civil War only to be whipped by well less than a hundred "shirttail Indians." But Lt. William H. Boyle was typical of a larger number of men and officers who still had faith in Wheaton. He was fiercely loyal to him and defended him strongly: "I am positive that no more could have been done under the circumstances we had to contend with. . . . Had the Volunteers maintained their line during the day and not fallen

A classic combat photograph of America's Indian wars is this picture of a picket post in the Lava Beds during the Modoc War. The troopers, wary of Modoc sharpshooters, peer gingerly over a barricade of volcanic boulders thrown up in imitation of Modoc defenses of Captain Jack's Stronghold.

The huddling pines and lush meadows of Fort Klamath were a great contrast to the Modoc Lava Beds, a waterless, treeless *malpaís* or volcanic badland in which the Modoc Indians chose to make their stand against Fort Klamath's horse soldiers.

Fort Klamath, Oregon, where California's Modoc Indian War began with the dispatching of a troop of cavalry to round up Captain Jack, and where the tragic conflict ended with the trial and execution of Jack and three of his chief lieutenants in the fall of 1873.

Cavalry troopers stand at ease at the base of Gillem's Bluff before an advance into the Lava Beds as foot soldiers during the Modoc War.

Even Coehorn mortars and artillery, like the battery of 12-pound howitzers in a volcanic-rock emplacement, did not overimpress the Modocs in the two sieges of their Stronghold in the Lava Beds during 1873.

When artist J. N. Marchand pictured the Battle of Hardin Butte, or the Battle of Black Ledge, called the Thomas-Wright Massacre by the Army, he unconsciously grouped the troopers—panicked by Scarfaced Charley's ambush—in the traditional circle of "Custer's Last Stand," gathered around their rash commander, Capt. Evan Thomas.

Thirty-five years after the Lost River raid of Fort Klamath cavalry of November 29, 1872, on Captain Jack's villages, artist J. N. Marchand sought to document the opening battle of the tragic Modoc War in oils.

Even the *London Illustrated News* had a war correspondent covering the conflict in the Lava Beds. He was William Simpson, a talented artist as well as a writer. No photographer was present at the Peace Tent on Good Friday 1873, when Captain Jack (left, center) murdered Gen. E. R. S. Canby while under a flag of truce, but Simpson's drawing is an accurate representation of the scene.

So heavy were casualties for the Army in the Modoc War, and so painful was their evacuation by litter bearers over the rocky trails of the Lava Beds, that the Army invented a mule-back reclining chair to take the place of stretchers or litters.

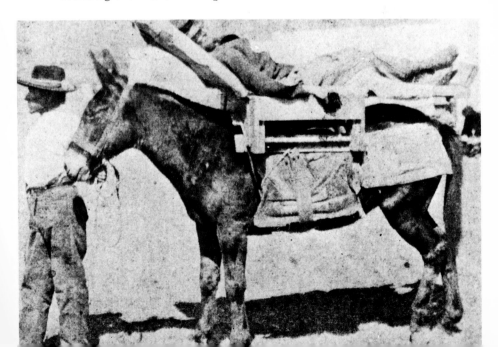

View of Gillem's Bluff from the stone corral of the 1st Cavalry, used briefly as a prison for the Army's sole Modoc prisoner, Long Jim. He did not like his lodgings and escaped one midnight.

Fort Klamath infantry stands at parade rest in front of one of the long barracks of the post, before or after the nightmare of the Modoc Expedition to the Lava Beds.

A panoramic view of Gillem's Camp, at the southwestern corner of shallow Tule Lake adjacent to the Modoc Lava Beds. Note the round corral of volcanic boulders built by the 1st Cavalry for its mounts.

Wisely, Alex McKay, war correspondent for the San Francisco *Evening Bulletin,* scribbles a dispatch in the Modoc Lava Beds near a sentry post, occupied by two nervous troopers armed with Spencer carbines.

War correspondent William M. Bunker likened the Fort Klamath guardhouse (on the outside) to a "comely" family home. Captain Jack of the Modocs did not find it a satisfactory lodge as he waited there for his October 1873 date with a U.S. Army hangman.

back, and the Indian allies under Captain Applegate been of any assistance, we might have succeeded in killing some Modocs. . . . Never did men fight better than did the Regular troops during that day's fight and, without exception, the officers did all that could be expected of them." However, Lieutenant Boyle was highly unimpressed by the Webfoot minutemen: "The Oregon Volunteers had learned that the Indians would fight and would not run at the approach of the soldiers. . . . They were not as anxious to shoot Modocs as they were in the morning."

New excuses for the size of Wheaton's debacle began to pile up. His supplies were inadequate. Just as there were no litters or stretchers for the wounded, so too there were no ambulances and the hurt men had to be jolted all the way to the Fort Klamath hospital in wagons. And although the entire effective strength of the Army for the whole United States in 1873 was only about nineteen thousand men, Wheaton could not find equipment a half-dozen years after the Civil War to fit out his several hundred men with such essentials as canteens and haversacks. When he ordered them from Fort Klamath in January, the C.O. of that ghost-post, Lt. Robert Pollock, had to reply that none were to be had in the Fort Klamath warehouses. (In April, Wheaton's successor again asked for them and again they were not available at Fort Klamath, his base.)

One story had Captain Jack's squaws acting as spies in an intelligence corps that worked the four-posters of Yreka and Linkville for information on troop movements. It is unlikely that Jack had even one Mata Hari. But the Klamath allies of the Army proved to be something of a secret weapon for Jack. They were judged so worthless that they were discharged and sent back to Fort Klamath in disgrace, although two of them had been captured and at least one, Chief Mogenkaskit, was wounded in one shoulder by a Modoc bullet that richocheted off his gun. The Klamath scouts were accused not only of cowardice but of aiding and abetting the enemy by informing them of the location of troops and even leaving powder and ball for Jack's snipers. According to Boyle, the Klamaths fired their rifles into the air and did some tall shouting, but no fighting. This was later borne out by Scarfaced Charley's testimony in the trial of Captain Jack. The Klamaths were a great disappointment to their commander, Oliver Applegate, if not to his lieutenant, Chief Dave Hill, who must have known what they were up to.

Curly Headed Doctor's fog storm took much of the blame for

the Army's defeat, although many soldiers blessed it for hiding them from the Modocs, as well as vice versa. Wheaton's succinct reports suggested that the fog, on balance, helped the Indians most. "The Modocs were scarcely exposed at all to our persistent attacks. They left one ledge to gain another equally secure. One of our men was wounded twice during the day but he did not see an Indian at all, tho' we were under fire from eight a.m. until dark."

The troops may have been plagued with misfiring weapons, to make matters worse. Trooper C. B. Hardin complained of the poor working of the extractor on the first issue of Springfield carbines and also criticized the other arms issued to the soldiers: "Once during an engagement in the Modoc War, when all was going well with me until a shell stuck in the Sharps carbine, I was almost in a panic until the shell was removed. Then all went well again. In another engagement in the same war, a certain troop, 1st Cavalry, armed with Spencer carbines, went into action with a bad lot of rim-fire cartridges. Several men of that troop told me that the failure of so many cartridges almost caused a panic and would have caused a panic had it not been for the fact that the other troops with them had Sharps carbines that never missed fire. Mortal man cannot withstand a well-armed enemy when his own weapon is not working properly. The few shots that he can fire must be ineffective while his nerves are unstrung."

Army marksmanship—or, rather, the lack of it—may have had something to do with Wheaton's defeat, too, as well as weapon malfunction and an ammunition shortage (although there was plenty for the picking up after the battle). Not until 1872 did the Army even adopt a course of small arms instruction including the firing of ninety rounds at a target with a service rifle. Green soldiers slammed back by the brutal recoil of a carbine would be unlikely to hit the Lava Beds in a pea-soup fog, much less an individual Modoc. Small wonder that the Indians could later boast to Albert Gatschet that Scarfaced Charley, the leader possessed of the best military and engineering capacity on both sides during the war, claimed that he held his station against a platoon of cavalry with only three squaws to help him load his weapons.

Although some officers, such as Stephen Jocelyn, believed Jack had a hundred men, the Indians told Gatschet that they had seventy warriors in the January 17 fight (and only fifty-one in April's second battle of the Lava Beds), but Meacham believed they used only fifty-three men—and boys—in the defeat of Wheaton. The Modocs told Meacham that they knew exactly how many soldiers and militiamen there were because the spirits pointed out each one to Curly Headed Doctor when he was in one of his medicine-making trances.

Not all the Modocs were satisfied, however, with Curly Headed Doctor's protective measures. Peter Schonchin, who fought beside his father, John Schonchin, concluded that the doctor's medicine had little of the power of, say, Jakalumas, the sorcerer of old, who brushed his hair at noon with porcupine quills, smoked the largest pipe ever seen, and filled it with self-igniting tobacco before causing the Modocs' Paiute and Warm Springs enemies to die in droves during a war. Young Schonchin saw the spell broken by advancing troopers. "We saw soldiers coming toward our camp. As they came closer we saw that one of the leaders had a sabre. Behind him, two other leaders were followed by the troops. As they came close to the [sacred, taboo] string the leaders shouted 'Mark!' and the soldiers dropped to their knees. They shouted 'Fire!' and the soldiers shot all around. They then ran over the string. The string did not kill the soldiers. Indian bullets did that. I saw it with my own eyes. After that, I did not believe it any more. My father, John Schonchin, was an intelligent man. The last time my father believed in doctors was when the soldiers crossed the string. He said, 'This is the last time we'll believe in doctors. We'll ask them no more!' Then my father and the others discussed the many times they had asked doctors to kill other people and it never happened; how many times they called doctors to cure and they didn't cure; and how many times they asked for rain and didn't get it. They spoke of how the doctors always claimed they were responsible when these things did happen. My father and the others were badly disappointed in the doctors."

But despite the agnosticism of Schonchin, *pere et fils,* many of the Modocs had their faith in Curly Headed Doctor's magic renewed by the great victory. He believed, even before the Ghost Dance craze, that the Modoc dead would be restored to life, soon, and would come to the aid of Jack's beleaguered band, while the "Americans" would be swallowed up by Mother Earth.

Wheaton's long withdrawal was not determined entirely by fear of a Modoc pursuit while his men were suffering, in the words of the *Army and Navy Journal,* a "morbid fear or panic," but perhaps as much because war profiteering was already rearing its ubiquitous and unlovely head. The Van Bremers were charging four bits for a single egg. Col. William Thompson recalled the ranch of the Van Bremer brothers on Willow Creek with sour humor: "From that time until our departure, I spent a considerable portion of my time in studying human villainy with the Van Bremers as a model."

The colonel was deeply distressed by his whipping, although the *Call* tried to dismiss the reverse as "nothing more than a forced reconnaissance," and the governor of Oregon wrote Gen. William T. Sherman that Wheaton retained the confidence of his officers and men, who felt that in the campaign he had accomplished everything possible for any officer to accomplish. But according to Dr. Bell of the Oregon volunteers, Wheaton's "forced reconnaissance" had not only wrecked the morale of civilians and military alike on the California-Oregon border but had cost him fourteen dead soldiers and twenty-three wounded out of some three hundred actually engaged. Captain Jack did not lose a man, of course, but may have had a few braves lightly nicked by some of the flying lead. The weapons and the thousand rounds of ammunition he garnered from his victory proved a real windfall. Until then, his men often had to fight with old octagonal-barreled Kentucky-style muzzle-loaders. At short range their trajectory was deadly even with the small ball they discharged, but Jack welcomed more modern armament.

Whether Wheaton was crushed by the failure of his regulars or was merely politicking in hopes of keeping his Oregon auxiliaries in arms, he praised the volunteers more than the career soldiers, thus speaking in opposition to Boyle (and the Modocs). If it was a political ploy, it failed. Both the California and Oregon companies mustered themselves out of existence with alacrity only surpassed by their sprint from the Lava Beds to Gillem's Bluff in the twilight of January 17, 1873. They were delighted to leave Captain Jack to the Lava Beds and the Lava Beds to Captain Jack. As far as they were concerned, Curly Headed Doctor's scruffy rabbit-skin and hawk-feather medicine flag could wave over the Lava Beds in lieu of Old Glory till eternity. (Later, new companies of Oregon volunteers would be mustered to help wind up the war.) But reinforcements of regulars were arriving, such as James Biddle's K Troop from Fort Halleck—a "hard-looking" bunch, according to Artillery Corp. Gilbert Davis. They had made a rough six-day march through ice and snow via Louis Land's abandoned spread near the southeast corner of Tule Lake.

Captain Perry was taken to Camp Warner to recover, since his family was there, but the remainder of the wounded were posted to Fort Klamath. In their hospital ward the men who had bragged that they would have "Modoc steak for breakfast" now made a combination of Metz and Hadrian's Wall of the Stronghold, with tales of its inexhaustible springs and ice caves, the bunchgrass pastures hidden in the volcanic jungle of rocks, the fresh water and fish in Tule Lake. How they snorted when someone read to them from the January 22, 1873, issue of the San Francisco *Call* that "Eight hundred or a thousand well-armed men ought to be able to bring the war to a close in short order."

Wheaton, while he awaited reinforcements and artillery, sent out a few cavalry detachments to intercept any raids from the Lava Beds upon surrounding ranches, but he certainly did not bottle up the Modocs. When Lt. David Ream took an escort of the last twenty-five Oregon volunteers to Bernard's Camp from Van Bremer's Ranch with the horses of Fairchild's disbanded company, he ran into a four-man Modoc patrol within six miles of Lost River. Civilians now began to fear that Jack would lead marauds against the Butte Creek Valley settlements only forty miles from Yreka and perhaps even down into Shasta Valley, heretofore considered as safe as Sausalito from Modoc raids.

All of Wheaton's plans for a return engagement with Captain Jack were aborted on January 23, 1873. He was replaced in command of the Modoc Expedition by a Tennessee-born West Pointer, Col. Alvan C. Gillem. The latter was his superior and C.O. of the 1st Cavalry Regiment. Wheaton was sent to the local Siberia (Camp Warner) again because of his failure. But the *Army and Navy Journal* prophesied with fair-to-middling accuracy that "Time will fully vindicate General Wheaton in every particular and those who have cried 'blunder!, blunder!' when there was no blunder will realize the fact of having done a brave officer a cruel injustice."

At the war dance of the Modocs following their victory, Shacknasty Jim said, "I can stand off twenty of them volunteers now because I have got me a nice Henry rifle and plenty of cartridges. I also have plenty of volunteer hats." The Modocs decided to try out their new weaponry on the disarrayed Army. They chose Bernard as their target for the second time. He had established a cavalry camp at Applegate's Ranch on Clear Lake and was receiving two wagonloads of grain in a repeat of the earlier incident. This time, however, he beefed his escort from six men to twenty-two troopers. But still the Modocs attacked, again about two miles from Land's Ranch. However, the strong escort not only fought them off while a messenger brought reinforcements, but suffered no casualties. Although the skirmish again documented an Army handicap— the Modocs could understand all the white's commands and could react to them while the reverse was anything but the case—the skirmish was a draw and almost a victory for the Army. Boyle claimed the wagons were partly burned by the Modocs before they fled, but the troopers pursued the raiders so hard that they abandoned their ponies and took to the Lava Beds on foot. Captain Bernard then rounded up forty-five cayuses, which Jack could not really spare.

Even before Colonel Gillem arrived on February 7, the whole complexion of the war changed. On the penultimate day of January, Secretary of War William Belknap ordered all hostilities against the Modocs to cease, although the Army could still protect settlers from attack. His fellow Cabinet member, Secretary of the Interior Columbus Delano, had decided to send a Peace Commission to end the Modoc War without further spilling of blood.

But the idea was not Delano's, nor President Grant's, but Meacham's, although Colonel Thompson wrote mordantly that eastern sentimentalists had shed a barrelful of crocodile tears and "the churches succeeded in hypnotizing the grim soldier in the White House and the result was the Peace Commission." Actually, Meacham and Lindsay Applegate met and talked in Washington while the former was a member of the Electoral College convened there. They persuaded Delano to give peace a chance, and the Secretary responded by naming Meacham head of the Peace Commission. He was very much in favor of negotiations rather than force, so he accepted. He agreed with his predecessor, Huntington, who had remarked: "Ten good soldiers are required to wage successful war against one Indian. Every Indian killed or captured . . . cost the Government fifty thousand dollars, at least."

The time was apropos to think of a commission for peace. Wheaton verified a rumor that Jack was interested in peace by sending Lt. John Quincy Adams to question Fairchild, who of all the whites had his ear closest to the ground. Fairchild told

Adams that Jack, Scarfaced Charley and a few others wanted peace but Curly Headed Doctor, Shacknasty Jim, Bogus Charley, Ellen's Man George and others violently opposed the idea, mostly because the Oregon murder indictments were considered death warrants. But Fairchild thought a powwow was worth a chance. So an intermission was declared by Washington in the Modoc War as the Army licked its still-stinging wounds.

The armistice did not put a stop to the arrival of reinforcements, and the strength of the Modoc Expedition continued to grow. One of the recruits was Corp. Gilbert F. Davis of a Fort Stevens artillery battery. If he was typical of the foot soldiers of the Modoc War (except for his literacy), the Army's rough going against such professional "soldiers" as Scarfaced Charley and Hooker Jim is explicable. All Davis ever thought about was girls. On the train from Portland to Roseburg he noted some nice towns and pretty women. Marching south, he scrawled in his diary on the last day of January, "Feel very lonely tonight. I am thinking of my girl. Saw a very passable girl today. Should liked to of kiss her." He liked Ashland. Why?—"Plenty of girls, splendid looking." After slogging through the snowy Siskiyou Mountains, he reached the Klamath Lake area on Lincoln's Birthday and noted, patriotically, "Saw two half-breeds girls. They was very pretty."

Once in camp, there were no girls. (Curiously, the Modoc War lacked one campaign element—no camp followers.) Boredom assailed the adolescent soldier: "Nothing doing about the Indians yet. Wish they would do something or send us home. . . . Captain Jack talks peace. Think we will go home soon. Some of the men wants to fight and some wants peace. As for myself, I don't care. One thing is as good as another to me." Later, as the pendulum swung, he almost became excited: "Strong talk of a fight. . . . Great excitement. Fight, we are bound to fight." It was with disgust that he wrote, a little later, of Canby, "The Gen'l seems to be afraid of the Indians." Monte and other card games and baseball—on the edge of the Lava Beds!—helped fill the time, but the hurry-up-and-wait tradition of the Army was palling on Davis, and he wrote in his diary, "Captain Jack says he will not talk any more. Things look bad. There is too much humbugging already. Something ought to be done."

CHAPTER NINE

THE PEACE COMMISSION

Shortly after the creation of the Peace Commission, which was to substitute doves and olive boughs for carbines and howitzers in dealing with the renegade Modocs, the new commanding officer of the Modoc Expedition, Col. Alvan C. Gillem, learned that Gen. E. R. S. Canby was coming to personally oversee negotiations as a kind of ex-officio commissioner.

Canby had originally taken command of the Army's Department of the Pacific in 1870 because he needed a rest from a tiring Civil War decade of active service. He found peace and quiet for two years, with his force of 1,225 men seemingly adequate to handle the policing demands of the Northwest Indian frontier. But in 1871 he asked for more men, and no wonder; the desertion of 268 men that year reduced his fighting force by twenty percent. By 1872, when 239 more men deserted, he knew that his command was inadequate to keep the peace. Captain Jack had left the Klamath Reservation in 1870 to find game thinned out in the Lost River country by the growing number of settlers and many of his best *camas* fields turned into pastures or crop lands, surveyed and settled under preemption laws in his absence. Were it not for the fish in the streams and lakes, the Modocs would have been reduced to two choices—starve or steal. During the winter of 1870-1871 Canby had helped the Modocs by authorizing them to draw rations at Camp Warner. Like Meacham, Canby was devoted not only to a sense of duty but also to an ideal of justice and compassion for the Indians. He was an outstanding example of the Victorian phenomenon of the Christian-soldier, like Chinese Gordon in England and O. O. Howard and Lew Wallace in America. Col. James B. Fry called Canby "one of nature's noblemen," and there is no doubt that he was an absolutely dedicated man. He intended to assist the Peace Commission in carrying out its two charges—to determine the causes of the Modoc hostilities and to devise measures to prevent their recurrence and to restore peace.

It would not be easy. Col. James Fry was not alone in thinking that Secretary of the Interior Delano's instructions to the commission were "artful," since they involved the department mediating between Army and Indians as if it were not only clear of any responsibility for the war but even ignorant of its causes. In Fry's view, the Indian Bureau, not the Army, with an assist from the dilatory U.S. Senate, created the Modoc War. Still, Canby was determined to win peace by using all of his prestige, power, patience and forbearance.

Over the months Canby's attitude toward the Modocs hardened somewhat, although he tried to be fair. He opposed using force on them unless they violated some agreement subsequent to the unratified Council Grove treaty, and he was not surprised at their unwillingness to return to the Klamath Reservation and the exactions of the Klamaths. But he swore he would not be hoodwinked by Jack's pesky band: "In no other respects are the Modocs entitled to much consideration, and although many of the complaints against them have been found to be greatly exaggerated, they are, without being absolutely hostile, sufficiently troublesome to keep up a constant feeling of apprehension among the settlers." By the second month of 1873, he was saying, "I have been very solicitous that these Indians should be fairly treated and have repeatedly used military force lest they be wronged, until their claims or pretensions were decided by proper authority. That having been done, I think they should now be treated as any other criminals and that there will be no peace in that part of the frontier until they are subdued and punished."

To make it easier for Canby and his commissioners to deal with the Indians, in mid-February Gillem moved Army headquarters from Camp Wheaton on Lost River back to Fairchild's ranch on Cottonwood Creek, about twenty-five miles from where the Modocs were snugly holed up. The climate, cold as it was, seemed just right for olive branches despite Canby's stiffening attitude. Lindsay Applegate's maxim that "jawbone is cheaper than ammunition" was a popular one. With wounded men still lying in the Fort Klamath hospital, only twenty to thirty able-bodied men to garrison Fort Klamath, and the Modoc Expedition far short of the one thousand men Wheaton had deemed necessary to storm the Stronghold, a peace policy made good sense. Lt. John Quincy Adams reported to Gillem that Captain Jack was personally so desirous of peace that he would seek an interview even though he dreaded being displaced by a more warlike Modoc as *de facto* chief.

The Peace Commission was finally organized at Fairchild's on February 18, 1873, by Meacham, its seemingly somewhat reluctant chairman. Actually, the idea of the commission had been almost as much Jesse Applegate's as Meacham's. The latter felt that the Modocs would scorn peace overtures after whipping Wheaton so badly. Col. James Fry was of the same opinion, feeling that the Peace Commission was constituted at the worst possible time—when it looked as if the Government was suing for peace after being defeated on the battlefield. But Applegate was a firm believer in "powwow policy," knowing like the rest of his pioneer clan that it was cheaper to either talk to Indians or feed them than to fight them.

It is not unlikely that the editor of the Portland paper, the *Bulletin,* reflected Meacham's original thinking, as well as that of the general public, when it editorialized, "When murder means not punishment but new treaties and concessions, massacre is likely to become a diversion of the savage mind and the employment of savage leisure." Although no one realized it at the time, the *Bulletin* editor was a prophet of chilling accuracy when he foresaw a massacre.

Yet when Applegate persuaded Interior Secretary Columbus Delano to form the body and also pressured Meacham into becoming its chairman, the latter assumed the post with some enthusiasm and hope. Applegate's other ideas were wrong-headed. He suggested that the Modocs be moved to the Coast Range Reservation between the Siletz River and Tillamook while, in almost the same breath, he posited that "different tribes of Indians can be better harmonized together where some can claim original proprietorship." Presumably it was Applegate also who nominated T. H. Odeneal and Simcoe Reservation Agent J. H. Wilbur to the commission. Delano actually appointed them, but he removed the two men in almost the next moment when Meacham made it clear he would refuse to serve with them.

Besides the chairman, the quickly reformed Peace Commission included Jesse Applegate, "the Sage of Yoncalla," and the Alsea Indian Reservation Agent, Samuel Case, whose hard-line obstinacy soon pleased the press more than Meacham's fair-mindedness. To editors, he seemed the only commissioner ready to stand firm for the interests of the State of Oregon. Seemingly, Meacham approved of both men, although Case was heard to remark pessimistically, "It is said the Modocs have a bitter enmity against Meacham and the Applegates and the general impression is that they will have nothing to do with either of them." General Canby was not a member, but Meacham considered him to be an advisor. The general made it clear, however, that he was used to running things in his neck of the woods, and he was soon acting like a super-commissioner, completely overawing Meacham.

The Peace Commission's first action was to send Matilda, the Modoc wife of ferryman Bob Whittle, accompanied by another squaw, Artina Choakus, alias One-Eyed Dixie, alias Long Legs, to the Stronghold on February 19-20 to reestablish contact with Captain Jack. It was a chancy operation since no one yet knew how Jack would react to peace feelers—perhaps murderously. Matilda, for example, left her rings and other jewelry with her husband when she set out. But the squaws proved to be a good, brave team. Stephen Powers described Matilda in flattering terms: "a woman of a strong, dark face, glittering eyes, slow and deliberate in speech and of an iron will—a good type of her race."

When Matilda Whittle returned safely to the Army camp, she reported that the Modocs were tired and running out of both clothes and provisions. She paraphrased Jack's words: "We want no more war and are ready to wash our hands of blood. . . . We were pitched into by the military and citizens when we were asleep. We did not intend to trouble the citizens. We wanted to fight soldiers. The citizens should not have troubled us. We went to the rocks for safety and the soldiers came and hunted us as if we were coyotes." Jack wanted the blockade of the Lava Beds raised and said he was against the whites using squaws as couriers, observing, "Women do not understand when men lie." There was some confusion in Matilda's report. When Meacham later passed word of it to reporters gathered in Gillem's Camp, he quoted Jack as saying, "I am ready to talk with these men that come from a long way [presumably, the correspondents] and I would like to see and talk with Judge Rosborough." But Matilda later said that Jack did *not* want to talk to reporters. One-Eyed Dixie told the San Francisco *Call* reporter that Jack still insisted upon a Lost River reservation. Mrs. Whittle also reported that Jack's influence appeared to be waning and that Johh Schonchin's star seemed to be rising. The latter was as garrulous as ever. Referring to Jackson's raid, he told the two women that his boys had gone wild when the soldiers attacked and that he had not been able to control them. But now he could handle them. He admitted that his own heart had been pretty wild, but now it was for peace. With a straight face, the old rascal told them that although he had a red skin, he had a white heart.

On Washington's Birthday, Whittle and "Commissioner Matilda," as the press corps dubbed her, returned from a second visit to Captain Jack's Cave. They had been met by forty-three Modoc warriors, armed like Mexican *bandidos* with cartridge belts and bandoliers draped all over them. Some of the men were sagging under the weight of two hundred rounds of captured ammunition. They were unanimous in saying that they did not really want to fight, although they now could fire ten shots for every one they had been able to spare in the January battle. They told the squawman, "We have not got mad yet. Your house is standing, so is Dorris', Van Bremer's, Fairchild's and Small's, because we are not mad. [However, they had celebrated Valentine's Day by partially burning down Crawley's cabin.] Captain Jack is still chief and is willing to talk to Steele, Fairchild and Judge Rosborough." The Modocs were curious about the commissioners, but said, "Their hearts may be good, but we don't know them. We won't talk with them unless we can get Rosborough, Steele, Fairchild and some of our friends to come with them."

And so it was that Fairchild, with Whittle and the squaws, met Captain Jack at the base of Gillem's Bluff. The talk began badly when the rancher declined to shake Jack's proffered hand. "No you don't," he said, "until we understand each other. We came here because we learned that you wanted to talk peace. We are not afraid to talk or to hear you talk. We were in the battle. We fought you and we will fight again unless peace is made." Jack replied, "We are glad you came. We want you to hear our side of the story. We do not want any war. Let us go back to our homes on Lost River. We are willing to pay you for the cattle we have killed. We don't want to fight any more." Although Fairchild had to explain that he was not a commissioner and not empowered to make terms of armistice, Jack understood what a truce was and vowed that he would commit no acts of war during peace negotiations. "I understand you about not fighting or killing cattle or stealing horses. My boys will stay in the rocks while it [peace] is being settled. We will not fire the first shot." Jack guaranteed the safety of the commissioners during negotiations—but no soldiers should accompany them. "They frighten my boys," he explained.

The emissaries returned to headquarters with Boston Charley and Bogus Charley, nineteen- or twenty-year-old warriors whom Jack designated as messengers. The commissioners felt it was too dangerous to trust Jack, and they refused to meet him at the bluff's base without an escort, as he had suggested. Instead, they recommended a compromise; they would meet on open ground, either armed or unarmed.

Ironically, after Fairchild risked his life to get peace feelers under way, irresponsible tongues wagged in calumny. He was accused of collusion with "the murderous Modocs." Meacham was particularly peeved by this, since he was a friend of Fairchild's and was also privy to the difficulty of dealing with Jack. He was disgusted that a person of such humane motives should be slandered and vilified by men who would not have dared approach the Stronghold for any sum of money.

Meacham acceded to Modoc demands for negotiators whom they knew and could trust, as the press derided his efforts. He even asked Washington for a copy of Steele's unratified treaty, for guidance. The Jacksonville *Sentinel* said sarcastically, "We stop the press to announce that General Canby has appointed the Fourth of July to meet Captain Jack and have a talk. Captain Jack replies through Modoc Sallie that he is very busy investigating the Crédit Mobilier affair and wants a few head of Mobilier stock if they are fatter than Fairchild's. Jack says he will meet the General at the Centennial Exhibition, if he don't change his mind, and in the meantime wants Secretary Delano to come and see him, without any arms, and promises that he will leave the Modoc Surgical Institute minus legs, also." Meacham brought Elijah Steele and his ex-law partner, Judge A. M. Rosborough, from Yreka and appointed the latter to the commission at Canby's urging. They joined Fairchild and Frank Riddle, the Kentucky-born rancher, ex-miner and hunter who was married to a Modoc, Toby. She was the daughter of Captain Jack's brother, Se-cot, and was a remarkable woman. Earlier, she had been called "The Strange Child" because she was unafraid of sacred places, and "The Little Woman Chief" because of her unfeminine bravery. Later, she would become the heroine of the Modoc War—a Far West Pocahontas—and would be given a sort of stage name, Wi-ne-ma. Colonel Fry described Riddle as having both intelligence and courage in good measure, and he lauded Toby, too, as "possessing more than ordinary personal attractions and intelligence. She loved her white husband and, Indian to the core, knew no law but his will and wish. . . . Holding the confidence of the whites . . . [she was], strange to say, trusted also by the Modocs."

Steele and Rosborough persuaded Meacham to open the commission meetings to reporters. There was opposition from some officers, such as Joel Trimble, who sarcastically reported that mail carriers and telegraphers were kept busy as all Peace Commission deliberations were leaked to eager editors' desks where they were "rehashed, recolored and fed to the community at large." Although Quentin Reynolds once described the Spanish American War's Richard Harding Davis as the father of the craft in America, there were a half-dozen war correspondents covering the Modoc War by the time of the Peace Commission. They disliked and distrusted Meacham because he liked to keep his own counsel. His reticence, in their eyes, was censorship.

During the next fortnight there was almost daily contact with the Modocs, but no news broke. Squawmen, whom Meacham designated as "whiskey-drinking white villains," were poisoning Jack's mind by harping on the murder indictments. And the go-betweens, Boston Charley and Bogus Charley, could not be trusted by either side. They were a pair of plausible, dissimulating scoundrels—perfect politicians. Boston was the more cunning of the two and was said to have been given his name not only because of his light complexion (a "Boshteena" was an American, a white) but because he had two tongues, one Indian and one white. And this meant more than the fact that he was relatively bilingual. According to Meacham, the Indians excused Boston's two-facedness by considering it to be a kind of act of God, beyond their control. They merely apologized for the fact that he was "a natural-born traitor." It was said that Bogus won his nickname not because he was born on nearby Bogus Creek but because he was a fraud and the jokester of the Modocs, although hardly a Lava Beds' Yorick to Captain Jack's Hamlet. He, too, was described by his kindred as a "double-hearted man." But he knew English better than any other Modoc, and Jack was thus obliged to use him as his courier—and spy. For all their duplicity, which was often transparent, the two scalawags became the favorites of the Army camp. Fed, clothed and otherwise "petted" by their enemies, Jack's half-overt, half-covert spies snooped about, hoping to find Gillem's battle plans, if any.

The press, both that small portion gathered at Gillem's headquarters and the editors at home, became impatient with the slow progress of Indian diplomacy and the boredom of a war without fighting. The *Oregonian* absurdly urged the commission to get cracking and find the nine thousand dollars that rumor said Jack stashed away in a Yreka bank. The San Francisco *Call* correspondent, Alex McKay, groused (February 23) that the commission was still determined to prevent the press from obtaining information except through its own hands. The Yreka *Journal* called the commission a perfect farce, and San Francisco *Chronicle* correspondent Robert D. Bogart created news by inciting a vendetta against the Applegates, particularly Ivan and Oliver. He accused them of profiteering at the expense of the Indians. This was not a new story and it was hard to kill. The *Call* later revived it and reflected that the Klamath Reservation was obviously quite a respectable one— from the number of whites it supported. The paper described the work of the staff, such as ex-Agent Lindsay Applegate: "The arduous labor of the whites is supposed to consist in teaching the Indians how to draw their rations." John McCall wrote Oliver Applegate on February 21, "I see the son of a bitch of a correspondent for the *Chronicle* is still at his abuse. . . ." Shortly, Jesse Applegate resigned from the commission, saying, "I am not a proper person to sit in judgment upon their conduct or to be a member of a tribunal charged to make investigations that might impugn it." Jesse was already soured on his diplomatic progeny, anyway, calling his commission "an expensive blunder."

Bogart, who bragged of U.S. Navy service and New York *Sun* by-lines, dreamed of emulating Henry M. Stanley's African adventure of the search for Dr. Livingstone. Bogart grandiosely reported on his progress toward "the seat of war," with what he termed the *Chronicle's* Indian War News Expedition. This amounted to a Yrekan guide, Ed Autenreith, and himself. He was often as content to use secondhand news as to libel the Applegate clan. He made the Yreka telegraph office his "seat of war" headquarters, and there he was hoodwinked by a bucolic prankster named Elijah H. (Lije) Heard. Heard filled him with the details of an imaginary interview with Captain Jack in his cave. Bogart not only swallowed the story but one of the

Chronicle's traditionally butter-fingered typesetters got the misinformant's name wrong (supposedly a cardinal sin of journalism) rendering Lije into T. H. Heard. The reporter then fudged by antedating his story to December 14, to make it a veritable scoop, and datelining it Van Bremer's Hill, which only illuminated his geographical ignorance. The Yreka *Union* spilled the beans on the humbugging of Bogart, who left for home.

But the Munchausen of the Fourth Estate was back in the field in January, where he joined some pretty fair correspondents. These were H. Wallace Atwell of the Sacramento *Record;* the New York *Herald's* Edward Fox; and an amateur reporter who submitted stories to the San Francisco *Call* and *Bulletin* as well as the Yreka *Union.* He was Alex McKay, a Siskiyou surveyor. Bogart eventually visited Jack in his Stronghold (as did the other newsmen), but suddenly disappeared on March 5, 1873, without explanation. Not that the Applegates demanded one. They were pleased with his mysterious departure and delighted with McKay's report that Bogart was drummed out of Army headquarters. Not only had Bogart fallen into editorial disfavor for his reckless charges against the Applegates, but he was arrested and tried by a Navy court-martial for desertion and embezzlement of either ten thousand or thirty thousand dollars (depending on which paper one read) while a paymaster's clerk aboard the U.S.S. *Vermont* in December 1869. The only thing that rendered the Applegates' pleasure less than complete was the December news that Bogart, after being found guilty and given a sentence of twenty-three months in the Mare Island brig, had either escaped from captivity on the old prison hulk *Independence* or had jumped his ten thousand dollar bail bond. In any case, he disappeared. Atwell took over for the *Chronicle.*

James Gordon Bennett, Jr., made an odd choice of a New York *Herald* reporter for the Modoc Expedition. Edward Fox was his yachting editor! But the Englishman was a veteran of the British Army and a first-rate newshawk. With the war at a standstill, he sat down and wrote the best account of the January battle in the Lava Beds—three weeks after it was all over. He used the text of original Army orders instead of hearsay and he interviewed survivors of the scrap in a brilliant piece of reporting, while his rival, Bogart, was creating a think-piece full of optimism about the commission. Fox's style was witty, too. When the governor of Oregon solemnly informed the commission that the state was the only jurisdiction competent to try the Modocs, he reported "remarks were made concerning the sanity of the aforesaid Governor." All of the press corps had to manufacture news during this dull period of inaction, of course—from McKay's description of his bed ("the soft side of the kitchen floor") to such local color as Fox's view of the sugarbowl at Fairchild's ranch ("an article of antediluvian extraction, coated with a brown crust of dirt which has accumulated by its constant service during the past few years without being introduced to water").

Fox was the most enterprising of the correspondents. When Fairchild prepared to visit Jack on February 24 to tell him Steele and Rosborough would be delayed, Fox asked permission to go along. Meacham refused and ordered Whittle (whom he had put in charge, for some reason, over Fairchild) not to allow any reporter to go with him. The redoubtable Fox faked a visit to an artillery encampment, circled around and picked up the trail of the party in the snow. He then bravely rode, all alone, into the Lava Beds. Joining the party, he was introduced as The Paper Man and made friends with the curious Modocs by passing around his pipe and tobacco pouch.

Although the Modocs quarreled over their visitors, they took them to see Jack, who was ill and leaning on a stick even while seated. The chief talked to Fairchild about Steele's delay, via Bogus Charley's translation. Then John Schonchin seized the floor and poured out grievances for two hours, till Bogus had to call on Steamboat Frank for help in translating the torrent of complaints. Fox then managed to interview Jack, and the visitors spent the night. Next morning, Jack was a little better but his wife had to support him with her arm around his waist when he stood up. He wanted The Paper Man to come to the big conference he planned to have with Steele and the others. Steele later told Fox that his presence at this preliminary conference had done much to establish confidence between the Indians and the whites.

The *Herald* treated Fox's scoop properly. The paper devoted all of page three to the story, which cost the *Herald* between five and six hundred dollars in telegraph tolls alone. (In the 1870s the first two pages were still reserved for advertisements.)

Elijah Steele consented to talk with Captain Jack. He was instructed, unwisely in the minority opinion of outvoted Meacham, to offer terms of peace to the Modocs although he was not a member of the commission. He was to extend amnesty to all of them if they would go to a distant reservation in a warmer climate, presumably Arizona Territory, Indian

Territory or Southern California, after a temporary stay on the Army's Angel Island in San Francisco Bay as prisoners of war.

Steele, Rosborough, Fairchild, the Riddles and reporters Atwell, Bogart and McKay were greeted by the taciturn Captain Jack, still sick, in his Stronghold. Toby Riddle told the Modocs that the group had come to have a good talk and would stay overnight. She showed him the food—hardtack, bacon and coffee—and the blankets they had brought. Sardonically, Scarfaced Charley quipped, "Yes, you folks might stay longer than you want to. . . . You know, we have been fighting the white people. We have not quit yet." Toby, unruffled, just said, "Charley, we know all what you say. But, listen, these men here are your friends and I am a Modoc. That is the reason we come here among you. We know you will not harm us. We are here to help you people, not to destroy you." Charley simply said, "All right, we will see."

Captain Jack added dried beef to his visitors' cuisine and instructed his men to care for their horses. After supper at Wild Gal's fire, Jack heard Rosborough's professions of friendship and some words from Fairchild and Steele, all translated by the Riddles. Frank Riddle then described Canby and Meacham as Jack's friends, adding, "Jack, I want you to make peace. The soldiers won't hurt you if you talk peace." Captain Jack then told the envoys to inform the Peace Commission that he was willing to hear them in council if Canby would protect him from his enemies among the whites. Next morning's conversation was again friendly, and Steele became convinced that peace was now assured. According to McKay, Jack boasted that the Snakes had offered him sixty warriors but that he had declined them.

Albert S. Gatschet in 1877 interviewed Toby Riddle in an early instance of recording oral history and got a description of Steele's visit to Jack in Toby's quaint English: "The Indians received us friendly and said, 'The palefaces had committed the first outrage. The whites were continually lying, reporting the Indians had attacked the troops for no reason. The Indians did not think, over there, that their folks had acted wrongly. The Americans had driven the Indians into the rocks and commenced firing at them, staying in the rocks.' The Indians declared, 'If ye will negotiate peace with us, we shall stop fighting. If we should fight again, the Americans would first start the war, the Indians not fire first.' Steele then said, 'Your hands are stained all over with the whites' blood. Canby will insist that ye give up. Canby will then remove you to a good land distant from here where the wicked Oregonians will not murder you. If ye here would remain, they would kill ye, every one.' The Modoc chief said, 'I do not want to leave my country. Not to any other country that I know of to live in. My father, mother, and brother also, are buried here. I desire to live and die in my own country. I myself have done nothing wrong so that anyone hence should take me away. This only I request—all to live in the same manner."

Hopes rose high in camp when Steele returned with his party and eight Modocs. He raised his hat as he neared the tents and shouted, "They accept peace!" In a euphoria of relief, couriers were sent galloping to the end of the wire in Yreka to flash the welcome news to the nation. The Peace Commission wired Washington: "Modocs to surrender as prisoners of war, to be removed to a southern and warmer climate and provided for. They accept the terms and have sent a delegation of eight to talk over details but not to conclude them. Captain Jack is sick. Everything looks favorable for peace. They ask small homes and to be located collectively. We think well of the request. Amnesty to all. Capt. Jack desires to visit Washington with one or two of his young men." Meacham recalled that happy moment: "We felt that a great victory over blood and carnage had been won and that our hazardous labors were nearly over." *Call* correspondent McKay also guessed that the Modoc War was now over.

John Fairchild shattered the optimistic mood. The gray-eyed, shovel-bearded pioneer insisted that Squire Steele had misunderstood Jack, who was not about to surrender as a prisoner of war. "I don't think the Modocs agreed to accept the terms offered. True, they responded to Steele's speech—but not in that way. I tell you, they do not understand that they have agreed to surrender yet, on any terms." Journalist Bogart was inclined to believe Fairchild, but Atwell, like McKay, backed Steele. When a puzzled Meacham tried to get confirmation from the Modocs who had come in, they were reticent and evasive, saying they had come to listen, not to talk.

The nervy Steele, steadfast in his conviction that he had read Modoc intentions correctly, decided to repeat his trip to the Stronghold to verify his opinion while Meacham held another session of the commission. The chairman was in favor of Steele's terms, but Applegate now joined Case in demanding unconditional surrender of the Modocs. Applegate then submitted his resignation, effective the moment that the Modocs should decide one way or the other, for peace or for war.

Atwell agreed to accompany Steele, but the other reporters said something to the effect that "We don't own any Indians in there." When Steele invited Fairchild to return to the Stronghold, the rancher declined with that slow swinging of his head, side to side, which was peculiar to him in times of crisis. Meacham noticed this. "That said a great deal, especially when he shut his eyes closely while so doing." Nor would Frank Riddle go with Steele on what he considered a fool's errand, although he grudgingly consented to his wife's going again as the Squire's interpreter.

To his horror, Steele found that he had indeed been wrong and Fairchild right. The wan light of a small campfire in the lava jungle revealed a circle of scowling, malignant faces. The Modocs were angry and distrustful, thinking that Steele had been party to some kind of trickery intended to lead to their capitulation. In the Squire's own words, his reception made his hair stand on end. Atwell learned the reason for the radically changed climate of opinion when a squaw, Lucy, asked him why whites told so many different stories. From her he learned that Oregonians ("cursed knaves," he called them) had told the Modocs visiting Fairchild's place that the commission was but a trick to draw them out of the Lava Beds so that they could be captured and hanged. One of Atwell's knaves was probably Charley Blair of Linkville, who had acquired a violent hatred of the commissioners. Although described as a worthless fellow and a jailbird by the Sacramento *Record,* Blair was Jack's choice for a commission envoy to Chief Schonchin and the peaceful Modocs at Yainax on the Klamath Reservation. Jack wanted them to come to the Lava Beds as intermediaries. The suspicious Yreka *Union* guessed that Jack intended to impress Old Schonchin's party into his army as involuntary recruits. But Schonchin hemmed and hawed and stalled and would not come. This may have been because Long Jim, one of Hooker Jim's Lost River murderers, went to Yainax with his family from the Lava Beds and told everyone there that Jack would never come in. Later, Chief Schonchin did attend a palaver with Jack during the first week of April, but he was not a factor. He said very little, only that he hoped the whites and Jack's Modocs would make peace.

Not a word was necessary to convince Steele that the slightest sympton of fear might cost him his life. He affected indifference to the hostility all around him and was heartened a little to find that Jack was less sullen than his men, who now numbered sixty-nine by Atwell's count, as compared to Fox's estimate of fifty to sixty at the earlier powwow. About twenty of them were strangers to Steele, and he guessed that some were Pit Rivers, Snakes and Klamaths, new allies attracted to Jack's banner by his success over the "Boston" soldiers.

Rumors swelled Jack's reinforcements to a battalion. Citizens of Lake City in California's Surprise Valley, jumping at shadows, felt surrounded by Paiute, Pit River and Snake allies of Jack. They reported that local braves had enlisted in his support. The *Call* printed a letter warning that news of Jack's success over Wheaton had spread like wildfire among the Indians of the Far West, making them insolent and defiant. The letter-writer predicted, "Any other terms than a full, complete and unconditional surrender to the Government will be but a signal to these other tribes to raise the war whoop and unsheath the scalping knife." Stock-raisers closer to the Lava Beds blamed their losses of cattle and sheep on the Modocs and other Indians emboldened by Jack's success, although in some cases the depredations were those of soldiers savoring a change of diet from Army rations and even teamsters who "boarded themselves," as they put it, by living off the land in this fashion. But alarms spread. A squaw was reported visiting Hamburg John and other Indians at Hamburg Bar on the lower Klamath River, asking them to join Jack, who would leave the Lava Beds as soon as the spring grass was up. He would then start a campaign of burning ranches. At least one Klamath near Leggett's ranch told whites that he was going to join Captain Jack, and residents predicted the spread of the Modoc War to their faraway area.

The Indian war scare spread further when Hooker Jim and three braves rustled fifty to sixty horses at Alkali Lake near Langell Valley on Washington's Birthday, then went to Yainax to try to recruit Modocs and Klamaths for Lava Beds duty. Hooker had no real success nor could he buy powder from a squawman named Jordan when he tried, telling him that Jack had lots of gold to exchange for gunpowder. But he alarmed the peaceful Indians on the Klamath Reservation as much as the skeleton force holding Fort Klamath, and jittery settlers in the Sprague River Valley prepared to pull out. Goose Lake citizens petitioned the governor of Oregon for protection, and in Siskiyou County, California, there was pressure on the grand jury to bring bills of indictment against the peace commissioners as accessories to the Indians in the stealing of stock and the killing of citizens.

While Gibraltar-safe settlements were panicking, a very scared Elijah Steele was trying to hide his fear from his hostile hosts. Only Scarfaced Charley and two of his confederates appeared to still be friendly. And, like Jack, they were in a difficult position, for the mood of the majority was an ugly one. Jack rebuked Steele for missing some of his words. He told him that the Modocs had not yet shown their hearts. The surly John Schonchin, looking for trouble as usual, accused Steele of duplicity and lying in a violent and inflammable tirade that led Modoc hands to play with pistol butts and knife handles. The Squire spoke only in English and Chinook, which had to be translated for many of the Modocs, in order that his adversaries might not know how much he understood of their threatening talk in the Modoc tongue. Testily, he said that he would never misrepresent his Modoc friends, then coolly terminated the interview by saying to the blackguard, "I do not want to talk to a man when his heart is bad. We will talk again tomorrow." Atwell described Schonchin John: "The old heathen chafed and fumed like a caged tiger." Shortly, the "old heathen" asked Steele if he was not afraid to sleep in the Modoc camp after talking to them with two hearts. The last subject Steele again denied, then said he was afraid of nothing. With good timing, Scarfaced Charley intervened to suggest that Steele and his companions bed down in Captain Jack's camp. With Queen Mary and Jack he then stood guard. Several times during a sleepless night, Steele looked up from his blankets to see one or the other of the threesome on alert sentry duty. Atwell swore, "To the protection of these three Indians, I am satisfied we owed our safety." The Modoc squaw, Artina Choakus, said the same thing. Although Jack was rather hostile when compared to Scarfaced Charley, he had a well-developed sense of honor and vowed that men who came to his campfire would be protected.

Morning, after breakfast at Wild Gal's, brought more angry words. Steele, understandably, decided to tell a whooping lie in order to save his skin. He promised to go back and bring the whole Peace Commission, along with Fairchild and the reporters, to the Stronghold—knowing that if he ever really did such a thing he would be transforming it into a slaughter pen. John Schonchin and Curly Headed Doctor were blinded to Steele's stratagem by their bloodlust and allowed the party to leave. They especially wanted to see their "particular friends," Applegate and Meacham.

A. B. Meacham recalled that morning of March 4 when Steele came back. "On his return he looked older than when he left the morning previous." Although only Boston Charley escorted them, with Queen Mary and some squaws, Atwell reported, "I did not draw a free breath until we reached the top of the bluff three miles from the Modoc camp." When the pair were safe, Atwell loosed a long whistling exhalation of breath to break the silence. "Wheeew! I'm glad to get out of that hole!" Steele, who had thought that the reporter was largely unaware of the gravity of their situation because of his lack of the Indian tongue, said "Why, did you know what was going on last night?" "Yes," answered the journalist, "but I don't care now. I can outrun them."

Steele admitted his mistaken opinion of Modoc attitudes and explained his ruse of promising to bring the commission to the Lava Beds. He warned that the peace body would be murdered should it venture there, and reported that only Scarfaced Charley really wanted to settle the trouble peacefully. (Perhaps Charley suffered from a major identity crisis. All he wanted to do was to "get away and behave like a white man.") According to Steele, the Modocs actually believed that the Government was afraid of them and was peace-dickering out of weakness. He advised Meacham to cease all negotiations until the Modocs should become the soliciting party.

Canby and the commissioners, of course, put the kibosh on Jack's terms for a meeting but the general, unwilling to give up, suggested instead that Jack and his headmen come to Fairchild's ranch to arrange peace terms. According to the reporters, he gave Jack until the end of March to accept his terms. Then he would refer the matter to the military. That was their choice. Canby guaranteed the Modocs safe passage back to their redoubt from the meeting.

Meanwhile, Meacham wired the Secretary of the Interior that the Modocs undoubtedly meant treachery and that the peace mission was a failure. The telegraphic reply that he received was an astonishing blow. From his viewpoint, three thousand miles east of the Stronghold, Secretary Delano refused to hear of Meacham's suspicions. "I do not believe the Modocs mean treachery," he wired. "The mission should not be a failure. I think I understood their unwillingness to confide in you.

Continue negotiations." Gen. William T. Sherman added the humiliating clincher to Delano's insulting wire. He telegraphed Canby: "All parties here have absolute faith in you but mistrust the commissioners." Small wonder the reporters began to call the commission a humbug, a farce and a packed tribunal.

But, seemingly, Delano was right. *Mirabile visu!*, Captain Jack sent his sister, Queen Mary, with word he would surrender. He and his men would become p.o.w.'s if the Army would send wagons for them to Point of Rocks on Lower Klamath Lake, a dozen miles from Army headquarters. Meacham opposed the scheme as both another abdication of responsibility by the commission and as a risky idea, to boot, in that the Modocs might not only steal the wagons but might kill the teamsters. But Canby took over completely, ignoring Meacham's protests. In the latter's bitter words, "The chairman could only look on."

Canby sent four wagons with Steele on March 10. Since the Riddles were as convinced that the Modocs were not sincere as the Squire was positive that they were, the general became prejudiced against Toby and Frank and began to use the wily pair of Charlies, Boston and Bogus, as his interpreters. This was so even though the former almost tipped Jack's hand at this point. He said to Toby Riddle as he left the Army camp, "If you ever see me I will pay you for the saddle I borrowed. . . ." Bogus, for his part, boasted in public that he was ready to handle twenty soldiers, himself, then zealously picked up cartridges dropped by soldiers as he made his way back to Jack with a can of powder he had stolen.

Rebuffed by Canby's strange attitude, Toby kept her strong suspicions of treachery to herself at first, but finally told her husband. Frank informed Meacham, who passed the word on to Canby. The general shrugged off the warning that the wagons would be seized. To him, it was proof that Toby was either ignorant of Modoc plans or else was being influenced by those opposed to peace. The Riddles were distressed by their lack of credibility with Canby. It was no wonder, observed Meacham, "Their warning had been disregarded, their opinions dishonored, their integrity doubted."

As it turned out, the wagons were not even met at the designated place, although Steele and his wagoners waited for four hours. Jack come up with an excuse—he had been busy with the cremation of a dead warrior. He set another date for the rendezvous. Again, Canby sent Steele with the wagons. Earlier, he had thrown up tents for the Modocs, grandly designating one of them "Captain Jack's Marquee," and had hay and firewood gathered for his guests' comfort. Once again, the correspondents guessed that the war was over. Even Jesse Applegate, this time, assumed that peace had finally broken out. He left for home, reporting en route, "The war is over. The Modocs have surrendered." Secretary Delano wired Meacham on March 11: "Modocs have surrendered. . . . Select a suitable reservation."

As usual, John Fairchild was the hirsute Cassandra of Gillem's Camp. He tossed a wet verbal blanket that effectively smothered the bright hopes of peace. "I don't think they will come. They are not going to Angel Island as prisoners, just yet." As usual, Fairchild was right as rain. That afternoon, as dusk fell, the watchers in camp descried Steele approaching with the wagons, empty.

Canby told General Sherman that the Modocs' hearts had failed them at the last moment; they could not bring themselves to abandon their old homes to go to a distant country. A Modoc delegation arrived to say that the band had not been able to agree on surrendering. Meacham learned that the hitch had been that the warhawks had not been able to bully Scarfaced Charley and Captain Jack into seizing the vehicles. Interestingly, Capt. James Jackson made a report that showed that Canby was not as naive as he seemed. He had taken the precaution, unknown to the press and commission, of sending a scouting party to shadow the wagons. They lay back at a considerable distance, hiding in the rocks, ready to rescue Steele were the arrangement a Modoc trap.

Reporter McKay gloomily filed a story: "The Peace Commission is a failure. Every promise made to the Indians was faithfully kept, every Modoc promise broken. . . . Everything points to war." Some papers, with blood in their eyes, were pleased at the breakdown of negotiations. The Yreka *Union* trumpeted that if war must come, let it come speedily and overwhelmingly. The paper predicted Canby would drag the Modocs out of the Lava Beds in short order, or leave their bodies there. The *Call*, four days later on March 18, advised, "The military will go for them with a vengeance and not leave two of them alive. . . ."

Editors were not the only ones enchanted by the idea of the Modoc War heating up again. A modest boom was beginning in Northern California. Farmers in Scott Valley prepared for larger crops during the 1873 season because of the increased demand

and higher prices for foodstuffs, with a hungry Army to feed. Ground long left idle was being ploughed up in March for planting to grain by speculating farmers, all of whom wanted the kind of business Gus Meamber was getting. His contract, for example, called for the delivery of sixty thousand pounds of oats at Army headquarters at ten cents a pound.

When Samuel Case followed Applegate in resigning, pleading the press of Indian Agency business, Meacham had to reconstitute the commission almost from the lava up. No one lamented the passing of the initial group. It had been ineffective, according to the *Call*, badly split, with Case for surrender and Meacham for compromise and Applegate wobbling in between. By the end of February the journalists believed that the Modocs would gladly go on the reservation if given a free pardon for the murder of the settlers. But by then Applegate had swung over to Case's adamant position.

Rev. Eleazar Thomas, a fifty-nine-year-old Methodist minister of Petaluma, California, and editor of California's *Christian Advocate*, was appointed. He had been recommended by Senator A. A. Sargent. Canby approved of him, saying, "I like his appearance and bearing very much and think he will be an addition to the commission that will be of some value." Klamath Agent L. S. Dyar replaced Case. Judge Rosborough was technically still a member, but his judicial duties had taken him back to Yreka and he had given Canby his proxy, as if the general needed more power when he was already running the show. Eventually the Interior Department not only gave Canby permission to replace any of Meacham's appointees, should he desire to change the makeup of the board, but ordered Meacham to submit his telegrams to the general for approval before sending them East. This downgrading of Meacham was an ill-kept secret; General of the Army William Tecumseh Sherman wrote Canby, "This actually devolves on you the entire management of the Modoc question."

Meacham swallowed his humiliation manfully because of his desire to bring peace to the Modoc country. The press was happier with the commission now, as reconstituted. McKay, impressed with Reverend Thomas' sincerity, thought that the divine understood his duties better than any other member. He praised the minister for being the only commissioner who dealt with the Indians as if he had no fear. This was the case; Thomas did not even have a *healthy* fear of the Modocs, although Steele advised him not to put himself in the Indians' power. Curiously,

Atwell seized on Dyar, not Thomas, as a "howling Christian" and then accused him of nepotism, stating that he kept his wife on the Klamath Reservation payroll as schoolteacher when there was, as yet, no school. Meacham, of course, remained a target of criticism. McKay, when he heard that Thomas meant to leave the area, giving his proxy to Canby should peace talks fail, quipped, "Very likely, Meacham will open a recruiting office for peace commissioners."

At this point, Canby engaged in some maneuvering that Meacham and others considered to be not only ill-advised strategy but downright unethical doings. As the weather warmed and the roads and trails began to dry out, the Army's *Hyas Tyee* (Big Chief) decided to squeeze Captain Jack a bit in hopes of forcing him sooner to the conference campfire. He tightened up the loose ring of troops he had thrown around the Lava Beds at the same time that he sent word to Jack that he would permit no "trifling" during the peace talks. This he did although the first message of the Peace Commission to Jack had been, "We come in good faith to make peace. Our hearts are all for peace; no act of war will be allowed while peace talks are being held, no movements of troops will be made." Canby was guilty of self-deception, of course. He described his troop movements in a St. Patrick's Day report as attempts to make it difficult for the Modocs to escape from the Lava Beds to raid settlers. In a telegram to Sherman from Fairchild's Camp (March 11), he advised, "Some movement of troops will be necessary in order to keep them under closer observation, but nothing more until authorized by you." On the twenty-eighth he added, "I think when the avenues of escape are closed and their supplies cut off or abridged, they will come in."

Canby moved troops closer to the Stronghold and increased the cavalry patrols on the outskirts of the badland. He also instituted a stricter censorship than Meacham had dared, because he now realized that the coming and going of such Indians as Boston and Bogus kept Jack perfectly posted on troop movements. He did not bother to inform the commission—not that there was anything Meacham could do, as the general took a commanding role now in civil as well as military affairs. Sourly, Meacham observed, "I was instructed to cooperate with General Canby and in no event to interfere with the movement of troops. A glance at this single proposition tells the whole story of the failure."

When Canby dispatched Capt. James Biddle and K Troop,

1st Cavalry, to reconnoiter the Tickner Road with its builder, H. C. Tickner, as his scout, the captain did a fine job. Too good. His action may have been the straw that finally broke Jack's resolve to work for peace rather than war. Biddle spied two Modocs guarding a horse herd. Trooper Maurice FitzGerald, who was with him, reported, "It was difficult to restrain some of the boys from pursuing them, but our orders not to fire or attack, unless fired upon, were imperative." Less imperative were orders about booty, however, and the troopers seized Jack's horses—either twenty-three, thirty-three or thirty-four ponies, depending on whether Jeff Riddle's, General Canby's or Meacham's count is accepted. In any case, Biddle drove the herd to headquarters, which had just been shifted from Fairchild's to Van Bremer's ranch. Meacham protested the bald-faced rustling of Modoc stock as a violation of the truce and urged the return of the animals. The general just tut-tutted him and said that they would be well cared for and turned over to the Modocs once they should sue for peace. Jack was furious, of course, but his protest fell on as deaf ears as had Meacham's. When he sent his sister, Mary, to ask for his own riding horse, at least, Canby sent her away with the cool remark, "When peace is made you shall get your horses."

A week after Biddle's modest but critical action, the Army, which had had a hard time even seeing an enemy in action, finally took a prisoner. Long Jim, Hooker Jim's accomplice who had gone to Yainax, was arrested there and brought to Gillem's newly relocated camp at the base of the bluff overlooking the Lava Beds. Since there was no stockade or guardhouse, he was kept a prisoner in the round stone corral that can still be seen today in the Lava Beds National Monument. It was brief captivity, for Long Jim escaped one midnight although the guards who chased him fired at least twenty shots at him.

In order to personally scout out Captain Jack's already fabled sanctuary, Canby joined Gillem on March 21 and accompanied a cavalry patrol to Gillem's Bluff, overlooking the Land of Burnt-Out Fires. Again FitzGerald was there to tell the story. The Irishman reported, "While leisurely gazing over the imposing landscape we suddenly heard a shot from the rocks near the foot of the bluff and then observed an Indian waving his cap." Also along with the officers was Dr. T. T. Cabaniss, a Siskiyou County surgeon who was a friend of the Indians although serving in the Modoc Expedition as contract surgeon "for the duration." He had set Captain Jack's badly broken arm some six years earlier when the chief's horse had fallen on him near Williamson River as he fled from the Snakes after a horse-raiding expedition. The doctor, taking reporter Fox with him, went to talk to the Indian. It was William (William Faithful), usually called Weium by the Modocs and Whim by the whites. They learned that Jack wanted to palaver with the big *tyee*, Canby, so the doctor and the journalist offered themselves up as hostages for the safety of Captain Jack during a completely unplanned, unscheduled powwow. They stayed with a guard of Modocs while Jack, Scarfaced Charley and six warriors climbed halfway up the bluff to meet the general at a lone juniper.

Canby later kept mum about the talk, merely saying that the meeting was unsatisfactory, but he did venture to Fox that the Modocs did not want peace unless they could stay on Lost River—and Canby had already decided that removal was necessary. He had written his wife, "It has always been a difficult matter to induce an Indian to leave his home and go to a new and unknown country but nothing else will do here and peace made on any other terms will not last a month." He also mentioned to the surgeon that Jack seemed restrained by the presence of the other Modocs and that he, Canby, was dissatisfied with the conversation. "Doctor, the Indians do not talk of peace," he said. "What do they say, general?" asked Cabaniss. "Captain Jack says that if we have anything for them, they will receive it at the Lava Beds."

The doctor and the reporter learned, as surely did Canby, too, that the Modocs were burning with resentment over Biddle's capture of their horse herd in a time of armistice. The Modocs at the bluff were stripped and painted for war and had cartridge belts filled with ammunition. Five warriors had Army carbines, three had muskets. Cabaniss noticed that two white men's scalps decorated the shot pouches of two of the warriors. One was brown and curly and the other light and wavy. He recognized the latter as the scalp of Private Brennan of the 21st Infantry, killed in January. Cabaniss called the scalps to Fox's attention, and the Englishman later said that his own hair stood on end at the sight. Fox tried to explain the seizure of the horses to the Indians and at the same time impress them with Canby's growing strength. He told them that Biddle's *one hundred men* were newcomers. "But," he reported, "I am grieved to say that they did not look very scared." (That night, the journalist got his hair cut so that his scalp should not be an attraction for the Modocs—or so he said.) When Cabaniss suggested the folly of resistance, the unimpressed warriors just shrugged and said, "The more men come, the more we kill."

If Jack's complaints of false dealing in the horse raid affected Canby, he gave no sign. Instead, he complained of the Modocs in a letter to his wife: "They are the strangest mixture of insolence and arrogance, ignorance and superstition that I have ever seen among Indians, and from this cause results the great difficulty in dealing with them in any way but by force. They have no faith in themselves and have no confidence in anyone else. Treacherous themselves, they suspect treachery in everything."

The general had Gillem order Major Mason to march three infantry companies and the howitzers from their Lost River camp to a new base at Scorpion Point at Tule Lake's southeastern corner, where it pinched out against the Lava Beds. There, Mason took command from Captain Bernard of all troops on the eastern front. Canby then dispatched another of the patrols that so annoyed Captain Jack and ordered Maj. John Green to Van Bremer's ranch. The Fort Klamath commander was to reassume direct command, under Gillem, of the troops on the western front. Thus General Canby, ironically called "The Prudent Soldier" by his biographer, continued a rash policy of containment of the Modocs, which he euphemized as "gradual compression."

Canby then moved his headquarters—on April Fool's Day—to the base of Gillem's Bluff, on the very edge of the Lava Beds. Meacham and his fellow commissioners were notified of the move in advance but were not consulted about its advisability. The new headquarters was first called Tule Camp, but soon its name became fixed as Gillem's Camp and the site is thus called, to this day. Canby tried to explain away these bellicose moves. He said the troop movements were for the purpose of interdicting Modoc egress from the Lava Beds and, thus, to prevent any raiding of ranches. But he candidly admitted, too, that his maneuvers were meant "to impress upon the Indians the folly of resistance." Meacham was so alarmed by these injudicious moves of Canby that his nerves got the best of him. He came to the general's tent during the first night in the new camp, convinced that Jack would attack the camp before daylight. Canby heard Meacham urge him to dig rifle pits for defense, then quieted his jumpy nerves and sent him back to his blankets. Meacham looked to the priming of his gun and slept with his boots on, if he slept at all that night, but no attack came. Apparently one of the squaws started the rumor of danger and practical-joking settlers, hanging about camp, decided to spook Meacham by playing on his fears.

Instead of an attack, the commissioners enjoyed a formal meeting with the Modocs next morning in the no-man's-land between Gillem's Camp and the Stronghold. As they left camp that April 2, a worried Toby and Frank Riddle warned them, "Be sure to mix up with the Modocs. Don't let them get you in a bunch." Meacham did not like the location of the talk, a sort of flat or swale of the Lava Beds that was hidden from field glasses in the Army camp, although within the view of men at the signal station on Gillem's Bluff. He thought that the peculiar location smacked of treachery. The Modocs said they wanted it far from Gillem's tents because they were afraid of the soldiers—with Boston and Bogus and others wandering in and out of headquarters as if they owned it!

The Modocs numbered three times as many as Boston Charley had promised, but they appeared cordial, and Meacham was relieved by the reassuring presence of squaws tending the council fire. The fire was a necessity that day, not just a symbol. Sitting patiently in the rain on an icy rock for four hours, listening to endless complaints and oratory, the long-suffering Canby thought back to an equally frigid day when the 10th Infantry had changed camps at Fort Bridger in March 1858. A pipe of peace was smoked but the talks did not go well. Hooker Jim at one point insolently told Riddle, "Stand aside! Get out of the way!" Toby reprimanded him for his discourtesy and Captain Jack spoke sharply to him, saying, "Stop that!" A good excuse to terminate the discussion, or rather bombast, which was going nowhere, blew up in the form of a sharp and cold snowstorm. But then Jack's attitude chilled and he ridiculed the whites, saying that Canby would not melt, like snow. The inclement weather led to the only agreement of the day, that the Army would erect a tent to shelter the council members during negotiations in bad weather. Soldiers pegged up a regulation Army wall tent the very next day, April 3, less than a mile—perhaps only nine hundred yards, so rough and broken was the terrain—from Gillem's headquarters camp. They were careful to locate it in no-man's-land between the Modoc and Army spheres of influence.

Many of the whites felt satisfied that the Modocs' angry talk was only a face-saving device prior to surrender. But reporter McKay disagreed. He did not believe the matter would be settled without a fight. When the Peace Commission loaded visiting Modocs with hard bread and other presents, he sarcastically observed, "all . . . will be useful to them in the coming fight." He could not help contrasting the peaceful Indians—who got nothing—with visiting hostiles. The Army fed the latter and their horses and loaded them with provisions and other gifts.

Already the Riddles had sniffed the stench of treachery in Modoc diplomacy. They learned of a Modoc war council held in the midst of the series of peace powwows. At this agitated conference, John Schonchin had seized the initiative. Declaring peace to be impossible, he reminded the warriors, "I have been trapped and fooled by the white people many times. I do not intend to be fooled again. You will see the aim of the Peace Commission. They are just leading us Mucklucks on, to make time to get more soldiers here. When they think there are enough men here, they will jump on us and kill the last soul of us. . . ."

Next to speak was Black Jim, so named for his complexion. Oregon old-timer Clyde Fairchild described him as being "black as a crow's wing." He agreed with John Schonchin, called Meacham's colleagues "peace shammers," and moved that the band kill them at the next conference. "Schonchin, you see things right," said Black Jim. "I, for one, am not going to be decoyed and shot like a dog by the soldiers. I am going to kill my man before they get me."

Those who favored the idea of murdering the commissioners stepped forward—Black Jim, John Schonchin, Boston, Bogus, Shacknasty Jim, Curly Headed Doctor, Steamboat Frank, Barncho or Boncho, Dave Rock, Little Steve, Ellen's Man and four or five more. The rest did not move, and one of them, Weium, protested, "Schonchin [John] is not head chief. Captain Jack is our chief. I have not seen him tonight." Weium found Jack and had him speak to his people. He urged patience and peace, then explained his strategy of passive resistance. "All I have to do is to hold the councils and stick to my point. I shall win. . . . I will hold out for a reservation on Hot Creek or right here in the Lava Beds as I have been doing. When they see I insist on either one of these places, they will offer us Yainax. Then I accept, with the understanding I take all my people, none to be tried for murder." But Jack's earnest words had no more effect than raindrops in the sea. His men badgered him, and Black Jim jumped on a big rock and shouted him down.

"Jack, you will never save your people. You can't do it. Are you blind? Can't you see soldiers arriving every two or three days? Kill them, next council. Then all we can do is fight until we die. . . . I am going to fight, and soon, too."

A dozen braves rushed Jack to persuade him to heed Black Jim's harangue. When he still refused to agree to murder the commissioners, they lost all patience with him. Dr. John McLaughlin's remarks about the Chippewas in 1805 were just as true about the Modocs of 1873: "As to their government, they live in an entire state of freedom and liberty, and the authority of their chiefs is entirely personal and no further obey'd by the others than suits their will and inclination." Captain Jack was very nearly deposed at this moment. Hooker Jim said, "You will kill, or be killed by your own men." Another warrior clapped a squaw's hat on Jack's head, and someone threw a woman's shawl around his shoulders. His men tripped him and sent him sprawling. As he lay on his back on the ground, burning with rage and shame, his men taunted him with accusations that he was a white-faced squaw who had gone back on his word: "You coward! You squaw! You are not a Modoc. We disown you. Lie there, you woman, you fish-hearted woman!"

Captain Jack tore off the offending garment and bonnet, leaped to his feet and shouted, "I *am* a Modoc! I *am* your chief! I will do it. *I* will kill Canby. But hear me, my people. This day's work will cost the life of every Modoc brave. We will not live to see it ended. But I will do it. It is a coward's work. . . . But I will do it."

CHAPTER TEN

PEACE TENT PERFIDY

After his worsting in the tribal power struggle, Captain Jack brooded in his cave, trying to find a way to wriggle out of his disastrous promise. He knew that the attempt would be suicidal, ultimately. Meanwhile, his less-sophisticated kinsmen threw a war dance that ran until daybreak. During the night, John Schonchin and his cronies chose their victims. Hooker Jim would assist John Schonchin in killing Meacham. Boston and Bogus, each of whom had just received the present of a suit of clothes from their friend, Reverend Thomas, naturally chose him as their victim. Shacknasty Jim was picked to kill Dyar, with the aid of Barncho. Black Jim, backed by Slolux, would murder Gillem. The plot was a complicated one. Curly Headed Doctor and Curly Haired Jack, with a Gumbatwas named Comstock Dave, would decoy Major Mason to his death on the other side of the Lava Beds from the Peace Tent. But when Frank Riddle's name came up, Scarfaced Charley finally broke his silence. He still refused to take any part in the ambush, saying, "It is unworthy of a Modoc to kill unarmed men." But then he warned his brethren that not only would he defend Toby and Frank Riddle's lives but would also avenge them if they were harmed.

Captain Jack asked Weium for advice, and that loyal retainer urged him to call a last council, and in the daytime when he could look his antagonists in the eyes. Captain Jack's steady gaze was almost as powerful as his oratory. But, though he held the meeting and, as his ally had predicted, the warriors dropped their eyes before his stare that day, he could not restore his shattered authority without going along with the clear majority that now opted for the ambuscade. No longer would his so-far successful policy of stalling suffice.

"You would have listened to me with willing ears a few years ago," he lamented, "but now it will all be in vain. But, nevertheless, I will say what I want to say to you all. You made

214

me promise you something a few nights ago I am sorry of. Do not hold me to it. . . ." But Hooker Jim interrupted, speaking the mind of the majority, now bent on a kind of regicide: "Chief, we hold you to your promise. You have to kill Canby. It is too late."

Captain Jack's primitive executive skills won him a weak compromise, which at least assuaged his feeling of guilt. He agreed to murder but hedged, "I'll do it if Canby refuses to give us a home in our country. I will ask him many times. But if he comes to my terms, I shall not kill him." He gave orders for Barncho and Slolux to hide seven or eight rifles in the rocks near the Peace Tent before daylight on the day of the meeting. Then, sadly, he said to his friend, Scarfaced Charley, "It is all over. I feel ashamed of what I am doing. I did not think I would ever agree to do this thing."

When Jack sent word on April 4 that he wanted to talk to Fairchild and Old Man Meacham, the latter took Rosborough, who was visiting headquarters, as well as the Riddles and Fairchild to the council tent. There Jack talked rather freely, for once, although at first he was haughty and given to offensive language and behavior. But he finally settled down and confessed a fear of Canby because he was a soldier and of Thomas because he was a "Sunday doctor" or priest. Then he said, "Now, I can talk. I am not afraid. I know you and Fairchild. I know your hearts." He reviewed the causes of the war, especially the bullying of the Klamaths and the failure of Agent Knapp, who, said Jack, had no heart for him. In regard to the November murders, he said, "No citizens been in the fight, no Indian women and children would have been killed, no citizens would have been murdered." He assured Meacham, "The soldiers taken away and the war will stop. Give me a home on Lost River." Meacham had to shake his head. "Since blood has been spilled on Lost River, you cannot live there in peace. The blood will always come up between you and the white man. The Army cannot be withdrawn until all the troubles are settled."

Jack sat, silently pondering, then replied, "I hear your words. I give up my home [on Lost River]. Give me this Lava Bed. I can live here. Take away your soldiers and we can settle everything. Nobody will ever want these rocks. Give me a home here." Patiently, Meacham explained that there could be no peace while Jack remained in the Lava Beds without surrendering the indicted murderers. "Who will try them?" asked Jack, "white men or Indians?" Meacham's answer was, "White men, of course," to which Jack countered, "Then, will you give up the men who killed the Indian women and children on Lost River, to be tried by the Modocs?" Sadly, Meacham had to explain that Modoc law was dead in California and Oregon; that only the white man's law now lived. But Jack was not through. "Will you try the men who fired on my people on the east side of Lost River by *your* law?" When Meacham could not even admit this as a possibility, Jack understood and said, "Governor of Oregon has demanded their blood and the law of Jackson County will kill them. . . . Law is all one side, is made by the white men for white men, leaving the Indians all out." He concluded, "No, my friend, I cannot give up the young men to be hung. . . . But take away the soldiers and all the trouble will stop." He laid his hand on Meacham's shoulder, saying, "Tell me, my friend, what am I to do? I do not want to fight." Meacham answered honestly, "The only way now for peace is to come out of the rocks and we will hunt up a new home for you. Then all this trouble will cease."

But Jack could only say, "You ask me to come out and put myself in your power. I cannot do it and am afraid—no, *I* am not afraid, but my people are. . . . I have kept my promise. Have you kept yours? Your soldiers stole my horses. . . . You say you want peace. Why do you come with so many soldiers—to make peace?" He pointed to the north shore of Tule Lake and recalled Ben Wright's Massacre. But Meacham then gestured toward Bloody Point and reminded him of the prior butchery of emigrants there. For seven hours the two men talked in the only full and open exchange of views between the opposing sides during the entire Modoc War. But it was a frustrating and a saddening meeting for Meacham. He was sure now that Jack had lost control of his men. Jack came back to the same point, again and again: "Tell your soldier *tyee* I want him to take his soldiers away. I do not want to fight but I am a Modoc. I am not afraid to die. I can show them how a Modoc can die. . . ."

Meacham reminisced, later, "Long as I have memory, I shall remember his last appeal to me, to give him the Lava Beds for a home, saying that if any other place were given him, white men would want it, some time, but the Lava Beds they would never want. There was something so sad in his face while he turned and swept the rocks with his hand as he made the appeal."

Toby Riddle also recalled her last interview with Jack at this time, when only thirteen of his men were for peace. In her curious, Germanic English, full of inversions, she told interviewer Gatschet, that she had said, "If you make peace, Canby will take good care of you," but her cousin had replied, "When the heart of my young people goes, I shall go with it. Tell your general. Here he will find me in the rocks and not for me around Shasta Butte he must hunt. Not about Yainax he must hunt. Only here will he find me. After I have fallen, many soldiers under me will lie."

When Meacham's long April powwow proved no more productive than those of March, Canby tried a new technique as he applied still more pressure on Jack. He actually notified him, in advance, that he was moving troops closer to the Stronghold. He had Mason order his five companies from Scorpion Point to Hospital Rock, well within the Lava Beds. In so doing, he captured four more of Jack's horses but, this time, Canby "telegraphed" (semaphored by flag) an order to return them to the Indians. The correspondents guessed again that the war would soon be over, with the surrender of Jack expected in about ten days. They did not know that he was building rock fortifications to strengthen his natural defenses.

Canby was delighted when Boston and Bogus stayed over in camp. He let them see his boats on the lake, his reinforcements of infantry, cavalry and artillery, his howitzers and mortars. He even let them examine the mortar shells. He told them one hundred Warm Springs Indian scouts, organized by Lt. Louis V. Caziarc, were coming with Donald McKay, their commander. But, strangely, Bogus and Boston were most interested, impressed and angry with the signal station that allowed Canby to talk over the heads of the Modocs to Mason on the eastern front of the Lava Beds. All of this display was to impress the Modocs with the Army's strength and to convince Jack to surrender. The general kept Washington posted about these moves: "There has been so much vacillation and duplicity in their talks. . . . All the movements of troops have been made deliberately and cautiously so as to avoid collision and to impress the Indians that we have no unfriendly intent. Thus far, we have succeeded very well but their conduct has given so much reason to apprehend that they are only trying to gain time that I have organized a party of [Indian] scouts to operate with the troops if they should go to the mountains or renew hostilities."

When Boston left camp this time, he bore not only the usual presents—two Army blankets and a sackful of provisions—but also the Peace Commission's last formal message to Jack: "If you will come in and surrender to us, we will take you to Yreka or some point adjacent thereto and allow you a voice in selecting your future home. If you do not comply with our wishes, we will resign and leave the matter with the military and you will have no voice in the selection of your future home."

Jack's response to Canby's veiled threats was hardly what the general expected. True, the chief sent a messenger to ask for another talk. But that was not all he sent, that eighth of April. Lt. John Quincy Adams forwarded a note from the signal station to Canby. It was quietly passed around and read silently, so as not to excite the ubiquitous Bogus and Boston. The spies were visiting headquarters, as usual. The message read: "Five Indians at the council tent, apparently unarmed, and about twenty others with rifles in the rocks behind them."

Such a threat did not bother troopers or reporters. As the commissioners grew despondent, the soldiers became cocky. The *Call* observed, "It is the general impression that if the Commission would withdraw, this farce would be ended within three days." On April 9, McKay reported, "The troops are fully prepared for an advance on a moment's notice." He chafed at Canby's inability to move without Washington's prior permission: "If left to himself, he would doubtless bring the difficulty to a close, speedily."

Naturally, after being alerted to Jack's clumsy trap, the commissioners did not accept his invitation to call at the council tent for a Big Talk. But, most unnaturally, with this bald act of treachery fresh in mind, they *did* accept an invitation to meet on April 11. Of course, it was trusting Dr. Thomas, as acting chairman, who accepted after he was conned by his friend Boston Charley's profession of grace: "God has come into the Modoc hearts and put a new fire in it." Unfortunately, Meacham was away on a visit to Lt. William H. Boyle's quartermaster's camp. The warnings of Toby and Frank Riddle went unheeded, although they had secretly been told, as they left the Stronghold after their last visit, that treachery was intended. Wild Gal's man, Weium, had sneaked out of the rocks to say, "Cousin Toby, tell Old Man Meacham and all them men not to come to the council tent again. They get killed." Meacham said of Boston, "He was shrewd enough to take advantage of my absence." But Dr. Thomas crowed, "Tomorrow will witness the triumph of God." Meacham shook his head sadly and retorted, "Doctor, if you keep this compact, you will never again keep one. I believe Toby, that the Indians intend to kill us. Nobody will ever say to you that Toby tells lies." But Thomas explained Meacham's fears by criticizing, "This Indian woman has frightened you. You do not trust in God enough."

Toby told her son Jeff (Charka), "My boy, in case I and your father get killed, stay with Mr. Fairchild. He will care for you till my brother comes for you. But if I can prevent it, the peace commissioners shall not meet Captain Jack and his men in council any more." Years later Jeff recalled, "She was crying as [if] her heart was broke." Meacham greeted the Riddles jocularly as they rode up, "Well, Jeff, I hope you and your mother brought Captain Jack to terms today." But the worried boy did not respond to the banter; instead, he blurted, "Mr. Meacham, I—and my mother—learned on our way to camp the intention of the Indians." His mother said, "Jeff, tell Mr. Meacham just what we were told by Weium." Meacham listened, asked the lad's mother, "Is that the fact?" and when assured that it was, he heard out Frank Riddle. "Mr. Meacham, I have known you for many years. That is the reason we took you into our confidence. My wife's life is in danger. I know you will keep what you have been told by my wife as a secret." The chairman replied, "Mr. Riddle, your confidence is not misplaced when you trust me."

Meacham then brought Canby, Dyar, Thomas and Fairchild to Toby, who addressed them: "I must ask you, before I tell you, not to tell any of the Modocs where you was told what I am going to tell you men, and by whom. My life and man's life and little boy's life will be in great danger. . . ." Meacham immediately promised again, "Toby, anything you tell me that's for our good, I will keep to myself. Depend on me." Canby was next. "Mrs. Riddle, as a man, I promise you not to say a single word to any Modoc of what you are to tell us." According to Jeff Riddle, Thomas got down on his knees in a prayerful attitude, clasped his hands and vowed, "Sister Toby, I am a minister of the Gospel. I have my God to meet and in the name of God, I will not divulge any secret that you may tell me." Dyar and Fairchild swore simply, matter-of-factly, not to betray her. Riddle prefaced his wife's remarks by saying, "I know she is right. I have been married to her for twelve years and she has never, in all that time, deceived me or told me a lie."

Toby then told them of Weium's warning and reiterated, "The next time you meet Jack and his men in council, you will all be shot to death. What I tell you is the truth. Take my warning. Do not meet the people in council any more. If you do, you will be carried to this camp, dead."

Canby smiled and indicated that he believed in the sincerity of Toby and her informant, but dismissed the whole idea of assassination as preposterous. "The little handful of Modocs dare not do that—kill us in the presence of a thousand men. They cannot do it. They might talk about such things but they would not attempt it." Reverend Thomas concurred. "God will not let them do such a thing. I trust in God to protect us."

Frank Riddle pleaded, "Gentlemen, I have known these Modocs for a long time. If they have decided to kill you commissioners, they will do it. I know it. If you men go tomorrow to meet them Modocs, you will never see the sun rise again in this world." Although Meacham, Dyar and Fairchild agreed with the Riddles, the general would only say, "We shall see in the morning what can be done." Meacham tried to cheer up Toby, saying, "I will see that Canby will not meet the Indians in council tomorrow. I will do my best to prevent it." Toby and Frank sat up until after midnight in their cave, trying to hit on a plan to save the commission. But they could not. As Colonel Fry summed up Toby's predicament, it simply was not in her power to overcome the weight of authority. And so, in Fry's words, the commissioners "stumbled on, half-blindedly to their fate."

Next morning, Bogus and Boston rode into camp and were greeted by the naive reverend. Thomas put his hand on each Indian's shoulder and with consummate foolishness, asked, "Why do you Indians want to kill us? Don't you know we are your friends?" Shamming outrage, the hypocritical Bogus demanded, "Who said we wanted to kill you . . .?" The preacher, without a thought for his promise to Toby, said, "Riddle's squaw, Toby." When Bogus, perhaps the cruelest and most treacherous villain in either camp, white or Indian, denied the allegation, the gullible Thomas took his words as gospel. "I thought she lied, Charlie. That is why I ask you." Boston immediately hurried to Jack to tell him of the "leak," while Bogus and the preacher walked arm in arm to Meacham's tent. There, the Modoc was assuring the whites that his people wanted peace when a runner returned from the Lava Beds to ask for a postponement of the arranged council until the next day, April 11, 1873, and to demand that Toby go to the Stronghold. "Toby," he said, "Captain Jack wants to see you at his cave."

Meacham pried the reason for the request out of him and then stopped Toby from mounting her horse. "It is dangerous for you to answer Jack's summons," he warned her. "If Jack wants to see you, we will ask him to come here. I don't want you to go." But Toby answered, "I'll go. I am not afraid to go, Meacham." He then let her proceed but pressed his derringer on her. "Here, take this, you may need it." He also loaned her his horse and overcoat.

Just then, Reverend Thomas walked in and cheerfully said in his asinine way, "Hello, friends, getting ready for council?" Much later in life, Jeff Riddle forgave Thomas' criminal stupidity and repented for not having done justice to the minister's goodness and sincere desire for peace. He wrote, "Since I have grown old, I have a warm place in my heart for Reverend Dr. Thomas and do not confound his name for not believing my mother's warning. I do not think of him with curse words for betraying mother." But Jeff's father on that April day of 1873 had no compunctions about speaking his mind. Angrily, Frank Riddle stared the man of God in the eye and swore, "Thomas, you lied like a yellow dog last night when you promised my wife that you would not say anything about what she was to tell. Jack has sent for her. You are the cause of it. I tell you this, Rev, if my wife ain't back here by sundown, I'll take my gun and shoot you in the right eye, you black-hearted son of a bitch!"

Thomas threw his hands toward heaven in the gesture so beloved of clergymen. "Brother Riddle," he chided in a shocked tone, "get down on your knees and pray to Almighty God for forgiveness. . . ." But Riddle interrupted his piety, snapping, "You lying yellow dog, you might get down and pray the caps off your knees. Then God would not forgive you for what you said last night!"

Toby's departure for the lava labyrinth was heart-rending even to the tough troopers who watched her leave. Meacham recalled the scene: "She parted with her little boy, ten years old, several times before she succeeded in mounting her horse. Clasping him to her breast, she would set him down and start, and then run to him and catch him up again, each time seeming more affected until, at last, her courage was high enough and, saying a few words in a low voice to her husband, she rode off." A distraught Riddle, wielding field glasses, watched her go and waited nervously at a vantage point for her return.

Later, Meacham said of Toby's voluntary meeting with Jack,

"In all the records of heroic actions, that of Wi-ne-ma's [i.e., Toby's] going, after the betrayal, into the camp of the most desperate men in the world stands alone, peerless as an act of heroism." The words are Victorian and pompous; the action Toby took was, nonetheless, courageous in the extreme.

At the Stronghold, Jack angrily demanded to know how Toby had learned of the Modoc machinations. She first talked of spirits informing her in a dream, but Toby was never very good at lying and she finally admitted the truth. "I didn't dream it. The spirits did not tell me. One of your men told me. I won't tell you who it was. Shoot me, if you dare. But," pointing toward Gillem's Camp, she warned, "there are soldiers there. You touch me and they will fire on you and not a Modoc will escape." When four or five gun barrels swung to cover her, she drew the pathetic little derringer which Meacham had given her. But Jack swept the rifles aside and eight men, including Weium, went to her to protect her. Jack then joined them. When the conjurer (Curly Headed Doctor) demanded her death, Jack forbade it, saying, "A woman she is. She knows nothing." He detailed the eight men as an escort to see her safely back to the Army camp, still insisting to her that he really meant to kill no one but only wanted to meet the commissioners, unarmed, with five of his men who would, likewise, be unarmed.

At the camp, a relieved Riddle treated his wife's guards to a hearty meal at the incongruous restaurant Charley La Booth had set up on the very edge of the potential battlefield. The supper must have cost Frank plenty; beef and flour were cheap enough, but oysters ran a dollar a can in the "village," eggs were a dollar a dozen, and whiskey stood at two-bits a drink.

Toby tried to warn the general again, "Canby, take my word. Do not go. You will be killed. I know that these Modocs will kill all of us tomorrow if we go. They may not kill me, but I am afraid of them. They are sure that the soldiers are going to attack them, soon as they get orders from Washington. You see, they are desperate. . . ." Once again, Canby thanked Frank's missus for her concern but said, "Where my duty calls me, I go as a soldier." And when Meacham implored him not to go, he said with a laugh, "Toby has got you scared. Do not show the white feather. If you don't go, I'll meet them alone tomorrow. These Modocs are not fools. They won't try to harm us only half a mile from our army, in plain view." Thomas also pooh-poohed Meacham's fears, telling him that the Modocs had had a change of heart. "God has put a new fire in them and they are ashamed of their bad hearts." They wanted to surrender, he said, and would do so if the peace commissioners would only show their faith by meeting them, unarmed. "God has done a wonderful work in the Modoc camp," he exulted. But Meacham shocked him by retorting, "God has not been in the Modoc camp this winter. If we go, we will not return alive."

In Gillem's marquee that evening, the general, his officers and Meacham were smoking cigars and "chewing the fat" on cots, camp chairs and boxes. Gillem remarked to Canby, "Well, general, whenever you are through trying to make peace with those fellows, I think I can take them out of their Stronghold with the loss of half a dozen men. Oh, we may have some casualties in wounded men, of course, but I can take them out whenever you give the order." Gillem had learned nothing from Wheaton's debacle; he was as cocksure as ever. Lt. William H. Boyle had sized him up upon his arrival, "He never asked any information or allowed Wheaton to give him any, but blustered around camp for a few days, bragging about what he would do and how he would capture and kill the Modocs, had he the opportunity."

Major Mason was less sanguine of an easy victory. "With due deference to the opinion of [brevet] General Gillem," he observed, "I think if we take them out with the loss of one third of the entire command, it is doing as well as I expect." The portly Captain Bernard took his side. "I agree with you, [brevet] Colonel Mason." Just then, Major Green came in. The Fort Klamath commander was asked his view. "I don't know. . . . Only we got licked on the seventeenth of January like. . . . Beg your pardon, general . . ."

In another tent, glory-hungry younger officers were denouncing the Peace Commission as Major Green passed. Throwing aside the tent flap, he poked his head inside and barked, "Stop that! The Peace Commission have a right here as much as we have. They are our friends. God grant them success. I have been in the Lava Beds once. Don't abuse the Peace Commission, gentlemen." But when Meacham returned to the commissioner's tent, he had a visitor, Capt. Thomas Wright, who obviously had something on his chest. Wright said that he had to "growl" to someone. Meacham said, "All right, pitch in."

"Well," began the young officer, "why don't you leave here and give us a chance at those Modocs? We don't want to lie here all spring and summer and not have a chance at them. Now, you know we don't like this delay, and we can't say a word to

General Canby about it. I think you ought to leave and let us clean them out." When Meacham told him of the heavy casualty guesses of Mason, Bernard and Green, Tom Wright exploded, albeit politely, "Pshaw! I will bet two thousand dollars that Lieutenant Eagan's company and mine can whip the Modocs in fifteen minutes after we get into position. Yes, I'll put the money up, I *mean* it!" Meacham replied that he was not at all sure that force would not have to be used—but he was sure of one thing: It would take nine hundred men in addition to Wright's and Eagan's stalwarts.

Quartermaster William H. Boyle visited Gillem's Camp that evening and found Canby and Thomas confident of success but Meacham in a funk. The latter wanted the Riddles as translators but Canby wished to accept Bogus's offer to interpret for him at the April 11 talk. Curiously, Boyle thought that it was Bogus who had warned Toby of treachery, rather than Weium. The quartermaster overstated the situation, too, when he recalled that "everyone" laughed at Meacham and intimated that he was a coward when he passed on Toby's warning to his colleagues. Reporter McKay told his editor that day that the week would probably settle the matter of the Modocs, one way or the other, war or peace. He expected orders for the troops to advance at any moment and that would bring a fight. He was convinced there was no chance of peace unless Jack was given Cottonwood and Hot Creeks.

Rumors that the peace moves were doomed to failure now swept the camp. Several soldiers promptly deserted. One of these was the man serving as the Peace Commission's cook. So Meacham and Dyar had to work out a schedule for each to take turns at the skillet. Thomas would do his part, of course, by asking the blessing. Meacham noted, "Those who have met the Modocs have no desire to meet them again. Those who have not are demoralized by the reports the others gave, and since the common soldiers serve for pay and have not much hope of promotion, they are not so warlike as the brave officers who have their stars to win in the field of battle."

Canby at this moment was writing his wife: "Don't be discouraged or gloomy, darling. I will take good care of myself and come home as soon as possible." In the evening of April 10, Canby again wrote his Louisa. It was his last day on earth. He ventured, prophetically and ironically, that he felt that the end of negotiations was very near.

Reverend Thomas did a lot of private praying as well as publicly pronouncing variations of his maxim, "One man with faith is stronger than a hundred with interest only."

On that tenth of April, Captain Trimble took Meacham and Cabaniss by boat to Mason's camp, giving them a thrill by deliberately skirting the Lava Beds, well within rifle range. But Jack's orders not to take potshots at the military were obeyed. Later, at a picket station, Scarfaced Charley came to Dr. Cabaniss and asked for a box of crackers and some matches. The doctor had none of the former but he gave his friend, whom he called "the Chevalier Bayard of the Modocs," some matches. Then, on impulse, he said, "Charley, I would like to see Captain Jack." "All right," said his friend, "you go to his house with me." Charley picked up his rifle, which he had laid aside to show his peaceful intent, and said, "Doctor, you take my rifle." But Cabaniss refused it, saying he was not afraid of Jack's Modocs. Captain Jack was not very communicative, except to stress his resolution to get a Lost River reservation. He was ill-mannered enough, also, to break off his conversation in order to take a sweat bath in his rude *temescal* or Modoc sauna. During the talk, which was translated by the glib Bogus, Jack and Black Jim fired at a gull on Tule Lake for target practice. (They missed.) Black Jim chuckled as the reports died away, "The soldiers think me kill you." He was right. When the doctor returned to camp, he found his friends fearful that he had lost his life.

The commissioners were up early on the morning of April 11, which some writers described as fair and calm but which later saw, according to Maj. John S. Parke (writing in 1908) the face of the sun hidden by dark clouds that hovered over the lava. But there was considerable optimism, and Lieutenant Boyle went back to Hospital Rock, expecting no more trouble from the Indians. He told friends that the Modocs were expected to treat with Canby that day; the war was over.

By one of those cruel ironies of fate with which the Modoc story is replete, Captain Jack had chosen a true day of sacrifice for his assassinations. It was Good Friday. Toby still begged the commissioners not to attend, as did Frank Riddle. In Thomas' tent Bogus and Boston were finishing off breakfast on the reverend's plates. Meacham was doubly sure treachery was afoot when, shortly, the two scoundrels, in their greed, could not help protesting as he switched to a worn pair of old boots for the hike to the Peace Tent. One of the Modocs asked, "What for you take 'em off new boots? Why for you no wear 'em new boots?"

Meacham was still opposed to going, as was Dyar. They wanted, at least, to arm themselves, but Thomas protested. The pious Petaluman reminded his colleagues, "The agreement is to go unarmed. We must be faithful on our part to the compact and leave it all in the hands of God." Yet even Thomas had some doubts for his safety; Meacham noted that the cleric paid the sutler for some goods he had bought for his Modoc pets, Boston and Bogus, and the preacher even confided to an officer that he was not sure he would return. But he said that he would do his duty faithfully and trust God to bring him out all right. According to the *Astorian*, Canby was worried a bit, too. Certainly he told Gillem to send a message to him via Cabaniss if Meacham's suspicions were verified by any overt action by the Modocs. The doctor was tense, remembering later that "all of us felt uneasy and anticipated that which followed," although some of this may have been hindsight.

Meacham asked Fairchild, "John, what do you think? Is it safe to go?" His friend suggested, "Wait a minute and let me have another talk with Bogus. I think I can tell." But when he returned, he shook his head. He could not advise him. "I can't make out from Bogus what to think. I don't like the look of things. Still, he talks all right. Maybe it's all on the square." Meacham then decided to go—after one more appeal to Canby. He told Fairchild, "I must go if the general and the doctor do." Then he hurried to his tent and penned a quick note to his wife, which he gave to Fairchild with one hundred dollars, two rings and his watch. The note, which reflected the price put on "honor" by Victorians, read: "You may be a widow tonight. You shall not be a coward's wife. I go to save my honor. John A. Fairchild will forward my valise and valuables. The chances are all against us. I have done my best to prevent this meeting. I am no wise to blame. . . ." To Fairchild he said, "John, I am going to my death. Send that package to my wife. I don't like to go, but I am not a coward."

Meacham questioned Dyar's going when he did not have to do so. Again it was the code of honor of the times that impelled the agent to go to what he thought might well be his death. He told Meacham, "If you go, I am going. I will not stay here if all the rest go."

Toby was weeping as she held Meacham's horse, Joe Lane, by

a rope. "Meacham, you no go! You get kill!" she cried. Winding the end of the rope around her waist, she threw herself on the ground, shaking. "You no get your horse. The Modocs mad now. They kill all you men. Meacham, you no go! You get kill!"

Although the general had made it clear that he felt the importance of the mission justified some risk, Meacham tried, one last time, to appeal to Canby. When he suggested that a well-armed Fairchild accompany them, saying, "I know Fairchild, I know he is a dead shot and he and I can whip a dozen Indians in open ground with revolvers," Canby's reply was negative. Such a precaution would be a breach of faith. Meacham persisted. "Gentlemen, my cool, deliberate opinion is that if we go to the council tent today we will be carried home tonight on stretchers, cut to pieces. I tell you, I dare not ignore Toby's warning. I believe her and I am not willing to go."

Canby sought to calm him. "Mr. Meacham, you are unduly cautious. There are but five Indians at the council tent and they dare not attack us." Meacham then blew up. "General, the Modocs dare do anything. I know them better than you, and I know they are desperate. . . ." The general patiently heard him out, then answered calmly, "I have left orders for a watch to be kept, and if they attack us, the Army will move at once against them. We have agreed to meet them and we must do it." Dr. Thomas seized on the last words, to add, "I have agreed to meet them and I never break my word. I am in the hands of God. If He requires my life I am ready for the sacrifice."

Thomas was deaf to Meacham's argument that they go armed. The minister castigated the chairman as being too much of a fighting man who should, instead, put his faith in God. Thomas reminded him that they were going to the tent to make *peace,* not war. "Put your faith in God," he said. "Pray more and think less about fighting." Meacham then blasphemed modestly by saying that he doubted *His* ability to drop revolvers down from on high when the commissioners would need them. Meacham's last hope was that Canby would agree to any demand, if it became necessary to extricate the party from a trap. But here, too, Canby was adamant, "No, in thirty years I have never made a promise that could not be carried out. I am not willing now to promise anything that we don't intend to perform." When Thomas added more of his moralizing, if suicidal sentiments, Meacham retorted that his own conscience would never condemn him for saving lives—even his own life—by dissimulation. "I don't want to die, but if you go, I must go, to save my name from dishonor." Canby's reply verged on sarcasm. "That squaw has got you scared, Meacham. I don't see why you should be so careful of your scalp. It is not much better than my own."

Meacham gave up and sadly walked to his tent. There he exacted a promise from Fairchild that, should his corpse be mutilated by the Modocs, the rancher would bury it in the Lava Beds and not torture his family by letting them view it. Fairchild handed him his revolver, saying, "Here, Meacham, you can bang brimstone out of 'em with it." But the commission's chairman had to refuse the weapon since he knew he would be accused of precipitating a fight by going to the council while armed. However, someone (never named in the accounts) dropped a small derringer in his pocket, saying in a low tone, "It's surefire. It's all right." Meacham said nothing and did not remove it. Dyar noted the action of Meacham's anonymous benefactor and ran to his tent and pocketed his own derringer.

Meanwhile, Frank Riddle had asked for an audience with Canby, his officers and the commissioners. He asked that he and his wife be absolved of all blame for whatever might occur at the Peace Tent. "I want you gentlemen to know. . . . I have been talking with my wife. She has never told me a lie or deceived me and she says if you go today you will be killed. If I happen to make my escape, I want my hands clean. I don't want any blame to fall on me or my wife, if she escapes. We wash our hands of all blame. . . . We did our best to save these men. . . . If you must go, go well armed."

Canby made a joke of Riddle's warning, saying gaily, "Well, brother-officers, I bid you all a last farewell. From what Riddle says, this is my last day!" Toby caught him by the arm and begged him for the last time not to go, but Thomas intervened: "Sister Toby, the Modocs will not hurt us. God will not allow it."

Tucking a box of cigars under one arm, Canby, resplendent in the full-dress uniform of a brigadier general, started on foot for the Peace Tent with the undoubting Thomas following dutifully at his heels. It was 11:06 A.M., April 11, 1873.

Meacham joined a pale but collected Riddle and gently took his horse from the still-crying Toby. Frank said, "I'm a'goin on foot. I don't want no horse to bother me." Actually, the ground was so rough that a man on foot could make better time than on horseback. Meacham made his good-byes and followed

Canby and Thomas. Dyar, riding a gray, followed him. Then came Frank Riddle, on shanks mare, preceding Bogus and Boston, both mounted. Toby, also riding, brought up the rear. Riddle was particularly uneasy about the two Modocs who accompanied them, although they had spent the night with him and Toby in their cave at Gillem's Camp.

Meacham reined up at the side of the surgeon and asked, "Dr. Cabaniss, do you think there is danger under the arrangement which we have made?" "What is the arrangement?" asked the doctor. "There are to be five unarmed Indians and five of us." Cabaniss replied, "Under that arrangement, there is no danger. But, Meacham, if you are suspicious of those Indians, remain here and let me go to see them." Meacham hesitated, turned in his saddle and saw Canby striding into the Lava Beds and shook his head. Silently, he followed the general. At the same time ten-year-old Jeff Riddle was bidding his parents a tearful good-bye and vowing, "If the Modocs kill you, I will avenge you if it takes a lifetime!"

The commissioners found a half-dozen Modocs awaiting them. With Boston and Bogus, who had hurried ahead, this made eight warriors, not the six men they had agreed to meet. And none of them made much of an effort to hide the pistol concealed in his waistband. Nor were they at the Peace Tent, but some distance beyond where a small council fire was more or less hidden from the Army's signal station by the bulk of the tent. To Meacham, this was no accident.

Captain Jack wore a slouch hat and a worn gray coat. He seemed anxious, ill at ease, unable to affect the excessive cordiality of some of his warriors. John Schonchin, black and gray-streaked hair framing a villainous face, was seated near him. Pacing restlessly to and fro like a cougar was young, muscular Hooker Jim, the very epitome of a cutthroat, and in Meacham's words, "a blot on humanity" and "an ugly customer in a fight." Near him was the untidy fellow, Shacknasty Jim, his hair parted neatly in the middle, however, for the occasion. His almost feminine features disguised a desperate man. Black Jim, Captain Jack's half-brother, was next; a bad-looking man who reminded Meacham of a snake and who was twice as mean as one. Ellen's Man rounded out the group. He was light-complexioned like Boston Charley, round-faced and fine looking. But he had a heart of dross. He had volunteered, eagerly, to take Jack's place if the chief still had qualms. Hidden from the commissioners in nearby rocks were Barncho and Slolux, with rifles ready to be rushed to their co-conspirators. Hidden from everyone was Scarfaced Charley, ambushing the ambushers, as it were. He waited with his rifle at the ready for any sign of an attack on his friends, the Riddles; ready to blow the head off the attacker.

Unknown to Scarfaced Charley, the plot almost aborted. Boston's nerve failed him at the critical moment. But he regained his determination to kill when his pardner, Bogus, offered to do his killing for him. He reminded his friend, too, "Kill these men and the war will stop. It will scare all the soldiers away."

As Canby approached the Peace Tent, three quarters of a mile from camp though seemingly closer because of the clarity of the air, the Indians could see the sun glinting off the brass buttons of his dress uniform. They rose to greet him with well-feigned warmth and camaraderie. He responded by passing around a box of cigars and soon all, except Thomas, who teetotaled in tobacco as well as spirits, were puffing away and chatting contentedly, even laughing occasionally. Riddle glanced at the Peace Tent as he passed it, half expecting to find a bushwhacker inside, but it was empty. Since Jack had no *chef de protocol*, individuals sat where they chose.

Although it was cool, Meacham took off his overcoat. He thought it would be hopeless to run, which he knew both Dyar and Riddle planned to do at the first sign of violence. But he wanted to be able to get at the derringer in the pocket of his coat, if need be. On the way out to the Peace Tent he had told his friends, "I cannot run. But I shall sell my life as dearly as possible."

From their hiding places, Barncho, Slolux and Scarfaced Charley watched a strange game, like a ritual dance. Their dissimulating kinsmen, smoking away on their stogies, tried to separate themselves from the whites, but Dyar and Riddle would have none of it and mixed with them. The proud Canby, of course, and Thomas stood erect and unmoving. Meacham noticed that when the fire needed renewing, there were no squaws for the chore. It was Bogus Charley who went to scare up more sagebrush, and he took his rifle, took his time, and took a long hard look back toward Gillem's Camp. Hooker Jim appeared to be in the role of a sentinel, too, and he suddenly gave an alarm. A white man was approaching. All the Modocs leaped to their feet. It turned out to be a man named Clark, out looking for strayed horses, who had blundered on the council.

Canby asked Dyar to send him away, and the powwow finally began with Toby translating English into Modoc and Frank rendering the Modoc into "Boston talk."

In an atmosphere soon crackling with electric tension, Canby opened the conversation by saying, "It is important that we should talk over the peace treaty." Captain Jack's reply was, "We want no more war. We are tired and our women and children are afraid of the soldiers. We want them taken away, *then* we can make peace. . . ."

Although his ears were taking in Jack's peroration, Meacham could not tear his eyes from the restless Hooker Jim. The latter virtually telegraphed his evil intentions by swaggering over and tying Meacham's horse securely to a sagebrush so that the animal would not bolt when shooting started. Meacham had dropped the halter to the ground, leaving Joe Lane free to escape. Hooker then tried on Meacham's overcoat, buttoning it carefully and smirking an insult, "Me Old Man Meacham, now. Bogus, you think me look like Old Man Meacham?"

The chairman, his heart pounding in his throat, tried to treat the implied threat like a joke. He said, "Hooker Jim, you had better take my hat, also." The Indian's words chilled Meacham's blood. "I will, bye and bye. Don't hurry, Old Man."

Dyar and Riddle were blanched of face at Hooker's sneering threats. Both made excuses to fiddle with the trappings of the horses in order to have the cover of the animals. Toby, with an exaggerated yawn, even threw herself to the ground and stretched out, resting on her elbows—hopefully out of pistol fire. Even Canby seemed to realize, finally, that he was in a trap. Meacham thought that he could tell this by the look that came on the general's face. He hoped against hope that the general, like Steele, would lie and promise Jack anything, including the removal of the soldiers. "All seemed to feel that if he assented to the withdrawal of the Army, the trouble would be passed over," Meacham recalled. But, although Canby's lips quivered a bit, he spoke firmly—and dashed Meacham's hopes of survival. "Toby, tell these people that the President of the United States sent the soldiers here to protect them as well as the white man . . . to see that everything is done right. . . . They are your friends and will not harm you. . . . They cannot be taken away without the President's consent." Thus the general pronounced his own death sentence.

Canby then began to reminisce about his younger days, when he had helped move some Mikasuki Indians from Florida during the Seminole War. He told the Modocs that they had become such good friends that the Mikasukis had adopted him and named him "Friend of the Indians." He ended, "I have no doubt that, sometime, you Modoc people will receive me as kindly." But the Modocs heard his sincere words with contemptuous and raucous laughter. The joke was, indeed, on Canby. Meacham relived that moment many times and recalled, "Whether General Canby realized the situation with all its fearful possibilities and would not swerve, even then, from his purpose, or if he still thought the Modocs had not the desperate courage to execute the plan, can never be known."

When Canby was finished, Meacham asked Thomas to speak. The latter dropped forward on his knees into an attitude of prayer and, grasping Meacham by the left shoulder, said, "Toby, tell these people for me that I believe the Great Spirit put it into the heart of the President to send us here to make peace. . . . We are all brothers and must live in peace together." When he finished, Jack got to his feet and said, "I don't want to talk further," and turned his back on Canby. Schonchin John then sprang up and shouted, "Take away your soldiers! We want Hot Creek for a home. Take away your soldiers, give us Hot Creek, or stop talking! I am tired of talking. I talk no more!"

Survivors Meacham, Dyar and the Riddles never made it clear whether they heard the sound of shots from Hospital Rock breaking into Schonchin John's bombast, but presumably Captain Jack heard them. They were the signal. Before Riddle could finish interpreting Schonchin John's hot remarks, Jack shouted in Modoc "All ready!" It was one-thirty in the afternoon. His words were answered by a war whoop from Barncho and Slolux who rushed forward, cradling the rifles in their arms, and by Schonchin John's cry of "*Chock-e-la!* (Blood!)."

Meacham barely had time to gasp, "Jack, what does this mean?" before the chief drew a six-shooter from under his coat. The sounds of shots on the eastern front were still echoing among the lava crags.

CHAPTER ELEVEN

AS GOOD A PLACE AS ANY TO DIE

At Captain Bernard's Hospital Rock encampment across the Lava Beds to the east, an eighteen-year-old sentry, Pvt. Charles B. Hardin of G Troop, was visited at his picket post by the officer of the day, Lt. William Sherwood of the 21st Infantry. The young lieutenant was a very popular officer with the rankers since he did not stand on ceremony and he liked to chat with the enlisted men. He had a lot more faith in the Peace Commission's efforts than Toby Riddle, and he explained why he was in a good mood. "Well, Hardin, this is the last day of the war and now we can go home and rest." Hardin was not so sure. He ventured, "This may be the last day of the war, lieutenant, but *I* don't believe it. I think we shall have at least one more good battle before the war ends." Sherwood laughed and said, "Nonsense! You must not be such a croaker; we shall have peace today." Then he told Hardin to keep a sharp lookout for Modocs who might want to visit the camp under a flag of truce.

Only a few minutes after he took his leave, Hardin saw two Indians waving a white flag some four hundred yards away. He put down his carbine, climbed to the top of a rock and waved and called to them. Sherwood, hearing his yells, retraced his steps and told the private, who could understand the Modoc shouts no better then the lieutenant, "I am going out to see what they want." He ignored the soldier's remonstrance: "Don't go, lieutenant; they will surely kill you!"

Fifty years later, that day was still clear in Hardin's mind as he recalled it to historian William S. Brown. He remembered Sherwood joshing him about his lack of confidence, and asking him if he did not know that the Modocs were meeting the commission that very day. Hardin's retort was that he knew it—and believed that it would be the end of the commissioners, too.

When Hardin pulled a stone out of the wall of his lava-rock breastwork, Sherwood asked the reason. The soldier explained

233

that he was a sharpshooter and that he was going to keep him covered from the loophole during his powwow with the Indians. Sherwood protested until Hardin assured him that the Modocs could not see him and that he would not fire unless they jumped him. As Sherwood left, Hardin sat down, adjusted the sights of his .50-caliber Sharps carbine to the proper elevation, and drew a bead on the taller of the two Modocs. This was almost certainly Steamboat Frank. At six feet in height, he towered over his kinsmen and, perfectly proportioned as well as tall, he approached the figure of the ideal redman of mythology. Hardin kept him covered during the brief interview, which ended without incident. The Indians disappeared back into the rocks and Sherwood returned to the outpost. He told the private that the Modocs would be back at one o'clock. "They wish to talk to the big *tyees,* Major Mason, Colonel Bernard and Major Jackson." He then told Hardin to turn his orders over to his relief and to have the man notify him, as officer of the day, when the Indians returned.

"I thought so," said Hardin cryptically. "What do you mean?" asked Sherwood. "I mean they let you go so they could catch bigger game." But Sherwood again laughed at Hardin's dire prophecies.

Shortly after noon the Indians reappeared, watched by Hardin and his comrades of the guard squad that had just gone off duty. Many of them perched atop Hospital Rock. Unfortunately for most of the men below the rock, they could not see the meeting under the truce flag. But a number of men in camp, apparently uneasy, rounded up their horses without any orders to do so and sat by their saddles, ready for action should it become necessary.

Wisely, Mason refused to meet any Modocs anywhere but at his camp's picket posts, so Sherwood took Lt. William H. Boyle, who had been Indian agent on the Umatilla Reservation and who spoke the Chinook Jargon fluently. The two officers, unarmed, walked about a half-mile from the point where Hardin's relief stood guard. They met Curly Haired Jack, out ahead of the truce flag. He asked Sherwood if Boyle was the big *tyee.* Boyle answered in the Chinook patois that he was not and explained, "He will not come." The Modoc then asked them to go to the white flag where Steamboat Frank and Comstock Dave wanted to talk to them.

Both men began to sense danger and declined the invitation. Boyle told the Indians to come to the Army camp for a *wa-wa.* This the Modocs refused to do. Lieutenant Boyle, recalling the sequence of events, years later, in the formal third person, wrote, "The officers saw at once that they were in for it and being some half-mile from the pickets and a good mile from camp, and in the power of three well-armed Indians, men chosen for the purpose, [saw] that their chances were very poor for getting back. So, after some more parleying with the Indians to show them they did not fear them, they bid [sic] them good-day, and started for camp."

No sooner had the two officers turned their backs than the Modocs began to fire at them. Boyle shouted to Sherwood to separate, so that they would make more difficult targets. "Run! Run for your life!" he cried. Each man broke into a zigzag dash over the rough terrain, one to the left and the other to the right. But Sherwood gained only thirty paces before Curly Haired Jack shot him in an arm and in one leg. The ball broke his thighbone close to the hip—dangerous enough—but the ball in his arm severed an artery.

The watching soldiers on Hospital Rock could no longer see the fleeing officers because of an intervening hogback, or lava ridge, but they scrambled down from their rocky perches to go to their aid. When Sherwood fell, the Modocs concentrated their fire on Boyle and followed in pursuit of him until a sentry began to fire at them and saved Boyle's skin. When the soldiers came to his rescue, they found him, in his own words, "sitting on a rock outside the pickets, very much exhausted by scrambling among the rocks to keep out of the range of the Indians' rifles."

In the pandemonium, the guard relief formed up, without orders, and started out to rescue the two lieutenants. An excited, bare-headed officer visiting Mason from Gillem's Camp ran after them and took command. It was probably the courageous Lt. C. P. Eagan, since the press later credited him with rescuing Boyle. Unfortunately, at the moment he was so rattled that he led the men off in the wrong direction. The sergeant of the guard tried to straighten him out but he would not listen. Desperately, the noncom turned to Hardin. "You know where they are. I cannot get away from this lunatic. You drop back and, when clear, run up this draw and hurry to that hogback. The officers are down behind that."

Hardin ran up the ravine and saw Boyle making his escape into the perimeter of the camp, but Sherwood lay on the ground. Hardin called to him, asking if he was badly hurt, and the lieutenant answered that he was. The private stood up and shouted, "Here he is!" as loud as he could. Some of his comrades, now two hundred yards away to his left with the blundering officer, broke away and came to help him carry the wounded man into camp. But Sherwood died of his wounds there. Boyle said of his friend, who had just returned from a European tour, "A better or more gentlemanly officer never wore the uniform of the United States Army, and all regretted his loss. . . . Young and energetic, with a long life before him, it was too hard to lose his life by such treachery."

The guard, under the sergeant (with the officer tagging along behind), deployed as skirmishers and took up prone positions in the rocks to cover the party removing Sherwood to the camp. From their advanced positions they could see across the arm of Tule Lake to the Peace Tent and, at that very moment, heard shots from the tent. Soon they heard the wild yells of men in Gillem's Camp, too. Hardin saw some of his comrades rush out toward the Stronghold, only to be halted—with difficulty—by their officers. He believed that Mason's prudence was well taken. "Had our commanding officer not kept his head, the war would have ended on that day, but at a fearful loss to the troops engaged." Major Mason's family thought that he had had a closer call than was actually the case, however, and his wife wrote a friend on April 21: "There is no doubt but it was their intention to shoot Edwin, too, when they shot poor young Lieut. Sherwood."

Mason hastily wigwagged Gillem's Camp, "Boyle and Sherwood attacked under a flag of truce." The message was hurried to Colonel Gillem by one of the signal station men. It was 1:30 P. M. Gillem sat down immediately to write a note to Canby at the same time that he sent his adjutant to fetch Dr. T. T. Cabaniss. "Will you take a message to General Canby?" he asked. "Yes, sir," said the doctor. Gillem said, "I have selected you out of this entire command but I do not want you to go under any misapprehension." Cabaniss said that he was ready. "I will write the message," continued Gillem, "because if you carry a verbal message, Bogus will tell the other Indians." Gillem was in the very act of handing the message to Cabaniss when the signal sergeant ran down the slope to camp, shouting "They're firing on the Peace Tent! They're firing on the commissioners!"

The shots fired by Steamboat Frank and his men at Sherwood and Boyle were the agreed-upon signals for Captain Jack to go into action. As the reports rumbled over the badlands, Barncho and Slolux rushed up with their rifles. Jack gave his cry and fired his pistol, point-blank, in Canby's face. But the hammer only snapped on a percussion cap in a harmless misfire. Quickly the Modoc recocked the revolver and fired again. This time the charge in the cylinder did not fail him. The pistol ball tore through the general's face under his left eye. But he did not fall. Instinct or the reflex action of motor nerves made Canby run. He broke into a shambling flight. Jack and Ellen's Man ran after him till he fell, mortally wounded and breaking his jaw as he pitched face-first onto the rough lava rocks. He was some thirty-five yards from the council fire. Jack held him by the shoulders while Ellen's Man stabbed him under the right ear with a narrow-bladed knife. Both men then speedily stripped the corpse, after which Ellen's Man took one of Barncho's rifles and shot Canby in the side of the head above the left ear.

While Canby was being killed, Dyar was sprinting for his life, chased by Hooker Jim. The agent bolted like a mule deer and outdistanced his pursuer. Several times Hooker Jim fired at him, as did Black Jim, but all their shots were wide of the mark. After covering about two hundred yards, Dyar managed to draw his derringer. He stopped, turned and aimed the peashooter at Hooker. Suddenly, the Indian's enthusiasm for the chase evaporated—along with his bravery—and he dropped to the ground.

Riddle ran for Tule Lake, chased half-heartedly by Black Jim, who was mindful of Scarfaced Charley's vow to revenge any harm done the Riddles. Black Jim fired a few shots. They were probably not in earnest but meant merely to scare the squawman away.

Boston Charley shot Reverend Thomas in the chest, near the right nipple. But he, too, was hard to kill. Bracing himself with his right hand, he lifted the other in supplication and begged his attacker, "Don't shoot me again, Boston! I shall die anyway." Boston just joked, "Not good now. You are a Sunday doctor." Bogus then joined Boston in tormenting their "friend." After letting Thomas clamber painfully to his feet to run, his two favorites tripped him and Boston taunted him as he fell, "Why don't you turn the bullets? Your medicine is not strong!" When Thomas again rose to walk a few unsteady steps, they pushed him down and continued to ridicule him as their guts rumbled in digestion of the food which he had provided them earlier in the day. "God damn you, you devil" cried one of them.

"Maybe so you believe what a squaw tell you, next time!" After the pitiable preacher fell for the last time, about eighty yards from the tent, Bogus placed the muzzle of a carbine to his head and blew Thomas' brains out before stripping him of his clothing. He had been careful not to scorch, puncture or bloody the fine tweed suit that he wanted so badly, after the unfortunate first shot in the chest.

John Schonchin, at Jack's signal, cross-drew a revolver from his left side with his right hand, then drew a knife with his left hand and started for Meacham with both weapons. The commissioner got his derringer out and jammed it against John's chest and pulled the trigger. But it did not fire; in his haste he had brought the hammer only to half-cock, to the safety position. Before he could thumb the hammer back to fire, the Indian thrust his pistol in his face. Meacham had time only to stoop but the movement saved his life. His face was powder burned, his whiskers were singed by the muzzle blast; but the ball only cut through the collar of his coat and the shoulder of his vest and shirt, barely bruising him. Meacham fell back about forty yards while Toby struggled with his assailant, who kept firing but missing.

Dropping his empty six-shooter, the Modoc drew another from his waistband but was fearful of coming too close to the derringer. Toby kept up her pleading, "Don't kill him! Don't kill Meacham! He is the friend of the Indians!" But John quieted her by striking her on the head with his gun. Now Shacknasty Jim took aim at Meacham but Toby recovered and struck down the gun barrel before he could fire. He threatened her with the weapon, drew aim again, fired, and crowed "I hit him!"

Just as Meacham was about to fire the single shot in his under-powered derringer, John Schonchin's pistol ball struck him smack in the forehead, but at an angle. Remarked Meacham, later, "After I fell, I raised my head above the rock over which I had fallen and, at that instant, Schonchin aimed at me so correctly that this shot struck me between the eyes and glanced out over the left eye, which was [temporarily] blinded." Meacham then fired and John Schonchin fell, wounded in the right side. But another slug, probably the one which Shacknasty Jim fired, tore into Meacham's right arm, forcing him to drop his little pistol. Another ball cut away part of his right ear and still another glanced off the right side of his head, knocking him unconscious. As Meacham lay quivering, apparently in his death throes, Schonchin John started to pull off his clothing and Slolux put the muzzle of his rifle to the white man's temple and began to squeeze the trigger. Just then, Shacknasty Jim unwittingly saved Meacham's life. He shoved Slolux rudely aside, saying "Don't shoot any more. Him dead. He no get up. I hit him high up. Save the powder." Hearing Jack calling to them, both men left Meacham, saying to Toby, "There lies another of your brothers, you white-hearted squaw. Go and take care of him. You are no Modoc!"

Boston Charley came scuttling up, like a buzzard after carrion, announcing "I am going to have Old Man Meacham's scalp to put on my shot pouch." Hooker Jim discouraged him, saying of the bald man, "He has no scalp." But Boston took out a small pocketknife he had looted from the corpse of a soldier killed during the January battle. He pushed Toby aside as she was wiping the blood from her friend's face and began what his victim later facetiously called "the difficult task of scalping a bald-headed man." Grasping what hair Meacham had, he began to make an incision in the scalp. But luckily for Meacham, Boston had not found a whetstone among the January booty and the clasp knife was dull. Toby shoved him away but he returned and threatened her with his pistol, then resumed his bloody work. Bracing his foot on his victim's neck, Boston cut a long half-circular gash prior to ripping off a side lock of hair and one ear. He commented, "Old Meacham, your hide is tough."

Suddenly, Toby Riddle clapped her hands and shouted, "*Ut nah sholgars kep-ko!* ("The soldiers are coming!"). Boston Charley abandoned his butchery, gave the "corpse" a final kick and fled without his grisly trophy. All of the Modocs now ran, except the wounded John Schonchin, who rode off on Meacham's horse, Joe Lane. Barncho grabbed the reins of Toby's horse and began to mount it, cursing because the saddle had two horns. (The Victorian Toby rode sidesaddle!) Mrs. Riddle pulled him off by his coattails but he swung his rifle and hit her across the back, knocking her to the rocks. He snarled, "You white man's sister, I'll leave you among your dead brothers if you bother me again!" Toby picked up a rock and slugged the warrior with it, crying, "You coward, you cannot fight your equal! You will not take my animal. Kill me first!" Barncho was annoyed enough to oblige her in this rhetorical request. He raised the butt of his rifle to his shoulder, but Captain Jack's voice cut through the air like a whiplash, "No, you won't!" And his hand knocked down the gun. "Barncho, if it was not for the good you will do in our war with the whites, I would blow your head off and leave you here to rot, you coward! What do you mean by striking that woman? If you ever say another word to her I will kill you!"

As the other Modocs bade her a friendly-enough good-bye, perhaps for the last time, Jack spoke to Toby. "I have thrown myself and life away today. I did something today that I thought I would never do, but I have done it. I killed an unarmed man. I know I will be killed, but when I fall there will be soldiers under me. Tell Gillem, if he wants to find me to come right over yonder (gesturing toward his cave); tell him not to go way off in the mountains to look for me. He won't find me in the mountains. I will be in my camp with my people. . . . Tell him I will be ready at any time to receive him and his soldiers. I am not afraid to die. I have committed a great wrong. I know it, but I was forced to do it by my men, and also by Canby himself. He did not talk straight to me."

Toby cleaned the blood off Meacham's face with her dress, muttered, "Him dead, him dead," in her grief (according to Meacham) and straightened out his body. She then rode off to alert the Army. (According to her son, Toby found a flicker of life in Meacham's body and rode to get medical help.)

Pvt. Maurice FitzGerald of K Troop was loafing about the signal station when the sergeant scrambled down the cliff with the alarm. Fitz followed him, as did many of his comrades, and ran to the line of tents where the troop's arms were stacked. Each man grabbed his carbine and started at full speed for the council tent. As the first puffs of white smoke were followed by the reports from the tent, young Jeff Riddle—on the bluff with field glasses trained and his father's revolver in his belt—shouted to the soldiers below, "The Modocs are killing the commissioners!" He then ran toward the council tent, swearing vengeance on the Modocs if they harmed his parents. But he was held back by soldiers, with difficulty, until he saw his mother and father coming safely into camp. According to Meacham's overdramatic recall, troopers threatened Toby's life with curses and menacing rifles and she cried out, "Shoot me! Shoot me if you dare! I am not to blame!" Then a corporal jumped in front of her, if Meacham's information was correct, and warned his mates, "I'll avenge her death!" In the general consternation, reporters Fox and Atwell rushed for their tents, the British Army veteran buckling on his revolver, ready to join the soldiers.

As they ran, the command "Fall in!" was roared by some officer. The troopers who were starting into the Lava Beds instinctively halted and returned to Gillem's Camp. Only a sergeant, an ex-Confederate in K Company, got very far with a few men, but he, too, was recalled to ranks. The bugle sounded Assembly and the men lined up ready to march out on the double.

With no fog and no snipers to slow them, Green's men could have repeated their move of January at double-quick time. But no order came to advance. All was confusion in camp. Gillem, too sick to attend the peace council, was petrified with indecision, although Captain Biddle told him, "I saw Canby fall!" Just how long it took the rescuers to make their move is impossible to say. Reporter Fox said it was five minutes; Atwell said it took an hour; FitzGerald merely reported a chafing delay. But the men and officers were frantic with impatience, the latter swearing they would march their men out without Gillem's orders. Finally the colonel snapped out of his funk and gave the command to advance. "Forward, march! Double-time, march!" was repeated along the line.

On their way into the Lava Beds the soldiers first met Dyar. The long-legged, tall and muscular Indian agent came bounding over the boulders and, almost out of breath, gasped, "They are all killed but me!" Leaving him, the troops next encountered Riddle and asked, "Where are the others?" "All dead, killed by the damned Indians," heaved Riddle. Catching his breath, he went on: "Oh, the devils! It has turned out just as I thought it would; and now I guess they will believe me, and her, when we tell them there is danger!"

Soon the soldiers came upon Toby, in tears, who sobbed, "Canby, Thomas, Meacham, all dead." Private FitzGerald recalled the next moment. "When we reached the tent, a gruesome sight was presented to our view. About twenty feet to the south lay General Canby, on his back. His body was pierced by three bullets and all his clothing had been removed." Next, the soldiers found the stripped body of Thomas, lying on top of his purse, which still contained sixty dollars, and then Meacham's body, naked except for a pair of red flannel drawers. The latter, in reporter Atwell's words, was "a terrible looking object" because of his gunshot wounds and interrupted scalping. Less than thirty minutes after Captain Jack's gruff command, Meacham had apparently staggered to his feet, so covered with blood that he was unrecognizable, and almost became a target for a trigger-happy trooper. "That's an Indian!" shouted the soldier, but Lt. William H. Miller's roar drowned him out: "Don't shoot! He's a white man!" Meacham was on the ground again by the time Dr. Cabannis reached him. The doctor ordered a stretcher and poured some whiskey down the wounded man's throat. Meacham sputtered a protest: "I can't drink brandy. I am a temperance man!" Cabaniss did not lecture Meacham on the difference between brandy and whiskey but just snorted, half in disgust and half in admiration, "Stop your nonsense! No time for temperance. Down with it!" It was probably pretty good whiskey. Meacham remained conscious and was so lucid that Atwell was actually able to interview him on details of the massacre while he awaited the litter.

Canby's orderly threw himself on the general's body, frantic with grief and raving like a madman, until Atwell and a soldier pulled him off. The reporter then used his coat as a shroud for Canby's corpse, but later cut a swatch of canvas from the Peace Tent to replace it as a winding sheet for the general. The bodies, dead and wounded, were placed on stretchers and started for camp, over which lay a pall of gloom. That very day a last letter had arrived at the general's tent from his wife Louisa. She had written, in part: "I hope you will come home soon. I think over all sorts of Modoc treachery till I am becoming a nervous, hysterical woman and will have to get away from Oregon to get over it. . . ."

To the consternation of his troops, Gillem now gave the order to withdraw, rather than pursue the fleeing murderers. Fox and others could still plainly see them, running in the distance. The men had not even fired a shot to revenge the cold-blooded assassination. FitzGerald typified the men in his thinking: "The Indians had to be punished and no time was to be lost." But Gillem had Recall sounded and, eventually, three days were lost. He absolutely refused his officers' pleas to be allowed to advance on the Stronghold. The troops were simply not ready, he said. "We shall not be ready to attack them until the Warm Springs Indians come." He added that he could not attack without orders from Washington, either, since he had been told to take no hostile action against the Modocs. This, of course, was an absurd interpretation of the limits of his freedom of action, with the commander of the entire Military Department killed before his very eyes. But he pulled his men back and reported to his superiors that he had advanced his men about a half-mile beyond the Peace Tent by 3 P.M. without encountering Indians. "To have followed the Indians into the Lava Beds would have been folly. The troops returned to camp and vigorously set about preparations for the attack." Even Private FitzGerald shortly came around to Gillem's point of view. He recalled, "The first impulse of the hot-headed young men was to press forward towards the Stronghold and inflict summary punishment upon the whole brood of accursed redskins. But, fortunately, wiser counsels prevailed. Had we then, in our unpreparedness, advanced into the Lava Beds, there would have been few, if any, left to tell the tale of the disastrous adventure."

The several war correspondents perched on rocks at Gillem's Camp, swiftly scribbling their dispatches. Leaping to their feet, one after the other, they pressed their reports on waiting horsemen, hired to rush them to Yreka. Atwell shouted to one, "Fifty dollars extra if you get my dispatch into the telegraph office ahead of the others!" Another Fourth Estater did not shout but whispered to his courier, *"One hundred dollars* if you get to the office in Yreka first." Shortly, a third rider climbed into his saddle for the eighty-three-mile ride to the Siskiyou County seat. This express rider bore Gillem's official telegraphic report to his superiors.

In Fox's story, the martyrdom of the two commissioners was attributed to the Indian Bureau's peace policy. For his part, Atwell described the Peace Tent tragedy as "the consummation of the most damnable plot that ever disgraced even the Indian character." Their stories made the Sunday editions and dumfounded and horrified the public. Col. William Thompson, a pioneer newspaperman himself, was a spectator not a correspondent at this stage, but he laid blame like an editor. To him, Meacham was responsible for the deaths, with his fool peace overtures—the only way he had of getting his job (Superintendent of Indian Affairs) back.

That night, carpenters transformed gun cases into coffins for Canby and Thomas. They waited impatiently for word to start on a third rude casket, for Meacham was expected to die momentarily. Doctors Semig and Cabaniss dressed his arm wounds; stitched his scalp, ear and face back together; and then debated whether or not to amputate his left forefinger. Meacham's brother-in-law, J. D. Ferree, looked in on him. He shook his head and said, rhetorically, "He will be blind if he recovers, won't he, doctor?" A hospital corpsman, standing by, put in his own two-bits worth: "He won't be very handsome, that's a fact."

With six hundred troops eager for action, correspondent McKay reported the Modoc War all but over. But while the Modocs divvied up their booty—Bogus and Boston claiming Thomas' clothes because he was *their* friend, and Shacknasty, Hooker and John Schonchin quarreling over Meacham's effects—Gillem first dillied, then dallied. (Captain Jack's prestige was so restored by his murder of Canby that he had no opposition when he claimed the general's dress uniform as rightfully his.) On the twelfth, the colonel held an impressive funeral ceremony with all of the troops lined up to salute the remains of the fallen commissioners, as muffled military airs were played.

After their medicine dance, sponsored by Curly Headed Doctor to celebrate the Peace Tent victory, the Modocs expected an attack. To their amazement, it did not come. Many were jubilant, thinking that the Army was afraid to attack them. For a time it seemed that the war hawks had been right; kill the commanders and the soldiers would go home. Probably only Jack and Scarfaced Charley knew the whites well enough to realize that it was the momentary paralysis of red tape, not fear, that held the troopers back.

The only action on the Army's part was the blasting away by trigger-happy pickets at shadows and the close call received by Major Green. The latter had his head bruised slightly and his cap torn by a bullet from an officer's pistol that discharged accidentally.

So, once again, the Modocs had to carry the war to the Army. Before the rude coffins were borne up the cliff to waiting ambulances, Modoc snipers began firing at Hospital Rock pickets. They actually forced the abandonment of one guard post. However, it was shortly reoccupied by infantrymen. One Indian was believed killed by the Army (*most* unlikely) and ten horses were claimed as having been captured from the Modocs. But when one brave mounted a lava ridge to wave a white flag insolently at the camp, Gillem permitted no response.

Mrs. Meacham was notified in Salem that her husband was mortally wounded. She started for the Lava Beds in order to tend him in his last moments. But Old Man Meacham was a tough coot and was being nursed back to health by the Florence Nightingale of the Modoc War—Toby Riddle. As Mrs. Meacham hurried south by stage on the fifteenth, her brother was writing her: "Your husband will recover. His wounds are doing well; but he will never be handsome anymore."

If Gillem's delay dulled the fighting edge of his troops, it served him otherwise. It gave the half-breed Cayuse scout, Donald McKay, time to bring his seventy-two picked Warm Springs Indians, neatly outfitted in Army uniforms, into camp. They were anxious to disprove the contention of many settlers that "the best Indians are all under ground." The three days of inaction also allowed public opinion to register itself. Unmistakably, it coalesced into a nationwide cry for vengeance. Force was now the only answer to the Modoc problem. Gillem was given a virtual carte blanche to deal with the Indians. Captain Jack's white defenders were stunned by the enormity of his treachery. For a spell, Quakers and other humanitarians were silenced by his dastardly deed. Secretary of the Interior Delano was hanged in effigy in both Yreka and Jacksonville, in the mistaken belief that he was the arch-architect of Grant's Indian peace policy. Placards attached to the pseudo-corpse parodied Grant's Civil War words: "Thus with the Quaker Indian policy. Make peace if it takes all summer."

The murder of one man, Canby, seized the imagination of the American public as no decade of attrition in the Indian wars could. The *Call* failed to recall a more treacherous and cruel act in the country's history. The *Army and Navy Journal* observed that no event since the Rebellion had caused so much excitement. The New York *Times* ruminated, "Seldom has an event of such a character created so deep a feeling of horror and indignation." Canby was destined to be the first—and the only—general to die in the Indian wars. Custer, who met his death three years later, was only a brevet brigadier general. He held the permanent rank of lieutenant colonel at the time of his suicidal blunder at the Little Big Horn.

The Army's general order lamenting Canby's passing was dignified. "Thus perished one of the kindest and best gentlemen of this or any other country, whose social equalled his military virtues." The men at arms recognized this, too. Private FitzGerald called him a genuinely superior officer, a man of unblemished character who was kindly and unassuming. Canby had earned the respect and esteem of every man serving under him—something that could not be said of Wheaton, Gillem or, later, Jeff C. Davis. General of the Army William T. Sherman, who wanted no more proffers of peace, who wanted, in fact, "no quarter" for the Modocs, mixed a dose of melodrama into his funereal prose: "He now lies a corpse in the wild mountains of California while lightning flashes his requiem to the furthermost corners of the civilized world." But from General of the Army to man-on-the-street, individuals were shocked and horrified that a man of peace like Canby could be murdered under a white flag of truce.

The San Francisco *Call* stressed the point that the Modocs had, in a sense, killed their best friend. It was Canby's amiability and kindness, his desire to exhaust every means to maintain peace rather than resort to war, which were taken advantage of by the Modoc plotters. Most of the press simply clamored for revenge. *Harper's Weekly* denounced the perpetrators of the massacre, and the San Francisco *Chronicle* now labeled the once-romanticized rebel (a sort of Rob Roy of the Lava Beds) as "the red Judas." The *Times* of London called the killings "a dastardly outrage"; the Philadelphia *Public Ledger* demanded an eye for an eye; the Chicago papers, the *Tribune* and the *Inter-Ocean*, demanded the extermination of the Modocs.

The *Call* next suggested that blood money be offered—a reward for shooting the ringleaders—while the Portland *Bulletin* urged that the Modocs, finally, be treated with the hemp or lead they had so long deserved instead of the consideration wasted on them. The *Bulletin* went so far as to accuse the Government of being an accessory to Canby's murder, by its misguided peace policy. The paper praised itself and the Oregon press in general for having been so clear-eyed, but maligned, when it had consistently warned the public of the faithlessness of "the bloody fiends." The paper observed, "The man who goes to Washington and talks sense about Indians is set down as a border ruffian." The editor urged the Government to stop worrying about saving Indians' souls, which was not its business, and to start protecting the lives and property of citizens, which was very much its business.

Nothing more was heard of the romanticizing of Captain Jack, as a Robin Hood, by eastern papers, like the Frankfort *Yeoman*, which had run a story that Jack was not a pure-blood Modoc but part-Kentuckian, the son of Capt. Jack Chambers of Franklin County, who had married a Modoc girl (daughter of a chief, naturally) in 1846.

When he was told that Oregon's "fighting editors' were blaming the deaths of Canby and Thomas on Steele, Dorris, Meacham and himself, John Fairchild snorted derisively and said to the wounded Meacham in his hospital tent, "Better send some more volunteers down here to eat up the Modocs like

Captain Kelly's company did the day that Shacknasty Jim held a whole company, for seven hours, in check. Damn 'em. If any of those 'fighting editors' come down here, we'll set Shacknasty Jim after them and then you'll see them git!"

Ferree read the papers to his bedridden brother-in-law, quoting, "Governor Grover will call out Volunteers to assist the Regulars. They will make short work of it. The Regulars are Eastern men and cannot fight Indians successfully." Ferree chuckled. "That's rich. One thousand soldiers here now, and more Oregon volunteers coming to whip fifty Modocs!"

The modern term, genocide, bandied about so carelessly by white-lipped critics of America's nineteenth-century Indian policy, for once fits the mood of the Government as of 1873. In the heat of rage and grief over the murder of his comrade, Canby, and with the backing of another old Army crony, President U. S. Grant, General of the Army William T. Sherman advised Gillem not to leave a Modoc man, woman or child alive to boast of Canby's murder. *Briefly*, his advocacy of the extinction of "the outlaws" was no mere figure of speech, although Sherman later came to his senses. He ordered Gillem to launch an attack on the Modocs "so strong and persistent that their fate may be commensurate with their crime. You will be fully justified in their utter extermination." He added, "I hope to hear that they have met the doom they have so richly deserved by their insolence and perfidy."

Gen. John Schofield went along with his superior, ordering Gillem to punish the Modocs with all the severity their treachery deserved. "Nothing short of their prompt and sure destruction will satisfy the demands of justice or the expectation of the Government."

Only a few faint voices could be heard, after Canby's murder, still calling for justice for the Indians, including the Modocs. *London Illustrated News* correspondent William Simpson found the one-time sympathy of the Sacramento Valley replaced by indignation and a cry for extermination of the whole tribe, like vermin. The Modocs' crime had placed them beyond the pale of mercy—this was the prevailing opinion. "Almost everyone expressed a desire to have the shooting of the Modocs reserved for his special satisfaction. Some wished that Captain Jack had a hundred lives and that they might be allowed to take them all. All kinds of terrible tortures were talked of. I began to speculate as to whether the Indians could be more bloodthirsty than these wishes indicated the white man to be." Then, curiously, he found that the closer he got to the Lava Beds the less violent were the cries for vengeance. At Abe Ball's ranch he found many rough Butte Creek ranchers who still defended the Modocs. "I heard of the frequent injustice which the Modocs had suffered." When he asked if they had not rustled beeves, they said the Modocs had not, and told him that when they found cattle mired they would rescue them and report them to the ranch owner. Fairchild and Dorris told Simpson that the Modocs were faithful to every engagement into which they entered.

The pioneer Indian agent of California, Edward F. Beale, countenanced the decidedly unpopular course of moderation, rather than blood for blood. The editor of the San Francisco *News-Letter* remained unconvinced that two wrongs could make a right: "The policy of the Government educated the Modocs into a contempt of its power and and no furious order of extermination can discharge it of responsibility for the murder of the Commissioners. . . . All the Modocs did not murder Gen. Canby and Dr. Thomas, and those who did not are guilty only of being Modocs. For this crime and the additional one of resisting when attacked, they are to be annihilated. Col. Gillem will, if possible, carry out his magnanimous resolve that 'no Indian shall boast that he or his ancestor killed Gen. Canby,' but men not quite so conscious of their own heroism cannot help doubting which are the civilized and which the savages in this miserable tragi-comedy of the Modoc War."

Another voice in the wilderness, opposing the frenzy of the hour, was that of E. C. Thomas, the murdered reverend's son. He wrote a letter to Senator A. A. Sargent which was picked up and published by the press. He called for punishment of the guilty *but* asked that it be tempered with justice, peace and security for the other, uninvolved, Modocs. The younger Thomas blamed not the Indians for their crimes but "the rapacious, lawless, perfidious whites with whom they have long been in contact." A chip off the old block, young Thomas shared his father's pathetic, inextinguishable optimism about human character. Still, he could hardly make himself believe that Jack had really killed his father: "How any man or beast could meet the kind smile of that face and do the old man harm, I cannot understand." Probably the younger man's solace was also a source of comfort to the pious parent, if comfort is possible beyond the grave, as he would have agreed with his son that "To few men, comparatively, is it given to die like a martyr."

While meetings were held in San Francisco and in Oregon towns to muster volunteers for militia duty as reinforcements for Gillem, the frontier grew uneasy. News of Canby's assassination excited the Indians as well as the white population. G. W. Kennedy, preaching in Washington Territory's Yakima country, reported, "So defiant was Chief Smohalla that he organized a sort of Indian 'Knights Clan,' sworn to defy the white man's rule. . . . This event [Canby's murder] set the Indians almost wild with hostile excitement." He reported the Kittitas Valley settlers as forting up in their sturdy log cabins and "listening with one ear to the preacher and with the other for the Indian war whoop." Kennedy led three unarmed men to Smohalla's *skookum wigwam* and, by dint of vigorous preaching and politicking (and hymn singing), persuaded the *tyee* not to become an ally of Captain Jack, but to keep the peace. Settlers in Oregon's Checowan Valley and California's Goose Lake Valley, were much closer to the Lava Beds and were even more alarmed when their local Snakes were made "saucy" by news of Jack's coup. These Indians began killing cattle in the settlers' herds, and the ranchers prepared to drive their stock away and follow the animals in a retreat to safety. Far away in the area of Fort Hall, Idaho, trouble was expected momentarily from Indians excited by Captain Jack's daring stroke. These Indians were particularly well posted on Jack's activities by the "sagebrush telegraph," and noted how many blankets had been given the unruly Modocs and how few had been given to peaceful Indians. On April 13, J. D. Ferree brought word to Gillem that the Klamath Reservation was quiet but that Fort Klamath was nervous, as the reservation Indians were watching the Lava Beds contest closely. If Jack should win another round, they might rise.

The nation, with its flags at half-staff, cried for action and vengeance. But the war correspondents could only file the frustrating sentence, "No news from the front," for all of Gillem's promise—"I shall at once commence active operations."

After an agony of inaction, the troopers were relieved of their waiting and given orders to attack on April 14. The incubus of gloom and frustration that was suffocating Gillem's Camp now lifted. The colonel issued his men three days' rations, overcoats, blankets and (according to the press) one hundred rounds apiece of ammuniton. FitzGerald's story was that the ammo dwindled in actuality to sixty rounds for his carbine and the rations to a mere fifteen hardtacks plus a small piece of fatty bacon to put in his haversack. On the eve of his attack, Gillem confidently wired General Schofield: "I shall close with the Indians tomorrow and endeavor to cut off all escape. No effort will be spared to make the punishment of the Indians commensurate with the crime. If possible, no Indian shall boast that either he or his ancestor murdered General Canby."

Without waiting for the arrival of Col. (Brevet Brig. Gen. and usually so addressed) Jefferson C. Davis, whom President Grant had appointed as Canby's successor, Gillem on the night of the fourteenth ordered Major Mason and Captain Bernard to reoccupy the latter's most advanced position of January. This was well into the Lava Beds. At 2 A.M. on the fifteenth, Gillem sent Troops F and K to occupy the neck of land protruding into Tule Lake's Canby Bay. All too soon it would have a name, too, reminiscent of a tragedy similar to Canby's. It would be called Hovey's Point for another innocent victim of Modoc murder. With these troop movements, the second battle of the Lava Beds, often called the Three Days' Fight, was under way. All of the men fought dismounted in the treacherous terrain, advancing in single file except for the skirmishers in the point, who spread out.

Gillem was supremely confident of victory although Wheaton had termed the Stronghold a perfect Gibraltar and even though the terrain forced him to duplicate his predecessor's plan of attack. Nor did he have the 1,000 men Wheaton thought necessary to carry Jack's volcanic redoubt. Gillem had about 745 effectives; perhaps even fewer serving as combat infantrymen. FitzGerald placed the number at 600, evenly split between Green's force on the west and Mason's on the east. Even so, the odds were at least ten to one in favor of the Army over Jack's fighting force. In addition to five troops of cavalry, five companies of infantry, four batteries of artillerymen and the Warm Springs Indian scouts, the Army had two mountain howitzers and four Coehorn mortars. Both the cavalrymen and cannoneers were fighting as infantrymen. The five hundred hand grenades ordered from Benicia Arsenal by Canby had not arrived, and the poison gas suggested by some persons was not given serious consideration by the Army. Gillem's whitehall boats on Tule Lake shortened his lines of communication for a repeat of Wheaton's pincers movement on the Stronghold from east and west. But now the fifty roundabout miles between command posts was shrunken to but five miles over water. Gillem had opposed the use of boats, fearing they would be exposed to Modoc fire and that the need for boatmen and guards would tax his combat strength. But he was agreeable to using the boats already on Tule Lake, if he would not order whitehalls transported all the way from Portland or Redding.

Their impatience ended, their morale restored after the battering of January, the common soldiers were eager to invest the Stronghold. They cheered Gillem's order to his officers: "Tell your men to remember General Canby, Sherwood and the flag!" This time there was no fog to blind the troops and screen the enemy. Although it was a moonless night, it was without a breath of wind and as beautiful as it was balmy. The sky was littered with so many bright stars that Gillem's men, even in the wee hours, could pick their way through the boulders, avoiding their rasplike edges in the silvery light. Cautioned to make not the slightest noise, the soldiers advanced in silence and in an orderly single-file formation. Dr. T. T. Cabaniss, attached by Surgeon McElderry to Capt. David Perry's command with an orderly and litter bearers, reported, "At the hour appointed, the troops left with so little noise that I did not know they were gone." But a soldier stumbled. His rifle accidentally discharged and the report was seconded by a cry of alarm from a Modoc sentry. His kin in the Stronghold soon picked it up. With the element of surprise gone, the Army's advance became slow. Even with daybreak and a warm and still morning, progress was measured in yards. At 6 A.M. the howitzers on Hospital Rock boomed, sending exploding shells into the heart of the Lava Beds, to soften up the defense. But the Modocs replied with their war cry—the "*Wow-wow-wow*" of children playing Indians, made by tapping the half-open mouth with the palm of one hand while uttering the cry. Or they would fire their rifles and salute the artillery with loud jeers. The few voices bounced off the rocks in echoes that made the number of Modocs seem to be thousands. The howling and war cries of the Modocs formed a useful part of Captain Jack's primitive psychological warfare. Doubtless he guessed that such ululation would scare the newcomers from Fort Halleck, like FitzGerald, who recalled, "When we heard that weird and awesome signal. . . the blood left our cheeks and great beads of perspiration stood out on our foreheads. . . as if the rocky peninsula were alive with ten thousand fiendish redskins ready to bear down upon, and annihilate, us."

Soon after sunrise, in the face of rifle shots as well as blood-curdling war cries, the main body of the west-side force came up, with Major Green in the center, Capt. William Miller on the right wing and Lt. C. P. Eagan on the left. As night paled and landmarks became visible, some of the soldiers' dread vanished, helped along by a brief barrage against the Stronghold from Lt. Edward Chapin's mountain howitzers. The men of Battery E, five paces apart in the eastward-probing advance, met no real opposition until about one-thirty, when they made a little charge. FitzGerald's Company K actually halted on a rocky eminence and became, largely, spectators. They watched the scrimmage on the right where an attempt to join Green's force to Mason's was being thwarted by hot Modoc fire from the flanks and even from the rear.

Carefully, a group of men would run forward to the security of boulders under covering fire from their comrades. They would then reverse the process. Still the ground covered was small. The soft "ping" of the Modocs' Henry repeaters contrasted with the sharp bang of the military arms. Only puffs of smoke were targets for the Army. No Modocs were to be seen. They were past masters of concealment.

Capt. Evan Thomas and Lieutenants Arthur Cranston and Albion Howe received orders to move the mortars forward at 2 P.M. But the first round was not fired until 5:10, with the sun sinking behind the gun crew. The bombardment was a fiasco and almost a tragedy. FitzGerald watched the mortarmen unlimber the thirty-inch-long Coehorns and place them into position to blast the Modocs' stone barriers or breastworks. Since they were set up just to the rear of K Troop, Fitz and his buddies were ordered to lie prone. But, to their horror, the very first mortar shell fired did not describe the slow, graceful arc into the Stronghold which the artillerymen expected. A defective round, the projectile fell only fifteen feet ahead of the cavalrymen and spun about, hissing and sputtering as if alive. Some of the troopers jumped to their feet and started to run. Others were too perplexed to move or else were hypnotized by the threatening shell. Just in time, an officer shouted, "Everyone lie close to the ground!" Hardly were the words off his lips when the shell exploded, sending steel fragments ripping through the air in all directions. Miraculously, no one was hurt. The succeeding shells were successful and the troopers enjoyed the show, watching the Coehorns pound the Stronghold. So slow were the projectiles that their courses could easily be traced from muzzle to target.

About 2 P.M. Major Green's men made what some witnesses described as "a beautiful charge." Reporter Alex McKay enthused, "Such was the rapidity of the onslaught, and so unexpected, that the troops were on them before they knew it and, in a few minutes, we were masters of the situation and our brave boys [were] behind the rocks, resting at their leisure." FitzGerald described the stirring event as merely "desultory fighting," but, in any case, the Modocs fell back to stronger positions nearer the caves of the Stronghold. They continued to annoy the attackers from these points and with flanking fire from snipers.

As the right flank of Green's force pushed eastward, the two troops of cavalry occupying the Hovey Peninsula advanced along the lakeshore to straighten out the line. FitzGerald now saw Modoc breastworks of piled-up volcanic boulders, with loopholes for rifles. As the men moved forward in a double-time charge, they found one of the little rock forts still occupied. Pvt. Charles Johnson looked over the top of one and received a bullet in the head, which killed him instantly. The Indian disappeared like a fox through the crevices in the lava. At least, mused FitzGerald, the Modocs did not seem to relish the idea of hand-to-hand fighting. At about this time Major Mason, across the Lava Beds, signaled "No one killed or wounded here yet," although a sharp volley of Modoc fire was rattling along his line.

The Modocs fired at the soldiers with Henry rifles, old muskets and rifles, captured Army carbines and rifles, and even hunting guns. Each weapon, Dr. Cabaniss noticed, had a distinctive report. Correspondents McKay and Fox, armed with rifles, made the advance with the troops till balls began to sing past their ears. Then "Mac" headed for the rear, telling Cabaniss, "The *Bulletin* having no one to fill my place, I am doing that paper an injustice by exposing my life." Fox continued onward until he was fatigued, although he later confessed to Cabaniss that he had been a damned fool to risk his life. The doctor concurred: "When a man hears the whistle of bullets about his ears and has no business there, he is a fool to remain."

Green asked Cabaniss to take a message to Miller and he did so, accompanied by a soldier who received a wound in one arm en route. Both had to hug the ground as rifle balls whizzed just over their heads. Then Cabaniss treated an artilleryman for wounds in the head and arm and sent an old soldier on a litter to camp. A rifle shot had shattered his thighbone. Next to be hit were Privates Rolla and Lamb. The latter, a boyish, modest twenty-four-year-old North Carolinian was one of the bravest men in battle that Cabaniss ever saw. Rolla behaved well too, although in 1877 as a noncom at the Battle of the Clearwater in the Nez Perce War he would be reduced in rank for faltering under fire. In spite of these casualties, the advance led by Miller, Throckmorton, Wright and Eagan began to drive the enemy back. Just then, Eagan was hit. Dr. Cabaniss asked nearby troopers to "lay down a barrage," and he ran and zigzagged across a fire-swept opening fifty yards wide. When the troopers saw him reach Eagan's side safely, they gave the doctor a rousing cheer. Cabaniss found four wounded men there in all. Eagan was shot through one leg; an Irish corporal, shot through the pelvis, died with his head resting on Cabaniss' arm as he took a last drink of water. The impetuous, courageous—and foolhardy—Major Green now started to cross the dangerous opening, but Cabaniss shouted and waved him back. The doctor bore a charmed life. He snaked back the way he had come, after first piling up rocks in a breastwork around Eagan and the other wounded men. He saw to it that they were removed as soon as possible. Cabaniss did not want any men left behind to be overrun by the Modocs, captured and perhaps tortured before being killed.

A sutler, Pat McManus, decided to mosey over to the front for a look. He started across the dangerous open space, rifle in hand, on his mule. The animal was speedily shot out from under him, probably by marksman Steamboat Frank. McManus was pinned down alongside his dead mule and was given up for dead. A message to that effect was even sent to his wife in Yreka. But the brash Irish civilian was only nicked in the neck. Since he was well under the influence of "the sutler's best," something more powerful than mother's milk, he never even felt it. After hiding in the sage till nightfall, Pat walked out on his own, cold sober.

At 2 P.M. on the fifteenth, Captain Perry was standing with his sixteen-year-old bugler when the lad was shot through the head. He lingered till morning in the field hospital, moaning all night to the horror of the nearby troopers, who were starting at shadows. Shortly another bugler was shot, this one through the neck. If Cabaniss was right, five trumpeters were thus hit in the

Lava Beds. The Modocs were selective of their targets. They preferred officers, noncoms and "music men," as they termed the buglers, to ordinary privates. No tears were shed for the buglers by the Warm Springs and Wasco Indian scouts. They thought that the Army did much too much bugling and not enough shooting. One of them once grunted, "Warm Springs don't like so much noise."

According to the sometimes undependable Col. William Thompson of the Oregon Volunteers, Gillem came up to the battle line and, rubbing his hands in glee, said to John Fairchild, "This is a splendid day's work. How long did it take Wheaton to get this far?" Fairchild, who may have disliked the Tennessean as much as did Thompson, replied, "General, I do not remember exactly, but as near as I can judge it was about twenty minutes."

Although even brave Eagan had failed to close the gap between the two wings of Gillem's army, Green was satisfied with the showing of his men. He halted them as darkness fell and adjusted his line to hold fast for the night. He also urged his men to throw up little rock redoubts as the Modocs had done. The men ate their ship's biscuit and sowbelly—and ached for the hot coffee, grits and gravy of civilian days. Nervous and tense, most of them sat up, or crouched, with carbines gripped tightly during all the long night, getting very little rest.

Green figured himself only two ridges from Jack's Cave. Mason's "drive" had been less impressive, and his linkup attempts less energetic. He said it was impossible without weakening his line too much. When Gillem checked Mason's estimate of his distance from Jack's Stronghold, he found it seven hundred yards, not four hundred. This, and the general timidity of Mason, annoyed the commander. His men were practically unhurt compared to Green's and he had the nerve to explain, "It was not part of my plan to expose my men unnecessarily." Perhaps his men's caution was understandable; most of the veterans of the January thrashing were with him, not Green.

Although he was hardly satisfied with his field commanders, Gillem still fired off a prideful telegram to General Schofield as his troops rested for the night. "I have fought the Indians all day and driven them to the immediate vicinity of the Stronghold. Our loss today is one officer, Lieutenant Eagan, wounded, three enlisted men killed, and nine wounded. I hope to surround them tomorrow." That night, Thomas pounded the Stronghold with mortar fire, extinguishing a campfire and eliciting cries of pain or dismay with one particularly well-placed round. It was followed by angry yells from the Modocs, inviting the soldiers to come and fight.

Gillem was not the only one sanguine of success; reporter McKay believed the Modocs' escape was now cut off. He reported them fighting with pluck and determination but thought that Gillem's well-laid plans would make short work of the war. The "savages" were doomed. But the so-called savages did not realize they were doomed. Fourteen of them, after drinking at the lake, bathed in plain view; when attacked, they beat off the troops and (according to one Oregon paper) killed three soldiers. They dodged the howitzer shells sent their way and patted their shot pouches in insolent derision. When the barrage ceased, the Modocs mocked the artillery by improvising a battery of their own by discharging their rifles high in the air.

During the second full day of fighting, April 16, Gillem had his howitzers and mortars soften up the Stronghold as his infantrymen probed (in vain) for a soft spot in the enemy's defenses. The usually dependable Bernard was unable to capture the gap separating the two Army units. Gillem then ordered Green to push out his right flank to meet Mason. The German obeyed, sending Capt. Marcus Miller of the Artillery to link up with the eastern force. Miller's maneuver failed even before Mason replied that he could not make the connection. He was much too occupied with enfilading fire. Miller broke off the attempt after he and thirteen men were cut off by the Modocs and forced to take cover. He managed to extricate his men with the help of a mortar barrage but lost two dead and several wounded. Briefly, the Warm Springs Indian scouts had a try at controlling the key area, but after one of their number was wounded, they also abandoned the attempt.

Once again, the tenacity of the Modocs forced the Army to revise its strategy. And, once more, the decision was to give up the idea of a junction on the south and to combine the two forces on the north. Gillem had little faith in the effectiveness of this lakeside maneuver, since it would not cut off the Modocs' escape. He did not realize how important was Tule Lake to the Modocs as a water supply. He crossed the lake by boat and met Mason, but according to some observers, like Colonel Thompson, never really gave his approval to the plan cooked up by Mason and Green. "I know what I am saying," insisted Thompson when he claimed the two subordinates disobeyed Gillem's orders. If this was the case, the disobedience of orders was hushed up by all parties. According to Cabaniss, Gillem nixed a plan of Donald McKay's to draw the Modocs out and to counterattack them. Cabaniss also felt that Mason was unjustly censured by Gillem for the failure of the southside linkup.

Green's left-flank advance went so well that some men had to fall back for fear of being hit by shells. Nevertheless, Private FitzGerald was skeptical. "We could make little headway and, judging from the distant report of firearms in that direction, the other command was not having any better success in its efforts to reach us. We straggled back, tired and hungry through the rocks, harassed all the time by galling fire, to very near the place we occupied the night before, although a little closer to the Stronghold."

The night of the sixteenth, howitzers and mortars again pounded the area of Captain Jack's Cave. The soldiers, with small-arms fire, turned back what appeared to be an attempt by the Modocs to secure the lake, for water. With stomachs as empty as their flapping haversacks, the troopers leaned on their rifles and waited for dawn. Gillem disbelieved Mason when the major reported that his line of jerry-built boulder fortifications now controlled not only the Medicine Rock of the Stronghold, from which flew Curly Headed Doctor's bizarre banner, but also the avenue of escape to the south. Both men were almost right. Mason *almost* had the key to encirclement of the Modocs. But, unknown to him and Green and Mason, the space between the detachments was occupied by a deep ravine.

That night a few Modoc sharpshooters kept the Army occupied. Others called the soldiers every filthy name in a pidgin-English vocabulary. A bonfire blazed until it was put out by a direct hit, in a scattering of embers. Meanwhile, the main body of Modocs stole down the lava gully past Mason's force to safety. As a waterless camp, the Stronghold was untenable to Jack.

If the Modoc obscenity and profanity, to which the soldiers replied in choice billingsgate, was not attractive, the blaze of musketry that night was like a fireworks display. A special messenger to Yreka again told the citizenry that the war was all but over. "The Indians are certainly disheartened. They were running from one point to another, back and forth, with no apparent strategic notice, seemingly bewildered by the advance of our forces." Gillem seemed to agree. He wired Schofield that he had driven the Indians back four hundred yards and was now about that distance from their caves. "They must now break through our lines or evacuate the Stronghold." He had to admit the latter possibility, excusing his inability to prevent it by stating, "I find it will be impossible, owing to the nature of the position, to surround the Indians with my present force."

On the morning of the seventeenth, some of FitzGerald's buddies raised their hats on their gun barrels and drew fire. But it was weak and sporadic. In FitzGerald's words, "Gradually, it dawned on us that the Indians had played us a foxy trick." Except for a few holdouts, all the Modocs had decamped to the south via the crevasse and the rough, "fresh" lava area called the Schonchin Flow. Both Green and Mason now began to move their men forward more rapidly as it became clear that the Modocs had skedaddled, that the Stronghold was abandoned. But the skirmishers still drew sniper fire—even from their rear. Gillem, advancing with Green, was furious that he could find none of Mason's units. He urged Green's men on, shouting, "Forward! Forward!" Finally, at noon on April 17, 1873, some of Bernard's men were met and the surround was complete, if rather late. Artillery Corp. Gilbert Davis, laid up with a fractured leg, cheered, "The boys has whipped them good."

The soldiers scoured the volcanic reefs and bluffs, but the birds were flown. The very day that they swept through the Stronghold, A. Hamilton of New Brunswick was advocating the use of primitive poison gas to flush them out. In a letter to Secretary Delano he wrote, "Permit me to suggest that gas-smoke from sulphur is the most sure means of forcing the savages out of their lava holes."

The troopers admired the natural trenches and Modoc-built galleries and rifle pits of volcanic rock. They ransacked the Stronghold for souvenirs, pawing through the litter of putrid fish, hides, bones and horns, which stank like a stopped drain. Besides sleeping mats and twig mattresses, they found human finger bones strung like clumsy beads as children's toys. To their astonishment, the crater called Captain Jack's Cave was unharmed by the shellfire and apparently bombproof. Only a direct vertical hit could have destroyed it. San Francisco *Evening Bulletin* correspondent William M. Bunker expressed the feeling of the touring troopers: "No soldier could have climbed within fifty yards of the Stronghold while the Indians were in possession without looking into the muzzles of guns, and nothing but a gun would be seen." The Londoner, William Simpson, was reminded of the defenses of Sebastopol in the

Crimean War when he viewed the redans and parapets planted by Nature in the Stronghold.

The victory in the Three Days' Fight (really a three-day siege) was not as hollow and anticlimactic as at first it seemed. The Modocs were now on the run, and without water. Frontal advances, sieges and trench warfare—so alien to Indian campaigning—were at an end. The Modoc War now reverted to traditional campaign techniques. From now on it would be a war of movement, of raids and reprisals and pursuits. This was the kind of fighting the frontier Army knew, and preferred, even if the crazy Modocs fought like "Rooshans."

Gillem mentioned five officers in dispatches, especially Green, and restrained himself from publicly blaming Mason for the failure of his strategy. But only one of Mason's subordinates, Eagan, had been wounded—and he had been fighting with Green. Mason had *no* casualties among his infantrymen. Only one Warm Springs scout was hit. Green had six men killed in his force and seventeen wounded. One of the wounded was a private who shot himself in the foot in the time-honored dodge to get out of combat. To his painful disbelief, Dr. Cabaniss refused to excuse him and sent him limping back into the line. There were only four sprained ankles—surprising in a battleground of crevices, funnel-like lava tubes and exploded volcanic craters. Curiously, Army opinion was that the toll taken by the Modocs might have been greater had they not switched to modern (captured) weapons. Unused to the rifles and muskets picked up in January, they tended to shoot high.

In a war in which no two estimates of casualties ever seemed to agree, it is impossible to know exactly what was the "body count" in the Stronghold area. Jeff Riddle angrily reported four old or crippled Indians murdered by the troopers. One of the victims, at least, was a squaw. The *Army and Navy Journal* gave a patently absurd figure of sixteen warriors killed and one squaw captured. Some participants in the second battle of the Lava Beds reported three men and eight women found (presumably dead) in the Stronghold. Lieutenant Boyle, probably more accurate than most, gave the figure as three dead and two squaws and an old man taken prisoner. The artist-correspondent of the *Illustrated London News*, William Simpson, reported four Modoc bodies found and three prisoners taken.

Whatever the casualty count, the "victorious" troopers behaved atrociously, perhaps because of Privates Brennan and

Hollis. Cabaniss found their remains under some piled-up rocks where they had been killed in January. Brennan had been scalped and his fingers cut off. Hollis had apparently been tortured before being killed. (It was later learned that this was the revenge of a squaw whose husband had been killed in Jackson's raid; therefore, Watchman's woman.) The doctor reported that three old Modoc men were found alive and one woman. Two of the men were shot by soldiers, as was the squaw. The third man was stoned to death by the Warm Springs.

A bitter Jeff Riddle claimed that all victims of the soldiers had been either old and blind or wounded or crippled, except for the woman. Of these cold-blooded murders he wrote, "God will surely punish such heartless people. It is sure a true saying with the white people when they say everything is fair in time of war. I have noticed, in the past, that the only time this saying is fulfilled or practiced is when the white man is fighting Indians."

Simpson drew a sketch of the scalp taken by a Troop K sergeant who insisted it was from the head of Scarfaced Charley, perhaps to enhance its sales appeal to credulous soldiers. A little later, Charley would again be reported dead—"without a doubt, from the description given"—but he survived the war. The scalp was also identified as Shacknasty Frank's. Schacknasty Jim's brother Frank had died as the result of wounds incurred in the battle. The sergeant cut up the scalp into swatches, or miniscalps, which he peddled to the souvenir-hunting soldiery. Meacham believed the scalp came from the head of a brave who had dressed like a woman to get water from the lakeshore, but had been shot.

During the April fight men sloughed off their veneer of civilized behavior like a rattler shedding an old skin. A shocked FitzGerald saw brutalized soldiers kicking the severed head of a Modoc like a soccer ball. The victim they believed (erroneously) to have been John Schonchin. Worse, Fitz saw an eighty- or even ninety-year-old woman begging piteously for her life: "Me no hurt no one, me no fight," she whined. In FitzGerald's presence, the officer in command of K Troop—who must have been Lt. Charles C. Cresson—snapped, "Is there anyone here who will put that old hag out of the way?" A Pennsylvania Dutchman stepped forward and said, "I'll fix her, lieutenant." He put the muzzle of his carbine to her head and blew it to pieces. At least, FitzGerald was not the only man horrified by the brutality of the blue-eyed West Pointer and the Pennsy-*Deutsch* common soldier. He was able to report, "I do not believe there was another man in the company, save the perpetrator of the deed and the epauletted officer, who did not feel shocked at such inhumanity."

Aside from murdered oldsters and squaws, the only casualties among the Modocs were the young son of Curly Headed Doctor and the brother of Shacknasty Jim, both of whom blew themselves to hell when they fooled with a dud shell that landed in the Stronghold. Some stories had them trying to draw the fuse with their teeth, but Colonel Thompson was probably more correct. He reported they attacked the shell with a file and a hatchet to get the highly prized powder inside, and it blew. Thus, their deaths were really accidental, and historian Harry Wells was correct when he stated that the Army's claim of sixteen "good" (i.e., dead) Modocs was just sixteen too many. Not a single Modoc warrior had been slain in the Three Days' Battle.

The major trophy of the battle, besides the grisly head and scalps, was the medicine flag of Curly Headed Doctor. He had erected it as a guarantee of victory on what the troops called Medicine Rock, one of the highest monoliths of the Stronghold's northeast end. This banner, on the end of a four-foot stick, was a mink skin decorated with hawk feathers and a white medicine, or magic, bead.

According to James Fry, the troops were absolutely worn out by their exertions in the badland. Some were dispirited, too, by the easy escape of the Modocs. FitzGerald was never so exhausted in his life as after two sleepless nights and three frenetic days of scrambling over crusted lava. Corp. Gilbert Davis wrote in his diary, "I feel very tired. Was where the balls flew thick.... A hard day's fight after the men fought all night...."

Pursuit of the Modocs over the half-melted country of the Lava Beds was impossible. The wounded were sent to Gillem's Camp to be cared for by hospital stewards and doctors and by that natural nurse, Toby Riddle. Gillem's failure to mount a vigorous or even prompt pursuit was laid by the press to strategy, not fear or incompetence. He now felt that he had only to hold Tule Lake until a thirsty Captain Jack should surrender or leave the area entirely. But Jack simply pulled back to some ice caves in the south end of the Lava Beds while one of his units—hardly a squad, with only seven men—gave the Army another painful lesson in guerrilla warfare.

Jack's little rear guard slipped out of the Stronghold just as the Army entered it. But they did not run for cover. Instead, the force passed neatly through the line of skirmishers without drawing a shot and then struck at the Army's rear. Heading directly for Gillem's headquarters, they overran two civilian teamsters at noon on April 17. Gillem had deemed an Army escort unnecessary since he had the Modocs "penned up" in the Stronghold. Sam Watson had his mule killed, but he managed to run to camp. His companion, Eugene Hovey, was less lucky. He was the proverbial "innocent bystander." Involved in the war only to the extent that he drove an Army wagon and occasionally handled mule-borne stretchers and thus impressed Surgeon McElderry with his diligence, civilian Hovey was a very well-liked twenty-one-year-old from Wisconsin. Unarmed, he was attacked by Hooker Jim and the others, hiding only fifteen yards from the trail. Hooker Jim shot him in the head, then stripped, mutilated and disemboweled the body. As a final atrocity the Modocs smashed his head between two boulders— the fate Capt. John Smith, more than 250 years earlier, barely escaped, thanks to the intervention of Pocahontas. The Indians took Hovey's animals and then turned their attention on Gillem's headquarters. FitzGerald and his pards found the body near Long Cave as they returned to their base. He described Hovey's smashed head as being reduced to the thickness of a man's hand. It is not known if the Modocs treated Hovey thus out of revenge for the Army atrocities in the Stronghold. Knowing of the Army's war crimes would not have been necessary for the monstrous Hooker Jim to act in such a manner. He was accustomed to it; he enjoyed it.

Like teamster Watson, reporters Fox and Atwell, as well as Dr. McElderry and some stretcher bearers, had to run for their lives from the tiny handful of Modoc raiders. They joined a makeshift defense force in Gillem's Camp, organized by the quartermaster, Lt. M. C. Grier, who wigwagged for help. Even reporter McKay took a turn at guard duty until Capt. Joel Trimble and some Warm Springs hurried in to relieve the little siege. McKay had to swallow some words he had just written: "The Lava Bed is ours. The Modocs are now guerrillas." Yes, *guerrilleros*, indeed, were the Modocs; but even Gillem's Camp was barely the Army's at that moment.

Once more, teamsters, settlers and other civilians were terrified at the idea of another Hooker Jim raid, suggested by the barbarous murder of young Hovey. Animals were already in short supply because of an outbreak of the epizootic but teamsters were ordered to go no closer to the Lava Beds than Ball's ranch, only forty miles from Yreka and about the same distance from the battle area. Gillem ordered Mrs. Meacham back to Linkville for safety, after the murder of Hovey, though she had traveled three hundred miles and was within three miles of her wounded husband. He sent Meacham by boat, with Cabaniss and Ferree, to the mouth of Lost River, where she waited. En route, one of Tule Lake's famous storms whipped up and her trip came close to being in vain. But shipwreck was narrowly averted. Dyar wrote Ferree from Fort Klamath that he had moved the white women and children from the reservation to Fort Klamath. "Be on your guard," he warned, "the Klamath Indians were in war council last night." Cooler heads reported, however, "Don't think there's any danger, though Dyar isn't yet over the scare he got in the race with Hooker Jim."

The Modocs made no secret of their new whereabouts. Smoke from their fires drifted up to the military, only a few miles away. And yet the Army claimed that the Indians were fleeing to either Willow Spring on the old Emigrant Road or the area between Clear Lake and Goose Lake. Reporters optimistically stated that the Army expected to announce the death of the last Modoc in a week, although the settlers were jittery and many officers were sick of Gillem's hesitancy and damned his "red-tape way of fighting Indians." Meacham was quoted as saying, "The Army in the Lava Beds is performing some masterly feats of inactivity that would have been a credit to General McClellan on the Peninsula."

But Col. Alvan Gillem smelled sweet victory. He crowed, "I have dislodged the Modocs from their Stronghold in the Lava Beds. They are moving southward. No effort will be spared to exterminate them. The cavalry will at once pursue. The country is exceedingly difficult to operate in. My loss is small, thanks to the howitzers and mortars. . . ."

Some of the military were cheered by the news from a Modoc squaw, who managed to survive capture, that John Schonchin was dead of Meacham's derringer ball. The old villain was as alive as Scarfaced Charley, of course, and the woman probably took pains to tell her captors exactly what they wanted to hear. Who can blame her? She reported eleven Modocs killed, including Shacknasty Frank (who was said to have chewed on the fuse of the dud shell) and John Schonchin, supposedly cut in two by the exploding missile. Other balderdash she supplied the Army had Hooker Jim dying of a wound through both hips and Bogus Charley crippled by a wound in his calf.

As the Army prepared to follow up on its hollow "victory" in the Stronghold, uneasiness increased on the California-Oregon frontier. Settlers around Ball's ranch and in the Shasta Valley feared a raid by Captain Jack. A traveler from the Klamath and Salmon rivers reported that the local Indians were better posted on Jack's successes than the whites: "It is evident that Modoc runners have visited all the tribes of Northern California and Southern Oregon." Rather than runners dispatched from his too-small force by Jack, this was the work of the ubiquitous Indian sagebrush telegraph. Even on the upper Columbia and the Snake, the Indians were well informed on the campaign. A nervous Governor Grover got five hundred stand of arms from Vancouver Arsenal to distribute to settlers and fifty more to arm a new Portland militia outfit, the City Guard. Settlers on Bogus and Willow creeks prepared to move into town, and the Indians of Scott Valley were reported donning war paint in sympathy with Captain Jack. The increasing hostility of Goose Lake Snakes or Paiutes ("vicious customers," they were termed) and Smoke Creeks, really Paiutes also, helped speed the panicky rumors of a general Indian uprising. So did the report of Captain John Mendenhall that 120 Pit Rivers were repairing an old bastion on the Pit in order to hold off any soldiers sent against them from Fort Crook.

At 6 A.M. on Friday, April 18, 1873, pursuit of the Modocs was begun. Captain Bernard took a patrol to the east and north and Captain Perry led 110 men south on a scout of the Tickner Road. The cavalry vainly beat the bushes of the Willow Springs and Sorass Lake area, doubtless naming the latter after a hard day in the saddle. Warm Springs scouts hunted east of the Stronghold. But when Captain Jack popped up, he was still in the middle of the Land of Burnt-Out Fires, only four miles south of Gillem's Camp, calmly herding his horses in plain view at the base of Sand Butte or Hardin Butte. Gillem rubbed his hands together and made plans for an attack once Perry was back. He hoped Jack would make a stand and not run for it and so extend the war. Reporter McKay put the general feeling into words for his *Call* readers: "Fifty desperate savages, roaming through the rocky fastnesses, can and will work incalculable destruction to property and cause a fearful loss of life. They will lay waste the country while the soldiers will be com-

paratively powerless because they cannot hunt them [well]. . . .
To find them is the trouble. . . . Extermination is the word, and
not until the last one bites the dust will the war be finished."

Although Jack's new headquarters was at Hardin Butte, his
braves were roaming widely. There was rifle fire into the
Stronghold, to keep sentries sweaty with nerves. Mason had
moved his camp there from Hospital Rock despite the stench of
death from unburied, unlocated bodies of the January fight.
There was sniping at Yreka-bound couriers, and firing by
Indians coming to Tule Lake for water. No civilian left Gillem's
Camp without an escort. The tracks of warriors were found at
Fairchild's ranch, where the Modocs apparently attempted to
rustle some horses. Although Perry reconnoitered for eighty
miles, the Modocs easily gave him the slip. He did not see a
single warrior in his circuit of the Lava Beds. Later, Bernard and
Jackson reported reconnaissances in which no sign of the enemy
was seen. Reluctantly, the correspondents had to admit that
Gillem's eight hundred men were insufficient to cordon off the
whole volcanic badland. But they still talked of a thousand
mounted men making short shrift of the Modocs.

As usual, Captain Jack did not wait to be found. Instead, he
found the Army. On April 20, some of his men not only
reached Tule Lake, to drink deeply, but took the time to bathe.
Supply Officer Boyle was disgusted. "Only a feeble attempt was
made to get them, or attack them." Next day, the Modocs
raided a pack train and its escort between Gillem's and Mason's
camps, in full view of the signalmen on Gillem's Bluff. Lt. Peter
Leary and his guards were still firing from the shelter of rocks
when their attackers also took on Lt. Albion Howe and another
detachment of twenty men sent out to escort the supplies safely
into camp. Leary lost one killed and one wounded. The train
was fired on as it entered and left the Lava Beds and was trailed
by the Modocs almost into Gillem's Camp. Howe's men were
reattacked on the side of Long Cave. From eight hundred yards,
the Modoc raiders peppered the pickets of Gillem's headquarters and threw a few rifle slugs into the camp itself. Capt.
Evan Thomas scattered the Modoc "force"—now said to have
grown to all of eleven men—with a well-placed shell. The excuse
for the Army being unable to control the Modocs was the
terrain, plus the fighting ability of the enemy. *Call* reporter
McKay asserted, "It is impossible to form an idea of the terrible
nature of the ground fought over. Colonel Green, an old
Arizona fighter, who commanded the line on this side, says he

never saw anything like it in Arizona, and General Gillem says the Modocs are the best fighters he ever saw."

Gillem was reluctant to believe that Captain Jack would make a stand at Hardin Butte, although his half-breed chief of scouts, Donald McKay, reported the Modocs still encamped there on the twenty-third. The colonel decided to reconnoiter the bunchgrass butte, but in sufficient strength to awe the Modocs, and to determine if Hardin Butte would be a suitable emplacement for his howitzers and mortars.

Gillem gave command of the strong contingent to Capt. Evan Thomas, whose artillery had kept the Modocs hopping. He was the son of Brig. Gen. Lorenzo Thomas, one-time adjutant general of the Army. The younger Thomas was a Civil War veteran who was given a major's brevet for gallantry on the field of battle in 1863. With Thomas were two other general's sons, First Lt. Albion Howe and First Lt. Thomas F. Wright, whose father was George Wright. The latter commanded the entire Military Division of the Pacific during the Civil War until his untimely death in the shipwreck of the *Brother Jonathan* in 1865. Howe was the son of Civil War general A. P. Howe.

Young Howe had been a major of volunteers in the Civil War and had won a captain's brevet in regular service (1867) Indian campaigns. It was Wright who had boasted and offered to bet two thousand dollars that his company and Eagan's could whip the Modocs in fifteen minutes. He shortly had admitted his error, describing the Modocs after the Stronghold fight as being "nearly lightning." Just before he marched with Thomas, he was quoted as saying, "The match for the Modoc Stronghold has not been built and never will be. Give me one hundred picked men and let me station them and I will hold that place against five thousand—yes, ten thousand—as long as ammunition and subsistence last. It is the most impregnable fortress in the world. Sumter was nowhere when compared with it. Captain Jack is the biggest fighter on this continent. See what he's done? We starved him out of the Stronghold. We did not whip him. He fought his way out in spite of one thousand soldiers and has killed forty or fifty, and [lost] only three or four of his Indians. He'll turn up in a day or two, ready for another fight." Wright was half right in his observation; it was Scarfaced Charley, not Jack, who turned up.

Other officers designated to accompany Thomas were Second Lt. George Harris, First Lt. Arthur Cranston, and Dr. Bernard Semig. Thomas was also assisted by civilians H. C. Tickner as scout and Louis Webber, packer. He took fifty-nine men of Batteries A and K, 4th Artillery, and C and E Companies of the 12th Infantry, all veterans of the Three Days' Fight. He was assisted by Donald McKay and fourteen Warm Springs Indians, but the scouts would march separately from the main force.

Neither Gillem nor Thomas expected any trouble. The reconnaissance would be in force; the terrain, while hardly an Eton playing field, was less jumbled than the Stronghold. This made for easier going by the troops and less cover for the enemy. The night before setting out, Cranston sat up late with Simpson, chatting about guns and projectiles, particularly the newfangled Moncrieff gun, and Wright jotted a note to his wife. He brought it to Grier's tent for posting and said, "That is something which will amuse her. That is the best way to keep her in good spirits."

The Londoner, Simpson, feeling that there was no immediate offensive in view, or other newsworthy action, decided he might get a better story out of the arrival of the new C.O. than in Thomas' patrol. So he joined the men detailed to Yreka to escort Canby's successor, Col. (Brevet Brig. Gen.) Jeff C. Davis to headquarters. New York *Herald* reporter Fox did the same. Toby had another of her premonitions, but when she told Wright about it he did not take her seriously. But she at least prevented sutler McManus from risking his neck in combat again. She drove away his waiting horse. When the Irishman, swearing a blue streak and carrying a Colt and a Henry rifle, demanded to know where his nag was, Toby replied, "I turned that horse loose, for the sake of your wife."

Starting at 0730 of April 26, 1873, Thomas' strong force advanced slowly southward over the ragged flat of an old, eroded lava flow between the more recent (geologically speaking) and almost impassable Schonchin Flow and Devil's Homestead Flow. The march was in a column of twos with E Company deployed in the van as a line of skirmishers. They moved out smartly, the morning sun striking sparks of light on the polished steel of their rifle barrels as they advanced. But before long, the wings of the line began to sag and contract on the point as the ruggedness of the terrain was felt. Soon the company became almost a huddle of men ahead of the main column. Even the surgeon, Semig, recognized this as sloppy soldiering. He called it to Cranston's attention. The lieutenant passed the word, and Thomas' other officers ordered the flankers to spread out again. But rather than climbing to the rough ridges and picking their way along them, they merely followed along the bases of the uplifts paralleling the line of march. First Sgt. Robert Romer of Battery A was so exasperated with the careless conduct of E Company that he appointed himself a flanker and clambered laboriously over the jagged ridges to afford his own men some protection from a surprise attack from the side. Now, Semig and Cranston began to worry anew as the column of troops began to sprawl out and merge with the broad—but not wide enough—line of scouts and skirmishers.

But there was no attack. In fact, no Indians were seen nor even any traces of them. When Thomas reached the rock-littered, sagey basin just west of Hardin Butte and two hundred feet below the summit of the whale-backed little mountain, it was noon of a very pleasant day. Surrounded by sixty-six well-armed men and with more than a dozen Indian allies within hailing distance, Thomas did not feel it necessary to post a guard. Although Wright protested, "When you don't see any Indians is just the time to be on the lookout for them," Thomas sent out neither flankers nor pickets. Unwittingly, he took no precautions after halting his command in a perfect trap—in the bottom of a bowl commanded not only by Hardin Butte but literally surrounded by close-in low bluffs of lava boulders called Black Ledge. Thomas had marched his command as if it were a ceremonial detachment, perhaps the Bank Picquet in London. Small wonder that his enlisted men began to act as if they were on a picnic, not dreaming that their reconnaissance-in-force would end as a panicky cortege.

The men laid down their rifles and relaxed. Some began to eat lunch. A few actually took off their boots and rubbed their tired feet. One man began to trim his toenails! Thomas and Harris, with a signal corporal and a private, started on a clambering stroll to Hardin Butte to signal from there the safe arrival of the patrol to the signal station on Gillem's Bluff. They never made it.

As Thomas took off in one direction, Cranston led a dozen men toward the surrounding Black Ledge, saying half-jokingly, "I am going to raise some Indians." He got his wish. A sudden blast of fire from the ridges and bluffs swept the rocky hollow. The lazing soldiers grabbed for their arms and dove for cover as a shocked Thomas beat a retreat to them. The fire was well directed and heavy. Realizing, too late, that they were surrounded and in a nigh-perfect trap, the soldiers panicked.

Men threw away rations, even weapons, and bolted—some of them barefoot—over the rough lava. It was *sauve qui peut*. In strong contrast was Wright's coolness. He ordered a "set of fours" to advance on the Schonchin Flow, only fifty yards away. But it did not work. Lt. Harry D. Moore reconstructed the action from survivors' accounts: "At the first fire the troops were so demoralized that officers could do nothing with them. Captain Wright was ordered with his company to take possession of a bluff which would effectively secure their retreat, but Captain Wright was severely wounded on the way to the heights and his company, with one or two exceptions, deserted him and fled like a pack of sheep. Then the slaughter began. . . ."

Cranston and five men now volunteered to dislodge the Indians from a position, but he and all five were killed without a chance. For the Modocs, it was like shooting carp in a cask. All discipline and order now broke down among the enlisted men. After the battle Gillem reported: "A portion of the command seems to have become panic-stricken and organization seems, in a great measure, to have ceased. . . . All the officers and a part of the men remained together and fought like heroes, but the Indians had secured all the advantages of position."

Lt. William H. Boyle was more blunt and more bitter than Gillem. He reported, "All the brave men remained and were killed, and the cowards ran away and were saved." When Gen. Jeff C. Davis arrived at the Lava Beds, to meet such disastrous news, he observed, "Those who stood to the fight filled true soldier's graves. The cowards who ran away disgraced themselves and the service."

Tickner was a civilian, not a soldier. He certainly saw no point in staying—and dying—to pay for Thomas' folly. He ran like a mule deer. Running for his life, he encountered McKay's Warm Springs. The chief of scouts told him that he was trying to get to Thomas' aid but was being fired upon by the befuddled soldiers as well as the Modocs. This was possible. But no excuses were necessary, whether McKay was hero or "arrant coward," as Colonel Thompson termed the half-breed. He had no more chance of rescuing the main force than would Reno be able to save Custer three years later. Private FitzGerald's anger and grief led him to berate the Warm Springs, undeservedly, for their "abject fear" of the Modocs. He described them as being worthless in emergencies. If so, then what of Thomas' men?

Even Colonel Thompson admitted that some of McKay's swarthy followers had guts, like the Wasco, Captain George.

Harris, Howe, Semig and a few enlisted men grouped around Captain Thomas as he withdrew to a pocket of boulders and brush a little to the west. When Harris was wounded and thought killed, even old soldiers wept. He was idolized by his men because of his bravery. Thomas thought that Wright had secured the low bluff and called to him. He was answered with Modoc rifle fire. Someone, perhaps Pvt. William Benham, though badly wounded, later described Wright's last minutes. Already wounded in the groin, he accidentally shot himself in one hand as he hurriedly rapped a percussion cap off the nipple of one cylinder of his revolver. He held some of his command together and cheered his men until he received a mortal wound in the heart. Even in death, Wright was still the fighter: "revolver in hand, his eye fixed in a glassy stare at the gunsight."

Thomas did not know how to fight Modocs, but he did know how to die. He called out, "Men, we are surrounded. We must fight and die like men and soldiers." After he received his mortal wound, he hid his gold watch and chain in the rocks and then emptied his revolver at the largely unseen enemy. Curiously, Wright was reported to have done the same thing, to keep his watch from falling into the hands of Modoc looters. By now the battle had turned from ambush into massacre, a slaughter. But Thomas died well. His last words were, "I will not retreat a step farther. This is as good a place to die as any."

One enlisted man, at least, won the Modocs' respect during Thomas' debacle, Jim Rose, whose leg was broken by a bullet in the first surprise fusillade, was separated from his rifle by the heavy fire and crawled into a crevice, pulling his pistol out of its holster as he did so. He lay on his back, listening to the firing and the war song of the Modocs. Slowly the firing tapered off and all was quiet. As the Modocs began to look for booty, especially weapons, ammunition and whiskey, one of them, Little Ike, or Dave (Kan-kush was his Modoc name), looked into Rose's hiding place. Before he could drop the trooper's blouse he was carrying and go for his gun, Rose shot him in the stomach and broke his back. As he fell and died, other Modocs rushed up. They shot into the hole several times and left Rose for dead, then buried Ike by putting him into a similar crevice and filling its entrance with rocks.

The Modocs were so close to the soldiers at all times that

they threw rocks at them, to flush them from cover, and called out to them. Scarfaced Charley took pity on the poor bloody troopers and called, "All you fellows that ain't dead had better go home. We don't want to kill you all in one day."

Long before the first shocked soldier stumbled into Gillem's Camp, to gasp out a wild tale of defeat at one-thirty, headquarters was aware of trouble at Hardin Butte. The rifle fire could be heard plainly at both Gillem's Camp and the Stronghold, and Lieutenant Adams at his signal station could see the puffs of smoke as well as hear the sounds of the action. But Thomas' force was such a strong one that there was no early alarm. Major Green, for example, reassured some worriers that the patrol could take care of itself. The story told by the first survivors to come in was discounted as the ravings of cowards. But as more and more men straggled in, their nerves broken, with the same tale of complete disaster, a sense of forboding settled over camp, like Wheaton's January fog.

Still, Gillem would take no action. Meacham reported that he made no attempt to rescue Thomas until almost three hours after he first learned of the unit's entrapment. "It is stated on good authority," accused Meacham, "that soldiers who escaped made their way into camp one or two hours before Col. Green was ordered to go to the scene with his command." Lieutenant Boyle was furious with the dilatory commander: "All the troops were at this time ready and anxious to go to their support. But General Gillem, as usual, lost all control of himself and would not act nor let others." Before the rescuers under Green and Capt. William H. Miller, with a contingent from Mason's Camp, reached Hardin Butte, darkness had settled over the serrated lava plain. The weather, which had been so pleasant, turned blustery, stormy and disagreeable. The troops were some six hours in making a distance of perhaps four miles. Sad to say, the first men who were actually rescued (not the sprinters who had abandoned arms, comrades and courage in a pell-mell dash for Gillem's Bluff) did not reach headquarters until thirty-two hours after the ambush.

It was a trail of blood and tears that led back to Gillem's Bluff. Even allowing for Private FitzGerald's exaggerating the number of wounds, his recall of one of the vanquished is awesome: "One splendid specimen of physical manhood made his way to camp over that awful trail (a wonderful feat) with more than twenty bullet wounds in his body, and lived thirty-six hours thereafter. It might truly be said that he was 'shot to pieces.' "

Green was afraid that he had missed Thomas' position in the dark. There was not a sound but the howling of the wind. The survivors, in their hiding places, were afraid to call out, not knowing if the noises they heard were made by Modocs or rescuers. Most of them shivered all night in dark crevices as Green's men threw up the already *de rigueur* rock shelters of Lava Beds warriors. Boyle learned "it was almost impossible to find the wounded as they were afraid to answer when called to, thinking it was a device of the Modocs to get them out and massacre them." But around midnight, five men—mostly wounded—took a chance, and they linked up with the rescue party. Green tried to use them as guides to their buddies, but they only floundered around in the darkness till the task was abandoned, Green waiting for daylight.

In the wan light of dawn, the redoubtable Lieutenant Boutelle, accompanied only by his sergeant, went out to locate the remains of Thomas' command. He found the swale and the bodies of Thomas (shot four times), Howe and a number of enlisted men. He also found Harris and Semig, the latter being the only officer to survive the fight (though he lost part of a leg), and reported, "It was the most heartbreaking sight it has been my fate to behold." Harry D. Moore, also with Green's relief force, described the scene in part: "One wounded man—wounded in the arms, both forearms broken—in the back and the heel, kept all the Indians from the wounded men and prevented them from mutilating the bodies of the officers. A brave man! And deserving of substantial notice by the Government." This was Pvt. William Benham.

Green continued to search the basin as occasionally a curious Modoc was seen against the skyline, but making no hostile moves. The Modocs were genuinely tired of killing. Wright (shot three times) and his comrades were found north of Thomas, but Cranston's group could not be found and were listed as missing. It took all day to recover the wounded and succor them and to bury the stripped, but not mutilated, bodies. Both Gillem and Green had been so rattled that a doctor was not sent with the rescue force. (Surely they could not have assumed that Dr. Semig was safe from Modoc rifle balls.) Finally, Surgeon McElderry was dispatched, but he did not arrive until noon, twenty-four hours after the action began. Nor had the rescuers brought water! Boutelle witnessed McElderry trying to nurse the wounded without even that essential. He reported the pleading of the wounded as being dreadful and continuous. "When it ceased we knew what had occurred. They were dead."

Possibly Green stalled so that his return to camp could be made under the cover of darkness. If so, he erred badly. (The Modocs, like most Indians, were not inclined to attack by night.) But the return march was a nightmare, even though the Modocs made no move. Green broke his command into three parts, one to carry the nine six-man stretchers and two to form relief parties. One would rest, the other would carry the guns of the litter bearers. According to Boutelle, some of the relief men, frightened by the darkness and their belief that the Modocs were lurking in every shadow, simply headed for camp instead of taking their turns with the wounded. A storm of sleet and rain came out of a night "as black as a wolf's mouth," in Boutelle's words, and turned the rescue force into a numbed mob hurrying for the bonfire marking Gillem's Bluff. Lieutenant Boyle observed, "That night's march made many a young man old."

Finally, Boutelle abandoned his exhortations and threats as useless and personally took up a handle on the stretcher carrying the dying Lieutenant Harris. Boutelle's demoralized mob reached camp an hour after sunrise. It had taken them twelve hours to cover four miles. At least the lesson of the inept rescue forced the Army into improvising reclining-chair type litters mounted on top of mules in place of the human-powered stretchers, but not till it was too late for them to do any good.

Back in his hole in the rocks, Jim Rose became conscious again. He found he could not move his hands or feet without great effort. It was as if great weights were on them. But there were no boulders toppled onto his limbs. If Jeff Riddle was right;* Rose found that both his legs were broken below the knees and both of his wrists broken, too. He decided to crawl to Gillem's Camp, more than three miles away. Jeff Riddle swore that he told the truth; Rose crawled all night in his wretched condition. At daylight he reached the picket posts and almost lost his life, then and there. When he did not have the strength to answer a guard's challenge, the latter opened fire on him, shouting, "Indian! See! He is crawling on us. Let's shoot him!" According to Rose, the guard and his companions fired at least a

---

*Army records list Private Rose as being found dead on the battlefield, his body carried into camp and buried there.

dozen shots before one said, "I guess we got him. He is still."
Finally, Rose spoke up. "You damned fools, can't you fellows
tell a white man from an Indian?"

The almost-dead soldier was picked up and carried to the
field hospital. He was shot through the intestines, according to
Riddle, and hit nine times in all by the Modocs. His kneecaps
were exposed by the grinding away of skin and flesh by lava.
The skin and flesh were worn away from elbows, too, and even
his chin. Wrote Riddle, "I saw his chinbone or jawbone. It was
bare, with no flesh on it at all. It is a sight I have never
forgotten and will never, as long as I live." If Riddle is correct,
the doctors amputated both his legs (below the knees) and his
hands. And yet the dying wreck of a man was able to tell his
friends, as he lay on his cot, about his escape: "I made up my
mind I might just as well die in my attempt to reach my
comrades as to die where the Modocs had left me for dead. . . .
After my leg was broke, I could do nothing but hide, which I
did in a crevice. I had not been hidden very long when an Indian
jumped on the edge of the crevice. I pulled up on that buck.
When I fired he leaped up in the air about fifteen [!] feet. I
plugged him right where he lived. You bet I did. I know I
plugged him. He was not five feet from me. I am satisfied, boys. I
got my Indian. I am ready to die. I know I cannot live. What good
would I be to myself or anyone else, handless and footless?"

Despite the efforts of the surgeons and Toby's tender
nursing, Rose died just ten days after his many wounds were
dressed. Young Jeff Riddle was at the side of his cot when he
breathed his last words—" I got my Indian." (If the story of
Rose is, indeed, apocryphal, Riddle supplied a lot of convincing
details.)

The ambush of Thomas was not the work of Captain Jack
but of his best warrior, Scarfaced Charley. With about twenty-
two men, he took on a force of sixty-six soldiers backed by a
dozen or so Warm Springs Indians. With the loss of probably
only one man, Little Ike, Scarfaced Charley could have wiped
out Thomas' force to a man, had he chosen to do so. But
Charley was the least hawkish of Jack's top warriors and he
deliberately let the survivors escape to Gillem's Camp, content
with having killed twenty-seven and wounded seventeen of the
force. Every officer but Dr. Semig died, and the surgeon lost a
leg below the knee and was partially paralyzed from a shoulder
wound.

The traditional Modoc account of the victory over Thomas is succinct: "Scarface Charley, having twenty and two Modocs under him, encountered Lieutenant Wright [sic] in an open field and fought. Long time they fought. Charley lost one man. Some Americans they killed, some they wounded. Twenty and three soldiers. Six officers also were killed. The Modocs, standing on watch on a little mountain [Hardin Butte] near the Americans seated on the ground, charged. Here they fought, at Sand-Covered Hill."

Scarfaced Charley's ambush and decimation of Thomas' force was perhaps the most perfect entrapment of troops in Indian war history. He utterly smashed a force three times the size of his own and within three miles of the field headquarters of an army. Lieutenant Jocelyn recalled the first word of the ambuscade was "sickening news." Col. Frank Wheaton, removed for far less cause, was aghast at the disaster to Gillem's scouting party. But he was not personally embittered toward Gillem, as were Boyle, the editors of the *Army and Navy Journal*, and others. Nor was Jeff C. Davis, the new supreme commander of the Modoc Expedition. He blamed the debacle squarely on Thomas for not properly using his skirmish line as a protection of his front and flanks before halting.

But, like most of the officers, he was scornful of the conduct of the enlisted men, considering them cowards. Gillem, for his part, praised the enlisted men who died, assuming them to have been braver than those who fled. This, of course, could be argued. They might simply have been paralyzed targets, sitting ducks. The colonel singled out two noncommissioned officers for special mention: "Their conduct was the subject of commendation by those who fled." Alex McKay had a good word for the enlisted men who "stood their ground," whether fighting or cowering (it will never be known), but would not excuse the cowards who fled so precipitously. "Of the men in the ranks who were killed or wounded, it is perhaps sufficient to say that they proved their bravery with their blood."

Colonel Thompson hoisted the blame for Thomas' debacle onto Gillem's epauletted shoulders. He did not like the colonel to start with, believing the Tennessean to be self-willed and opinionated (*a` la* Thompson!). But now he was sure that Gillem was not only ignorant of Indian warfare, to boot, but was incompetent, too. He spread the story that Gillem owed his "shoulder straps" to able officers he was lucky enough to command in the Civil War and to the treachery of a woman in the killing of Confederate Gen. John Morgan which made his reputation.

Scarfaced Charley's victory over Thomas could have been absolute, had his heart not softened so that he heard himself telling the soldier boys to go back to camp while they were still alive to do so. As it was, his destruction of Thomas' force was devastating to the Army. It negated all of Davis' efforts to restore *esprit* to the Modoc expeditionaries. Davis wrote his superiors: "It proved to be one of the most disastrous affairs our Army has had to record. Its effects were very visible upon the morale of the command, so much so as that I deemed it imprudent to order the aggressive movements it was my desire, and intention, to make at once upon my arrival."

One wonders if the newcomer-commander, unable even to get a straight account of Thomas' defeat with all officers dead but Semig, and the latter in pain and losing his leg, knew what the cynical soldiers were now calling Gillem's Camp, where he made his headquarters, not far from the rude, stone-walled cemetery. It was "Gillem's Graveyard."

CHAPTER TWELVE

MODOC BLOODHOUNDS

As predictably as a knee-jerk, the American press clamored for more troops as details of Captain Thomas' ambuscade came in, and as Colonel Wheaton grumbled of his successor, Gillem, "I told you so!" It would be almost twenty years before the Army-apologist magazine, *United Service,* would dare to euphemize the disaster as "a gallant but unfortunate reconnaissance." Correspondents in the field argued that it was better to have ten thousand men campaigning for one month than one thousand for ten months. General of the Army William Tecumseh Sherman offered the Modoc Expedition a group of raw recruits headed for San Francisco, and also the entire 4th Regiment of Infantry. There was only one hitch; the Fourth was stationed in Arkansas and might be on the road for some time, if called to the Lava Beds.

Some of the public wished fervently and loudly for the return of Gen. George Crook, who had put the fear of God into the Paiutes and Pit Rivers at Infernal Caverns in 1867. Others, forgetting the mediocre showing of California and Oregon volunteersmen in January, demanded militiamen to supplant the "overmatched" regulars. Jesse Applegate agreed that such a call was desirable but wanted frontiersmen—old Indian fighters—recruited, not ribbon clerks from Portland. He topped the idea with a suggestion of his own—that a bounty be offered for each Modoc captured or killed, venturing that this plan would buy peace in three months.

A story datelined Chicago urged that bloodhounds be used to hunt down the Modocs, reminding readers that they had been employed against the Seminoles in the Florida War. But this suggestion found no favor in Washington, which probably did not want memories of the Seminole War (as unpopular as the Modoc War, if not more so) revived. Sherman opposed the bounty on scalps, if for no other reason than that he was sanguine of ultimate Army success and saw no advantage to scalping dead Modocs.

Once again, Gillem seemed paralyzed by crisis. The colonel made no move against the Modocs. He was censured, unfairly, for Thomas' blunder, although Dr. Cabaniss and others at the front tried to refute this unjust criticism. Gen. Jeff C. Davis, no fan of Gillem's, did not blame him but Thomas, and rightly. He pointed out that the latter would not have been surprised had he extended his skirmish line to front and flanks before nooning. And even without this precaution, he could have extricated himself, Davis believed, had his men stood by their officers and obeyed orders instead of running for their worthless lives. But this time Gillem probably acted, or, rather, failed to act, with good reason. His troops' *esprit de corps* had turned to *esprit de* corpse. There was much antiwar sentiment in the ranks.

An anonymous pacifist's letter was published in the *Call* on May 10 under the headline *A SOLDIER'S VIEWS*. It read: " 'He who enters here leaves hope behind' is a quotation that applies most aptly here. . .after the horrible massacre that occurred last Saturday and the rash and useless manner in which our men have been rushed into the very jaws of death by the governing authorities ever since fighting commenced. . . . All the men feel that unless there is a complete change in the administration of affairs in this country and more effective means are adopted to conquer the red fiends, we will gradually be sacrificed by detail . . ." Then the unknown soldier dropped a bombshell on the public by questioning even the real necessity for the Modoc conflict: "As long as this war proves a source of profit to contractors and others, so long it will continue; and that gain and money-making is the chief cause of its prolongation there can be no doubt." The soldier ended his epistolary diatribe by predicting that the time would soon come when sacrifices of comrades would so disgust the common soldiers that they would refuse to take the field. "We will leave those who made the war to fight it out, themselves."

Gillem was still sitting on his hands when Canby's successor, Gen. Jeff C. Davis, arrived. Some of the troops, such as Corp. Gilbert Davis, were, frankly, more interested in the shipment of canned fruit from the ladies of Yreka which accompanied him. Davis' retinue included Maj. Garret J. Leydecker of the Army Engineers, sent to sketch and map the Lava Beds, and Eadweard Muybridge, a San Francisco photographer chosen to record the Modoc War on glass negatives. Muybridge was following in the steps of Roger Fenton of the Crimean War and Matthew Brady and Timothy O'Sullivan of the American Civil War in pioneering in the role of combat photographer. The San Franciscan was long thought to have been the only cameraman covering the war, but actually he had competition in Louis Heller of Yreka and Fort Jones. But Heller sold his pictures to a San Francisco rival of Muybridge's, Carleton Watkins, and the prints and stereopticon slides that appeared bore Watkins' name. Apparently, some of the photos purchased by the Army were Heller's as well as Muybridge's. The Army used the work of both men to show the public what a godforsaken terrain it was up against in its Lava Beds campaign.

For a week after the Thomas-Wright disaster not a shot was fired by either side as the troops got used to their new commander. Jeff C. Davis, no relation to the Confederate President, was a no-nonsense officer, tart as a Newtown pippin. He was experienced, too. Davis had been a noncom in the Indiana Volunteers during the Mexican War before entering the Regular Army in 1848. In the Civil War he became a brigadier general of volunteers and was breveted a major general. His career, naturally, was somewhat slowed when he shot to death his commanding officer, Gen. William Nelson, in an argument. He was not promoted to major general of volunteers nor brigadier general in the Regular Army. It was as colonel of the 22d Infantry Regiment that he received Alaska from the Russians at Sitka in 1867. Doubtless, he was elated at the promotion, and expected the new command to improve his military reputation with a resoundingly successful conclusion to a war which had been badly bungled, so far.

Settlers at Goose Lake, Surprise Valley and the John Day country were made nervous again by renewed rumors of impending Modoc raids after the Thomas defeat. Indian Agent Dyar applied to Fort Klamath's C.O., Lt. Robert Pollock, for a detachment of soldiers to be stationed at the Klamath Agency to protect employees and their families. Pollock informed his superiors that he believed there was a genuine danger of a general Indian uprising, but he squelched the rumor that the Modocs had cut off all communication between Jacksonville and Linkville. He forwarded Dyar's request to Gillem, asking for a company of troops from the Lava Beds, and added, "I would urgently recommend that more troops be sent to this point for, in the event of an attack upon the Klamath Reservation or this post, we are but ill prepared to defend either place .... In the event of immediate danger, I have proffered the shelter of this post to the families at Klamath Agency." Gillem would have been out of his head to release fifty men from his battered, demoralized army for garrison duty, and he refused the request. General Schofield in San Francisco took alarm now and asked Fort Klamath for a weekly statement on the peacefulness of the reservation Indians. Pollock dutifully complied.

Meanwhile, Gillem's Camp was becoming a boomtown. Curiously, there were no prostitutes, but the village had all of the other attributes of civilization. Besides Charley La Booth's restaurant, a brand-new hotel was flourishing and a sutler, Walbridge, was erecting a general store close to the quartermaster's warehouses, presumably in competition with Pat McManus' establishment. Heavily laden wagons behind straining teams rumbled about frequently, and reporter Alex McKay of the San Francisco *Call* compared the hustling-bustling camp to a settlement in the diamond fields. The swarm of civilians included Lieutenant Harris' mother, who arrived the day before her son died of his wounds, and Maj. James Biddle's six-year-old son, Dave, who had been a good friend of General Canby. Young Biddle visited every wounded man and attended every funeral. He and an Indian boy, one day, were fired on by Modocs as they were fishing in Tule Lake. The youngster was a cool one; before leaving for camp, Dave strung his catch.

For all the activity and movement of supplies, there were shortages. When the campaigners ordered saddle blankets from Fort Klamath, Lieutenant Pollock had to send troopers' blankets to take care of the horses, since he had none of the former. And when the wounded were moved from the boomtown to the fort, there were not enough ambulances or even spring wagons for the task. Consequently, D. J. Ferree took Meacham across Tule Lake by whitehall boat to meet his wife at the mouth of Lost River. Pollock actually had to authorize the hiring of Indian canoes to convey the wounded from Ferree's ranch on Klamath Lake's Modoc Point across Agency Lake to Wood River and, finally, Fort Klamath's hospital.

Even when a courier to Ball's ranch was fired upon and forced to lie in concealment all night long, General Davis was not ready for offensive action. He was not as timid as Gillem, but he knew that his demoralized army was unready, as yet, to march into combat. He found that his men, even prior to the Thomas affair, had been in depressed spirits as the result of cheerless winter camps, the loss of friends in the campaign and the repeated failure of their best efforts against the wily Modocs. Mediocre marksmen that they were, the troopers were probably better rifle shots than the Modocs, and trench warfare should have been their cup of tea. Yet, each time they were matched against the Modocs, they failed. After April 26, their sagging morale touched bottom. "So much so," reported General Davis, "that I deemed it imprudent to order the aggressive movements it was my desire and intention to make at once." Like Wellington, Davis had the lowest regard for his troops. "A great many. . .are utterly unfit for Indian fighting of this kind, being cowardly beef eaters." But he was determined to hammer them into soldiers, soldiers who would snuff out the fires of the Modocs in the Lava Beds. Actually, Davis was under orders to be cautious. On April 30 General Schofield wired him: "Let there be no more fruitless sacrifices of our troops. . . . We seem to be acting somewhat in the dark."

According to a local war correspondent who later became a judge, Charles B. Bellinger, Davis helped to restore morale by marching a Modoc prisoner around camp at the muzzle of a double-barreled shotgun, to show his men that the renegades were but mere mortals. Unfortunately, the tale seems apocryphal, even if related from the bench. Where in the world would Jeff Davis have found a Modoc prisoner? Captive Modocs were about as common around Gillem's Camp as nuns. Long Jim, the Army's sole prisoner so far, had long since escaped from the stone corral. But if Davis never strutted with a scattergun, he certainly used his time to investigate the Lava Beds as he awaited reinforcements and the mending of morale. He pronounced the craggy badlands a formidable obstacle but not insurmountable. Davis' efforts paid off. Cuban-born Oregon pioneer Samuel A. Clarke, war correspondent for *The New York Times*, wrote in his notebook that Davis had definitely restored the solders' morale. As for Gillem, Clarke wrote him off: "I am satisfied that the most of them who served under him had lost all confidence in his capacity to compete with Captain Jack's strategy. The common soldiers were terribly demoralized and it is not too much to say that only for the presence of the Warm Springs Indians the demoralization would have been greater and so would the number of killed and wounded."

Davis' new reinforcements were two batteries of the 4th Artillery from the San Francisco Presidio. With both yellowlegs and infantrymen in short supply, the cannoneers of Battery B were transformed into cavalrymen, while those of Battery G were pressed into service as foot soldiers. Restoration of morale was much slower in coming than the reinforcements, however; on May 5, Davis was still reporting that his men were in poor fettle to attack Captain Jack. But he thought they soon would be ready.

As ever, Captain Jack chose not to wait for the Army. He struck first. While Donald McKay and his Warm Springs and Wascos were finding on May 9 the deserted Modoc camp of twenty-five burned-out campfires and a natural cistern, drained dry by thirsty warriors, Jack's renegades made a sortie. They struck a supply train from Lt. William H. Boyle's new quartermaster's camp on Tule Lake's Island, now The Peninsula, on its way to Scorpion Point. The Indians captured at least eleven mules and three horses. (According to some accounts, the Army recaptured the stock.) They looted and burned three or four wagons, wounded three of the fifteen-man escort and may—again, according to some reports— have made off with two precious kegs of whiskey. All this was carried out with the Modocs receiving not so much as a blood blister in return. In high dudgeon and higher disgust, Davis had to inform his superiors, "Escort whipped with three wounded. No Indians known to have been killed." At Camp Warner, Lieutenant Jocelyn shook his head over "the usual stampede of the troops."

That same day, Asst. Surg. Henry H. McElderry started the convalescent wounded for the wards of the Fort Klamath hospital. Luckily the Modocs did not strike at this party, which included Lieutenant Eagan, so badly wounded that he was relieved of duty and ordered to Angel Island in San Francisco Bay for specialized medical treatment. Had Jack hit this party, he would have wiped it out to a man.

So disorganized was Davis' army, still, that even in strength he did not dare reconnoiter Hardin Butte, or Sand Hill, in order to collect the bodies of Thomas' dead. Instead, he fell back on the tried-and-true services of Modoc squaws such as One-Eyed Dixie (Artina Choakus). He sent the ladies out on May 4 to find the missing Lieutenant Cranston and to ascertain, if possible, Jack's position and strength. The squaws were gone three days and spent eighteen hours without water. But they found the corpses and reported to Davis that Captain Jack had left the area. Probably, he was out of water. They brought one quite unexpected bit of good news. The morale in Jack's little army was beginning to decline. Even with repeated victories, the endless running was beginning to tell on the Modocs, especially since they were encumbered by women and children and short on both horses and water. Factionalism was beginning to plague Jack's leadership.

Gillem sent out a patrol to bring Cranston in but the bodies were too decomposed for transfer and were buried where they lay. Next, he sent the Warm Springs scouts to find Captain Jack's trail. They located it, trending toward the southeast, as if he were leaving the Land of Burnt-Out Fires. Actually, the Modocs were holed up in the ice caves of the Lava Beds using melted ice for drinking water. Finally, on May 9, Davis was ready to loose his troops again. Curiously, he chose a newcomer and an artilleryman, Capt. Henry C. Hasbrouck, to lead the reconnaissance. Perhaps Hasbrouck was not as much in awe of Jack as officers who had already been bloodied by him. In any case, he proved to be a wise choice. With B and G Troops and Battery B he went to Sorass Lake, south of the Lava Beds, and dug for water in the dry lake bed. When his men's efforts resulted only in empty wells, he dry-camped there and ordered McKay to take his Warm Springs, next morning, to Boyle's Camp, seventeen miles away, for water.

Captain Jack, for once, decided to personally lead a surprise attack. He chose Hasbrouck for his victim. This time he would not send Scarfaced Charley, who was getting too much prestige from his battlefield successes. (Curiously, the whites did not realize that Charley and Hooker Jim, *et al.,* were the real fighters, even if Jack would be considered the tactician as well as civil chief of the insurgent Modocs.) This time, Jack wanted to be in on the kill. He had a strong forty-five man force; his attack would be a total surprise, like the Thomas ambush; his opponent was grass-green as an Indian fighter. Jack was right in this last assumption. While his braves were stripping to breechclouts and he was dressing in Canby's uniform, Hasbrouck was splitting his force! He bivouacked his cavalrymen on the west side of the *playa* but took his battery of artillerymen almost a mile away from the lake bed to the scrubby cover of junipers and mountain mahogany below Timber Mountain. But unlike Thomas, Hasbrouck took proper precautions. He posted guards on a rock bluff four hundred yards north of the cavalry camp and some thirty feet above the level of Sorass Lake, which he now gave a less vulgar name—Dry Lake. Below the bluff was a line of rocks, amounting almost to another very low bluff about sixty yeards from the bivouac. This he did not guard since the higher ground controlled it.

It was as still as a church on Wednesday as Jack and his men took up their positions on the higher bluff, studied the guards' movements and easily infiltrated the line of pickets to reach the rocks between the lake camp and the guard posts. A dog belonging to Hasbrouck's packer growled an alarm that alerted his owner, who barricaded his campsite with *aparejos* and saddles, swearing and shouting, "Let the mules go to the devil. We must look out for ourselves." The officer of the day just laughed when he was warned of nearby Indians by the muleteer. Not a redskin had been seen. Still, he awoke Hasbrouck, reluctantly. It was almost too late. The roosters of Yreka were calling up the sun as the stillness of the dead *playa* of Sorass Lake was broken by a blaze of gunfire. The Army horses stampeded. To all appearances, Hasbrouck was headed for a repetition of the Thomas-Wright disaster.

But something went wrong for the Modocs—or, rather, right for the Army. The soldiers did not really panic this time, although some of them bolted from their blankets and were shot down on the lakeshore as they dashed for cover. Others hardly flinched. They rolled behind whatever cover they had in camp and returned the fire of the hidden Indians. Someone later said that it was Corp. James D. Totter of B Troop who turned the battle around by leading a charge ordered by Hasbrouck. The latter sent Captain Jackson to the right and Lieutenant Moss to the left. According to Pvt. Charles B. Hardin, who was there, it was Quartermaster Sgt. Thomas Kelly of G Troop who really tipped the balance, however. Sick of running from unseen Modocs, he decided to fight. And the Irishman fought like hell. Recalled Hardin, "I saw a line of Modocs pop up their heads and fire a volley. This at first caused some confusion. Men rolled over behind saddles and bundles of blankets—no covering, however small, being ignored, fastening on belts and pulling on boots under a hail of bullets. There was a possibility of panic but this was happily averted by Sergeant Thomas Kelly of our Troop, who sprang up and shouted, 'God damn it! Let's charge!' "

Charge they did, and the Modocs faltered. Hasbrouck then split his Warm Springs unit into two detachments to flank the Modocs. Corporal Totter and others fell in their advance, but the line of bluecoats kept moving forward. The skirmishers swept the lower rocks, then the bluff, and chased the fleeing

Modocs clean across the sagebrush plain to the west. Some of the raiders were heard crying, "The Warm Springs! The Warm Springs!" as McKay tried to outflank them. The scouts failed to cut off the Modocs' retreat, and the tired cavalrymen, now acutely conscious of their shortage of water, gave up the pursuit after three or four miles of running. Hasbrouck had a total of only twenty gallons of water, which he rationed out to his wounded. All able-bodied men had to go thirsty.

Captain Hasbrouck praised Lieutenant Kyle and the omni-present Boutelle, (whom Private FitzGerald also lauded as a splendid officer in contrast to the cruel Cresson) for holding their positions so well. He also praised Jackson and Moss for the charge or countercharge that they had led. He was proud, too, of the way B and G Troops scaled the twenty-foot ridge in the muzzles of Modoc rifles. In truth, everyone fought well at Sorass Lake—except unlucky Battery B, which was just far enough away to get to the scene too late to take part in the engagement. The glory was the cavalry's and the Indian scouts', but the leadership was artilleryman Hasbrouck's.

The rout of Captain Jack was complete. Not only did Hasbrouck drive the Indians back into the cover of the timber, he captured twenty-one of their ponies and three pack mules loaded with six cases of cartridges—practically the entire Modoc armory. Even more surprising, the Modocs lost at least one and possibly two warriors and had several wounded. They left a man on the battlefield—something unheard of in Modoc history. This signaled a real decline in Modoc morale. Hasbrouck did not yet realize it, but his little victory had turned the tide of the Modoc War.

One of the jubilant Warm Springs scouts tied a rope around the dead Modoc's heels and dragged the body all the way to Boyle's Camp behind his pony. Some thought the victim was Boston Charley, "the meanest of the outlaws," but the face was too disfigured by the dragging to be identified. Surrendered Modocs later said it was the body of Ellen's Man George, whom Jeff Riddle termed "the bravest of the Modocs." Ellen's Man had been Captain Jack's assistant in the killing of Canby. But Riddle claimed the corpse was that of Little Steve, and that George died later. Historian Keith Murray believes that Ellen's Man George was gravely wounded at the dry lake but died some three and a half miles away and was cremated there by his comrades, along with Canby's watch.

When Modocs fled they left, for the first time, a bloody trail to follow. It led off toward the mountains south of Sorass Lake. Hasbrouck did not get off easily; he had eight horse-soldiers wounded, three of them mortally, and two Warm Springs scouts killed. But he sensed the effect of his fight on Army morale although he was unprepared for its disastrous effect on Modoc spirit. The Army was suddenly charged with enthusiasm and self-confidence. All it had needed was a victory. Men now began to volunteer for hazardous patrols; a fortnight earlier they would have deserted first. Hasbrouck was a newcomer as an Indian fighter but he instinctively knew that he had to keep the Modocs moving now that he had them on the run. He needed no orders to this effect from Davis, although they came. He sent his wounded to the Peninsula Camp, led the rest to the nearest water at Scorpion Point or Promontory Point of Tule Lake, then turned back on the Modoc trail like a sleuthhound. Davis in his report of the pursuit suggested the sudden reversal of Army morale: "It partook more of a chase after wild beasts than of war, each detachment vying with the other as to which should be first in at the finish."

The Sorass Lake victory caused the press to flip-flop from doom and gloom to sunny optimism. The *Call*, for example, editorialized: "At one time the courage of a portion of the Army was doubted. It was thought the sudden attacks made by the Indians had intimidated and more or less demoralized them. Such seems not to have been the fact. Our latest information is to the effect that they behaved themselves with courage on every occasion and in every encounter." Hasbrouck's victory was, in a sense, "retroactive." The *Army and Navy Journal* soon noted, with relief, the soaring morale of the expedition. It attributed it, however, to Davis' mere presence rather than to the presence of mind of Hasbrouck under surprise attack.

If any Utah Goshutes, California Pit Rivers, Nevada Shoshones or Fort Hall Snakes in Idaho really planned to join the Modocs in a kind of Amerindian *jihad*, Hasbrouck's spunky fight quickly cooled their ardor. Fort Klamath still reported younger Klamaths being tempted to go to war with the whites if Jack continued his winning ways, but that danger, if it ever really existed, was extinguished by Sorass Lake. On May 17, Chief Allen David obsequiously made a point of calling on Lieutenant Pollock at Fort Klamath to reassure him of the tribe's good feelings toward its white neighbors. Pollock was so impressed by David's fealty that he recommended the chief be given some remuneration for his efforts as chief in behalf of peace. The lieutenant wrote, "I believe in the good feeling of the Klamaths towards the Government. And I think that, as long as the authority of Allen David is recognized and respected by them, that there is no danger to be feared from that tribe."

No one quite realized it as yet but the Modoc War was virtually over, and all because of the scrimmage at waterless Sorass Lake. Some officers, such as Lieutenant Boyle, realized that it *might* end the war, even if it was only a draw. Davis saw it as more than a draw. It was a square fight in which, for the very first time, the Modocs were whipped.

Incredibly, Jack's tightly knit little band of rebels began to fall to pieces. Hot Creeks Bogus, Hooker, Shacknasty and Steamboat all denounced Captain Jack for Ellen's Man George's death while the cremation rites were still going on. Reluctant to join the fight in December, then the most hawkish of the Modocs from January through April, the Hot Creeks or Cottonwood Creeks now reverted to a hypocritical pacifism. Black Jim not only blamed Captain Jack for the death of George but almost shot him before Weium intervened. Colonel Thompson insisted that Hooker Jim contemplated shooting Jack, too. The band then split in two. The Hot Creeks pulled out and headed west.

As early as May 8, Bogus Charley was reported to have abandoned his chief. He went with his wife to Four Creeks, about thirty miles northeast of Yreka, and there met and talked to three whites. While he declined to give up his gun, he said that he was tired of fighting. He reported thirteen Modoc warriors dead, including John Schonchin's son (from the dud shell). But Schonchin senior he reported to be very much alive. Bogus next popped up on the Klamath Reservation where he told the Indians that he had killed three soldiers and a Warm Springs during the Three Days' Fight. Again he said that he was ready for more fighting, if need be, but was really tired of it. He predicted that his fellow Modocs would begin drifting in, to surrender. A Yreka posse searched for Bogus, dead or alive, but he easily gave it the slip.

After dodging his pursuers for some time, Bogus turned up again, to talk with ex-Sheriff J. C. Burgess and to disclaim any knowledge of the Peace Commission murders. He told the ex-lawman that Captain Jack had about thirty men left and that they would probably fight to the end. However, he guessed that the end was not more than two or three weeks away. Bogus then wandered back to join Hooker Jim and ten other warriors, with their families, who were heading for the mountains west of Van Bremer's ranch.

With his Army's confidence restored, Davis knew that he did not need the thousand men Wheaton had thought necessary for victory. With half that number he had an adequate force. Reporter Alex McKay agreed, stating in the *Call* on May 14 that the Modocs were nearly starved out and, with their ammunition almost gone, would be subjects of easy capture if the Army had good guides. As the pursuit was pressed, Davis moved his headquarters from Gillem's Camp to Boyle's Camp on the Peninsula, alias Miller's Island. He nearly drowned himself and Gillem in a swamped boat on May 12 when the lake roused itself in a storm, as usual, when the brass started across it.

All the while, the dogged Hasbrouck stuck to Jack's trail like a clover burr. He had found horses useless in the volcanic rock quarry that was the Lava Beds, so he marched his men as foot soldiers, but with pack animals carrying food, medical supplies and water kegs. He had 210 men living on beans, hardtack and a quart of water a day. Mason was coming up with a reinforcement of 170 men. Despite Gillem's jaundiced opinion of Mason, the latter's subordinate officers, such as Boyle, had confidence in him. Reporter William M. Bunker wrote, "Mason is one of those quiet, quick, discreet officers who are always ready for orders; a man without oath or bluster, and one who never wastes time or words." An old soldier vouchsafed the accuracy of this feeling: "Colonel Mason fights like hell in the morning and in the afternoon says nothing but 'Forward! Forward!'" When Capt. David Perry returned from a leave of absence, Davis sent him out on a scout with one hundred men, with orders to cooperate with Mason and Hasbrouck. He then abandoned the Stronghold as a camp and put every man in the field that he could, holding back only fifty men for a headquarters guard. Davis also relieved Gillem of his command of the Modoc Expedition and restored Wheaton to the command, but actually took personal control himself of the entire campaign.

The hard-marching pursuit of Mason and Hasbrouck caught Jack, who had returned to the Lava Beds from Sorass Lake and the defection of the Hot Creeks of his band. He found himself pinched between the two Army forces at a treeless, brushless hill of pumice called Big Sand Butte. Jack hesitated, prepared to fight, but with only thirty-three effectives, thought better of it. As the soldiers converged, he easily slipped out of the trap and disappeared into the torn-up terrain.

When the Modocs escaped from the Army pincers movement at Big Sand Butte, they left the Lava Beds. Their campfires winked out forever in The Land of Burnt-Out Fires. The Army had them where it wanted them, on the run and in the open.

Hasbrouck remounted his men, who were tired from scrambling over the pedregal on foot, and, though short of water, searched for the Modocs' track. When he found it, he led his men on a hard eight-mile dash through juniper and mahogany to a ridge of Sheep Mountain, or Fairchild's Mountain. Unwittingly, he had picked up the Hot Creek quitters, not Jack's band. They fought but not well, and at Hole-in-the-Ground a squaw was killed, two warriors "claimed" by the self-deluding Jackson, and five squaws and an equal number of children captured. The death of the squaw, Limpy, was termed accidental by Hasbrouck, but the Modocs later contended that the woman had actually been a messenger conveying their desire to surrender. (Hence, the poor showing of the Hot Creeks in the scramble at Sheep Mountain.) According to them, she was killed by the Warm Springs and scalped. Revenge may have been involved; Stephen Powers later reported that Modoc tradition had a warrior-squaw killing at least one soldier in the April battle for the Stronghold.

The captured squaws told One-Eyed Dixie that Captain Jack's contentious band was now definitely breaking up. Dissension had been synergized by the Sorass Lake defeat into more than warweariness, into out-and-out disloyalty. The reason was a curious one to Hasbrouck, but it made good sense to the Modocs. It was not so much the deaths, even of strategist Ellen's Man George, nor the wounding of Curly Headed Doctor and Little John. It was not even so much the growth of the suspicion that Jack was putting the Hot Creeks in the front line rather than his own Lost River kin. No, it was the simple failure of a prophecy that he had made in a burst of overconfidence. Stealing a leaf from Curly Headed Doctor's book of conjuring, Jack had consulted a captured chronometer just before the battle of Sorass Lake. The strange instrument, which he had used like a Scottish peep-stone, had divined good medicine, good fortune in battle. He then had told his men that he would cast a spell that would render them bulletproof. Naturally, the warriors were indignant and felt betrayed when the spell failed them, miserably, at Sorass Lake.

When the squaws reported that the Hot Creeks were ready to surrender but were afraid of the Warm Springs with their boasting, singing of war songs, and endless sharpening of scalping knives, John Fairchild stepped in again. Correspondent S. A. Clarke found him a man of judgment and character, well versed in Indian affairs and influential with the redmen. Observed Clarke, "He seems to be confident that the war will soon end, with considerate management." Fairchild sent the squaws out once more, after persuading a skeptical Hasbrouck to postpone his search-and-annihilate mission. When they returned, he got them an audience with General Davis. The Hot Creeks were only fifteen miles away, eager to surrender and to live in peace, but still afraid of being killed by trigger-happy soldiers or Warm Springs scouts. They asked *hyas tyee* Davis to come see them. Mindful of past traps, Davis bluntly refused all terms. Instead, he rudely offered them only a safe-conduct to come in and surrender—or else. He set a time limit after which he would shoot every Modoc found packing a gun.

At 1 P.M. on May 22, 1873, the squaw, Matilda, galloped into Fairchild's ranch, her horse completely blown. Excitedly, she told the rancher that the Modocs, very near, were now ready to surrender if he, alone, would escort them in. No soldiers, they insisted. But they still had faith in Fairchild. "Where is Artina?" asked Davis. Matilda explained her delay: "Tied up. Long ride. No water. No good." Some suspected foul play, but tensions relaxed when Artina swept in on a foam-covered horse, to verify her friend's claim. Fairchild, his majordomo and a few cowhands saddled up and rode off to the hills and Indian Springs with the squaws. Davis, with Colonels Wheaton and Sumner, sat in front of the headquarters tent to await developments. Gillem, alas, was not present. He was robbed of the spectacle of surrendering Modocs by a case of rheumatism atop his humiliation, so he left for Yreka before Fairchild brought in the Hot Creeks.

Late in the afternoon the soldiers began to shout, "Here they come! Here they come!" An uncanny hush fell over the normally busy camp as Fairchild's majordomo, or ranch foreman, led a procession into camp. He looked hard at the soldiers as he passed, for the first sign of hostility or treachery. Fifty yards behind him rode Fairchild and twelve "bucks," including Curly Headed Doctor, Bogus Charley and Steamboat Frank. The watchers were disappointed to find that only a segment of the rebel band was surrendering. All the Modocs were in motley garb, including parts of Army uniforms. But each man carried a sound rifle. They were followed by twenty squaws and thirty-one children, all on worn-out ponies they had scraped up from somewhere. Each Modoc, man, woman and child, wore a daub of pitch smeared on his or her face. Clarke thought it was for decoration or to prevent chapping, but probably it was a sign of surrender. The good physical condition of the warriors surprised the onlookers. McKay, for example, reported, "Strange as it may seem, the young captives are as stout and hearty as if they had been living in peace and on the fat of the land." Clarke, for his part, thought the warriors looked "horrid," except for handsome, light-complexioned Bogus Charley.

No Indian said a word. Nor did the watchers talk much as General Davis advanced to a point fifty yards from Fairchild's house to receive the surrender. He was formally introduced to the loquacious Bogus, who now assumed leadership because of his fluent command of "Boston talk." The slender and athletic youth smiled ("sweetly," thought Alex McKay), but a poker-faced Davis took his proffered hand. All of the Modocs then came forward and ceremoniously laid their rifles on the ground next to Davis. According to Clarke, fifteen rifles were piled up. Davis broke the impressive silence of the capitulation by ordering, "Give up your pistols and all your other arms." But each man signified that he had no other weapons. "Now then," continued Davis, "I shall give you a camp where you may remain tonight. If you try to run or escape, you will be shot dead."

The Modocs promised to obey, then crossed Cottonwood Creek into a clump of trees to draw rations and prepare a big *muck-a-muck* (feast) under the security of seven guard posts. Fairchild, counting off the sixty-three Indians, reported twenty braves missing from the Hot Creek or Cottonwood Creek band. Bogus told him Boston was dead and that Hooker Jim was out looking for his body. Fairchild knew this was more of Bogus' usual hogwash. Even reporter McKay could not swallow such a yarn; he called it an "Indian romance."

S. A. Clarke saw an Indian sign shortly, on the road near Ball's ranch, and assumed it had been made by one of the surrendering band. In fact, it was the trail of Hooker Jim, lurking in the sagebrush to see how the surrendering men fared. Satisfied, he jumped from hiding, raced across the camp and burst into Davis' tent. There he threw his gun at the startled general's feet and grunted, "Me Hooker Jim. I give up." Davis later told Col. William Thompson that Hooker's sudden apparition was the grandest sight he had ever witnessed.

The *Call* reported some regret in camp at the fact that Col. Alvan Gillem had not been allowed to close out the Modoc campaign. On the other hand, some "face" was restored to Col. Frank Wheaton by Davis. He let him participate in the surrender ceremony.

Next day, Bogus told Fairchild that his people were worried by the curses and fierce looks of some of the common soldiers. But he said his men were impressed by Davis' strong control over them, in contrast to Captain Jack's weak leadership. "The *tyee* must be a great man if he can make all of them do as he pleases," said Bogus to Fairchild. The latter immediately seized the opportunity to lecture him on the immense power of the general-*tyee*.

Davis found a new ally in Steamboat Frank. The rogue was eager to turn his coat. He yearned to join the Army in hunting down his erstwhile chief. Here was the guide the Army had been looking for. Steamboat believed (or so he said) that Jack had let the Hot Creeks bear the brunt of the fighting while his clique of Lost River friends, to which the "westerners" were not welcome, stood by. Bogus also accused Jack of deceiving him and his friends; Jack had a lying tongue in his head. Some of this was transparent fence-mending, but Bogus still resented the failure of Jack's promised immunity to .50/.70-caliber Army slugs. But self-preservation loomed largest in the tricky minds of Bogus and Steamboat.

All of the Modocs wanted to meet the brave new *tyee,* Hasbrouck, who was little-known to press and civilians as well as the Indian enemy. They said he had "hustled" them lively at the place they called Dried-Up Lake. During the Lava Beds sieges they had lived fairly comfortably, but once Hasbrouck was on their trail it had been a mean life. They had run and run until their winded nags refused to carry them further. Said Steamboat Frank, "No eat. No sleep. Soldiers around, all the time, night and day." Sorass Lake and the subsequent harrying of the Modocs proved to be the high point in the career of the West Pointer from New York, although Hasbrouck was already a veteran of sixteen years in the artillery, had taught at West Point and had captained a battery in the Army of the Potomac during the Civil War.

Davis treated his captives well, considering them to be bait to draw in more hostiles. He assured them of protection from the wrath of soldiers who had lost friends to their deadly rifle fire. He fed them Army rations and forbade visits to their compound without a pass or his own express verbal orders. Still, the Warm Springs made the captives uneasy. The nominal Christians, who sometimes refused to march on Sundays, yelled, gesticulated and chanted war whoops at their traditional enemies. This they did even on Sunday. They particularly liked to hone scalping knives on their moccasins while glaring in the direction of the distrustful prisoners. Toby took informal charge of the Modoc squaws, who were as fearful for their lives as their menfolk. The women had good reason. S. A. Clarke sampled camp sentiment and wrote: "Several of those who surrendered are very bad Indians and should certainly be hanged for their murderous acts. It is possible that some of them may be saved from that fate, as the worst that can be said against them is that they fought in open battle."

Bogus Charley, Hooker Jim, Shacknasty Jim and Steamboat Frank, not inaptly titled "the leading ruffians of the tribe," now came forward to volunteer their services as scouts to help run the foxy Captain Jack to his hole. Artina and Matilda had visited Jack and found he had only about twenty-five loyalists and their families now, and just eighteen ponies. The general kept his confab a secret, but the four prisoners caused a sensation when they passed through camp at noon of May 25 en route to the headquarters tent. Each was curiously adorned for a "captive" with a Springfield rifle over his shoulder and an Army belt with cartridge box on his belt. Rumors flew, but Davis kept mum.

With the four "hounds," as the turncoats were now called, Davis and a party rode off, to be joined by correspondent McKay. The general visited Capt. John Mendenhall at his foot-artillery camp at Gillem's Bluff. Mendenhall was aghast at his commander putting himself in the bloody hands of the quartet. Leaving Mendenhall, Davis' party entered the Lava Beds. More than a dozen times the "prisoners" ordered their captors to halt while they crawled through gulleys and peered over ledges. Later they either relaxed (or tired of their sport with the whites) and proceeded to bang away with their new rifles at pelicans and ducks, to show off their marksmanship. Hooker was the best shot, killing several of the big-billed birds at a range of seventy-five to one hundred yards and once bringing two of them down with a single shot. He told the whites that, when he got used to his new Springfield, he would be able to do some good shooting.

The traitors failed to cut Jack's track on this reconnaissance but, their dubious "loyalty" tested sufficiently, Davis let them go out again, alone. The *Call's* McKay noted, "Hooka Jim, the Lost River murderer, is the best reconstructed Modoc alive. He fairly dotes on Gen. Davis." Sarcastically, the journalist commented, "Perhaps he wants the appointment of Collector of Customs at the Lava Beds, or some other sinecure."Unlike Davis, McKay was unwilling to forgive and forget. He indulged in some wishful thinking about Hooker: "Desperate work is the only thing that will save him from the halter." Probably Dr. Cabaniss felt the same way. He recalled that Hooker Jim killed Henry Miller and perhaps seven other men. The doctor called him the meanest man in the whole tribe.

Captain Jack and his diehards were now making east from the Lava Beds on the ridges between Tule Lake and Clear Lake. They stopped at a favorite old campsite on the east side of the Bryant Mountains and there hunted with the bows and arrows of Long Jim's father, so as not to give their position away with rifle shots. Then they headed for Steele Swamp, a hideout east of Clear Lake; but they did not reach it.

From his new Scorpion Point headquarters, Davis reorganized his entire force into three highly mobile squadrons under Perry, Hasbrouck and Jackson. Each consisted of two cavalry troops, twenty Warm Springs and thirty pack mules. His orders to his officers were: "Find and fight or capture the Indians, and stay by them if possible. Do not return to camp without a brush with the foe. I will forward rations to the front." His orders to his turncoat spies were the same he had given Artina and Matilda—Find Captain Jack and persuade him to come in.

The four sellouts easily found Jack's camp, where the chief ordered them to surrender their weapons. They refused and a stalemate ensued. During the standoff they tried to convince the chieftain that he should capitulate. Bogus was forbidden to talk by Jack, but the latter's authority was now so eroded that even his best friend did not respect his wishes. Scarfaced Charley spoke up. The 150-pound fighter, "the boldest warrior of the band" to most whites, said that he was tired of living like a dog. Someone else then bitterly assailed the "bloodhounds" for turning traitor and leading the Army. Bogus just shrugged and said the soldiers and Warm Springs were going to come anyway.

When Jack saw that the conversation was beginning to demoralize his comrades further, he broke it off. He ordered the four deserters to clear out or he would shoot them. S. A. Clarke closely paraphrased the report the foursome brought back to Applegate's ranch, now a temporary Army headquarters. "He [Jack] said he would never surrender. He didn't want to be hung like a woman without resistance, but was determined to die fighting, with his gun in his hand as a warrior should." Davis' Modoc spies reported Jack and his small coterie to be hiding in Willow Creek near the old South Emigrant Road, about fourteen miles east of Clear Lake and Applegate's ranch. According to a rumor they picked up, Jack was thinking of raiding the ranch in retaliation for the meddling of the Applegates—and to re-horse his broken-down band.

Hasbrouck and Jackson hurried to Willow Creek. They found it a natural hiding place with its thick brush, its junipers, the fish and game there, and its wild celery and *camas* roots. Green, in overall command, divided his force, equipping each with Warm Springs scouts as well as Modoc spies. Hasbrouck, guided by Hooker Jim, led his men along the high ground on the north edge of the deep, sheer canyon. Jackson, with Lieutenants Charles C. Cresson and John G. Kyle, plus Bogus, Shacknasty and Major Green, moved up the south or left bank of Willow Creek canyon, guided by Steamboat Frank. Hasbrouck's terrain was rougher, and his squadron fell behind the one on the opposite bank. Jackson finally found the Modocs at three in the afternoon. Captain Jack was caught napping; he just could not believe, considering past experience, that the Army could move so fast. The Modocs were across the defile on Hasbrouck's side. They saw Jackson's men and fled, shouting in Modoc, "Run quick! Run quick! Soldiers coming!"

Because of the depth of the gorge and its steepness, communication between the two squadrons was almost impossible. But Jackson ordered Lt. Henry N. Moss to dismount his men and to take them as skirmishers down and across the canyon to seize Jack's camp. Just then, three Modocs appeared and yelled from the far side of the creek that they wished to surrender. They cried, "Don't shoot!" in English. "Surrender! Surrender! We no fight. We want to talk peace. We like peace talk." One of them, his rifle cradled casually under one arm as if he were out hunting mule deer, was Boshtinaga or Boston Charley. He was wearing Cranston's cap. Immediately, he was covered by a dozen rifles. Laying down his own weapon at Fairchild's feet, he then shook hands with Steamboat Frank and the Warm Springs. Next, he offered to bring in all the Modocs. They were hidden in the rocks and timber nearby, he indicated, but were dispirited and ready to give up. Fairchild and Cabaniss assumed responsibility for him and sent Boston back to fetch in his fellow warriors.

The Modoc War should have ended at that moment. Unfortunately, someone accidentally discharged a rifle. Stories differ; either Steamboat Frank did it or a Warm Spring scout named, ironically, Modoc Frank. In any case, someone turned his horse in the thick brush; the hammer caught and cocked itself; the weapon discharged. The Modocs scattered like quail. They thought the soldiers had shot Boston.

Jackson sent Boston back, post haste, to persuade his comrades that all was well. Unfortunately, in the process of seizing Jack's abandoned camp and a surprising amount of arms, ammunition and captured Army mules, Hasbrouck ran into Boston and held him prisoner along with four hungry squaws and some children. One of the women was Jack's sister, Queen Mary or Princess Mary. By the time Donald McKay convinced Hasbrouck of Boston's peaceful errand, two hours had passed and further dickering, or even pursuit, was impossible. The Modocs had decamped, the country was rugged; a chase was out of the question in the penumbra of twilight. The two squadrons encamped.

On Friday, the penultimate day of May 1873, the chase was resumed across fragmented lava in which the cavalry left a trail of ripped-off horseshoes and bloodied boulders. The Warm Springs lost the Modocs' track but the troopers overran it in Langell Valley north of Clear Lake. Just before dark they spied three warriors running into Black Jim Canyon in the bluffs on the east side of the valley on the ranch of Simpson (Simp, or Horsefly) Wilson. San Francisco *Evening Bulletin* correspondent William M. Bunker described the scene: "Along the crest of the bluff and down the steep trail on its side charged the entire force of 230 men. Never have I seen a more beautiful military movement." Scarfaced Charley was obviously impressed, too. After directing four rifle shots in token defiance, just for the record and well over the heads of the charging troopers, Jack's chief warrior laid down his rifle. He came to the crest of a hundred-foot bluff with a "moat" of loose basalt at its base—"a Gibraltar for the Modocs" in Dr. Cabaniss' terms, had Charley chosen to defend it. There he carried on a long-range but not long-winded conversation with his pursuers. He offered to surrender to the doctor and volunteered to try to get the rest to give up their hopeless fight.

Giving up his gun, Scarfaced Charley took Cabaniss to Jack for a talk. The doctor remembered, "I found the chieftain sitting on a rock, a white blanket around him and a carbine by his side. We shook hands but he was very dignified and had little to say." Jack agreed to surrender since his people were tired and without food and adequate clothing. But, because it was getting late, he said he would bring them in next morning. Green had no choice but to agree. Cabaniss and One-Eyed Mose took a supply of hard bread to Jack's hungry camp and spent the night there. The chief kept men posted to fire on the soldiers should they attack, and he hid his women and children in the rocks. Cabaniss almost lost his life about the time he arrived. Captain Jack took a bugle call to mean an advance, whereas it was sounded to recall the soldiers four miles to Wilson's ranch in Langell Valley for supper, where there was water and forage. Actually it was a closer thing than Cabaniss suspected at the time. A surprise attack was actually suggested by glory-lusting officers. Wrote Cabaniss later, "Col. Green was urged by a few rash officers to do this but he refused and said 'If I do, they will kill the Doctor.' "

Next morning, the thirty-first, "the old villain," John Schonchin, formally surrendered, as did the villainous looking but honorable Scarfaced Charley. In all, fourteen braves, twelve squaws and ten children followed them in. But not Captain Jack. The chief just could not bring himself to accept the humiliation of surrender. Somehow, the press transformed his trauma into lunacy, reporting Jack to be suffering from "emotional insanity." Scarfaced Charley put it more kindly and accurately: "His heart failed him." While nine warriors fled in one direction, he and his last three followers took off in another direction in the pre-dawn shadows.

S. A. Clarke observed the surrender of Scarfaced Charley, whom Elijah Steele insisted was not really a Modoc at all but a Rogue River of Tipue Tie's tribelet, which had become extinct, and thus only a "naturalized" Modoc. Said Clarke: "He did it with exceeding sorrowfulness, as if he felt and understood all that he surrendered in doing so. Scarface is more respected than any other Indian, and there is much sympathy felt for him among the whites, as he went to war unwillingly and has done his work in open warfare and has not been engaged in any savage and merely murderous work. He is considered the best and bravest of the entire Modoc brand of braves." Cabaniss called Scarfaced Charley the Modoc's Chevalier Bayard because he fought so well and was so generous and free of cruelty. Sergeant McCarthy dubbed him the Paladin of the band. As for Schonchin John, Clarke wrote: "All his fears and half of his hate of white men were visible in his sullen manner."

The San Francisco *Evening Bulletin,* in its long-distance wisdom, chided Dr. Cabaniss for his recklessness. General Davis and some younger officers were critical, too, of the doctor's "meddling." But Hasbrouck congratulated him for saving many lives that would have been spent in an attack in the face of Captain Jack's last stand. Earlier, he had won commendations from Gillem, Green and Surgeon McElderry for his coolness under fire while dressing wounds, for shaming litter bearers into action by carrying stretchers himself into a field of fire when they balked, and because, as Gillem said, "He never hesitated to meet the Modocs or enter their Stronghold." Still, Wheaton would complain to Green, "Would it not be well in future, to keep Dr. Cabaniss at his legitimate business? It would appear that his unauthorized action has delayed and embarrassed your operations." Cabiniss' reasons for his actions should have satisfied even an old warhorse like Wheaton: "I did not want to see any more men killed."

Three companies of Oregon volunteers now joined the hunt. Into their hands fell Black Jim, Dave and three other braves, with their families. Their trail had been easy to follow because one of them was hobbling along with the aid of a crutch, the result of a wound incurred on January 17. According to Colonel Thompson, the man had been wounded by Fairchild. One of the Modocs was treed in a juniper, the others were trapped in some rimrock between Tule Lake and Langell Valley. Only Black Jim showed an interest in resistance, and even that was momentary. In Thompson's words, "The muzzle of a .50-caliber Springfield answered as a magnificent persuader." The Modocs were turned over to the Army, but not until Lieutenant Lindsay had to stop some of the militiamen from lynching them. Bunker, of the *Evening Bulletin,* predicted assuredly that Black Jim and Dave would "swing," shortly, in any case.

As June opened, Captain Jack was still to be netted. By chance, the honor fell to the so-far unlucky 1st Squadron of Capt. David Perry. He and Capt. Joel G. Trimble found nothing on their scout the morning of June 1. But a Warm Springs Indian picked up the trail in the afternoon. It was almost impossible for Jack to hide his tracks now. Sergeant Michael

McCarthy explained, "He was evidently out of provisions, for he had to dig *camas* for food and make frequent halts for that purpose." McCarthy noted that the Warm Springs scouts could read freshly turned ground like a book.

When the trail split, Perry broke his command in two. Surprisingly, each lead looped back across the tableland to Willow Creek. Perry took most of the squadron up the north side of the creek while Trimble beat the opposite bank. They moved upstream in concert until Willow Creek bent to the north in a sharp angle. Something told Perry that he had run Captain Jack down, at last. He stood on a ledge jutting out from the cliff's rim and studied the deep canyon. Suddenly, only a hundred yards away but across the chasm, he saw an Indian dog appear at the top of a ravine and, just as quickly, disappear as a hand and arm snatched the cur back out of sight. Perry's men now lined the canyon rim as it was obvious that the prize would fall to Trimble. The latter, with about twenty men, worked his way up the canyon slowly, beating the brush. They were taking a shortcut across a small promontory when an old soldier, Jim Shay, captured a Modoc, Humpy Joe, Jack's hunchbacked half-brother. He was hiding in a clump of junipers. Humpy threw away his gun and came out when a Warm Springs scout shouted in Chinook, "Come here! We won't hurt you!" (Some say that Warm Springs George and four other scouts actually made the capture.) The soldiers started to rush forward but were signaled back by McKay's Indians, who crawled about like reptiles, looking for moccasin tracks. The troopers restrained themselves and sat down to watch the anticlimactic denouement of the Modoc War.

Humpy asked Trimble's civilian guide, Charley Putnam, who was Jesse Applegate's nephew, if he could speak to Fairchild. Putnam said the latter was across the canyon and Jack would have to surrender "now." Humpy told him that Jack was hiding almost below them in the canyon bottom in some rocks on the edge of the creek. Putnam got the hunchback to test the bonds of Modoc consanguinity by yelling to his half-brother, *"Ha ka-i shishuka ka-i mish kshaggayuapka!* (if you do not fight, they will not hang you!). This was misleading since the Army had not promised Jack anything. But Steamboat Frank later said that he believed it to be the case, too. This was his excuse for becoming one of "Davis' bloodhounds"—he wanted to save Jack's life by talking him into surrendering! Boston Charley said the same thing, but anthropologist Albert Gatschet, normally sympathetic to the Modocs, could not swallow this story of Boshtinaga's. He believed the glib twenty-three-year-old half-Shasta, half-Modoc was ready "to sell himself for a few coins to the enemy, body and soul, and then to commit upon his own chief the blackest kind of treason."

And so the six-month-old Modoc War ended on the morning of June 1, 1873, with a parley with Jack, in hiding, after which he came up the slope and surrendered. He shook hands with Shay and told his captors that his legs had given out. An eyewitness to the surrender was Sergeant McCarthy: "On the promise that we wouldn't shoot, he came, preceded by two squaws and one or two boys and his little girl, about four years old. He held the girl in his arms, as a shield, I guess." Trimble asked him for his rifle and Jack hesitated a moment and asked for his old friend, Fairchild. Told that he was nearby, Jack handed over his trusty old Springfield, a muzzle-loader converted to a breech-loader. He coolly walked up to some Warm Springs and shook hands, but he let Humpy do the talking, in broken English and Chinook. Once Trimble was sure that it was really Captain Jack, he threw his hat in the air and gave a yell of triumph that was picked up by his men and the cheering soldiers across the canyon.

Jack had none of Schonchin John's hangdog sullenness, though he was in shabby and dirty clothing rather than Canby's dress uniform—which had proved to be such bad medicine at Sorass Lake. Still, reporter Bunker said, "Although dressed in old clothes, he looks every inch a chief." The officers let him change from his ragged shirt and old cavalry trousers (cut down to knee breeches) to better clothing in his pack, which also contained Canby's hat cord. He chose a clean pair of pants and a calico shirt. His favorite squaw, Lizzie, put on a new delaine dress over her rags, but his number-two wife had to make do with her tatters. Jack should have appeared crestfallen as he rode to camp, humbly sharing a spotted cayuse with his squaw and closely watched by Warm Springs scouts, as Perry and Trimble packed him off to Davis' new headquarters at the so-called Applegate mansion.

But S. A. Clarke was impressed by the captive's presence. "He still bore himself with dignity and sat there like a Roman hero. . . . He never moved a muscle or bore evidence in his look that he felt humiliated at his defeat. He bowed to Fairchild as he passed him but made no other sign." Trooper McCarthy was less impressed. He thought the thirty-six-year-old Modoc looked too young to be the leader of sixty-odd Indians who had held off an army. In the Irishman's opinion, he was only "a passable-looking buck." But Clarke watched him more closely and reported, "He showed no timid fear or trepidation and his conduct commanded the admiration of those who were his captors, for a certain sort of native dignity was apparent and, even in defeat and at the moment of surrender, the great Modoc chief was self-possessed and acted a manly part." Correspondent Bunker was amazed at Jack's self-control. The chief never said a word. Even when curious spectators peered into his face he did not heed them. "He is as still as a statue."

At the Applegate ranch, a pleasant mid-afternoon siesta was broken by cavalrymen galloping and a sergeant shouting, "Captain Jack is captured!" Davis, Wheaton and other officers joined the gawking enlisted men. Bunker thought Schonchin John was a dead ringer for the character from Victor Hugo's pen who climbed through walls by main strength (Jean Valjean), but added that John had the villain depicted in every line of his face. He thought Boston Charley looked half-witted, with his face vacant of any expression. But Captain Jack impressed Bunker as he had Clarke. The reporter did not believe the romantic bosh already welling up around the mythical Captain Jack, such as that he was the son of Capt. Jack Chambers of Kentucky and a Modoc princess (as the Frankfort *Yeoman* had it). No, wrote Bunker, "He is a thorough Indian. . . .His countenance is not an agreeable one to gaze upon. . . . A striking man, place him among a thousand Indians and he would be thought the chief by any observing stranger. Those who have seen him marvel not that he is the leader of the Modocs. Though in chains and on the brink of eternity, he is yet feared and respected by the Indians about him. . . ."

Bunker's reference to a chieftain in chains was not figurative speech. Jack first showed fright when an unfeeling Davis marched him and Schonchin John to the smithy under a six-man guard. Jack apparently mistook the detail for a firing squad. To explain that Jack was going to be shackled to prevent escape, Fairchild drafted Scarfaced Charley as an interpreter, since the chief refused to have anything to do with his old interpreter, the treacherous Bogus Charley. His protests that he had surrendered in good faith fell on deaf ears and his humiliation at being ironed was lost on the unrelenting Davis. Jack absolutely refused to talk while fettered, but he made no resistance. To Clarke, he appeared resigned to death. He seemed to have less regard for life than his warriors, and the reporter predicted a hero's death for him. He was a stoic among stoics. Alex McKay interviewed Boston Charley, since his chief would not speak. He asked him if Jack was worried about his fate. "No," was the reply. "Captain Jack does not care for anything; he will not speak to any person save his sister, Mary. Captain Jack is a brave man. Women care for death; warriors never."

Boston Charley was ironed to One-Eyed Mose, and Sam was manacled all by himself, but the other Modocs were not fettered, although kept under close guard. Finally, through Mary's intervention, Bunker was able to interview Jack in his Peninsula prison tent. The chief complained of the irons. He resented being hobbled like a horse. Wrote Bunker: "As he spoke, his eyes fairly snapped and he looked a very lion in rage." Scarfaced Charley interpreted as Jack explained his actions as being revenge for Ben Wright's massacre of his people twenty years before. Bunker, like Davis, thought the irons were necessary, for Scarfaced Charley told him Jack had planned to escape, till hobbled. Davis also told him that one of the other Modocs had almost filed through one of the rivets of his shackles during the night of June 3 in an unsuccessful escape attempt. And on the march to Fort Klamath later, the weakened rivets of Captain Jack's irons had to be replaced. Davis just would not believe Schonchin John, who protested the irons, saying that none of them intended to escape even if opportunity should offer itself. In Bunker's words, "He obtained little satisfaction and retired in disgust."

The usual Sunday services of the piously Methodist Warm Springs were postponed for an atavistic, howling war dance around a bonfire till midnight, as Davis had the great pleasure of writing his superiors (June 1), "I am happy to announce termination of the Modoc difficulties." But Brig. Gen. John E. Ross of the Oregon Volunteers would not let this go unchallenged. On the fourth he wrote Gov. Lafayette Grover, "The Modoc War is ended by Oregon Volunteers," since his men had rounded up what they took to be the last five warriors and some women and children after Jack's capture. Actually, a handful of Modocs were still at large, and the last man was not made a prisoner until July.

Davis moved his headquarters again, this time to Camp Tule Lake Peninsula, usually called Boyle's Camp. There a crowd of soldiers and civilians lined the so-called Barricade, a rock wall built across the narrow neck of land to protect the camp from possible Modoc attack. Lt. Edward S. Chapin led the caravan into the camp. As the Warm Springs howled their victory war whoops, the craning crowd cried, "Where is Captain Jack?" But the stolid chieftain disappointed them, remaining concealed in a wagon, wrapped in a blanket. Sergeant McCarthy, however, described Jack's followers: "After they came in, they were treated with great kindness by the soldiers, and such a jolly, good-natured lot of fellows, all young but Scarfaced Charley, (he was thirty-five or older) it was hard to find. They were all dressed like white men, hair clipped fairly short, and dressed mostly like herders or buckaroos, or cowboys. Scarface wore a suit of soldier's clothes and was the quietest of the lot. His record was free from any of the murders or from any cruelty."

Although his men, rather surprisingly, treated the captives well, Davis was planning to inflict summary punishment on the Modoc ringleaders for their crimes. General Sherman wanted no quarter shown them, and Davis was happy to oblige. The General of the Army had gone on record as favoring court-martialing and shooting the leaders. He wanted the others to be either turned over to Oregon civil authorities for trial or dispersed—"so that the name 'Modoc' should cease." He suggested that those who escaped the noose should be deported to the land of an alien people, like the Winnebagoes of Lake Superior, where they might be easily guarded. "Thus the tribe of Modocs would disappear, and the example would be salutary."

To identify the bloodiest of the band, Davis brought to camp Mrs. Boddy and her daughter, Mrs. Schira, although they had been unable to identify Black Jim for the Oregonians. On June 6, the suspects were paraded before them. Already, Hooker Jim had admitted robbing the ladies' home, though he accused Black Jim of taking "the long purse," containing eight hundred dollars, while he had contented himself with "the short purse." According to Colonel Thompson, New York *Herald* reporter Fox, bunking with Sutler McManus, came hurrying to Davis to warn him that the two women were going to kill themselves some Modocs. Davis rushed from his tent just in time to see a sobbing Mrs. Boddy draw a pistol from concealment and aim it at Steamboat Frank. At the same time, Mrs. Schira lunged at Hooker Jim with a knife. Neither Indian made a move to save himself from the amateurish assassins. Each stood as stiff as a piece of statuary. But Mrs. Boddy did not even know how to properly cock her pistol, and Davis was easily able to disarm her. However, he received a cut in one palm when he took the knife away from Mrs. Schira. The surgeon dressed the wound and Davis joined his officers for dinner in Boyle's mess. There, one of the younger officers criticized the women's actions as a lack of respect for the general. Davis rose and blistered him with a lecture on the bloody ranch massacres.

CHAPTER THIRTEEN

"UNWORTHY TERMINATION OF A WAR"

Jeff C. Davis received word on June 5, 1873, to hold his prisoners until further orders should arrive. This effectively frustrated his plans for quick vengeance. He obeyed, of course, but he growled a protest to General Schofield in San Francisco: "I have no doubt of the propriety and the necessity of executing them on the spot, at once. I had no doubt of my authority as Department commander in the field to thus execute a band of outlaws, robbers and murderers like these, under the circumstances. Your dispatch indicates a long delay of the cases of the red devils, which I regret. Delay will destroy the moral effect which their prompt execution would have had upon other tribes, as also the inspiring effects upon the troops." Later, talking out of the other side of his mouth, Davis would explain how pleased he had been by the order to spare the Modocs: "I was glad to be relieved from this grave responsibility."

United States Attorney General George H. Williams pondered the case of the Modoc Indians and decided they should stand trial before a military commission for crimes committed against the laws of war, just as had Missouri jayhawkers and bushwhackers during the Civil War and Confederate Henry Wirz of Andersonville Prison notoriety. The Army disregarded the demands of Governor Grover that the "Modoc outlaws" be turned over to Oregon courts for trial. The vengeful Davis found himself opposing a surrender of his prisoners to civil courts because the Oregon public had already prejudged the Modocs—guilty, of course—and a trial would be just a farce.

The general feeling in camp at the news of Davis's orders from Washington was one of profound disgust. Many felt the Modocs would now escape justice. Their fear of a revival of public sentiment in favor of the "underdog" Modocs was justified. As early as March, a New Yorker had written President Grant to urge that the Army be turned on the greedy and covetous Oregonians rather than the Modocs who were defending their worthless Lava Beds. Now, a letter from a Tom Haines of Boston, addressed simply, "Capt. Jack, Lava Beds, Cal.," was promptly delivered to Davis' headquarters. The Bostonian offered his heartfelt sympathy for Jack's cause, wished him and his band success, and offered his "brother" any assistance he could give. Newspaper correspondent Clarke took one look at the letter, shook his head and muttered, "The fools are not all dead, yet."

Hatred was more commonly felt toward the Modocs than sympathy as an immediate aftermath of the war, especially in Oregon. This was made brutally clear when four warriors surrendered with their wives and children at the ranch of John Fairchild. None of them had played much of a role in the fighting so Fairchild sent them to the Army's Peninsula camp in an unescorted wagon driven by his brother, James. At Lost River Ford, Oregon militia let him pass a check-point but, just seven miles beyond, at Adams Point on the north shore of Tule Lake not far from the bloodied ranches of Hooker Jim's raid, two men rode up. Their identity is unknown to this day. If Fairchild recognized them, he kept mum—to save his neck. He claimed that they were strangers, and it is likely that they were vengeful Oregon militiamen. They did not wear uniforms but few if any of the volunteers were not in mufti. The strangers reined up in front of Fairchild's team and ordered him down from the seat at gunpoint. While one man covered him, the other cut the traces and slapped and whooped the mules into a run. Then, methodically, they fired at point-blank range into the stolid Indians packed into the wagon. It was cold-blooded murder. Tee-hee Jack, Pony, Mooch and Little John were killed outright; the latter's wife was wounded, perhaps accidentally. A noncom and a squad of artillerymen, attracted by the shots, rode up as the blood of the dead Indians was still seeping through the cracks of the wagonbed and puddling in the alkali dust of the road. They guarded the survivors against any further attack but made no effort to pursue the fleeing murderers. Nor did Captain Hyzer of the Oregon volunteers or the commanding general, Jeff Davis, attempt to apprehend or punish the guilty parties. Superintendent Odeneal went through the motions of ordering Dyar to investigate the atrocity but the sub-agent made half-hearted excuses, knowing that local public opinion would not tolerate an investigation. President Grant received a flurry of angry letters denouncing the butchery of the unarmed and peaceful Modocs by the Oregon "border ruffians", but nothing was done to bring the murderers to justice.

Captain Jackson went ahead to Fort Klamath to build a strong 150-foot-long and fifty-foot-wide stockade to hold the 155 prisoners—forty-four braves, forty-nine squaws and sixty-two children. Then Davis and his command followed, with the captives. Black Jim and Curly Headed Doctor tried to escape while en route to Fort Klamath but were easily apprehended because of their crippling leg irons. After this escape attempt, stronger measures were taken for security. The chain binding Black Jim and the doctor together was staked into the ground at night. Even peaceable Whim or Weium, William Faithful, was ironed. But Davis was cheated of his revenge on one of the so-called outlaws by the "escape" of Curly Headed Jack, one of the murderers of Lieutenant Sherwood. Curly Headed Jack got away—all the way to the Happy Hunting Ground, in fact—during a Sunday layover at the Natural Bridge on Lost River. Depressed at the thought of being hanged, imprisoned or even exiled from his Modoc homeland, the Indian retrieved the pistol a squaw had hidden for him in her petticoats, and blew his brains out. Soldiers came on the run, carbines at the ready, as the loud report blasted the peace and quiet of a sabbath rest. But the word quickly spread that it was only a Modoc becoming "a good Injun," as the men callously put it.

Davis let Curly Headed Jack's womenfolk mourn him properly (while an ill-mannered Captain Jack and his Lost Rivers chatted and ignored the sad ceremony), and the officer of the day attended his burial on the right bank of the river below Natural Bridge. Hooker Jim, who owed the dead man two dollars, scurried around among the soldiers, changing some paper money into silver. He threw the coins into the grave before Army shovels began to fill it.

Reporter Bunker watched the Indians as they bade farewell to the Land of Burnt-Out Fires, forever. "As we neared a hilly point that must shut from view the distant Lava Beds, they stood erect and talked rapidly among themselves and then took one long lingering look at the lava fastness and watched until nothing of the awful retreat could be seen. . . ."

The seven large freight wagons, loaded with Modocs, deserters and stores, passed Council Grove and a particularly ironic monument to dashed hopes on the Klamath Reservation. This was the rough-hewn log foundation for a cabin that was to have become Captain Jack's home. Escort and prisoners arrived at the fort on June 14, by which time the last straggling holdouts were being turned over to the Army by Pit Rivers, with whom they had tried to find sanctuary. Only one warrior remained long at liberty, none other than Long Jim, the stone corral escapee. He was finally captured at Yainax on July 10 by an Indian, Charley Riddle, and brought to Fort Klamath by the chief, Old Schonchin.

Bunker was impressed by Fort Klamath after the bleakness of the lunar Lava Beds. "Klamath is justly reputed one of the prettiest and most attractive military stations on the Pacific slope, and certainly is a grand place for the closing scenes in the Modoc drama," he enthused. In describing the green meadows, lofty pines, snow-covered mountains and whitened barracks, he saw it as Constable might have: "A landscape beautiful to behold, harmonious in its various phases and impressive in its character." He was surprised to find *objets d'art* and other "relics of gentility" on the Oregon frontier—even in the B. O. Q. (bachelor officers' quarters). Bunker's mood changed with the weather, however. When clouds closed in on the post and the heavens opened to sluice the parade ground into a fair replica of a rice paddy, a shivering Bunker found Fort Klamath to be about as dismal a place as he had ever seen, and he was hard put to understand the cheerfulness of its contented garrison.

On June 15, Lt. Robert Pollock asked authority to issue fifteen pounds of candles per month to the vigilant stockade guards, figuring that they would need three tapers a night for the safekeeping of the Modocs. That very day, Hasbrouck succeeded him in command of the fort. He continued the lieutenant's religious filing of weekly reports on the attitude of the reservation Indians. Davis, meanwhile, chose his military commission. It was composed of Lt. Col. Washington L. Elliott, who as senior officer was its president; Captains Henry Hasbrouck and John Mendenhall; and Lieutenants Robert Pollock and George W. Kingsbury. Maj. H. P. Curtis, Judge Advocate of the Department of California, became Judge Advocate of the commission. Davis announced that the proceedings would follow those of a court martial except that those on trial were not soldiers and would not be represented by counsel. Moreover, the War Department had directed him to try only those directly involved in the killing of Canby, Thomas and Sherwood. The murderers of the hapless ranchers were not to be tried.

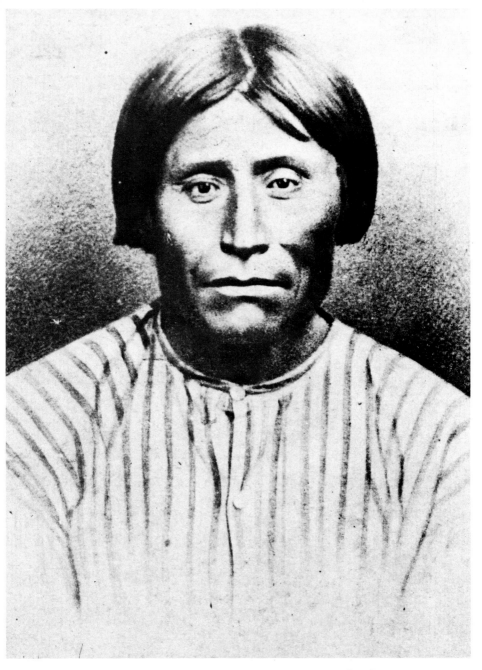

Captain Jack, also called Kientpoos or Kintpuash, the tragic leader of the so-called renegade Modocs, ironically was a man of peace driven not only to war but to murder and then betrayed by the war hawks of his tribe.

The photographer labeled this Modoc War photograph "Lost River Murderers," probably because the Modoc on the right, the shaman Curly Headed Doctor, was a bloody lieutenant in Hooker Jim's massacre of helpless ranchers. But Curly Haired Jack (left) was the ambusher of Lieutenant Sherwood and the only Modoc suicide in the war. Weium or Whim, center, was a peaceable Modoc who warned the whites of Captain Jack's plan to assassinate General Canby.

Captain's Jack's family—his wife Lizzie, his sister Mary (Queen Mary), and his old wife, name not recorded, with his daughter —shortly after the surrender of the Modocs in the summer of 1873.

These Indian scouts, hired by the U.S. Army from the Warm Springs Reservation in Oregon, north of the Modoc and Klamath country, proved themselves as valuable allies of the regulars as the Klamath scouts had proved themselves worthless earlier in the Modoc War.

Oregon photographer Louis Heller grouped three typical Modoc warriors, Shacknasty Jim, Hooker Jim and Steamboat Frank, with their sometime-friend, sometime-enemy, John A. Fairchild. Fairchild was the California rancher who worked so hard to avoid war, and is today one of the unsung heroes of the Modoc War.

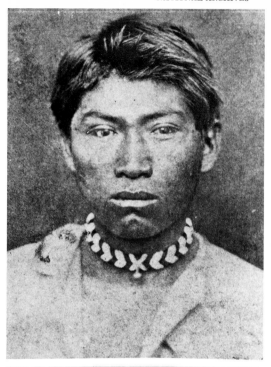

This youthful warrior, not blustering John Schonchin or scowling Curly Headed Doctor, was the bloodiest murderer of Captain Jack's band, a Modoc who seemed to kill for the pleasure of it. In his trial, Captain Jack said, "Hooker Jim is the one who always wanted to fight, and commenced killing and murdering." Jack was hanged and Hooker was spared, because he had turned traitor and hunted down his chief for the Army.

Capt. Reuben F. Bernard's biographer credited him with 103 fights and scrimmages in the Civil War and Indian wars. But the Apache-chasing cavalryman, who worked his way up through the ranks from farrier and blacksmith, won few laurels in the Modoc War. Captain Jack and, especially, Scarfaced Charley fought rings around the veteran officer.

Captain Jack was a skilled strategist—even in ambuscades. At the same time that he attacked General Canby and the Peace Commission on the west side of the Lava Beds, he had another attack made on the east side, in which Lt. William L. Sherwood (left) was trapped and shot to death.

The Crazy Horse, Geronimo, Sitting Bull of the Lava Beds, was not Captain Jack, as is often supposed, but his chief warrior and tactician, the little-known but brilliant Scarfaced Charley. Charley never lost a battle to the Army, and his defeat of Capt. Evan Thomas at Black Ledge, near Hardin Butte, may be the classic Indian victory of our history.

One of the would-be peacemakers of Yreka was Judge A. M. Rosborough, friend of Squire Elijah Steele, who tried to stop the Modoc War before it started. Captain Jack said at his trial, "Rosborough never gave me any advice but good advice. He always told me to be a good man."

Even when all the romantic nonsense about a "Pocahontas of the Lava Beds" is stripped away from folk-history, Frank Riddle's Modoc wife, Toby (alias Wi-ne-ma), remains a bona fide heroine of the Modoc War.

Donald McKay, the hard-drinking Scots-Cayuse chief of scouts for the Army (center) during the Modoc War, poses for a photographer with some of his Warm Springs and Wasco scouts on the edge of the Modoc Lava Beds.

One of the most bellicose of Captain Jack's warriors was John Schonchin, brother of the legitimate chief of the Modocs, Old Schonchin. (Captain Jack was a sub-chief who became a *de facto* war chief in the Lava Beds.) Something of a blusterer, John Schonchin talked tough in victory but was rather craven in defeat, at his trial and execution.

Captain Jack's fondness for sod-
buster's and cowboy's clothing
was not acceptable to eastern and
midwestern editors. When an
Illinois mugbook pictured Jack,
he was much more buckskinned
than the chief of reality.

The stars of A. B. Meacham's post-Modoc War lecture troupe on
tour of the U.S.A.—Steamboat Frank, Shacknasty Jim, Toby Riddle
and Scarfaced Charley, standing, and Frank Riddle and his son,
Jeff (Charka), seated.

The American public split into factions again. Many people, seeking an eye for an eye, were angered at the military trying a handful of the "culprits" and feared an absolution, a whitewash. Oregon would hang them neatly enough, was their feeling. They were furious (and were joined in this sentiment by many less vengeful people) when word got around that the very worst killers would be spared—"Davis' bloodhounds." The latter were being well repaid for their services in shortening the war, though they had been promised nothing. On the other hand, humanitarians began to speak in favor of the Modocs again, as the horror of Canby's murder began to fade with the passage of time. As before, Californians were more likely to favor clemency; Oregonians demanded a stern reckoning.

California Congressman J. K. Luttrell went to the Lava Beds with Elijah Steele on June 11 when the Army asked the latter to question Captain Jack about valuables stolen during the massacres. The legislator blamed the war on the wrongful acts of bad whites, speculators who desired Lost River land and wished the Modocs removed. He was on the right trail. Only a month and a week later, the Portland *Oregonian* noted how the Link River country was settling up since the conclusion of hostilities. The paper reported the area to be a hard one to beat for stock raising. Luttrell demanded an investigation of the conflict, saying, "We have lost so many valuable officers and men in this contest; justice demands that, if any particular individual or individuals are guilty of inciting the Modocs to war, that he or they should be punished." Still, he demanded the hanging of the actual Modoc murderers.

H. Wallace Atwell, the slovenly, long-haired reporter who called himself Bill Dadd the Scribe, and who was never seen without a pipe clenched between his teeth, now took a part in the controversy. In the shock of Canby's assassination he had come out for the extermination of the Modocs. Now his reason returned, and the writer who had covered the campaign for the San Francisco *Chronicle*, New York *Herald*, Chicago *Inter-Ocean* and Sacramento *Record* called for genuine justice and objected to what he saw as a drumhead court-martial.

Quickly the California-Oregon frontier began to return to normalcy. As settlers squatted on Modoc lands, the Warm Springs scouts were being paid off. Although they received only thirteen dollars a month, plus twelve dollars for the use of their horses, it was quite a windfall for The Dalles. The Portland

Bulletin reported that they had shouted war cries as they rode through the streets. Doubtless the merchants had shouted little cries of joy themselves when the scouts finally adjourned to an old woolen mill for a war dance after leaving most of their money on the bars and counters of The Dalles.

The captive Modocs found their stockade, built by Lieutenant Cresson, to be a strong one. It was formed of twelve-foot high pine logs sunk three or four feet into the ground. It was broken into two sections, each with its own door, so that the Lost Rivers would not be at the Hot Creeks' throats, or vice versa. Army tents were erected for the noblest Romans of them all, the turncoat "spies" and their families. They were given the run of the fort as well as new clothing, but were required to retire for the night in the tents. Twenty-four soldiers guarded the prison compound, standing post in front of each door and manning platforms raised at the corners of the stockade. In its crowding, the pen somewhat resembled the later concentration camps of Valeriano Weyler's Cuba or Hitler's Germany. But the captives were not ill-treated in any way. They were fed well and clothed and, if not actually comfortable—for they chafed at confinement, of course—they made no trouble for the guards. In fact, they even helped civilian employees chop firewood for the oncoming winter. Doubtless, many visitors to the stockade came away with the same thoughts as Lt. Stephen Jocelyn: "They are a sorry, pitiful-looking set to have given so much trouble."

Most of the Modocs no longer feared for their own lives, but they were convinced that Captain Jack would hang. Many of them believed that his death would atone for the sins of all of them and would also become the signal for their freedom. The more sophisticated and skeptical souls among them, like Bogus and Steamboat, knew better. The latter, overhearing snatches of soldiers' conversations about the probability of their being banished to either Alcatraz or Angel Island in San Francisco Bay, set his squaw to work making beaded moccasins which he hoped to try on the San Francisco curio market.

The sturdy guardhouse at Fort Klamath held Captain Jack and Schonchin John in one whitewashed cell, Ike and Buckskin Doctor (Curly Headed Doctor) in another, and Black Jim, Dave, Boston, Mose, Pete and Curly Headed Doctor's son all jammed into a third cell. All were securely shackled. The cell windows were high up near the ceiling and covered with gratings. The neat white building with its porch was "comely" in Bunker's view and resembled a small family home (on the outside), but it was virtually escape proof.

Although the cells were clean, light, and well ventilated, the prisoners could hear little and see nothing of the outside world, and it began to tell on them. The natural result of imprisonment of as free a people as the Modocs was a state of depression. Bunker accompanied an officer one day who was searching the captives for contraband. He noted how disgusted Jack was. He had thought he was to be given an airing. "The prisoners look bad," wrote Bunker. "They huddle together and make no noise. . . .Every captive wore a dejected air and some looked as if death, in any form, would be welcomed as a measure of relief. . . .Jack grows thin and so do others of the band, and the Curly Headed Doctor is a very sick man. . . .Indians rapidly wear away when cooped up in a building. . . .Three months in the guardhouse will probably serve to 'turn up' Jack and render a funeral necessary." James Fry's estimate of the prisoners' condition was the same. He found them "a sickening sight. . . manacled, haggard and folorn." But New York *Times* reporter Samuel A. Clarke did not find Jack so crushed by his plight. He wrote, "I have seen the favorite wife of Captain Jack during the days of his captivity when he wore chains, sit by his side all day long and embroider a moccasin skillfully as she strove to beguile the tedium of his captivity. It was his only wish that Lizzie might sit beside him and it must be concluded that there was a warm attachment. While the favorite was thus winsome and beguiling, the old wife—the wife who shared his joys with him when Captain Jack was young—took care of the favorite and was a drudge."

Six men were labeled ringleaders by the Army and arraigned for trial. They were Captain Jack, John Schonchin, Black Jim, Boston Charley, Barncho (alias Watch-in-tate or One-Eyed Jim) and Slolux (alias Cok or Cox). There were only two charges—the murder of Canby and Thomas and the attempted murder of Meacham and Dyar. No one was ever tried for Sherwood's murder. The trial, which began on July 1, 1873, and ended July 9, was well documented, thanks to the shorthand skills of a professional court reporter, E. S. Belden, seated at the end of the narrow commissioners' table opposite the Modoc bench.

Usually Barncho and Slolux flopped on the floor, bored with the proceedings although they were translated into the Modoc idiom by Frank and Toby Riddle, the official, ten-dollars-a-day interpreters. Reporters occupied a side table and soldiers stood guard at both ends of the room with Springfields topped by polished angular bayonets. Near the door, unguarded, slouched Davis' pets, Hooker, Bogus, Schacknasty and Steamboat.

The proceedings were formal. The Modocs were asked if they objected to any member of the commission and were then asked if they intended to introduce counsel. No, they said, they were not going to have a defense attorney because they had been unable to obtain a lawyer. (The Army would not provide them with one.) In his memoirs, A. B. Meacham claimed that he offered himself as their counsel so that it would not be an ex parte trial. And Commission President Elliott had said, "It would be an act of magnanimity on your part that is without precedent." But, according to Meacham's story, when he consulted an Army doctor about his defending the men who had tried to murder him, the surgeon told him that the effort would probably kill him. Reluctantly, he said, he gave up the idea. (Belden made no mention of any of this.) All of the Modocs pleaded not guilty to the charges—murder and attempted murder in violation of the laws of war—and to the specifications.

Frank Riddle was the first witness called, so briefly he was translating his own remarks from English into Modoc, with the help of his wife. The interpreter identified all of the Modocs as having been at the Peace Tent but said that he had not known Barncho and Slolux at the time. Under questioning by the Judge Advocate, he stated that he thought Captain Jack had been a chief since 1861, that John Schonchin was a commoner until 1872 and then became a sub-chief, a *sajint* or sergeant. He said Black Jim was a watchman and Boston a "high private." Asked about Barncho and Slolux, Riddle answered in each case, "He is not anything." Riddle added some details to the story of the Peace Tent murder plot. Hooker Jim had taken him aside to warn him, "If you ever come with them peace commissioners to meet us any more and I come to you and push you to one side, you stand back, one side, and we won't hurt you, but will murder them." Then, said Riddle, he had told the peace commissioners of this warning and had advised them, "I think the best way, if you want to make peace with them, is to give them a good licking and then make peace." At a March meeting, he testified, Hooker had actually taken hold of him and shoved him, saying, "You come out here and sit down." But Riddle had refused and kept his place.

Frank also testified that when he took a note to Jack from the Peace Commission and translated it for him, the chief threw it on the ground and said that he was not a white man; he could not read. He had no use for it. But he had agreed to meet the commissioners—but a mile beyond the council tent. The Judge Advocate interrupted to ask, "What did he say about the propostion to move him from the Lava Beds?" Riddle answered, "He said he knew no other country, only this, and he did not want to leave it. . . . He said if they would move the soldiers all away, he would make peace then, and live right there where he was, and would not pester anybody." But Riddle had seen them preparing for war—butchering beeves and forting up lava gullies—so he had told the Peace Commission that it was useless to try to make peace. "If I was in your places, I would not meet them anymore," was his advice. It was at this time that he had advised Canby to secrete twenty-five or thirty soldiers in the rocks near the tent as a precautionary measure. Canby had refused, of course, fearing the Modocs would see them and be insulted. Such an affront might even provoke the Modocs into harming the commissioners, he had felt.

Step by step, under Curtis' prodding, Riddle reviewed the events leading to the assassinations. Toby had cried, "Meacham, don't you go! They might kill you today! They may kill all of you today!" and the interpreter reiterated his reply to Reverend Thomas' banal "Put your trust in God." "You might trust in God, but I don't trust any in them Indians!" Riddle then repeated, as best he could remember, the words of his last warning to Gillem. (The latter had answered, with a laugh, that if the Indians started anything, he would take care of them.) "General Gillem, these men are going out to hold council with them Indians today and I don't believe it is safe. If there is anything happens to them I don't want no blame laid on me hereafter because I don't think it is safe for them to go and after it is over I don't want nothing laid on me. I am not much afraid of the Indians but I will go before I will be called a coward."

Curtis then asked, "What did he mean by giving up Lost

River?" Riddle replied, "He said there was where the fight had taken place, and that he didn't want to have anything more to do there. He said he thought that was what the [November 29] fight took place about—that country there, he said the whites wanted it."

Riddle continued his description of the bloody Peace Tent affair. Meacham had tapped Captain Jack on the shoulder and in a fatherly tone had said, "Jack, let us talk like men and not like children. You are a man who has common sense. Is there any other place that will do you except Willow Creek or Cottonwood?" Meacham was talking so loudly that Schonchin John told him to shush up. He wanted to talk. He said that he would talk a "straight talk." But Jack, saying that he had to answer a call of nature (though he put it more crudely), walked away. Behind Dyar's horse he pulled a pistol from his shirt and then shouted, "*A-tuck!* (all ready, boys!)." The interpreter finished: "Before you could crack your finger, he fired. . . .I saw General Canby fall over and I expected he was killed, and I jumped and ran with all my might. I never looked back but once. . . .They commenced firing all around. I did not turn back to see who it was. I thought it was warm times there. . . .There were three Indians running after me. . . .I could see the dust flying ahead of me from the bullets. . . .One ball came by my ear and grazed it a little. . . ."

There were no questions in cross-examination from the defendants so Riddle was excused and Toby and Dyar were called. They offered little new information. Schacknasty Jim was the next witness to be sworn. He was followed by Steamboat, Bogus and Hooker as Fort Klamath offered the rare spectacle of Indians turning state's evidence. The first two admitted their presence at the Peace Tent—but as bystanders, of course, not plotters. Hooker did not bother to deny that he had been there to kill a commissioner for Captain Jack. The Judge Advocate asked him, "Are you a friend of Captain Jack?" The innocent replied, "I have been a friend of Captain Jack, but I don't know what he got mad at me for. I had a quarrel and a little fight with him over to Dry Lake." Asked "Do you like Jack now, or dislike him?" Hooker replied firmly, "I don't like him very well now."

Weium or Whim was called but speedily dismissed, not even having been at the Peace Tent. Meacham next took the stand. His right hand was useless, its nerves being paralyzed by a ball through the wrist. His left forefinger was still twice its normal

size, and a scar on his forehead and a visible lump on the right
side of his head were further evidence of the foul play at the
council tent. His ear and side wounds had healed. He had
arrived in time to visit Jack in the guardhouse where he refused
the chief's hand, saying, "No, Captain Jack, your hands are red
with Canby's blood. I cannot, now." When he urged Jack to tell
his side of the story, the chief said, "I cannot talk with the
chains on my legs. My heart is not strong when the chain is on
my leg. You can talk strong. You can talk for me." Meacham's
answer was, "No, Captain Jack. I cannot talk for you. I saw you
kill General Canby." Even John Schonchin, after pinching his
arm to see if he was really alive, tried to get Meacham to help
him. When he refused, the Modoc blustered, "I did not kill you.
You did not die. I am old man. I was excited. I did not shoot
good. The others all laugh at me. I quit. You shoot me. You
don't want me to die. You did not die."

On the witness stand, Meacham had little to add to the
already well-known story. He made one point, however: Canby
was less naive than many critics thought. Just before his last
walk on earth, to the Peace Tent, he had said to Meacham, "I
think there is no danger, although I have no more confidence in
these Indians than you have. I think them capable of it, but
they dare not do it; it is not to their interest." And when
Hooker brazenly took his coat, Meacham had looked hard at
the general. He recalled, "I sought to get a glance at Canby's
face and I am very confident, although no words passed, that
General Canby understood the act and knew what it meant. . . .
I asked General Canby if he had any remarks to make, partly
for the opportunity to look him in the face and partly to see
whether he could say something to avert the peril." It was
Canby's sense of honor, more than his naiveté, which doomed
him. Meacham reminded the commission that he had suggested
they lie, if necessary, to save their skins. Dr. Thomas had
answered, "I will be a party to no deception under any
circumstances; this matter is in the hands of God." Canby had
agreed. "I have dealt with Indians for thirty years. I have never
deceived an Indian and I will not consent to it—to any promise
that cannot be fulfilled."

Meacham was followed as a witness by Canby's aide-de-camp
and by Dr. McElderry. Then the first witness was called for the
defense. It was Scarfaced Charley. He brought his listeners up in
their chairs as he answered a question put to him by Captain
Jack, acting more or less as his own counsel. "Tell about Link

River Jack coming and giving us powder and stuff." Scarfaced
Charley's rambling testimony did no good in exculpating Jack
for the murders, but it certainly helped explain Wheaton's
debacle of January and the disgust of soldiers and volunteers
with his Klamath auxiliaries. "The first time was down there at
Ellen's, at the east end of the Lava Beds. We were attacked
there by the soldiers and there were some Klamath Lake Indians
along with the soldiers there, and they told us not to shoot at
them but to shoot at the soldiers, the Klamaths did. . . .

"The Klamath Lake Indians told me that they did not expect
to be friends of the soldiers all of the time, that they would be
our friends after a while. After that, they came with the soldiers
to our Stronghold in the Lava Beds and fought us. . . .In the
fight there were ten of them came to us and they gave us most
of the ammunition we had. We took some of it and some of it
was given to us. The Modocs got it from the Klamath Lakes.
One in particular, One-Eye or Link River Jack, gave us
ammunition and guns. They got back one gun from us. They
came to talk to us, and Scarfaced Charley got eighty [percus-
sion] caps from one Klamath Lake Indian. They bought them
of the Klamaths. The Klamath Lakes said to us, 'Don't shoot us.
Shoot the soldiers and let us alone; we are your friends.' The
Klamath Lakes told me that Allen David told them when they
went to shoot up in the air. They said, 'I don't want to shoot
any of you. I listened to what Allen David told me. I held up
my gun and I didn't want to shoot any of you.' That is what the
Klamath Lakes said.

"One-Eye Link River Jack gave [Captain] Jack twenty caps.
One-Eye Link River John then gave his powder horn full of
powder to Indian George, a Modoc. He poured it all out and
gave it all to him that was in the horn. My tribe took one gun
and one pistol away from them and the reason of it was they
had stolen our horses and taken them away, the Klamath Lakes
had.

"I never knew of Allen David telling the Indians to murder
Canby. I came up on the eleventh of April after the commissioners were killed. I was speaking of the powder and caps. Our
tribe caught Little John and took him to our camp. Little John
talked a long time to us and told us not to fight them; that they
would never fight the Modocs. The day before the fight of
January 17, Little John told me to fight hard the next day and
whip the soldiers and kill all we could, that Allen David had
told him to tell us so, and to shoot up in the air and [for us]
not to shoot at them. . . ."

Apparently Scarfaced Charley had feared being played for a fool, à la Wheaton, by the double-dealing Klamaths, for he had said to Little John: "Don't you lie to us. You are the first ones who have tried to raise a fight and now you come and tell us you are our friends, [and] to come and fight the soldiers. Little John said, 'I don't lie. Allen Dave sent me here with the message. . . .' "

Referring to the accusations that Steele, Rosborough and Fairchild had urged the Modocs to go to war, Charley added, "No white man ever told us to fight. Little Link River John told me the Indians on the Yainax Reservation were mad at us and wanted to kill us, but Schonchis never advised us to fight— Schonchis of the Yainax Reservation, I mean. Not this one [indicating John Schonchin]; he would not talk with us. Link River John told us that the Indians of Yainax were all afraid but that the Klamaths were not afraid, and advised us to fight. . . . The way we got most of our ammunition was after the fight of January 17 last. We went round and picked up the cartridges and the Klamath Lakes gave us some and we opened the cartridges and got out the powder [for their old muzzle-loaders] and then made bullets out of the lead in them. We had plenty of caps.

"In the fight of the seventeenth the Klamaths laid down and after the soldiers moved on, then I came to them and asked them who was their chief and they told me that Link River John was. There is where they gave us the ammunition and stuff. They said they came there to lay down behind the rocks to see us so that they could get a chance to give us ammunition and powder. After the soldiers quit fighting, we were then going home to our Stronghold, all going along together, and we saw three Indians lying down behind the rocks. This was after they had given us the powder. The Klamath Lakes told us not to shoot them, that they were our friends, and I drew my pistol out and I told them that they were the cause of the fight, that they had urged it on, and they said no, that they were always our friends. We had a long talk. I told them then to leave all the ammunition that they had and could get, to pile it under a rock where they were and I would get it. I told them, 'You say you are our friends, and I want to see whether you are or not. To see whether you will leave your cartridges and things here, or not.' I went the next day and found the ammunition there. There was a flour sack, half-full. I got a hundred rounds of ammunition myself that they had left there. I then asked the Klamaths if they were telling the truth and they said they were, that Allen David had told them to tell me that they would not fight us; that when they went there they went to shoot up [in the air] to make the soldiers believe that they were our enemies, but they were our friends.

"That is all I know."

That should have been plenty. But the military commission was interested in just one thing—the guilt in the Peace Tent murders. Scarfaced Charley's damning indictments of the conspiring Klamaths, including Chief of Scouts Link River John and tribal chief Allen David, were ignored by the tribunal. The only question put to Charley by the board was in regard to his whereabouts at the time of the murders. He said he was about a half-mile away at the bend of Tule Lake's shore.

Dave and One-Eyed Mose were called next. They reiterated briefly what Scarfaced Charley had said at length, about the help the Modocs had received before and during the January battle from their "adversaries," the Klamaths.

There was a stir in court as Captain Jack was finally called to testify. "I will talk about Judge Rosborough, first," he began. "He always told me to be a good man. . . .Rosborough never gave me any advice but good advice. . . .I considered myself as a white man; I didn't want to have an Indian heart any longer; I took passes from good white men who gave me good advice. I knew all the people that were living about the country and they all knew I was an honest man. . . .I never accused any white man of being mean and bad; I always thought them my friends and when I went to anyone and asked him for a pass, he would always give it to me; all gave me passes and told those people who had to pass through my country that I was a good Indian, and had never disturbed anybody. No white man can say that I ever objected to their coming to live in my country; I always told them to come and live there, and that I was willing to give them homes there. I would like to see the man that ever knew me to do anything wrong heretofore; I have always dealt upright and honest with every man; nobody ever called me mean—except the Klamath Indians. I never knew any other chief who spoke in favor of the white men as I have done, and I have always taken their part, and spoken in favor of them. I was always advised by good men in Yreka, and about there; to watch over white men when traveling through my country and I have taken their advice and always done it. I would like to see the man who started this fuss, and caused me to be in the trouble I am in now.

"They scared me when they came to where I was living on

Lost River and started this fight. I cannot understand why they were mad with me. . . .I have always lived on what I could kill and shoot with my gun and catch in my trap. Riddle knows that I have always lived like a man and have never gone begging. . . .I should have taken his advice. He has always given me good advice and told me to live like a white man, and I have always tried to do it, and did do it until this war started. I hardly know how to talk here. I don't know how white people talk in such a place as this, but I will do the best I can."

Judge Advocate Curtis encouraged him, "Talk exactly as if you were at home, in a council."

Jack continued: "I didn't know anything about the war—when it was going to commence. Major Jackson came down there and commenced on me while I was in bed, asleep. When Meacham came to talk to me, he always came and talked good to me. He never talked about shooting or anything of that kind. It was my understanding that Ivan Applegate was to come and have a talk with me and not to bring soldiers, but to come alone. I was ready to have a talk with any man that would come to talk peace with me. The way I wanted that council with Applegate to come off was I wanted Henry Miller to be there and hear it. He always talked good to me and gave me good advice. Miller told me he wanted to talk with me and wanted to be there when Applegate met me, and wanted to talk for me, and with me. Dennis Crawley told me he wanted to be there to talk with me when Applegate came. He told me I was a good man and he wanted to see me get my rights.

"It scared me when Major Jackson came and got there just at daylight and made me jump out of my bed without a shirt or anything else on. I didn't know what it meant, his coming at that time of day. When Major Jackson and his men came up to my camp, they surrounded it and I hollered to Bogus Charley to go and talk, until I could get my clothes on. He went and told them that he wanted to talk; that he didn't want them to shoot. Then they all got down off their horses and I thought we were going to have a talk, and I went into another tent. I thought then, 'Why are they mad at me? What had they found out about me that they came here to fight me?' I went into my tent then and sat down, and they commenced shooting. My people were not all there; there were but a few of us. Major Jackson shot my men while they were standing round. I ran off; I did not fight any. I threw my people away that they had shot and wounded. I did not stop to get them. I ran off and did not want to fight.

They shot some of my women and they shot my men. I did not stop to inquire anything about it, but left and went away.

"I went then into the Lava Beds. I had very few people and did not want to fight. I thought I had but few people, and it was not of any use for me to fight, and so I went to the Lava Beds. While I was on my way to the cave, there was a white man came to my camp. I told him the soldiers had pitched onto me and fired into me while I was asleep, but I would not hurt him—for him to go back to town, home. I went into the Lava Beds and stayed there. . . .John Fairchild came to my house and asked me if I wanted to fight, and I said no, I had quit fighting; that I did not want to fight any more—him or anybody. The Hot Creek Indians then started for the reservation and got as far as Bob Whittle's on Klamath River and there the Linkville men scared them and they ran back. They were going to kill them. Then the Hot Creeks came to my camp and told me the whites were going to kill them all. They got scared by what the white men had told them, that they were going to kill them all. . . .

"I didn't know anything of any settlers being killed until Hooker Jim came with his band and told me. I didn't think that they would kill the whites when they went around that way. I did not believe it. I did not want them to stay with me. None of my people had killed any of the whites and I had never told Hooker Jim and his party to murder any settlers. . . .I always advised them *not* to kill white people. I told Hooker that I never had killed any white person. . . .[and asked], 'Why did you kill those people for? I never wanted you to kill my friends. . . .' I knew that the white people would be mad at me just on account of this Hooker Jim killing so many white people when he had no business to do it. . . .Fairchild told me. . .the chances were the soldiers would all come on us again and kill us all, if we did not make peace then. . . .I told Fairchild that I did not want to fight any more, that I was willing to quit if the soldiers would quit.

"Fairchild then never came to my house any more for a long time after the Indians that were stopping with him had run off. He was afraid to come then, any more. It was a long time that I heard nothing from him. Nobody came to my place and I could get no more news. After a great while, Fairchild came again with a squaw and told me I had better make peace, for the white people were all mad at us. . . .When the soldiers came they came fighting and fought all day. . . .Link River John came and told me not to be mad at them [i.e., the Klamaths]. . . .

When Fairchild came in. . .I told him there had been blood spilt on Lost River and that I did not want to live there; that I would hunt some other place and live, and that I was willing to quit fighting if they would let me alone. . . .

"While the peace talk was going on there was a squaw came from Fairchild's and Dorris', and told us that the peace commissioners were going to murder us. That they were trying to get us out to murder us. A man by the name of Nate Beswick told us so. There was an old Indian man came in the night and told us again. . . .This old Indian told me that Nate Beswick told him that, that day; Meacham, General Canby, Dr. Thomas and Dyar were going to murder us if we came at the council. All of my people heard this old man tell us so. And then there was another squaw came from Fairchild's and told me that Meacham and the peace commissioners had a pile of wood ready built up and were going to burn me on this pile of wood, that when they brought the news to Dorris', they were going to burn me there. All of the squaws about Fairchild's and Dorris' told me the same thing. After hearing all this news, I was afraid to go and that is the reason I did not come in to make peace.

"Riddle and his woman always told me the truth and advised me to do good, but I have never taken their advice. If I had listened to them, instead of to the squaws that were lying all of the time, I would not have been in the fix that I am in now. . . .Bob Whittle's wife lied to me. . . .She always gave me bad advice. . . .

"I didn't consider myself, when you came to have a talk with me the chief, then. . . .I didn't know anything about fighting, then, and didn't want to fight. *Your* chief makes his men mind him and listen to him, and they do listen to what he tells them, and they believe him; but my people won't. My men would not listen to me. They wanted to fight. . . .By my being the chief of the Modoc tribe, I think that the white people all think that I raised the fight and kept it going. I have told my people that I thought the white people would think that about me, and I did not want to have anything to do with it; that if they wanted to fight, they would have to go on their own hook.

"Hooker Jim was the one that agitated the fighting, that wanted to fight all the time. I sat over to one side with my few men and did not say anything of fighting. Now I have to bear the blame for him and the rest of them. Schonchis [sic] was with Hooker Jim; he was on Hooker Jim's side. . . .I would talk to them but they would not listen to me. . . .Hooker Jim is the one that always wanted to fight, and commenced killing and murdering. When I would get to talking, they would tell me to hush, that I didn't know anything, that I was nothing more than an old squaw.

"I and Hooker Jim had a fuss. . . .I got my revolver and if I could have seen him through the canvas I would have killed him. I thought that I would kill him, and I wanted to kill him, for he is the one that murdered the settlers on Tule Lake. I [had] thought that the white people were mad because I was living on Lost River and that they wanted the land there. . . .

"I then had a fuss with another Indian. . . .George and I had a quarrel and he told me I was nothing but an old squaw, that I never had killed anybody, that he had killed white people and had killed lots of soldiers—him and Hooker Jim. Hooker Jim said, 'You are like an old squaw, you have never done any fighting yet. We have done the fighting and you are our chief. You are not fit to be a chief. . . .What do you want with a gun? You don't shoot anything with it. You don't go any place to do anything. You are sitting around on the rocks. . . .' I told them that they run around and committed those murders against my will."

Jack admitted that even his friend, Scarfaced Charley, had become disgusted with him at that time. "Scarfaced Charley told me that he would go with Hooker and them; that he could fight with them; that I was nothing but an old squaw. I told them then if that was what they were going to do, why, they could go on their own responsibility; that I did not want to go with them, that I did not want to live with them.

"Scarfaced Charley will tell everything that he knows. He don't want to keep anything back; neither do I want to keep anything back."

Captain Jack tired of talking and asked to be allowed to continue next day. John Schonchin then described himself as a peace-loving duck hunter at the time of Jackson's raid, a man who had wondered why the soldiers came to kill his children. He claimed to have tried to talk both Hooker and Curly Headed Doctor out of the massacre of the settlers.

Next morning, Captain Jack continued his pathetic appeal for justice, as he saw it. "The four scouts have told you they didn't know anything about the murder of General Canby. . . .They all talked to me and were all in with it, because we didn't want to move off to any country that we didn't know anything about. I would like to know why Hooker Jim could not tell who he wanted to kill when he went out there. . . .Meacham was the man he wanted to kill. The four scouts knew all about it. . .they all wanted to kill the peace commissioners; they all advised me to do it. . . .Hooker Jim, he said that he wanted to kill Meacham, and we must do it.

"That is all I have got to say."

The tribunal had nothing to say about the evidence, but Judge Advocate Curtis felt that he had to defend Capt. James Jackson against the Modoc's words. He reminded all present that the captain had operated in compliance with direct orders. The only major speech by Captain Jack ever recorded made little impression on its hearers. Meacham took it as an attempt by a pettifogger to shift blame to others.

After the Modocs were led back to their cells, the commission deliberated briefly in executive session. They found all six Modocs guilty, sentenced them to be hanged by the neck until dead, and adjourned, *sine die*. General Davis approved the proceedings and forwarded them to Washington just as volunteer counsel belatedly arrived for the Modocs in the person of "a Colonel Lewis of Colusa, California," probably Edward Jefferson Lewis of Tehama County. He was greatly disappointed to find that he was too late.

Davis had promised nothing to his scouts or "bloodhounds". But he had implied that the traitorous Modocs were entitled to some consideration for shortening the war. Since Davis was in the field on an "intimidating expedition" en route to Portland, the Judge Advocate decided their fate. He pardoned them without even bringing them before the commission, explaining, "I believe that there could be no better policy than that of teaching these savages that treachery to their race, under such circumstances as those which obtained here, would merit its own sure reward." Later, Davis hedged on the issue of impunity for the four, probably because of the public outcry at the worst of the Modocs being spared. He reiterated, "They were promised no rewards for this service." And of Hooker Jim he said, "He was an unmitigated cut-throat and for this reason I was loath to make any use of him that would compromise his well-earned claim to the halter."

Friends were allowed to visit the condemned men in the guardhouse and, several times, the latter were allowed to visit the stockade. Scarfaced Charley was given the freedom of the post. He could not bring himself to join the four card-playing traitors, however, and usually sat alone in gloomy silence. As a result of Curtis' recommendation of mercy for Barncho and Slolux—"It will be an unnecessary outlay of national vengeance to put them to death"—the two had their death sentences commuted by President Grant on September 12, after he set October 3 as the date of the executions. Cruelly, the President ordered Wheaton *not* to reveal the reprieve to them until they were at the scaffold. Graves would be dug for all six men, although two of the excavations would not receive bodies. Wheaton was proud of his gallows, completed some time before September 30. Since he intended to execute all four of the Modocs at once, he made it large and strong—thirty feet long, of dressed pine logs each a foot in diameter.

While the date of execution was waited out, Fort Klamath returned to a humdrum existence. The Modocs in the stockade exchanged their rags for clean, though used, Army clothing. Lt. J. B. Hazelton was confined to quarters and later court-martialed for habitual drunkenness. Lt. Arthur Cranston's remains were brought to the fort, en route to the San Francisco Presidio. Bodies of the fallen enlisted men had been interred in the rude graveyard at Gillem's Camp. Almost every day, Modocs and Klamaths from the reservation, sometimes as many as fifty, visited friends and relatives in the stockade.

Meacham left the fort before the hangings. He finally forgave Captain Jack and shook hands with all of the condemned men. Jack clearly showed his dread of being hanged. He looked twenty years older than he was; his face was thin and haggard. Always nervous for an Indian—indeed, his name, Kientpoos, meant "Having-the-Waterbrash" (i.e., pyrosis or heartburn), Jack was in failing health from melancholia. The Army doctors were dosing him with opiates, which did not help matters. Bunker reported that his hands shook like an aspen and his whole body seemed palsied. Small wonder; like a good Modoc, he believed that hanging would suffocate his soul within his body, preventing its escape to the Happy Hunting Ground of immortality. But Jack still looked the eagle to some, his eyes often clear and steady, his attitude more nervous and anxious than sullen or abject. Meacham tried to commiserate with him and promised to tell his story to the public.

Bunker grumbled at the amnesty given the four treacherous scouts. The reporter complained that their pardon cheated the gallows of several "brilliant and distinguished ornaments." He also hated to see the buffalo-maned shaman, Curly Headed Doctor, escape the death penalty. He considered him to be the devil incarnate, the man whose evil counsel had forced Captain

Jack to both war and murder. Bunker, in his dispatches, likened the silent, powerfully built medicine man to a cruel and untamed beast. He considered the witch doctor's escape from hanging to be downright robbery of justice.

On October 2, Capt. George B. Hoge tested the strength of the six dangling ropes with some sandbags, as the "bloodhounds" and Scarfaced Charley watched with great curiosity. Mrs. Boddy and Mrs. Schira arrived, and Hooker Jim made himself scarce in the stockade. Wheaton, the post chaplain, and others then visited the condemned men with Oliver Applegate and Klamath sub-chief Dave Hill as interpreters. They told the six men that they had only another day of life. The Fort Klamath chaplain spoke to them about God, and then Jack bitterly blamed the war on others, particularly General Davis' card-playing friends, who loafed about the guardhouse. He asked for an audience with President Grant, and when this could not be promised he went on at some length. "I have heard the sentence and I know what it means. When I look in my heart I see no crime. I was in favor of peace. The young men were not ready for peace—they carried me with them. I feel that while these four men—Bogus, Shacknasty, Hooker and Steamboat—are free, they have triumphed over me and over the Government. When I surrendered, I expected to be pardoned and to live with my people on Klamath Land." But Jack was affected by the padre's prayer, translated for him by Donald McKay, and he added, "A long time since, I was a good man and was willing to forgive the injuries of the white man, but the whites made my heart black and I have been a bad man since, and have done bad things. I would like to be a good man again and have all forgotten."

Wheaton asked whom he wished to take charge of his people. Captain Jack hesitated and said, "I can think of no one. I cannot even trust Scarfaced Charley." So embittered was Jack now that he turned his hate on his most loyal subordinate and urged that Scarfaced Charley be executed in his place. Bunker, Stephen Powers, Capt. James Jackson were all surprised if not shocked by this *volte-face* and mentioned it in their writings. There were two reasons for Charley's fall in Jack's esteem. First, while he had not led the troops to Jack, he had surrendered and then persuaded some of Jack's last-ditch holdouts to quit. And, second, he had tried too hard to make Jack's last days on earth easy. He had predicted a fine life for him after death. Jack offered to trade places with Charley, and the scarred warrior of course declined.

Thus, Bunker heard Captain Jack say, "Scarfaced Charley is a bad man and was always ready for any enterprise during the war." Jack was paranoid now; he feared and hated everyone. Stephen Powers was not awfully surprised, for he had never romanticized him into a Rob Roy of the Lava Beds; to him, the chief had always been the opposite of Scarfaced Charley. Jack was irresolute, insincere and cowardly, or so thought Powers. Bunker was almost in that frame of mind, now, and noted that most of the visitors to the guardhouse entered with pity and admiration for Captain Jack but left it with contempt for him.

Only Boston Charley of the six condemned men appeared genuinely unmoved, indifferent to fate. The baby-faced killer continued to chaw his tobacco as if he had a century of life remaining. Bunker observed, almost admiringly, "He has the nerve of a devil." Boston created a mild sensation. Scornfully, he said, "Although a boy, I feel like a man, and when I look on each side of me I think of these other men as women. When I die and go to the other world I don't want them to go with me.... I am not afraid of death. I think I am the only man in the room...." And yet, when asked why he had attacked the peace commissioners, he made excuses like the rest—his heart had been wild and he had thought the deaths of such powerful *tyees* would end the war.

A tight-lipped Black Jim said that he was anxious to live in order to take care of Jack's band. But he added, "If the white chiefs' law says I am guilty of crime, let me die. I am not afraid to die. I am afraid of nothing. I should like to hear the spirit man's [the padre's] talk." Brawny, broad-chested Barncho and Slolux denied any part in the assassination.

Captain Jack's last recorded words were hardly dignified and lofty. "It is terrible to think that I have to die. When I look at my heart, I would like to live till I die a natural death." He then again gratuitously offered Scarfaced Charley as a substitute on the scaffold. According to Bunker, Jack's very last words were, "He is worse than I am and I propose to make an exchange and turn him over to be executed in my place."

John Schonchin tried to get in the last word, of course. He blamed the war on the younger men, too, and admitted to Boston's claim that he was "a woman," always interested in peace, not war. He even suggested that he had been insane at the time of the Peace Tent murders. He whined a bit, "I have always looked on the younger men of our tribe as my special charge and have reasoned with them and now I am to die as a result of their bad conduct. . . . It is doing a great wrong to take my life. I am an old man and took no active part." He blamed Odeneal for the war, and might not have been too far off the mark. One moment he vehemently wished that Hooker and the pardoned Modocs were in chains and condemned, the next moment he was urging that they be allowed to grow up to be good men. He asked that his children be taken care of and thus won the sympathy of onlookers, then lapsed into his pleading: "My heart tells me I should not die, that you do a great wrong in taking my life. War is a terrible thing. All must suffer—the best horses, the best cattle and the best men." But finally he straightened up and boldly closed with, "I can now only say, *let Schonchin die!*"

The chaplain's prayer was translated from English to Chinook by Oliver Applegate and from Chinook to Modoc by Dave Hill. At its end the reverend burst into tears and buried his face in his hands. Wheaton allowed the families of the condemned men to visit them one last time and also invited in the four turn-coats. Only Shacknasty Jim accepted. In Meacham's words, his appearance "roused the nearly dead lion into life again." Jack showered him with recrimination. The other blackguards, in keeping with their character, contented themselves with asking Wheaton for a good viewing point for the executions.

Oregon newspaperman C. B. Watson witnessed the familial visit. The women and children gathered around each man and sang the traditional death chant. But Jack and his stolid comrades said not a word.

Next morning, Sheriff McKenzie of Jackson County went through the motions of presenting warrants for the surrender of the prisoners indicted for the murder of the Tule Lake ranchers. Wheaton ignored them, likewise the writs of habeas corpus issued by the Jackson County Circuit Court. They all had been held invalid by the Army; the Modocs were prisoners of war and war criminals, not common felons. If Meacham is to be believed, the sheriff then offered Wheaton ten thousand dollars for Captain Jack's body after execution. If true, Wheaton spurned the offer. But this was far from being the last such incident of ghoulish souveniring in a shocking post-climax to the Modoc War.

Bunker noted that both Black Jim and Scarfaced Charley were on the Oregon "wanted" list, though neither had been along during Hooker Jim's murderous rampage. The former, shot through the body during Jackson's raid, had been recuperating at the time; Charley had been in the Lava Beds, far from the ranches, and in fact warning settlers about the war during the atrocities. Bunker, however, lumped Charley with the so-called "bloodhounds" as a sort of traitor, apparently because Charley had tried to end the war as early as possible by "talking in" some of Jack's last men at Langell Valley and Willow Creek. Still, he was fair to Charley, saying, "Scarfaced Charley, the chief advisor and interpreter of Captain Jack and really the Bismarck of the band, has only been a warrior in arms against our troops and today there are no regrets that he should be pardoned and at large."

To the end, there were efforts to spare all of the Modocs. While preacher Henry Ward Beecher offered prayers from the pulpit of his famed Plymouth Church in Brooklyn for "that poor, persecuted people whose long pent-up wrongs have driven them to acts of violence and diabolical murder," reporter Atwell was urging Secretary of the Interior Delano to stay all action till a full investigation of the causes of the war could be made. He reminded him that the Modocs had been without benefit of counsel at their trial. In his zeal, he maligned two good friends of the Modocs, the Riddles. Cuttingly he observed, "We know he [Frank] is illiterate, can neither read nor write, cannot translate the idioms of our tongue, cannot even understand good English. We know the squaw with whom he cohabits has shielded her relatives in his interpreting, at the expense of others. . . ." When he abandoned his attack on the Riddles, he made more sense: "We know that gross wrongs have been committed by whites on these Indians, and will show them, if permitted to do so."

Elijah Steele and the Modocs' other California friends did not give up the fight either. On July 30, 1873, Steele first wrote Delano to urge a delay in the execution until a full and fair investigation into the war could be made. He sent a petition, signed by himself, reporter Atwell, John Fairchild and William H. Morgan, ex-sheriff of Siskiyou County, California. The document asked that Modoc prisoners of war such as Scarfaced Charley, Miller's Charley and even the punishment-exempted "bloodhounds" be allowed to work on Morgan's ranch. The Modocs had asked this favor; they wanted to make their living as farmhands, not be a burden on the Government. Steele reminded Delano, "These Indians are used to take care of themselves; talk our language; and understand all kinds of farm work."

Steele again begged for a halt of the executions and the exile planned for the mass of Modocs. "This war was brought about by designing men, for selfish purposes. . . . I have been in the campaign from the first. . . . Having been on this coast for twenty-two years, having a good knowledge of Indians and their ways, I cannot, in common with thousands, avoid the feeling that a great wrong has been committed and should be investigated for the honor of our Government, which is supposed to protect the weak."

But leniency was not to be permitted. Grant intended to make an example of the Modocs, and not just those chosen for execution. Incredibly, cruelly, the President wanted even the individual exiled Modoc families *scattered* among other tribes of Indians in the Indian Territory. Banishment as a tribe was not enough. (At least he drew the line at splitting up individual families.) Delano concurred. In his 1873 *Annual Report*, the Secretary of the Interior reminded the President, "You deemed it advisable, if possible, to make this the occasion of furnishing the other Indian tribes an example calculated to deter them in future from the commencement of hostilities. . .to remove the entire remnant of the tribe. . .to break up its tribal relations and divide the members thereof among certain friendly Indians in the Southern superintendency. . . . The Indian is greatly attached to his tribal organization and it is believed that this example of extinguishing their so-called national existence and merging their members into other tribes, while in reality a humane punishment, will be esteemed by them as the severest penalty that could have been inflicted, and tend by its example to deter hostile Indians in future from serious and flagrant insurrections."

A year later, Delano was still optimistic: "With a judicious and efficient execution of the present mode of treatment, it is not believed that we shall see another general, or even serious, Indian war." Two years after these words came Custer's "last stand" at the Little Big Horn River.

Since there was no telegraph at Fort Klamath, correspondents Edward Fox and Col. H. S. Shaw of the New York *Herald* and the San Francisco *Chronicle*, respectively, conspired to set up a line of courier stations to rush the news of the execution to Jacksonville's telegraph office. They estimated nine horses and seven hours' time would be needed to get a message through. Wheaton, to whom they offered their services for his official report, guessed it was more like a twelve-horse, nine-hour ride over the mountains. Fox and Shaw, with Atwell, opposed William Turner of the San Francisco *Evening Bulletin* getting the news on the wire first, because he represented the Associated Press and its Western Union monopoly. Turner, for his part, quietly cleared an old Indian trail to Jacksonville of its windfalls and other obstructions, since it would cut the ninety-five-mile run to only seventy-five miles. Atwell tried to beat all of them by sending his courier not to Jacksonville but to Ashland. Fox tested his run by sending a preliminary story ending with the tag line, "More to come."

Not everyone looked forward to the day of execution. Lt. Stephen Jocelyn, commanding F Company, 21st Infantry, at Fort Klamath was disgusted by the hanging and fearful of drawing special duty on October 3, 1873. He wrote, "The officer of the day will have charge of the unpleasant duty but I hope to so arrange it that the detail will not fall to me." Whether his machinations worked, or he was blessed with good luck, Jocelyn did not draw the detested duty. That fell to Capt. George B. Hoge.

A little after 9 A.M. on hangman's day, October 3, the troops formed up on the parade ground, both the cavalry and artillery mounted. They moved to the guardhouse as the band played a quick march, then escorted the prisoners' wagon back to the scaffold as the bandsmen played the Dead March with muffled drums.

Earlier, Jack's wife, daughter and sister Mary had visited him. He had clasped the child to his chest, obviously deeply affected, as the women wept. He then gave his long string of beads, worn around his neck in several loops, to George S. Miller, in a gesture reminiscent of Anne Boleyn's tipping the headsman of Tower Green with twenty pounds. The captives were puzzled as six of them sat on only four coffins in the wagon bed. A chisel cut off their irons, and Wheaton motioned Captain Jack, Schonchin John, Black Jim and Boston Charley up the gibbet's steps while troopers held back Barncho and Slolux. The four sat on the deadly platform, Jack looking wretched and miserable, according to Bunker, while Captain Hoge read the execution order and the reprieve of Barncho and Slolux. The two men were led away; like Scarfaced Charley, they were not obliged to witness the death throes of their leaders. (Charley sat on a bench on the far side of the stockade, his head in his hands.)

The captive Modocs had a good view of the proceedings from the stockade. There were also 200 soldiers and 150 civilians present, plus many Modocs and Klamaths from the reservation. Wheaton reported the entire Klamath nation as being present, perfectly orderly and much impressed by the ceremonies supervised by Post Adjutant Lt. George W. Kingsbury. At 10 A.M., the four men were led onto the trap, where their arms and legs were tied as six mounted patrols circled the crowd. Two corporals placed the nooses around the necks of Captain Jack and Schonchin John, after some of the former's hair was cut for a better fit. Two other hangmen, privates this time, did the honors for Boston and Black Jim. The chaplain prayed and was echoed in translation by Dave Hill. With stiff and solemn formality the Officer of the Day moved from man to man, bidding each one farewell in a gesture perhaps left over from the days of knighthood and chivalry. Black hoods were slipped over the heads of the four Modocs, and at exactly 10:10 Fort Klamath time (but 10:20 by some watches), Hoge dropped his handkerchief in a signal. The shiny, honed blade of an axe dropped on the single hempen rope holding the trap door. Four bodies dropped with a jerk and writhed and twisted in the air, tightening and loosening the taut ropes as half-smothered wails of anguish burst from the stockade Modocs.

Captain Jack and Black Jim died instantly, but Boston and Schonchin John struggled and may have choked to death. Still, Boston was the hero of the last sad act of the Modoc "difficulty." Private FitzGerald observed: "Charlie mounted the scaffold at Fort Klamath with firm step and seemingly the most stoical indifference. His only request was for a 'chew' of tobacco. . . . He died like a brave man and upheld the traditions of his race." At 10:28 a surgeon pronounced the Modocs dead, and the crowd, some of it shocked and horrified, began to break up. Wheaton was proud of the way his men had carried off the ceremony. With solemnity, with every possible formality, it had gone off without a hitch.

Meacham mused on Captain Jack's fate: "In view of Jack's record as a warrior, no one will ever say he was a coward, but had he refused to accede to the demands of the cutthroats and they had, then and there, enforced the threat of death, it would have been better for the interests of justice, and today his name would be enshrined as a martyr instead of being used as a watchword against his race." Stephen Powers could not forget Jack's attempts to switch the blame for war and murder to Scarfaced Charley, to *anyone*. He was still severe in his criticism: "They deserved a better leader than they had. Captain

Jack was not a hero and does not deserve to be mentioned with Tecumseh and Pontiac and Red Jacket."

At almost the very moment that the trap dropped from beneath the feet of Captain Jack and his comrades, the newspaper couriers sped off. The *Herald's* man held the lead until he reached the Rogue River. There he found what he suspected was sabotage. The saddled horse that should have been awaiting him on the ferry was in the stable, and unsaddled, and the ferryboat was on the opposite bank. He was delayed a full twenty minutes and he lost perhaps ten more to a bucking mule. The Evening *Bulletin's* special courier, B. Evans, who also served the *Call*, won the race in world-record time of six hours and thirty minutes. But still he arrived too late to make the afternoon edition. Twenty minutes behind him was the *Herald's* man. Poor Atwell's run of bad luck continued. In June, trying to get a scoop out of Captain Jack's capture, he had bought a three hundred dollar mule and started cross-country to Ashland by a shortcut. The lava proved too rough for even as sure-footed a critter as a mule, and the beast stumbled and fell, breaking its neck and injuring Atwell. He had managed to get to Boyle's Camp, where he was patched up, but later had to undergo medical treatment in Yreka. This time, he did not lose a mule, but one of his riders got so drunk that he fell off his horse and lost six hours to his rivals. Nor was Atwell's lousy luck over yet. On his way south from Yreka, the stagecoach in which he rode was held up by road agents. The passengers and Wells, Fargo's treasure (express) box were robbed of four thousand dollars. But, at last, Atwell's luck changed. When he told the bandits that he had only two-bits to his name and was a long way from home, they let him keep the quarter as a grubstake.

Colonel Shaw backed up the couriers with two carrier pigeons. He loosed them as Bunker watched. Later, Bunker wrote, "One of them made a splendid start, circling round for a while and then darting off southward. The second lost his message and alighted on a pine tree a hundred yards distant, where I left him gazing at the Modoc funeral."

General Schofield wrote to the War Department to report that the effect of the Army's administration of justice in what General Davis liked to call "the Modoc insurrection," even though tardy, had had a most salutary effect on other western tribes. He could not praise Davis highly enough: "The inspiriting influence of his presence, example and judicious orders speedily changed disaster and defeat into complete success."

CHAPTER FOURTEEN

AFTERMATH

Morbid souvenir hunters had a field day at Fort Klamath on October 3, 1873. Hardly were the Modoc corpses stiffening in *rigor mortis* before a memorabilia market was thriving. Strands of the rope that had hanged Captain Jack, and locks of his hair, sold for as high as five dollars apiece. Lt. George W. Kingsbury later mounted short lengths of the hangman's hemp on printed cards reading "The Rope That Hung the Chief of the Modoc Indians, Captain Jack, Oct. 3rd 1873." He either gave them away to friends or sold them. One can be seen today in the keeping of Dr. Bernard Fontana of the Arizona State Museum, Tucson, along with two Modoc bows, one made by Jack's brother-in-law, Miller's Charley, and the other by Steamboat Frank's wife. There are also vesicular lava samples collected by Kingsbury, two Modoc pipes, a tobacco pouch made of a deer's foot, fish spear points, moccasins, a basketry hat and a beaded buckskin jacket with red *bayeta* (baize or flannel) collar and sleeves and with brass buttons. Col. William Thompson managed to get John Schonchin's bow and arrows, and Dr. Cabaniss claimed the hangman's knots from around Jack's and Schonchin's necks. He sent them to a friend, Dr. F. G. Hearn of Yreka, a dentist whose cabinet of Indian curiosities was given to the State of California. The knotted ropes are now in the Indian Museum at Sutter's Fort, Sacramento.

A more macabre aftermath of the trial and execution shortly seized the public's imagination. A reporter, probably Colonel Shaw, peeked into a tent at Fort Klamath and saw a table covered with a black india-rubber sheet similar to those used in dissecting rooms of medical colleges. Nearby was a barrel of water and a case of surgical instruments. He was told that the heads of Captain Jack and Schonchin John had been cut off for shipment to Washington. The *Chronicle* was (or, at least, affected to be) horrified. Aghast, it called such actions by the Army atrocious and barbaric. However, the editor of the loyal magazine, the *Army and Navy Journal,* leaped to the defense of the head-hunting service, claiming that there was nothing barbaric about it since the decapitated heads were being sent to Washington for scientific study—craniology. During the 1870s, the Secretary of War was inordinately proud of his anatomical museum. He reported that anthropologists from France and Germany and elsewhere were coming to Washington in order to study the world's largest collection of American Indian skulls.

Nor were these the first such anatomical specimens collected during the Modoc War. On April 14, 1873, a San Francisco embalmer, R. M. Taylor, put in his bid for the bodies of Captain Jack, Schonchin John, Boston and Hooker Jim in the event they should be killed, or captured and executed. He asked General Schofield for a permit to embalm the dead Modocs and to bring them to San Francisco for exhibit "in the cause of science and with a desire to gratify the curiosity of the people." Whether Schofield bothered to reply or not is not known (the embalmer enclosed a stamped, self-addressed envelope). San Francisco did not get any Modoc bodies for a freak show. As early as May 6, however, the *Call* reported the sending of some skulls and bones of anonymous Modocs to Washington (where they are still to be seen in the Smithsonian Institution). These skeletons were, early, confused by the public with the remains of Captain Jack and his three comrades.

The Army tried to hush up the story of its vandalizing and indecent burial of the Modocs, to shut off the rush of bad publicity, but only fostered more and wilder tales of horror. First came a story that not only had Jack's head been sent East, but his body as well. This led a horrified Meacham to exclaim, purplishly, "His bones—despised, dishonored, burnished, sepulchred in the crystal catacomb of a medical museum—represent his ruined race in the capital of a conquering nation." Albert S. Gatschet was similarly shocked: "The unworthy termination of this war is well typified by the fact that the skeleton of the Modoc captain is now dangling as an anatomical specimen in the Museum of the Surgeon General's Office." Lending substance to this yarn was the report of a teamster, loading a wagon with stores at the Roseburg, Oregon, railroad depot, who showed the editor of the Roseburg *Plain-Dealer* a cask that he said contained the headless corpse of Captain Jack, addressed to the "Society of Natural History." There was no such society, of course, but he may have seen the actual cask sent East, which bore a label "Specimens of Natural History."

Another hideous story was bandied about and then given new life in 1914 when Jeff Riddle's book, *The Indian History of the Modoc War,* appeared. Riddle acknowledged that four coffins were lowered into the ground that Friday afternoon and six graves filled, but he claimed that a ghoul came that night and disinterred Jack's coffin, stole the body and hurried it to Yreka by wagon for embalming. Historian Keith Murray seemed to half-accept Riddle's yarn, which ended with Jack's mummy being exhibited in a sideshow in Washington, D.C., at a dime a look.

Actually, Dr. McElderry had written Washington on July 13 that he had great hopes of obtaining the heads of John Schonchin and Captain Jack. He finally took all four, scalped them, removed all soft parts and placed them in a barrel which he sent to the Surgeon General's Office, along with a box of pathological specimens from two typhoid victims at Fort Klamath. Lt. John Quincy Adams signed Post Surgeon McElderry's receipt for the two packages at Fort Klamath on October 20. An old Form No. 5, *Invoice of Stores Transferred,* can be inspected today at the Smithsonian. The printed phrase has been crossed out and replaced by the handwritten words, "Receipt for two packages transferred." McElderry's receipt-invoice was received in Washington on November 10 along with an accompanying letter dated October 25: "I have the honor to enclose herewith the Post Quartermaster's receipt for two packages of specimens for the Army Medical Museum, this day turned over to him for transportation. The barrel contains the heads of the four Modoc Indians, Captain Jack, Schonchis [sic], Boston Charley, and Black Jim, executed on the 3d inst. at this Post for the murder of Maj. General Canby and Rev'd Thomas, Peace Commissioners. The heads are labelled with the respective names of each." The remains themselves arrived in the District of Columbia on January 24, 1874.

Almost a hundred years after the hanging, you can still read the penciled names of their rightful owners on the skulls, but inventory numbers were assigned to them, too—Jack's was 1018, Schonchin's 1019, Boston's 1020 and Black Jim's 1021, so that they would not be lost in our national golgotha. But for a scientific organization the Surgeon General's Office was awfully casual about determining the ages of the executed four—Jack was put down as fifty years of age and all the others, including John Schonchin, who looked the oldest, were estimated to have been forty years old. Long ago, the skulls were transferred from the Surgeon General's custody to the Smithsonian Institution of the United States National Museum, where, assigned specimen number 225070, Captain Jack's skull can still be seen, by arrangement, along with the other anthropological remains in the Department of Physical Anthropology. This collection on the "Peoples of the United States" is maintained, by law, for scientific and scholarly study.

Part of what might be called the American historical souvenir syndrome is the sudden multiplication of specimens, where the proper commercial climate permits such vigorous growth. Thus, Billy the Kid's pistol has reproduced itself perhaps a half-dozen times and now can be seen in several states of the Union. Captain Jack, however, was able to contribute two heads to history. Besides the one resting in the cabinet drawer of the Smithsonian, another was for years in the custody of the University of Oregon. When Col. Robert A. Miller of Portland died, his will left his effects to his lodge brothers, but three skulls in his basement went to the university. One was plainly labeled "Captain Jack." Today, university officials report that neither of Captain Jack's heads is to be found in Eugene, only Modoc leggings, armbands and feathers and an iron knife that was Jack's.

In recent years, graves of the four Modocs have been found at old Fort Klamath, which is slowly being restored by the Klamath County Historical Society. The four sunken graves at the end of the parade ground near Highway 62 are now protected by a fence. From south to north they are believed to be those of Captain Jack, Schonchin John, Black Jim and Boston Charley—except, of course, for their missing crania. Oregonians who once believed that the plots were filled with rotting coffins loaded with stones by the "resurrectionists" now are convinced that only the skulls were sent away. But, as yet, no one has checked the buried remains.

As the time came to move the remaining Modocs into exile, new rumors flew. This time, so went the stories, there would be an attempt to rescue the Modocs while they were en route to Fort D. A. Russell in Wyoming Territory, their first destination, which was subsequently changed. Just who was going to pull off the rescue has not been determined. Wheaton felt it necessary to advise his Portland headquarters that he put no stock in the "dread" of the settlers in regard to the threatened rescue. He also turned down still more writs of habeas corpus and bench warrants for some of the prisoners, delivered to him from the judge of the District Court of Jackson County by the never-say-die sheriff.

Captain Hasbrouck and his battery on October 12, 1873, escorted the 153 surviving Modoc "renegades"—less Barncho and Slolux, who were sent to Alcatraz—out of Fort Klamath and into exile. Thirty-nine were men. Old Schonchin and his peaceful followers were allowed to remain at Yainax. The banished Modocs proceeded to Yreka and Redding, where they entrained for Fort McPherson, Nebraska, rather than Fort D. A. Russell. Gen. Phil Sheridan genuinely wanted to make the Modocs as comfortable as possible, and he changed their destination to McPherson because Russell had so few amenities, not even wild game to hunt. Sherman then suggested Brady's Isle in the Platte River near Fort McPherson, but the decision was to put them on the Quapaw Indian Reservation in Indian Territory, now Oklahoma.

On the twenty-ninth, Col. J. J. Reynolds gave Hasbrouck a receipt at Fort McPherson for his charges. He then sent them to Seneca Station, Indian Territory, on Shawnee land near the Quapaws. The Shawnees were less indolent than the Quapaws and would set the Modocs a better example. Moreover, Baxter Springs, Kansas, "a notorious place for corrupting Indians," was too near the Quapaws. Indian Agent H. W. Jones, a Quaker, put them in barracks which they built themselves and put them also under his friendly wing, hoping that the Shawnees would adopt them. The Modocs impressed him greatly, and he reported to the Indian commissioner that they were obedient and ready to work and that they cheerfully complied with his police regulations. In fact, they proved to him, over and over again, that they only required just treatment, executed with firmness and kindness, to make of them "a singularly reliable people."

On June 23, 1874, the Indian Bureau concluded an agreement with the eastern Shawnees for a four thousand-acre site for six thousand dollars, to be the Modocs' permanent home. The contract was submitted to Congress, but since there was no authority for such agreements, the Interior Department did not even approve it. Instead, it substituted a simple lease; for five thousand dollars the Government got the land in question at the northeast corner of the Shawnee Reserve for a five-year term.

There the transplanted Modocs lived, and died. They raised corn and wheat on 180 cultivated acres and left the rest to prairie grazing or timber. They built cabins and sent their children to school and Sunday school. Many took white men's names. When Slolux came to the Quapaw area after serving only five years of his life sentence on Alcatraz, he became George Denny, for example. Scarfaced Charley—"the best educated and most civilized of them all"—was made chief, but the scarified bachelor had little desire for leadership, although he was a willing and indeed obliging servant of his people. When he would not put a stop to his Modocs gambling away even their clothing and blankets, the Indian agent replaced him as chief with the rascally Bogus Charley. The latter remained in office for several years, probably until his death on October 25, 1880. Before being deposed, Scarfaced Charley received blankets and clothing from a fifteen thousand dollar appropriation, to get the Modocs through the winter and early spring. But his people suffered from the strange climate, from poverty and disease. One by one they fell. When Meacham visited them in November 1874 and found the once-bloodthirsty warriors playing croquet, he said 139 were still alive. But Gatschet counted only 103 survivors in 1878, and James B. Fry reported that 50 of the exiles had died by 1880. Hooker Jim passed away in 1879; the escapee, Long Jim, was dead after only six years of exile. Steamboat Frank "got religion" and, now calling himself Frank Modoc, attended Oak Grove Seminary at Vassalboro, Maine, where he died of consumption in June 1886. Scarfaced Charley—"a good Indian in bad company," as Pres Dorris' ranch foreman described him—became a Christian. Like so many other Indians, he not only got religion but TB to boot, and was dead by 1888. According to Jennie Clinton (a Modoc), Curly Headed Doctor lasted till 1890, when he was killed by spirits "because he didn't do anything for them." On the day of his death, spirits in the form of wild pigeons flocked to the Modoc Reservation, filling the trees. The doctor warned, "Don't kill those birds or you will suffer. They have come to bid me farewell. As soon as I die, the spirits leaving me will cause the greatest storm you have ever seen." Curly Headed Doctor was more accurate in this prophecy than he had been in the Lava Beds, with his bullet-proofing incantations. Quapaws, Modocs and Shawnees were lashed by a great storm as life flickered out in his body. When the tempest was over, the doctor was cremated according to his wish, although most of the tribe, now Christianized, preferred burial. According to Jennie, it was the most unusual fire the Modocs had ever seen, as the flames not only jumped very high but were of many colors.

In 1909, the Government permitted the Oklahoma Modocs

to return to the Klamath Reservation. A few did so, such as One-Eyed Mose, only to be greeted again as interlopers on private Klamath property. The localized xenophobia which, in large part, had caused the Modoc War, was still endemic there. Today, only a handful of Modocs in Oklahoma (the forty of 1940 were thirty in 1970), with the three hundred in Oregon and perhaps a few in California, fight against total extinction.

The survivors summed up the end of their melancholy tribal history for investigator Gatschet: "Then to distant land they brought a portion of the Modocs, to the far-off Indian Territory, to Quapaw Indian Reservation. Some at Yaneks [Yainax] in Oregon live, close by the former Indian country." Even the stoical, fatalistic Modocs could not help being impressed by the greatness of their last stand and the enormous efforts necessary to crush them. To put down a guerrilla war carried on by probably fifty-three braves (at *top* strength), they recalled proudly: *"Kank she'sha nánuk maklasham shellualsh vunepni millions tala* (so much did cost the whole Modoc War, four millions of dollars)."

Even with the hidden cash costs, the war probably did not run that high in *tála*. It was usually overestimated by whites as well as Modocs. While not America's most costly war, or even Indian war, it may well have been that in terms of the number of enemy committed to combat action—possibly sixty-odd but probably never more than fifty-three. (Simpson of the *London Illustrated News* insisted there were never more than forty-five.) Only 161 Modocs in all—men, women and children—surrendered in 1873. Perhaps the estimate of M. C. Meigs, quartermaster general (June 26, 1874) is as close to an accurate money-cost as any—$411,068.18 beyond normal operating costs of the Army in the Department of the Columbia.

But this was not the whole cost of the Modoc War, by a long shot. There were the lives squandered; the lives ruined; the widows and orphans on both sides. There were the war claims of greedy settlers, the graft and corruption that always thrives in a wartime climate. Most of all there was the psychic or spiritual damage done to both the Indians and white Americans. If *any* war is worthy, the Modoc War was a senseless, needless and unworthy conflict.

In terms of lives lost, the war is wildly misrepresented by people who have grown up bemused by pulp magazine, movie and TV dramas of Indian wars in which redmen and white men drop like the proverbial flies. The Indian commissioner in 1874 gave the total of Modocs killed as eighteen–but only seven of them were men! The Modocs themselves admitted only *five* casualties from battle–three in the Three Days' Fight from rifle fire and the exploding dud shell; one at Sorass Lake; and one in the Thomas-Wright ambush. Perhaps the other two "claimed" by the commissioner were boys. Several squaws and a child or two were certainly killed, whether deliberately or accidentally. General Davis, in his final report on the war, dated November 1, 1873, gave the Army's dead as seven officers, thirty-nine enlisted men and two Warm Springs scouts; its wounded as four officers, sixty-one enlisted men and two Warm Springs scouts. To these figures he added sixteen civilians killed and one wounded, a figure that seems low when the Oregon and California volunteer losses of January are added to the murders of Hovey and the Tule Lake settlers. Thus, his grand total of 132 men killed and wounded is probably a low estimate. (Some accounts run as high as 163 casualties.) Custer, for comparison, lost 264 men at the Little Big Horn.

Whatever the body count, the Modoc War remains one of the most difficult campaigns ever fought by U.S. Army elements, ranking in its impossible terrain with the Everglades and hammocks of Florida's Seminole War. General Schofield was correct when he described it thus: "The Department of the Columbia has been the scene of a conflict more remarkable in some respects than any other before known in American history."

California's costs were minimal, only $4,621.33 for its militia participation. But Oregon paid its citizens $130,728.44 for military services or supplies, then turned around, supplicated Congress, and was reimbursed a whopping $72,637.83. Individuals began to file war-damage claims for losses, real or imaginary, which were the result of the war. George S. Miller was perhaps typical. Modocs (presumably) stampeded the Langell Valley rancher's Arizona-bound herd of three to four hundred fat steers, of which he retrieved only thirty to forty head. Next, the Indians ran off his horses. Miller filed a depredation claim and, after much delay, won three thousand dollars. Although Simpson (Horsefly) Wilson did not enlist in the Oregon Volunteers and did little service beyond carrying a dispatch or two and letting the Army bivouac on his property as Jack's capture was imminent, he was awarded a pension on May 29, 1924, in Calvin Coolidge's Presidency. John Fairchild did not prosper like a carpetbagger, but neither did he lose money on the war. He was paid only $455 for his services (and his efforts were worth ten or twenty times that sum), but he received another $2,000 for the hay and horses he had supplied the Army.

Perhaps Gen. John Pope's words of 1864 can be applied to the Lava Beds "difficulty" of almost a decade later. "Then begins an Indian war which the greed of contractors and speculators interested in its continuance, playing upon the mutual apprehensions of the people and influencing the press, makes it very difficult to conduct successfully or bring to an end." Or the words of John Wool in regard to the Oregon militiamen of 1856: "They appear to be running a race to see who can dip deepest into the Treasury of the United States. I have never doubted for a moment that as soon as the volunteers ceased their depredations and savage barbarities on the Indians, arrangements could be made satisfactory to all concerned." Perhaps the words of Gen. William T. Sherman, who ordered "no quarter" in the Modoc War, were as right in 1873 as when they were uttered in 1866: "All the people west of the Missouri River look to the Army as their legitimate field of profit and support."

Although the fickle press soon abandoned the Modocs for new headlines about California *bandido* Tiburcio Vásquez, or the bucko mates of the hellship *Sunrise,* the "rebels" were not forgotten. The San Francisco *Call* reported a gang of hoodlums in the lumberyards area "south of Market" (Street) to be calling themselves Modocs and their chief Captain Jack. Back in the Blue Ridge of Virginia, a band of outlaws similarly dubbed themselves Modocs, according to the Warrenton, Virginia, *Index* and the Philadelphia *Star,* and named their hideout, in a rough spur of the Blue Ridge only four or five miles from Culpeper, "the Lava Beds." In Denver, the *Tribune* reported that the younger boys had abandoned their kites and balls to take up tin tomahawks and scalping knives carved of shingles. Little girls were left out of the campfires, death chants and simulated scalpings (the tots had never heard of Toby), and were said to be singing, mournfully, "When this Modoc War is over, we will have good times again."

As early as May 1873, a melodrama titled "Captain Jack" was performed in New York at Apollo Hall and Wood's Museum, with W. H. Halley in the title role and T. W. Keene his understudy. The New York *Times* applauded the show as "sensational drama." Halley was not the last to take the Modoc

War to the boards. White America had not done with its exploiting of the poor Modocs. Anatomical specimens, morbid souvenirs and diaspora were hardly enough to "gratify the curiosity of the people," as the Frisco embalmer had put it so well.

A. B. Meacham perhaps demeaned himself somewhat by capitalizing on Modoc notoriety and his own semiscalping. He organized a lecture tour of the Midwest and East under the management of James Redpath of the Boston Lyceum Bureau. But Meacham was almost certainly well-meaning, even if his theatrical replaying of the Modoc War cheapened the sacrifices on both sides in the bloody conflict. It may be that he had a bit of Parson Weems—even P. T. Barnum—in his makeup. But if self-interest or, at least, self-importance somewhat threatened principle and loyalty to the Modocs in Meacham's character, he eventually overcame such temptations. Indian reform was not a mass crusade until at least the 1880s. It was the result of individual effort, and from 1875 until 1881, when Meacham died and was replaced as the Indians' champion by Helen Hunt Jackson, author of *Ramona* and *A Century of Dishonor,* he was the outstanding person in the field. He shrugged off such attacks as that of the Dolores, Colorado, *News,* which labeled him "a coward by nature, a thief by instinct, a hypocrite by choice." After all, he was called the most faithful and generous friend the Indians ever had by Secretary of the Interior Carl Schurz.

Strangely, Meacham was woefully ignorant of Modoc customs and language in 1874, so he had to hurry a request to Oliver Applegate for a few choice Modoc and Klamath phrases that he could memorize in order to "embellish" a series of lectures. He then signed up some Klamaths, plus Lindsay Applegate and even a Rogue River Indian. He hired Frank and Toby Riddle and changed the latter's name to the more romantic Wi-ne-ma, meaning (more or less) Little Woman Chief. According to Oliver Applegate, Meacham lifted the new name for Mrs. Riddle right off the pages of a poem by Joaquin Miller. He got permission from the Indian commissioner to borrow some of his erstwhile enemies for an eastern tour, but Secretary Delano balked. Meacham stressed to President Grant that he meant to tell the Modocs' story, not just exhibit and exploit them as a showman, and Grant overruled Delano.

In November 1874, Meacham went to Indian Territory and

signed up Scarfaced Charley, Steamboat Frank, Shacknasty Jim and others. They were all pleased to see and oblige their old friend, who had been killed by John Schonchin and then brought back to life by the Great Spirit. Meacham and his (unconsciously) self-parodying troupe toured Sacramento, St. Joseph and St. Louis, Terre Haute, Louisville and Lexington, Washington, Philadelphia, Reading, Morristown, Camden, Trenton, Elizabeth, Newark and New York City. Meacham's show resembled more the educational lyceum-chautauqua type of performance—like that inflicted on the redeemed Apache captive, Olive Oatman, by her pious protector-promoter, Royal B. Stratton—than the true Wild West show of Buffalo Bill Cody. It was partly educational, partly pro-Indian propaganda, partly a publicity stunt. But as a commercial venture it was hardly a yowling success. Meacham blamed the lukewarm reception of his troupe on the cheap, sensational "Indian shows" that had preceded him on the road and had ruined his market. (By the end of the nineteenth century, there were five hundred companies traveling the country's theatrical circuits, and not a few of them in feathers, moccasins and war paint.)

Very much to his credit, A. B. Meacham asked his audiences for justice for the American Indian and let some of his company, particularly the glib Dave Hill, make impromptu speeches criticizing the laws of the land that protected newly arrived immigrants but offered no justice to native Americans. In March 1875, for example, Hill—alias The Left-Handed Chief Who Lives Between Two Rivers—explained to a Philadelphia audience his disillusionment with the Great White Father and his helpers: "I went to see the President. He looks just like any other man. I was not afraid of him. I intended to tell him what my people wanted . . . but his ear was too small; he could not hear me. I brought all the things in my heart away. Then I went to see the commissioner [of Indian Affairs]. He had large ears. He *seemed* to listen to what I had to tell him, but I looked him in the eye. He did not put the things I told him in his heart. My heart got sick, because I had come a long way with Colonel Meacham to see these men, but they would not take the words I gave them."

With apparent sincerity, Meacham tried to explain the Indian's religion and philosophy to city audiences, taking along a medicine man to help him. He soon admitted defeat. "I knew that his [i.e., an Indian's] religion controlled him more than do the religious pretensions of any other people. . . . [But] who ever heard of a white man standing up in the face of the world and declaring that the Indian had any right to his religious practices and beliefs?"

Expenses more than gobbled up the profits of Meacham's lectures and serious charades. Finally, he had difficulty in getting enough money together for railroad tickets home. He refused to prostitute his Indians when a New York theater manager offered to bail him out financially if he would put his show into vaudeville. Meacham shouted at him, "I came here on a *mission*, not a *speculation!*" He did better, perhaps, when he switched his affections from the stage to Clio. His books of popular history, although prosy, romanticized, fictionalized and melodramatized, were rather well received. He write *Wig-wam and Warpath* in 1876 and *Wi-ne-ma* in 1877. The crusading magazine *The Council Fire*, which he started in 1878 with Dr. T. A. Bland's help, was probably his greatest contribution toward the reform of Indian policy.

Not to be outdone by a paleface, Donald McKay, the half-breed chief of the Warm Springs and Wasco scouts for the Army, further corrupted the record of valor that was the Modoc War by taking a Wild West show to Europe in 1874. As if that were not enough in the way of exploitation of his role in the campaign, he next hit the old Snake Oil Trail. In 1888, T. A. Edwards wrote a two-bit booklet titled *Daring Donald McKay, or the Last War Trail,* which was a fanciful, farcical account of the war. In a sense, it rubbed the noses of all Modoc War participants in the commercial dirt of America. In this penny-dreadful, the *métis*, naturally, made the capture of Captain Jack personally. The dime-novel prose alternated with an overwhelming pitch for the various nostrums of the Oregon Indian Medicine Company of Corry, Pennsylvania. Its manager was none other than author T. A. Edwards. The latter's cure-alls included Nez Perce Catarrh Remedy, the Warm Springs Consumption Cure, Modoc Oil ("The Greatest Pain Remover on Earth") and, the top of the line, Donald McKay's Great Indian Worm Eradicator. These panaceas were priced at five dollars a bottle, fifty dollars a dozen.

Edwards liked to offer a one thousand dollar reward to any consumptive who did not cure his TB with liberal dosages of Daring Donald McKay's favorite firewater, the pulmonary cough syrup called the Warm Springs Consumption Cure. This surefire remedy for ulcerated lungs was made not only of roots, herbs, maple sap and water (and, probably, whiskey) but also a rare moss found only above timberline in the Rockies. There, somehow, the Umatillas and Warm Springs had found it. (Doubtless Edwards meant the Cascades rather than the Rockies, but his weakness in geography betrayed him.) Edwards offered testimonials by the sheaf that his Indian medicines really routed stiff joints and female weakness.

Possibly Dave McKay put too much faith in Edward's medications, if they were as fortified as was the custom. Logger Dick Breitenstein once was a passenger on a launch on Klamath Lake with McKay. An oncoming boat failed to respond to McKay's signal, a raised and lowered lantern. The ex-scout, in his cups from either redeye or Worm Eradicator, hauled out his pistol in pirate fashion and shot the other craft's smokestack full of holes.

After the heat of battle cooled following the Modoc War, both the military and civilians began to offer ungrudging praise to the Modocs whom they had been intent on killing off only a short time earlier. Back on June 3, 1873, an apprehensive *Call* editor was worrying aloud that such villains as Boston Charley would soon be "toasted and feted" by a Government he considered always too lenient toward offending redmen. He was not far off. Even earlier than his editorial, the iconoclastic San Francisco *News-Letter,* always jaundiced about the need for the Modoc War anyway, used the Modocs to attack the socio-political climate of the times. The *News-Letter* printed a parody of a letter to the editor in which Count Von Moltke supposedly ranked Captain Jack with Hannibal and Wellington. The paper said of the Prussian general who had conquered Napoleon III, "He is of the opinion that Jack must in the end triumph and the great American Republic will succumb to his well-directed fury and be absorbed by him and carried to the Lava Beds. In a few weeks, predicts the Count, he will come out of his fortifications and move deliberately on Washington. . . . Crédit Mobilier swindles will be less frequent, elections will be conducted with diminished political disturbances, society will be elevated, religion purified and the laws administered with improved vigor and impartiality."

But few could take the war as a joke, as the *News-Letter* seemed to do. Capt. Joel G. Trimble, who had actually captured Captain Jack, was cool in his regard for the emerging folk hero but sharply critical of the causes of the Modoc War: "A long dreary winter, and for what? To drive a couple of hundred miserable aborigines from a desolate natural shelter in the wilderness, that a few thieving cattlemen might ranch their wild steers in a scope of isolated country the dimensions of some several reasonable-sized counties."

By 1908, the Modocs were heroes, indeed, and Maj. John S. Parke wrote in the *Journal of the United States Infantry Association,* "Few men can boast the heroism, the bravery and the success of these savages under circumstances so adverse and disadvantages so great. There never were, at any time, more than fifty-three warriors among them and yet they killed and wounded, from first to last, one hundred and thirty-two men with a loss to themselves of only four in actual hostilities. Including those that were executed, five that were foully murdered after surrendering by unknown parties, and a few others who died from accident or suicide, their total loss was seventeen."

Some individual Oregonians now began to defend the Modocs, in the fashion of their neighbors across the line. George Masterson Miller, for example, stated publicly that the Government and its agencies, not the Indians, were to blame for the Modoc War. But, by and large, Oregonians remained unreconstructed; they refused to forgive and forget the murders committed by Hooker Jim and his ilk. Governor Grover, in his final report on the war to General Schofield (February 13, 1874), characterized Captain Jack's Modocs as murderers, the most bloodthirsty savages west of the Rockies, who had occupied a land admirably suited to protect them in their slaughtering of settlers and to shield them from punishment. A decade after the war, one of the state's newspaper editors sneered, "Captain Jack and Scarfaced Charley were not considered very desperate when they made occasional visits to Yreka to clear the clothes lines for clean sheets and clothing for their squaws." As for Captain Jack's sis, the Queen Mary of such easy virtue, the editor snorted, "She had a beautiful crushed mushroom complexion and was as graceful as a sack of carrots trying to climb over a ten-rail fence and her sale, at any price, proved the great scarcity of women in the region."

After the Modoc War, more people heeded Meacham. He said that the Modocs had learned a terrible lesson and would never go on the warpath again. But he was not surprised that other Indians, everywhere, were being driven by a fury of hopeless despair such as the Modocs had felt, and were ready to throw themselves on the bayonets of an advancing, God-fearing nation that sang "Peace on earth and goodwill to men" as it marched westward. To Meacham, it was the Government that had learned nothing from the bloody lessons of the Modoc War: "It has not hunted up and executed or exiled the white murderers who outraged humanity by killing four unarmed warriors in Fairchild's wagon. . . . It has not won the confidence of the Indian tribes of America. It has not made war with them less probable in the future. It has not heard the silent muttering of the Indian for vengeance." Meacham called the Modoc War a conflict without counterpart in either history or living tradition, one which bemused civilization as half a hundred braves moved from success to success. And now, "The remnant band of savage heroes shout back their anguish to the bleak winds of their prairie home in a land of exile. The maimed victims of both races hobble on, seeking to forget the past."

James Fry wrote in a similar vein in 1879. "As a tribe, the Modocs have ceased to exist. Suffering from wrongs that entitled them to sympathy and assistance, they took the law into their own hands and worked savage vengeance not upon the men who had injured them but on those striving to save and provide for them. In blind fury, they treacherously entrapped and murdered their two best friends. . . . The remainder, in banishment, are fast fading away by disease and despair. . . . They do not increase in numbers, the deaths exceeding the births. . . . When asked of their welfare, they answer they are sick, that many die and, pointing to the graveyard, say sadly that too many lie there."

After the execution of the Modoc "ringleaders" and the exile of their followers, Fort Klamath resumed its traditional dozing. The snooze was briefly broken on November 22, 1873, by an earthquake that did no damage but rattled dishes for two and a half minutes, opened and closed doors and shook hats off pegs. Some of the troops felt giddy, and Wheaton found it hard to stand. He reported, "My floor seemed to be moving like the deck of a ship at sea, influenced by a grand swell." No one, alas, seemed to consider the seismic disturbance to be a belated spasm of revulsion by Mother Nature at the treatment accorded her Modocs by the whites.

After the war, L. S. Dyar reported the Klamath Reservation not only quiet but prospering. He had 1,120 Indians, of whom 100 were Modocs of Old Schonchin's band. But the reservation's human population did not grow, although livestock reproduced well. By 1881, there were only 1,018 souls. Seven years later, the Indians were running 2,201 animals, tilling

1,400 acres of the potential 20,000, and had about 500 more broken to the plough. Oats, barley, hay and vegetables were the main crops. The Indians continued their lumbering and also did some freighting in the lake basin. Meacham felt that their lumber mill was so successful it should be a model for similar projects on other reservations. A flouring mill was being finished, Indians were becoming Christianized, the schoolhouse was completed and a boarding house was under construction. Except for a handful of greedy land speculators, everything looked bright for the Modocs and Klamaths to Agent L. S. Dyar. The Military Road Company, which had cut its way right across the reservation, was advertising every odd section of Indian land for three miles back from the road for sale. Dyar urged the Government to buy the land back if the company had prior rights to it. He was afraid of trouble, even war, because he found it impossible to convince his wards that, when a certain tract of land was set apart for them, presumably forever, the Great Father could take it away and give it to settlers.

One curious by-product of the war was the creation of Modoc County, California. When W. T. Cressler of Cedarville was elected to the California legislature for the 1873-1874 term, he introduced a bill to create a new county named in honor of Canby. His opponents offered an amendment that changed its name to Modoc County, thinking that the name of the tribe that murdered Canby would kill the bill, too. To their surprise, Cressler accepted the change of name, the bill passed into law, and Dorris Bridge, eventually renamed Alturas, became the county seat.

At Fort Klamath itself there was the usual round of duties and details, the occasional purchase of cavalry horses, the visits of travelers. Tragedy struck in the winter of 1875 when Joseph Frankl, the first Bohemian (Czech) argonaut of the California Gold Rush, was found face-down, dead, in the snow. He was buried in a now-lost grave at Fort Klamath on December 10, 1875. By 1877, the reservation needed a *skookum*-house or jail of its own, patterned after the fort's guardhouse. A Klamath headman, Ball, was shortly lodged there for abandoning a wagon in the woods to chase his straying wife. Earlier, he had cut off her hair for adultery. That time, the winter of 1876, she had done the impossible—had made love to a soldier in a canoe on the cold bosom of Klamath Lake—and then had stolen the canoe.

Some of the reasons for the Modoc War belatedly came to

light in 1878 when an Ashland *Tidings'* correspondent, Perkyns, described how cultivation, drainage and irrigation ditches, and threshing machines were turning the land of sage and alkali into a pleasant landscape, with its rough volcanic features smoothed out. Only a few years before, he had traversed the lakes basin with a pack horse, coffee pot and frying pan. Now he could stay in hotels and even enjoy bath houses where once Klamaths and Modocs had dug *camas* roots to survive. In 1881, when Corp. Herman Werner of Fort Klamath talked to Lost River settler George Miller, he found him bitter and resentful of new "raiders" more eager to run him out of the country than the Modocs had ever been. Miller complained, "Now the Indians are all gone but we have a couple of 'big fellows' in the valley. They drive a lot of horses and cattle into the valley. They want the whole valley for themselves. They have tried their best to get me to move because I keep a few hundred heads of sheep. Maybe they will burn me out, some of these days."

It was probably reporter Perkyns who wrote finis to a chapter of frontier military history when the *Tidings* bade a fond farewell to Capt. James Jackson's B Troop, 1st Cavalry, in September 1878: "This company has been stationed at Fort Klamath for seven years and fought for us with genuine gut during the Modoc War, and the solid old captain, genial lieutenants, and many of the men will be missed by the sagebrush people. May good luck and prosperity be their lot!"

Captain Jack's Stronghold briefly became a magnet for visitors after the Modoc War. The English writer-traveler, J. W. Boddam-Whetham, was properly awed by the Lava Beds, remarking "One man could keep a hundred at bay in the volcanic caverns." The Sage of Yosemite, John Muir, paid a call in 1874 and noted so much bony litter in Captain Jack's Cave that he predicted that some eager archeologist of the future would startle the world with his discovery of a Stone Age site in the Lava Beds. But, as a tourist attraction, the Lava Beds had a short life until the twentieth century and their designation as a National Monument, and by 1880 the Modoc War was almost forgotten. That year, a history-minded officer, Capt. John S. Parke, visited the old battlefield with John Fairchild as his guide. He rode a little old mustang, *Ya-muck-o-nee,* which had been captured from Captain Jack seven years before but was still tough as a pine knot. The two men dropped down Gillem's Bluff via the old Army route, now a decidedly "blind" trail. They found a foot-long board marking the Peace Tent site. Parke even collected some of the old tent pegs that had witnessed the massacre. Fairchild then led him into the Stronghold, past the heaped-up stones of the loop-holed barricades of both soldiers and braves. The rancher found Captain Jack's Cave with difficulty and pointed out Jack's bed of tules among a litter of cattle bones. It was just as John Muir had described it, just as Captain Jack had left it. On the way back, they renewed the lettering on the signboard, which had become obliterated with weathering, and passed the bleached bones of a horse whose rider, Fairchild remembered, had been shot to death as he went to the assistance of some wounded men.

That same year of 1881, in August, Capt. Stephen G. Whipple, commanding Fort Klamath, sent out a reconnaissance party to the Lava Beds. Corp. Herman Werner was along. Although he was more impressed by the burnt and abandoned homesteads in Lost River valley than by the *malpaís,* he was a gullible listener when the unit's guide, a Modoc, regaled him with myths of the Modoc War. The dragoman had Scarfaced Charley on January 26, 1873, raiding Gillem's Camp with six braves, killing two sentries and cutting the throats of five wounded soldiers as they lay in their hospital beds. The storyteller also bragged of Boston Charley's March 14 attack on John Fairchild's California Rangers, in which the Californians (who had disbanded, of course, much earlier) were supposedly wounded and scattered.

In September 1882, Captain Parke was ordered to Fort Klamath on temporary duty, and he secured permission from Departmental Commander Nelson Miles to mark the site of the Peace Tent more adequately. Fairchild could not guide him this time but had his carpenter make Parke a cross of six-by-six lumber. It was twelve feet high with four-foot arms. Parke and his helper took it by buckboard to the brink of Gillem's Bluff, where they gave it a priming of paint, then carried it down to the Lava Beds in an unconsciously grotesque parody of Christ at Calvary. They erected the cross on the council tent site, gave it another coat of paint, and heaped loose volcanic boulders halfway up its height. Lastly, Parke added the inscription, "General Canby, U.S.A., was murdered here by the Modocs, April 11, 1873." Replicas of that original cross have stood there ever since, and one will be seen there (unpainted, however) today.

In 1881, Professor Rudolph Virchow wrote a letter from Germany to Dr. George Martin Kober of Washington, in which he indicated that he was interested in studying the pigmentation of the American Indian. Once again, Fort Klamath was only too eager to oblige science. Just as it had once sent heads and skeletal remains to Washington, now it dispatched samples of Indian skin. Just who was flayed is not clear from the existing records.

Thirteen years after Captain Jack's surrender, Washington deemed that Fort Klamath had outlived its usefulness. With the Modocs exiled or cowed and the Klamaths as docile as so many nuns, there was no need for a military presence in the basin. On May 4, 1886, the military reservation was transferred to the Interior Department; Fort Klamath was abandoned. Steps were taken to open the post's lands for public sale but were suspended because of a howl of protest from the people of Klamath County. A caretaker detachment was stationed there for a time but finally removed in 1890. Again there was a great demonstration by the local people who had not, after all, forgotten the Modoc War and its horrors. They forwarded their fears of a general Indian uprising to Washington, reminding the Government of the messiah craze sweeping Indian America in the form of the Ghost Dance religious revival. But their protests were unavailing and Fort Klamath died in 1890, the same year that the pigeons took away the spirit of the Modoc shaman, Curly Headed Doctor, in Oklahoma; the same year that the frontier ended, by decree of the Census Bureau and Frederick Jackson Turner; the same year that the Indian wars of the United States were ended by the atrocious murder of the Sioux by Colonel Forsyth's 7th Cavalry at Wounded Knee.

ACKNOWLEDGMENTS

I am indebted, as usual, to many people for research aid and comfort. Doubtless, I have forgotten some names but here are those that leap most readily to mind: J. Lawrence Angel, Edwin Bingham, John B. Blake, C. William Burk, Elgin C. Cowart, Jr., William N. Davis, Jr., David C. Duniway, Ferol Egan, Marty Egan, Elliott Evans, Bernard Fontana, Barbara S. Friedman, Mary Hanley, Lois McKee Hardy, Herbert M. Hart, Joseph G. Henrich, B. William Henry, Jr., James J. Heslin, Mary Hill, Kenneth L. Holmes, John Hussey, Priscilla Knuth, Millard McClung, Ken McLeod, David Myrick, Irene Simpson Neasham, Allan R. Ottley, Elmer O. Parker, Mrs. S. N. Partridge, Lucile E. St. Hoyme, Samuel Stark, Barre Toelken, Thomas Vaughan, Egon Weiss, Allen Welts and, of course, my patient wife and children.

RHD

BIBLIOGRAPHY

There are only a handful of absolutely essential books on the Modoc War—the volumes of Keith Murray and Erwin N. Thompson in the following bibliography, A. B. Meacham's two works, Jeff Riddle's Indian view of the conflict, and H. H. Bancroft's *History of Oregon* (II) and *California Inter-Pocula*, with an account of the Modoc War actually by Frances Fuller Victor rather than by Bancroft, which is detailed, if sometimes erroneous, and often biased—especially versus Meacham. Meacham's volumes must be used with care, not only because of his Tyrian prose and his suspiciously total recall of events but also for a Parson Weemsian penchant for embroidering a narrative and inventing or "perfecting" dialogue. Riddle has to be used with even more caution for very much the same reasons, plus naiveté, but his illustrations and their captions alone make his book essential. Hearsay and totalized recall loom large in Riddle's reconstruction of events and his knowledge of details and lengthy conversations must be taken with a grain of salt since the half-Modoc author was only nine years old at the time of the war. Probably his 1914 volume was a too-hasty rebuttal to the careless and very anti-Modoc memoir of Col. William Thompson, published two years earlier. It is regrettable that Erwin Thompson's monograph, with its excellent factual detail, maps and photos, was an "intramural" publication of the National Park Service and thus is virtually unobtainable even in large libraries. However, Sacramento antiquarian bookseller Herb Caplan has reprinted it for public sale, albeit in a limited edition.

The half-dozen or so necessary books are neatly balanced out by a similar number that will not be found in the following bibliography, even though they are sometimes cited by historians. They proved useless to my research. Doris Palmer Payne's *Captain Jack, Modoc Renegade,* for example, is too fictionalized for service, as is James Michael Allen's *Wi-ne-ma.* William F. Drannan's *Thirty-One Years on the Plains* is an interesting humbug but a compote of lies and legends, while Joaquin Miller's *Life Among the Modocs* is not only a mishmash of bad prose and worse history but is not very much abot the Modocs, to boot. T. A. Edwards' penny-dreadful *Daring Donald McKay* would have been ignored were not McKay and his silly little booklet participants in the story of the Modoc War. The book is relevent to the denouement of the story itself, if the text is rather less trustworthy than the New Testament and Koran.

(Applegate is Abblegee, Boutelle is Bartell, and Bernard becomes Beard. The yarn ends with this howler by McKay: "Captain Jack, I call upon you to surrender [in clear, ringing tones]. You are my prisoner." [Jack] "Ugh! Captain Jack surrender to the Mighty Hunter—to no one else.")

At first blush, Herman Werner's little book appears to be worthwhile, but it barely deserves inclusion since its poppycock almost outweighs its factuality, with nonexistent battles described as well as imaginary deaths of women and children during Hooker Jim's Lost River raid. Col. William Thompson's memoir is an untrustworthy title but useful for some campaign details and contemporary viewpoints. (For example, the colonel has Hooker Jim being hanged with Captain Jack, forty-two soldiers dying in the first Lava Beds engagement, and only two survivors of Thomas' sixty-two trapped troopers at Hardin Butte, although he blasted Drannan as a "wild romancer." Even when he was right, the colonel was wrong—he called Drannan "Captain Drehan.") *Caveat lector!*

Few Modoc War manuscripts of value remain unpublished. An exception, perhaps, is the Henry E. Huntington Library's newly acquired William Murray memoir. Unfortunately, there was a *tabu* on the document when I sought to publish parts of it. Gen. John E. Ross's manuscript in Bancroft Library is disappointing. Don Rickey made good use of Col. William H. Miller's unpublished memoir, placing extracts in his *Forty Miles a Day on Beans and Hay*. I must thank the Manuscripts Division of the Library of Congress for permission to use the journal of Sgt. Michael McCarthy. Several manuscripts mentioned by H. H. Bancroft in his histories have not survived the move of Bancroft Library to Berkeley from San Francisco, if they really existed as more than rough notes from an interview. Examples are Oliver Applegate's "Modoc History" and Elijah Steele's "Modoc Question." Perhaps some archival sleuth of the likes of John F. McDermott will yet turn them up.

American newspapers for 1872-1873 are full of excellent material on the Modoc War, providing a surfeit of minute (and, thank God, not always conflicting) detail about the campaign and its consequences. Eastern, midwestern and English newspapers joined the California and Oregon press in covering the incredible conflict, even sending war correspondents into the Lava Beds. Between December 2, 1872, and October 5, 1873, for example, *The New York Times* ran fifteen stories on the far-off guerrilla war in California and Oregon. San Francisco's Fourth Estate contributed the largest body of information on the campaign, and I have used all of the city's papers, plus some Oregon and Sacramento sheets, but I have made the San Francisco *Call* my "control," examining every page of every issue from long before Jackson's Lost River raid to a point well beyond the hanging of Captain Jack and his cohorts. With a daily circulation of thirty thousand copies in 1873, it claimed to have about double the circulation of any other newspaper. Thus, more people learned about the tragedy of the Modoc War from the *Call* than from any other source.

The volume of information in government documents seems scarcely inferior to the reams of newsprint on the Modoc War. Most useful to me were the Annual Reports of the Secretary of the Interior and, thus, of the Commissioner of Indian Affairs, and those of the Secretary of War and Adjutant General. Most of the important documentary material on the war, scattered over the years and Congresses, was gathered together in one handy and essential volume (Serial Set No. 1607) as House Executive Document 122 of the 1st Session, 43d Congress: *Official Copies of Correspondence Relative to the War with the Modoc Indians.*

Books
Bancroft, Hubert Howe, *California Inter-Pocula.* San Francisco: The History Company, 1888.
_____*The History of Oregon,* II. San Francisco: The History Company, 1888.
_____*The Native Races,* I. San Francisco: A. L. Bancroft, 1882.
Battey, Thomas C., *The Life and Adventures of a Quaker Among the Indians.* Norman, Okla.: University of Oklahoma, 1968.
Beach, W. W., ed., *The Indian Miscellany.* Albany, N. Y.: J. Munsell, 1877.
Bensell, Royal, *All Quiet on the Yamhill,* ed. by Gunther Barthe. Eugene, Ore.: University of Oregon, 1959.
Bland, T. A., *Life of Alfred Meacham, Together With His Lecture, The Tragedy of the Lava Beds.* Washington, D.C.: T. A. and M. C. Bland, 1883.
Boddam-Whetham, John W., *Western Wanderings.* London: R. Bentley & Son, 1874.
Brady, Cyrus, T., *Northwestern Fights and Fighters.* New York: McClure, 1907.
Brown, Dee, *Bury My Heart at Wounded Knee.* New York: Holt, Rinehart and Winston, 1970.
Brown, William S., *California Northeast, the Bloody Ground.* Oakland, Calif.: Biobooks, 1951.
Carey, Charles H., *History of Oregon.* Chicago: Pioneer Historical Publishing Co., 1922.
Curtin, Jeremiah, *Myths of the Modocs.* Boston: Little, Brown, 1912.
Dillon, Richard H., ed., *William Henry Boyle's Personal Observations on the Conduct of the Modoc War.* Los Angeles: Dawson's Book Shop, 1959.
Downey, Fairfax, *Indian-Fighting Army.* New York: Scribners, 1941.
Dunham, Wayland, *Blue Enchantment, the Story of Crater Lake.* Caldwell, Idaho: Caxton, 1942.
Dunn, J. P., *Massacres of the Mountains, a History of the Indian Wars of the Far West.* New York: Harper, 1886.
Frémont, John C., *Memoirs of My Life.* Chicago: Belford, Clarke, 1887.
Fry, James B., *Army Sacrifices, or Briefs from Original Pigeon Holes.* New York: D. Van Nostrand, 1879.

Gatschet, Albert S., *The Klamath Indians of Southwestern Oregon.* Washington, D. C.: Government Printing Office, 1890.

Glassley, Ray H., *Pacific Northwest Indian Wars.* Portland, Ore.: Binfords and Mort, 1953.

Hagemann, E. R., ed., *Fighting Rebels and Redskins.* Norman, Okla.: University of Oklahoma, 1969.

Hart, Herbert, *Pioneer Forts of the Northwest.* Seattle: Superior, 1963.

———— *Pioneer Forts of the West.* Seattle: Superior, 1967.

Heitman, Francis B., *Historical Register and Dictionary of the United States Army.* Washington, D. C.: Government Printing Office, 1903.

Heizer, R. F., and M. A. Whipple, eds., *The California Indians.* Berkeley, Calif.: University of California, 1951.

Heyman, Max L., Jr., *Prudent Soldier, a Biography of Major General E. R. S. Canby.* Glendale, Calif.: A. H. Clark, 1959.

Hilleary, William M., *A Webfoot Volunteer,* ed. by Herbert Nelson and Preston E. Onstad. Corvallis, Ore.: Oregon State University, 1965.

Hunt, Aurora, *The Army of the Pacific.* Glendale, Calif.: A. H. Clark, 1951.

Jackman, E. R., and John Scharff, *Steens Mountain in Oregon's High Desert.* Caldwell, Idaho: Caxton, 1968.

———— and R. A. Long, *The Oregon Desert.* Caldwell, Idaho: Caxton, 1964.

Jackson, Helen Hunt, *A Century of Dishonor.* New York: Harper, 1881.

Jocelyn, Stephen P., *Mostly Alkali.* Caldwell, Idaho: Caxton, 1953.

Klamath County Museum, *Research Papers, No. 2: The Samuel A. Clarke Papers.* Klamath Falls, Ore.: Klamath County Museum, 1960.

Knight, Oliver, *Following the Indian Wars.* Norman, Okla.: University of Oklahoma, 1960.

Kober, George M., *Reminiscences.* Washington, D. C.: Georgetown University, 1930.

Kroeber, Alfred, *Handbook of the Indians of California.* Washington, D.C.: Government Printing Office, 1925.

Lewis, Oscar, *The War in the Far West.* Garden City, N. Y.: Doubleday, 1961.

Lowe, Don and Roberta, *100 Oregon Hiking Trails.* Portland, Ore.: Touchstone Press, 1969.

McDowell, Irwin, *Outline Description of Military Posts.* San Francisco: Presidio, 1879.

MacLeod, William C., *The American Indian Frontier.* New York: Knopf, 1928.

Meacham, Alfred B., *Wigwam and War-path.* Boston: John P. Dale, 1875.

———— *Wi-ne-ma.* Hartford, Conn.: American Publishing Co., 1876.

Merrill, James M., *Spurs to Glory.* Chicago: Rand McNally, 1966.

Muir, John, *Steep Trails.* Boston: Houghton Mifflin, 1918.

Murray, Keith, *The Modocs and Their War.* Norman, Okla.: University of Oklahoma, 1959.

Nash, Philleo, "The Place of Religious Revivalism in the Formation of the Intercultural Community on Klamath Reservation," in *Social Anthropology of North American Tribes*, Fred Eggan, ed. Chicago: University of Chicago, 1955.

National Park Service, *Soldier and Brave*. New York: Harper, 1963.

Odeneal, T. B., *The Modoc War*. Portland, Ore.: Portland *Bulletin*, 1873.

Peterson, Ethel M., *Oregon Indians and Indian Policy 1849-1871*. Eugene, Ore.: University of Oregon, 1939.

Physical and Economic Geography of Oregon. Salem, Ore.: Oregon State Board of Education, 1940.

Powers, Stephen, *Tribes of California*. Washington, D.C.: Department of the Interior, 1877.

Priest, Loring B., *Uncle Sam's Stepchildren*. New Brunswick, N. J.: Rutgers, 1942.

Prucha, Francis P., *A Guide to the Military Posts of the United States, 1789-1895*. Madison, Wis.: State Historical Society of Wisconsin, 1964.

Ray, Verne F., *Primitive Pragmatists, the Modoc Indians*. Seattle: University of Washington, 1963.

Rickey, Don, Jr., *Forty Miles a Day on Beans and Hay*. Norman, Okla.: University of Oklahoma, 1963.

Riddle, Jeff C., *The Indian History of the Modoc War and the Causes That Led to It*. San Francisco: Marnell Co., 1914.

Rodenbough, Theopholus, *The Army of the United States*. New York: Merritt & Company, 1896.

Whitman, S. E., *The Troopers: An Informal History of the Plains Cavalry*. New York: Hastings House, 1962.

Williams, Howel, *Crater Lake, the Story of Its Origin*. Berkeley, Calif.: University of California, 1951.

Wilson, Hugh R., *The Causes and Significance of the Modoc War*. Tulelake, Calif.: Tulelake High School P.T.A. Scholarship Committee, 1953.

Wormser, Richard, *The Yellowlegs: the Story of the United States Cavalry*. Garden City, N. Y.: Doubleday, 1966.

Periodical articles

Brown, J. Henry, "The Biggest Little War in American History," *Oregon Historical Quarterly*, Vol. 43, No. 1 (March 1942) pp. 37-39.

Brown, William S., "The Other Side of the Story," *Overland Monthly* (New Series) Vol. 82, No. 4 (April 1924) pp. 156-59.

Bunker, William M., "In the Lava Beds," *The Californian* (New Series) Vol. 1, No. 2 (February 1880) pp. 161-66.

Clarke, Samuel A., "Klamath Land," *Overland Monthly*, Vol. 11, No. 6 (December 1873) pp. 548-54.

Dillon, Richard H., "Costs of the Modoc War," *California Historical Society Quarterly*, Vol. 28, No. 2 (June 1949) pp. 161-64.

Edgerton, Ralph P., "Our Biggest Little War," *The Pacific Northwesterner,* Vol. 5, No. 4 (February 1961) pp. 49-57.

FitzGerald, Maurice, "The Modoc War," *Americana,* Vol. 21, No. 4 (October 1927) pp. 498-521.

Jackson, James, "The Modoc War—Its Origins, Incidents and Peculiarities," *The United Service Magazine* (New Series) Vol. 8, No. 1 (July 1892) pp. 1-12.

Klamath Echoes, Klamath County Historical Society, Klamath Falls, Ore. 1964-date. (Especially No. 6, 1968, "Fort Klamath Issue.")

Larson, Rupert L., "California Pocahontas," *Westways,* Vol. 34, No. 10 (October 1942) pp. 10-11.

Lockley, Fred, "How the Modoc War Started," *Overland Monthly* (New Series) Vol. 81, No. 7 (November 1923) pp. 12-14, 43.

McLeod, Edith R., "Two Kegs of Whiskey," *Westways,* Vol. 44, No. 6 (June 1952) pp. 6-7.

McLeod, Ken, "The Beginnings of the Modoc War," *The Pacific Historian,* Vol. 3, No. 4 (November 1959) pp. 74-80.

Parke, John S., "A Visit to the Lava Beds," *Journal of the United States Infantry Association,* Vol. 4, No. 5 (March 1908) pp. 710-38.

Powers, Stephen, "The California Indians: The Modocs," *Overland Monthly,* Vol. 10, No. 6 (June 1873) pp. 535-45.

Santee, J. F., "Edward R. S. Canby, Modoc War, 1873," *Oregon Historical Quarterly,* Vol. 33, No. 1 (March 1932) pp. 70-78.

The Siskiyou Pioneer, Siskiyou County Historical Society, Yreka, Calif. 1957-date.

Steele, Rufus, "The Cave of Captain Jack," *Sunset,* Vol. 30, No. 5 (May 1913) pp. 565-68.

Stern, Theodore, "The Klamath Indians and the Treaty of 1864," *Oregon Historical Quarterly,* Vol. 57, No. 3 (September 1956) pp. 229-73.

Trimble, Will J., "A Soldier on the Oregon Frontier," *Oregon Historical Quarterly,* Vol. 8, No. 1 (March 1907) pp. 42-50.

Turner, William V., "Scraps of Modoc History," *Overland Monthly,* Vol. 11, No. 1 (July 1873) pp. 21-25.

Various articles in:
Army and Navy Journal, 1872-1873
Harper's Weekly, 1873
Illustrated London News, 1873

Manuscripts
Applegate Papers. Eugene: University of Oregon.

Ayres, Irvin, "Notes . . . [on] the Indian Question . . . [and] the Modoc War." Berkeley: Bancroft Library, University of California.

Hagen, Olaf T., Olaf Hagen Papers. Washington, D. C.: National Park Service.

Kingsbury, George W., Scrapbooks. Tucson: University of Arizona Museum.

McCall, John M., Manuscripts. Salem: Oregon State Library.

McCarthy, Michael, Journal. Washington, D. C.: Manuscripts Division, Library of Congress.

Oregon Miscellany. Berkeley: Bancroft Library, University of California.

"Record of Medical History, Fort Klamath, 1872-5," Record Group 94, Vol. 432. Washington, D. C.: National Archives.

Records of Adjutant General's Office. Washington, D. C.: National Archives.

Rinehart, William, "Oregon Cavalry." Berkeley: Bancroft Library, University of California.

Ross, John E., "Narrative of an Indian Fighter." Berkeley: Bancroft Library, University of California.

"Siskiyou County Affairs," Manuscripts and clippings. Berkeley: Bancroft Library, University of California.

Newspapers

New York *Herald*
New York *Times*
Portland *Oregonian*
Sacramento *Daily Union*
San Francisco *Call*
San Francisco *Chronicle*
San Francisco *Evening Bulletin*
San Francisco *Examiner*
Yreka *Union*

Government documents

Federal
Annual Reports, 1864-1874
    Adjutant General
    Board of Indian Commissioners
    Commissioner of Indian Affairs
    Secretary of the Interior
    Secretary of War
Condition of the Indian Tribes (report of the Joint Special Committee appointed under Joint Resolution of March 3, 1865). Washington, D. C.: Government Printing Office, 1867.

War of the Rebellion Records, Series I, Vol. 50, Parts I and II. Washington, D. C.: Government Printing Office, 1897.

Oregon
Annual Reports
Adjutant General of the State of Oregon, 1864-72
Grover, Lafayette, *Report of Governor Grover to General Schofield on the Modoc War.* Salem, Ore.: State Printer, 1874.

Dissertation
Davis, William N., Jr., *California East of the Sierra.* Berkeley: University of California. Doctoral dissertation, 1942.

INDEX

361

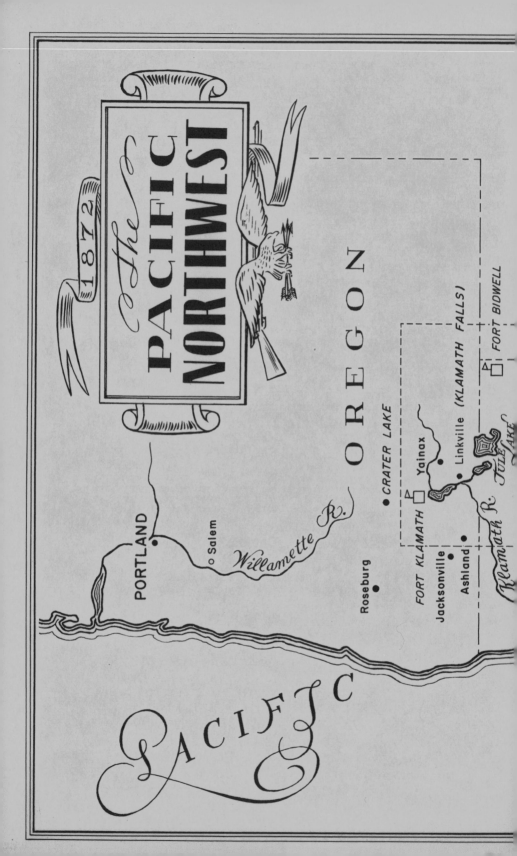